Advances in the History of Rhetoric

Advances in the History of Rhetoric

The First Six Years

Edited by
Richard Leo Enos and David E. Beard
with
Sarah L. Yoder and Amy K. Hermanson

Parlor Press
West Lafayette, Indiana
www.parlorpress.com

In cooperation with
The American Society for the History of Rhetoric,
Texas Christian University, and the Rupert Radford Trust

Parlor Press LLC, West Lafayette, Indiana 47906

© 2007 by Parlor Press
All rights reserved.
Printed in the United States of America.

S A N: 2 5 4 - 8 8 7 9

Library of Congress Cataloging-in-Publication Data

Advances in the history of rhetoric: the first six years / edited by Richard Leo Enos and David E. Beard, with Sarah L. Yoder and Amy K. Hermanson.
  p. cm.
"In cooperation with The American Society for the History of Rhetoric, Texas Christian University, and the Rupert Radford Trust."
Includes bibliographical references and index.
ISBN 978-1-60235-038-0 (acid-free paper) -- ISBN 978-1-60235-037-3 (pbk. : acid-free paper) -- ISBN 978-1-60235-039-7 (ebook : acid-free paper)
 1. Rhetoric--History. I. Enos, Richard Leo. II. Beard, David E. III. Yoder, Sarah L. IV. Hermanson, Amy K.
PN183.A38 2008
808'.009--dc22
                              2007045890

Cover design by Letter Five Studios.
Engraving by Cornelis Cort, "Rhetorica." © Museum Boijmans Van Beuningen, Rotterdam. Used by permission.
Printed on acid-free paper.

Parlor Press, LLC is an independent publisher of scholarly and trade titles in print and multimedia formats. This book is available in paper, cloth and Adobe eBook formats from Parlor Press on the World Wide Web at http://www.parlorpress.com or through online and brick-and-mortar bookstores. For submission information or to find out about Parlor Press publications, write to Parlor Press, 816 Robinson St., West Lafayette, Indiana, 47906, or e-mail editor@parlorpress.com.

Contents

Preface: Our Title Is Our Mission Statement ... ix
   Richard Leo Enos

1 Beyond Dichotomy: The Sophists' Understanding of Antithetical Thought ... 3
   Valerie V. Peterson

2 Hermagoras' Theory of *Prose Oikonomia* in Dionysius of Halicarnassus ... 12
   Robert Stephen Reid

3 The Teaching of the *Progymnasmata* of Pedro Juan Núñez (Valencia 1529–1602) ... 30
   Ferran Grau Codina

4 Erasmus's Irenic Rhetorical System ... 40
   Bohn D. Lattin

5 Neglected Texts of Olympe de Gouges, Pamphleteer of the French Revolution of 1789 ... 50
   Mary Cecilia Monedas

6 Samuel P. Newman's *A Practical System of Rhetoric*: The Evolution of a Method ... 62
   Beth L. Hewett

7 Visions of the Probable: The Transition from Rhetorical to Mathematical Models of Probability ... 76
   Terri Palmer

8 A Rhetorical Liturgy: Ephesians I and the Problem of
   Race Relations in the Early Christian Church   87
   Gary S. Selby

9 "Danced through Every Labyrinth of the Law":
   Benjamin Austin on Rhetoric as Virtue and Vice
   in Early American Legal Practice   98
   Sean Patrick O'Rourke

10 The Human Genome Project: Novel Approaches,
   Probable Reasoning, and the Advancement of Science 112
   Charlotte A. Robidoux

11 Let's Re-Enact Rhetoric's History   133
   John C. Adams

12 Leading Lady or Bit Part: The Role of the
   History of Rhetoric in Communication Education   144
   Glen McClish

13 *Encomium on Helen* as Advertisement: Political Life
   According to Gorgias the Barbarian   154
   Michael William Pfau

14 Upholding the Values of the Community:
   Normative Psychology in Aristotle's *Rhetoric*   167
   Ulrike Zinn Jaeckel

15 Enacting the Roman Republic: Reading Pliny's
   Panegyric Rhetorically   175
   Davis W. Houck

16 Hrotsvit, Strong Voice of Gandersheim   187
   Janet B. Davis

17 Classical and Christian Conflicts in Keckermann's
   De rhetoricae ecclesiasticae utilitate   199
   Jameela Lares

Contents

18 Rethinking the History of African-American
Self-Help Rhetoric: From Abolition to Civil Rights
and Beyond ... 209
Jacqueline Bacon

19 Historical Continuity and the Politics/Rhetoric
of Democracy: Solonian Reforms and the
Council of 400 ... 221
Davis W. Houck

20 Recognizing a Rhetorical Theory of Figures:
What Aristotle Tells Us About the Relationship
Between Metaphor and Other Figures of Speech ... 235
Sara Newman

21 Disciplinary Relations in Ancient and
Renaissance Rhetorics ... 248
Robert Gaines

22 Walter Pater and the Rhetorical Tradition:
Finding Common Sense in the Particular ... 261
Lois Peters Agnew

23 Contemporary Pedagogy for Classical Rhetoric:
Averting the Reductionism of Classical Opposition ... 273
David Timmerman

24 Rhetoric, Civic Consciousness, and Civic Conscience:
The Invention of Citizenship in Classical Greece ... 286
Christopher Lyle Johnstone

25 Motives for Practicing Shakespeare Criticism as a
"Rational Science" in Lord Kames's
Elements of Criticism ... 296
Beth Innocenti Manolescu

26 Sentimental Journey: The Place and Status of the
Emotions in Hugh Blair's Rhetoric ... 308
Sean Patrick O'Rourke

27 Who Measures "Due Measure"? or, *Kairos* Meets Counter-*Kairos:* Implications of *Isegoria* for Classical Notions of *Kairos* 326
   Jerry Blitefield

28 "Time Appeases Anger": The Rhetorical-Political Temporality of the Paradigmatic Passion of *Orge* in Aristotle's *Rhetoric* and *Politics* 337
   Renu Dube

29 Augustan Rhetoric: The Declining Orator 351
   Ilon Lauer

Afterword: Moments of Opportunity in the History of Rhetoric 369
   David E. Beard

Appendix: A Brief History of the American Society for the History of Rhetoric 373

Bibliography of Classical Authors 375

Bibliography 379

Index 409

Preface
Our Title Is Our Mission Statement

Richard Leo Enos

I would like to begin by thanking the Rupert Radford Trust and Texas Christian University for providing the funding that made it possible to publish the first six issues of *Advances in the History of Rhetoric* (1997–2002) in this single volume. I am pleased to have edited the first six issues of *Advances* and very thankful to be editing this collection with David Beard. In several ways, this collection, and even the founding of *Advances in the History of Rhetoric* itself, reminds me of an event that I experienced thirty years ago. In 1976, a colleague of mine had the enviable task of introducing Lloyd F. Bitzer. My friend asked what he should say in his introductory remarks. I promptly suggested, "Tell the audience that Lloyd Bitzer's essay, 'The Rhetorical Situation,' is probably the single most widely-read essay in our discipline." Bitzer's insights help us to understand that rhetoric can solve problems of value and preference, especially when we are sensitive to the context within which these needs emerge. I feel that Bitzer's observations still ring true today and bear directly on the mission of our journal. In 1995, we believed that having a journal for the American Society for the History of Rhetoric would meet a number of needs that faced our academic organization.

The early years of *Advances* are best characterized as a "rhetorical response" to our discipline's need to "advance" in three respects. First, we felt that a journal provided a tangible resource that would complement the objectives of our annually presented conference papers; the journal made rhetoric visible in a real sense. To that end, all ASHR conference papers were eligible for consideration in *Advances*. The result was overwhelming. In the first six years, thirty different rhetoricians published essays in *Advances*.

Second, *Advances* provided a rhetorical solution to another critical need: a place for developing historians of rhetoric to publish their research. Our intent was to provide a national journal that concentrated on "advancing" the work of emerging scholars. With the exception of occasional guest contributors, *Advances* became a place where competition for publication would be among developing researchers and not with established scholars. This emphasis on nurturing the work of beginning researchers had tangible benefits. Over the years, several institutions used the research of these emerging scholars in hiring, tenure, and promotion evaluation reviews.

Third, we also encouraged a diversity of methods, disciplinary perspectives, and research procedures. This emphasis on diversity helped to overcome one of the major constraints in our field: the belief that historical topics must employ "traditional" research methods. The consequence of this self-imposed limitation is that important historical questions are either never asked or are not answered thoroughly, because conventional research methods are not adequate for such tasks. Over the first six years of *Advances*, we sought diversity and encouraged new, innovative methods for researching historical topics. We welcomed participants from a variety of fields, including but by no means limited to: Communication, English, Philosophy, History, Religion, and Classical Studies.

Readers will note that this diversity is reflected in several ways. Texts that are disputed and neglected have been studied, with researchers often seeking to resolve issues that conventional literary approaches have left unresolved. These authors have re-examined the presumptions of disciplines and their relationship(s) with rhetoric. Such studies have included not only the humanities, but mathematics and the sciences as well. Efforts to provide sensitive explanations accounting for the voices of women and other groups have been an ongoing concern. Finally, the appropriation and modification of non-traditional research methodologies have redefined the range and province of rhetorical historiography. In sum, this collection reveals an exciting diversity of topics and approaches that helps us to remember that the title of our journal is also our mission statement: advances in the history of rhetoric!

Consistent with Bitzer's notion of rhetorical situations, in each of the six years of *Advances,* we sought to respond rhetorically to the disciplinary needs outlined above. Yet, disciplines—as well as situations and their solutions—change over time, while new ones emerge annually. The intent is that, with each year, *Advances* will respond to the recurring needs that come because our field is active, diverse and engaged in advancing the study of the history of rhetoric. Our purpose here is to put forth the work of those first six years so that readers will have this research readily available, and so that the progress made by these authors will be recorded in a single collection.

Acknowledgments

The articles collected in this book and that continue to be collected in *Advances* under its current editor, Robert Gaines, represent the kinds of innovations in research in the history of rhetoric that are possible when departmental affiliations and disciplinary lines matter less than quality research. I encourage those who have valued this collection to seek more information on current issues of *Advances* as it moves research into the 21st century.

—David Beard

Advances in the History of Rhetoric

1 Beyond Dichotomy: The Sophists' Understanding of Antithetical Thought

Valerie V. Peterson

Antithesis has been both a rhetorical scheme and a structuring concept of thought at least since the days of the sophists. As a figure of speech, antithesis generates dichotomies by setting one word or category in opposition to another, separating and differentiating the two. As a mode of thinking, antithesis allows people to organize and reorganize their ideas and the world around them. Antithetical thinking is an important concern for modern scholars because it plays a significant role in the way we understand and operate in democratic society.

Antithesis is generally valorized as a means of understanding. Like metaphor and irony, it has earned a place in rhetorical theory and practice. As structuralism suggests, dichotomy may be a universal property in all human thought—a basic means by which humans come to know and deal with their surroundings. With this connection to the nature of human reason, antithetical thought and practice are seen as creative and useful ways to come to understand the world and people's places within it.

Yet unlike other rhetorical strategies, the modern notion of antithetical thinking has been particularly divisive. Often, when two words or categories are set against each other rhetorically, they are also set against each other substantially. As a result, dichotomized categories take on a "real" meaning in the world and a separate existence for the people who recognize and use them.

When dichotomies become ossified, only two opposing categories remain. As Frazer and Lacey argue, "our analyses and judgments . . . tend to be structured in terms of binary oppositions which find their roots deep in western culture and philosophy: subject/object; mind/body; reason/emotion; culture/nature; individual/community; form/substance; public/private; male/female.[1] Middle positions, those between dichotomized categories, are marginalized as mere compromises and are deemed unprincipled. "Third" categories have little chance to challenge the perspective of the dichotomy itself and gradations between categories are denied, forgotten, or rendered impossible.[2]

Frequently, one category of the dichotomy is devalued. Traditionally oppressed or marginalized groups are well aware of the problems this devaluation produces—problems related to their status as "the other" (the devalued member of an antithetical pair). Many feminists, for example, have brought attention to the problems women have had with antithetical thinking. According to Frazer and Lacey, "the identification of women with emotion and hence unreason, and as objects or bodies, creatures of nature in the private sphere as opposed to creators of public culture, is one of the clearest and most widely analyzed aspects of this dichotomized thinking and its social implications."[3] These feminists and other critical scholars have "noted and deplored the extent to which western social thought [and perhaps also non-western thought] tends to be carried forward in terms of dichotomized categories."[4] They question the value of a rhetorical device that can be used pre-discursively to devalue particular voices, contribute to the inequitable distribution of power, and stand in the way of fair democratic practice.

The problems of antithetical thinking need to be addressed and we can look to antiquity for help. By examining the classical roots of antithesis, we may find a richer understanding of the notion than our more recent understandings allow, one based on a viable epistemological outlook. In so doing, we may find a way to make our dichotomies less divisive and devaluing and more conducive to fair democratic exchange of ideas and resources.

---

[1] Elizabeth Frazer and Nancy Lacey, 167.

[2] Frazer and Lacey, 168. For further discussion of the problems with dichotomized conceptual categories, particularly in relation to gender, sex, and sexuality see Judith Butler's *Gender Trouble* and Monique Wittig's *The Straight Mind and Other Essays*.

[3] Frazer and Lacey, 168.

[4] Frazer and Lacey, 167.

The History of Antithetical Thought

Classical Greece holds the key to many Western traditions of language, thought, and practice. A number of cultural, political, philosophical, and rhetorical traditions were conceived there, including antithetical thought and practice.

Antithesis was originally used by the rhapsodes in the pre-literate seventh, sixth, and fifth centuries BCE. The rhapsodes were poets, singers, and performers who generated extended and extemporaneous productions for special people and special occasions. The rhapsodes used antithesis as a way to add emphasis to their work through exaggerated differences. Little could be remembered, or a plot followed, or a poem coherently delivered, unless it took advantage of binary oppositions, since that is one of the ways the mind works. In the performance of word and song, these exaggerated differences added emphasis to the rhapsodes' artful performances and helped listeners remember what was sung.

Early public speakers (in the fifth and fourth centuries) consciously inherited the methods of the rhapsodes. They also relied on techniques of memory and emphasis such as antithesis. As Scenters-Zapico points out, speakers used "formulary expressions and mnemonic devices to ensure that both messenger and receiver could retain the message."[5] Since the use of text and other types of "artificial" memory were not yet widespread, antithesis became a popular and commonly used rhetorical technique.

Sophists of fifth and fourth century Greece recognized the importance of mastering rhetorical techniques in oratory. Taking advantage of the growing need to improve speaking skills required for the acquisition and maintenance of power in a developing democracy, they taught and practiced rhetorical techniques that moved audiences in the law-courts, assemblies, and games. Sophists were the first recognized and paid teachers of wisdom and their practices were later codified into influential theories of rhetoric. As Kennedy notes, "rhetoric was in no real sense an invention of the sophists, but their speculation helped crystallize its theories and show its significance."[6]

In addition to the rhetorical techniques of the rhapsodes, the sophists were influenced by a culture filled with conflict and opposition.

---

[5] John Scenters-Zapico, "The Case for the Sophists," 359.
[6] George Kennedy, *The Art of Persuasion in Ancient Greece*, 26.

To the constantly fighting Greeks, life was among other things a struggle, an agonistic contest to attain excellence amongst and against others—man against man, polis against polis, alliance against empire. This perpetual contest, experienced as a series of opposing forces both figuratively and literally, and the "agonal drive" it generated, could provide the key to understanding the Greeks' entire mentality.[7]

The Sophists' Understanding of Antithetical Thought

The sophists of the fifth and fourth century BCE practiced antithetical thinking, making use of its mnemonic and artful qualities as they reflected the combative, competitive, and comparative tendencies of Greek culture. Yet despite its agonistic roots, the antithetical thinking of the sophists worked situationally and thus constructively as well as divisively. It owed its flexibility and perhaps also its success to a rich intellectual context of relativistic epistemology and *kairos*.

As Kennedy has argued, "[t]o many sophists a confrontation of opposites may have been the fundamental process of reasoning."[8] Some early Greek thinkers, particularly eleatic monists and Pythagoreans, may have believed that they could transcend antithetical thinking, relativism, and time to discover larger (or smaller) truths of the world or universe. However, those who have been called sophists were less optimistic.

Unlike other thinkers, the sophists did not hold that antithetical thought could be transcended. What they did argue is that antitheses could be finessed, negotiated, and handled by some sort of relativizing move. As Guthrie has argued, "(t)he legitimacy of taking either side in an argument according to the circumstances was founded on theories of knowledge and being which constituted an extreme reaction from the Eleatic antithesis of knowledge and opinion, the one true and the other false."[9] As such, Empedocles, Democritus, Heraclitus, Gorgias, Hesiod, and others used antithetical argumentation, that is, the method of taking either side of an argument, in the context of relativistic theories of existence and knowledge and against the universalizing positions of other thinkers.

---

[7] W. E. Sweet, *Sport and Recreation in Ancient Greece*, v.
[8] George Kennedy, *The Art of Persuasion*, 34.
[9] W. K. C. Guthrie, *The Sophists*, 267.

These relativistic sophists saw no use in debating over objective or ideal truth. Perceived properties had no objective existence. To bridge the gap between the sensory world and other individuals, standards of advantage and disadvantage were substituted for those of truth and falsehood. Things were "true" or "false" only in the mind because total knowledge was limited by sensory experience and perspective. With this sort of understanding, sophists like Gorgias (and Protagoras) developed what Enos has called a "nonformal epistemology of rhetoric which would allow for the contingencies of interpretation and human nature that are inherent in any social circumstance lacking 'ideal' or universally affirmed premises."[10]

To many, Gorgias exemplifies the sophist's inheritance of techniques from the rhapsodes. His emphasis on style and stylistic techniques (including antithesis) reveals his appreciation for the "truths" of appearance. For Gorgias, truth was dependent upon circumstances, and knowledge was, in a sense, impossible.

In *On Nature,* Gorgias argued that knowledge is impossible by claiming "first and foremost, that nothing exists; second, that even if it exists it is inapprehensible to [hu]man[s]; third, that even if it is apprehensible, still it is without a doubt incapable of being expressed or explained to the next [hu]man."[11] For Gorgias, truth depended on the proof providing belief and was never "there" in any concrete sense. However, Gorgias thought probable knowledge could be achieved by means of discourse and situated consensus between individuals' perceptions of the "real."[12]

Gorgias' understanding of existence and knowledge allowed him to claim that the art of rhetoric was, itself, morally neutral. Throughout his career Gorgias steadfastly maintained that he was not in the business of teaching moral excellence. Gorgias could conceive of an amoral rhetoric because his notion of truth was situational, contingent, and flexible.

Protagoras, another sophist and a contemporary of Gorgias, shared Gorgias' relativistic understanding of existence and knowledge. Like Gorgias, Protagoras rejected the notion of an absolute truth and understood truth in terms of advantage. For Protagoras, truth was rela-

---

[10] Richard Leo Enos, "The Epistemology of Gorgias' Rhetoric: A Re-Examination," 51.

[11] See "Gorgias." Translated by George Kennedy, 43.

[12] Richard Leo Enos, "The Epistemology," 50.

tive to individual humans, and a statement like "A=B" made no sense without a reference point by which to judge. "A" could only equal "B" to some "C" where "C" was a person with a particular perspective on "A" and "B." In that way, truth was linked to power, the power of person "C" and his or her perspective. Protagoras' treatise on Truth reveals this connection—its title was translated from a Greek word for "throws," referring to the tactics used by wrestlers to gain advantage over their opponents.

Protagoras taught his students how to argue both sides of a case and believed in the value of entertaining antithetical arguments. Though he denied the existence of an ultimate truth, Protagoras did not deny the existence of wisdom. In Plato's *Theaetetus* he is quoted as saying, "I call 'wise' precisely that [hu]man who, by working a change in us, makes what is good appear to be to any one of us to whom what is evil appears and is."[13] In other words, the wise person is the person who can see and argue both sides of a case, showing how there is advantage in every disadvantage, evil in every good, falsity in every truth.

Protagoras maintained that whatever custom or policy a particular state believed was right would be right only as long as the people of that state were willing to accept it. For Protagoras, there was no ultimate or divine law by which humans should conduct themselves. The denial of divine logic and the notion that humans are the measure of all things is expressed in Protagoras' treatise *On The Gods*. There, he stated that believing in gods was real and even good for those who believed in them, but as to the objective reality of the gods he could only speculate because life is short, and the subject obscure.[14]

Gorgias, Protagoras, and other sophists had understandings of existence and knowledge that were relativistic but not skeptical or nihilistic.[15] These perspectives allowed for a stable yet flexible way to deal with both antithetical rhetorical schemes and antithetical concepts of thought and practice. Dualities were only dualities for a particular situation and their truth was contingent on the consensus of individuals and their understandings of the real. This situated reasoning allowed reality to shift and evolve as individuals' conceptions of the real changed, and as consensus emerged or eroded. Such reasoning left room for change in a democratic society; it was stable enough to pro-

---

[13] See "Protagoras." Translated by Michael J. O'Brien, 4.
[14] "Protagoras." Translated by Michael J. O'Brien, 4.
[15] Richard Bett, "The Sophists and Relativism," 139–169.

vide a way to judge what was true for a particular situation, and it was flexible enough to allow for changes over time in "truth" itself.

The sophists' understanding of antithesis was also closely tied to *kairos* (timeliness). In order for antithetical reasoning to work, not only did appropriate words have to be spoken, they had to be spoken *at the proper moment*. Protagoras believed that two opposing *logoi* exist in every experience when . . . considered *abstractly*.[16] Yet antitheses would enhance meaning and make messages powerful *only when kairos occurred*. As Scenters-Zapico (1993) observed, "(w)hen *kairos* occurred, the sophists appear to have created a form of *short-lived order*."[17]

In the *Dissoi Logoi*, an anonymous collection of what seem to be student notes of a sophist's lesson, particular pro and contra arguments are assembled and the importance of the *proper timing* of an utterance is discussed. Specifically the *Dissoi Logoi* states that, "nothing is always virtuous, nor [always] disgraceful, but taking the same things the opportune moment made disgraceful and after changing [them made them] virtuous."[18] In other words, what might be disgraceful at one moment might be virtuous in the next. As Scenters-Zapico put it, "[t]he Sophists' use of antithesis . . . combined with *kairos*, could cause a hearer to come to a different belief on virtually any topic."[19]

It was in conjunction with *kairos* that the early sophists avoided the traps of both skepticism and idealism. The sophists and their listeners gained knowledge that was revealed by a timely juxtaposition of the diametrically opposed.[20] The sophists did not make this opposition permanent, but recognized that members of a dialectical pair were interrelated and coexisted necessarily; one would be impossible to conceive of without the other. Thus, antithetical thinking acted as a *temporary stepping stone* to generate larger understandings of the world and people's place within it.

The sophistic understanding of antithesis worked better in early practice than it did in later rhetorical theory. As Greek culture went from oral to oral and literate, theories of rhetoric lost the relativistic focus of the sophists and were less able to account for contextual and temporal situatedness. Unlike the sophists' understandings, Plato's

---

[16] Edward Schiappa, *Protagoras and Logos*, 200.
[17] John Scenters-Zapico, "The Case," 362.
[18] John Poulakos, "Toward a Sophistic Definition of Rhetoric," 41.
[19] John Scenters-Zapico, "The Case," 363.
[20] Richard Leo Enos, "The Epistemology," 44.

theories were based on timeless, idealistic truths and Aristotle's on a scientific desire to discover, codify, and describe "natural" or stable categories of differentiation. Plato and Aristotle perhaps also feared the sophistic notion's potential for democratic change as well as its power to undermine and possibly usurp (their) aristocratic privilege and control.

Those hostile to sophistic notions of rhetoric tried to control rhetoric by turning it into a specialized intellectual discipline of concepts, rules, and practices. In doing so, they maintained the agonal dimension of antithetical thought and practice, but divorced these from their temporal and contextual situation. As Kennedy and Poulakos have noted, holistic fifth-century concepts such as *kairos* were deemphasized once rhetoric became a discipline. *Kairos,* by nature, could not be reduced to rules, and it could not receive great attention in the handbooks.[21]

This unsatisfactory translation, conceptualization, and codification of antithetical thought and practice turned process into product. Antitheses turned into ossified dichotomies: oppositional and bounded categories that tended to develop unequal valuation. The more complicated understanding of antithetical reasoning—as generator of an insightful moment in time—was lost . . . at least for the moment.

Conclusion

As Kennedy suggests, "conceptualization of great art is . . . always partial and incomplete."[22] One casualty of rhetoric's conceptualization was the sophists' understanding of antithetical thinking. Relativistic epistemologies and an appreciation for the importance of proper timing made the sophists' understanding of antithetical thinking practical and holistic, constructive as well as divisive. This understanding was degraded when separated from its epistemological and temporal underpinnings.

The sophists' understanding of antithetical thinking provided both flexibility and stability—a flexible means of negotiating temporally and contextually situated "truths" and a framework in which to (re)construct them. These dual qualities should make it particularly

---

[21] John Poulakos, "Toward a Sophistic," 200.

[22] George Kennedy, *Classical Rhetoric and its Christian and Secular Tradition from Ancient to Modern Times*, 6.

attractive to a democracy such as our own. Its value as a means of reasoning that destabilizes ossified dichotomies and allows for difference and change is well suited to the indeterminate nature of human existence and preferable to other, less flexible alternatives which are more likely to exacerbate conflict, distance and "otherness."

If it is time to generate a new democratic rhetoric (like a new language or new algebra), then encouraging a richer, sophistic approach to antithetical thinking should be part of such a project, particularly for those who wish to transcend rigid categories and people's places within them. Such a project would need to address the epistemological assumptions behind existing rhetorical schemes and tropes, and one way to do this is with antithetical thinking. Having people think and argue "other-wise" encourages intellectual humility, a healthy relativism, and an appreciation for the contingency of "truth." By rediscovering and putting into use the sophists' flexible yet stable, contextualized understanding of antithesis, we might help equip our democracy to do the kind of work it needs to do without curtailing its ability to discover its own (situated) truths and without relegating its constituency to categorical prisons of language, thought, and practice.

2 Hermagoras' Theory of *Prose Oikonomia* in Dionysius of Halicarnassus

Robert Stephen Reid

The ancient rhetorical theory of prose *oikonomia* has had a shadow existence in the rhetorical tradition at best. Quintilian tells us that "Hermagoras places *judgment, division, order* and everything under the heading of *economy* [*oikonomia*], a Greek word meaning the management of domestic affairs which is applied metaphorically to oratory and has no Latin equivalent" (3.3.9).[1] Kennedy states that "grouping these matters under economy was unusual and was not adopted by later rhetoricians, even when they followed Hermagoras in other ways."[2] Though generally correct, Kennedy's assessment obscures the fact that the term actually does occur in rhetorical contexts. For example, at the outset of his treatise *On the Sublime*, the author states that "Inventive skill [τῆς εὑρέσεως] and the proper order [τάχιν] and disposition [οἰκονομίαν] of material [τῶν πραγμάτων] are not manifested in a good touch here or there, but reveal themselves in slow degrees as they run through the whole texture of the composition" (1.4).[3] This distinction, which places *taxis* and *oikonomia* on equal footing, seems

---

[1] For ease of access, all citations unless otherwise indicated are from the two volumes translated by Stephen Usher, *Dionysius of Halicarnassus: The Critical Essays in Two Volumes*. However, following Russell, I refer to Dionysius' essay Περι Συνξεσεως Ονοματον as *On the Arrangement of Words* rather than Usher's rendering of *On Literary Composition*; see D. A. Russell, and M. Winterbottom, eds. *Ancient Literary Criticism*.

[2] George Kennedy, *A New History of Classical Rhetoric*, 100.

[3] *Classical Literary Criticism: Aristotle, Horace, Longinus*. Translated and edited by Dorsch, T. S.

to follow similar presentations that can be found in the *Ad Herennium* (3.8.16), in Sulpitius Victor (14) and as late as Athanasius.⁴ The former is generally termed Natural Arrangement (*ordo naturalis* for τάξις) while the latter is said to represent principles of Artistic Arrangement (*ordo artificiosus* for οἰκονομία)⁵ or theory in which the "cause itself obliges us to modify with art the Arrangement prescribed by the rules of the art" (*Ad Her.* 3.8.16).⁶

If we want to find evidence of the Arrangement theory in which *order* is subsumed as part of the larger theory of *economy*, Quintilian is helpful in one additional reference (7.10), but for a full development and exploration of the theory, the rhetorician must necessarily turn to the critical essays of Dionysius of Halicarnassus (*ca.* late first century BC). Dionysius not only discusses and makes extensive use of this approach in his own comparative criticism of Attic composition styles, but he also assumes that his reading audience is thoroughly familiar with the theory as well. And it is this latter sensibility that should give pause when considering how extensive the influence of this theory may have been. This is especially true when we recall that, together with Hermogenes, Dionysius' essays were *the* authoritative texts for rhetorical theory in late antiquity.⁷

Dionysius' overall project, outlined in the brief essay *On the Ancient Orators* was to examine critically the effective style of expression (λεκτικὸι τόποι) and treatment of subject-matter (πραγματὸι τόποι) of selected ancient Attic orators/authors so that students of political thought could practice imitation of these characteristics. The first four of these projected critical essays are extant, providing us with one of the earliest collections of applied rhetorical theory and critical practice. To these four studies can be added letters on theory as well as two extant essays on theory, an epitome of *On Imitation* and the full essay, *On the Arrangement of Words*.⁸ *On Arrangement* is the only intact an-

---

⁴ Hugo Rabe, *Prolegomenon Sylloge*, 176.

⁵ Translated and edited by H. Caplan. [Cicero]: *Ad C. Herennium de Ratione Dicendi*, 184–85.

⁶ On οἰκονομία as a rhetorical term, see D. Matthes, 111–114. The narrowing of the concept of *oikonomia* as an unusual approach to arrangement is found only in the late sources; see Roos Meijering, Literary and Rhetorical Theories in Greek Scholia, 142.

⁷ George Kennedy, *Greek Rhetoric Under Christian Emperors*, 49.

⁸ Surviving fragments of the epitomator's version of *On Mimesis* are in Usener-Radermacher VI, 197–217. Three chapters cited from the work can

cient treatise devoted entirely to the subject of arrangement theory we possess, and therefore must provide the starting place for comprehending any theory of word arrangement in the late Republican era.

Taken together, Dionysius' body of critical practice constitutes the largest collection we possess of criticism in antiquity. But despite this impressive body of rhetorical theory, practice, and criticism, he has not fared well in the estimation of contemporary critics. Prior to Gabba's very recent rehabilitation, historians generally rejected the multi-volumed *History of Archaic Rome* as too rhetorical. With similar objections, modern literary critics and classicists alike have generally expressed frustration that he is not Longinus, that his concern with criticism is preoccupied with obscure, typically Greek issues of classification for its own sake—in sum, that "he inevitably shared the rhetorical slant of his contemporaries."[9] For quite different but equally damning reasons, he has fared little better among rhetoricians. Dionysius has been dismissed as having little interest in the true art of persuasion because he only "touches on traditional theories of invention and arrangement"[10] and because in his approach he is too tightly focused on style.[11] Dionysius' contribution to rhetorical theory has generally been treated as a shift away from practical and philosophical rhetoric focusing, instead, on classroom rhetoric, declamation, and representing little more than an interest in the ability to speak well.[12] Only recently have there been significant efforts to rehabilitate his reputation.[13]

In this essay I want to trace how Dionysius makes use of the existing theory of *prose economy* as one of his primary critical systems in the comparative criticism of orators and historians. Beyond these

---

be found in Gn. Pomp. 3–6. Beyond his critical texts we also have most of the first eleven books of his twenty-volume *The History of Archaic Rome*, the primary identifying feature of which is the declamatory epideictic speeches placed on the lips of its characters.

[9] G. M. A. Grube, *The Greek and Roman Critics*, 205; see also S. F. Bonner, *The Literary Treatises of Dionysius of Halicarnassus*, 72.

[10] George Kennedy, *The Art of Rhetoric in the Roman World*, 362.

[11] *The Art of Rhetoric*, 342.

[12] *The Art of Rhetoric*, 342, 347.

[13] See Emilio Gabba, *Dionysius and the History of Archaic Rome*; Cecil Wooten, "The Peripatetic Tradition in the Literary Essays of Dionysius of Halicarnassus," 121–130; and Robert S. Reid, "Dionysius of Halicarnassus' Theory of Compositional Style and the Theory of Literate Consciousness," 46–64.

obvious uses, I also want to demonstrate how he then extrapolates a theory of word arrangement (*sunthesis*) from the threefold division of the theory of *oikonomia*. Because he believed that the theory of *prose arrangement* and his "recovered" theory of *word arrangement* was the implicit ideal in Attic theory, Dionysius proposed a set of divisions in rhetorical theory in which arrangement was considered as important as invention in the strategic development of the argument of a speech. For this reason, I argue that the theory of *prose economy*—a theory of strategic arrangement rather than the concern for style with which he usually dismissed—is at the heart of the Dionysian rhetoric. The question, of course, is whether this approach to rhetorical theory has any precedent. In the search for antecedents, I look beyond Hermagoras to the articulation of what Isocrates calls his First Principle of Oratory. The result of the inquiry suggests that Dionysius' place in the contemporary reception of the rhetorical tradition may well be misunderstood precisely because he was still a participant in a theoretical tradition in which invention was collapsed in arrangement.[14]

PROSE OIKONOMIA AS CRITICAL THEORY IN DIONYSIUS

Dionysius turns to a technical analysis of the historian Thucydides' art of *prose economy* in handling of subject matter (πραγματοὶ τόποι) in two extended texts. The first can be found in part of the epitome of *On Imitation* cited in the *Letter to Gnaeus Pompeius*. The second occurrence is in his essay *On Thucydides* where he provides us with eleven chapters of comparative criticism according to the precepts of *prose economy*.

At *Gn. Pomp.* 3–6, Dionysius offers five precepts for method in the art of historiography and then uses the principles to assess the degree to which the historians, Herodotus, Thucydides, Xenophon, Philistus and Theopompus, are worthy of imitation. Briefly summarized, his precepts are as follows: the first task of method in historiography is, "to select a noble subject that will please . . . readers"; the second is control of *division:* "to decide where to begin and how far to go"; the third is control of variety and proportion by choosing "which events he should include and which he should omit"; the fourth is control

---

[14] See Kathleen Welch, *The Contemporary Reception of Classical Rhetoric: Appropriations of Ancient Discourse*; Richard Leo Enos, *Greek Rhetoric Before Aristotle*, 87.

of *ordering*, "to distribute [διελέσξαι] the material of his account and arrange [τάξαι] each item in its proper place"; and the fifth task presents Dionysius' case that the governing philosophy of historiography should be to serve the moral concern of showing "pleasure in the good and distress at the bad" (3). Note that, in this poetics of historiography, the inventional task of selection of subject flows very smoothly into the compositional tasks of *division, variety,* and *ordering* (cf. Arist. *Poetics* 1451a35–b6 and 1459a17–29). The ease with which Dionysius turns this theory into critique can be seen in his brief, summary recommendation of Xenophon's approach to the task of writing a history: "But it is not only for his subjects, which he chooses in emulation of Herodotus, that Xenophon deserves to be praised, but also for his arrangement of his material [τῆς οἰκονομίας]. Everywhere he has begun at the most appropriate place, and he has concluded each episode at the most suitable point. His division [μεμέρικεν] is good, and so is the order [τέταχεν] and variety [πεποίκιλκε] of his writing. . . . Such, then, is his manner in the treatment of subject-matter" (*Gn. Pomp.* 4). After first praising selection of subject matter, he simply commends Xenophon's division, order, and variety in composing narrative.

In *On Thucydides,* after three chapters of praise for certain aspects of Thucydides' treatment of his subject matter, Dionysius provides what amounts to a clear thesis and preview for his extensive discussion of compositional problems with Thucydides' treatment: "The defects of Thucydidean workmanship and the features that are criticized by some persons relate to the more technical side of his subject matter, what is called the economy [οἰκονομικόν] of the discourse, something that is desirable in all kinds of writing, whether one chooses philosophical or oratorical subjects. The matter in question has to do with division [τὴν διαίρεσιν], order [τὴν τάξιν] and development [τὰς ἐξεργασίας]" (*On Thuc.* 9).[15] Throughout Chapters 9–20, the critique of Thucydides' compositional style is conducted according to the theory of *prose economy*. Chapter 9 critiques aspects of the historian's practice of *diairesis*, or division, of subject matter. Chapters 10–12 are devoted to critiquing his practice of *taxis*, or his ordering and positioning of the parts of the text in relation to one another. Chapters 13–20 analyze Thucydides' method of *exergasia*, which is to say, his manner of development and balance in the final composition.

---

[15] Translated and edited by W. Kendrick Pritchett. Dionysius of Halicarnassus: *On Thucydides: An English Translation with Commentary.*

Meijering has already provided extensive philological analysis of the rhetorical dimensions of this threefold system in his study of *Literary and Rhetorical Theories in Greek Scholia*.[16] Therefore, I will simply clarify Dionysius' usage of the terms here with a minimum of argument and illustration from the texts. Of the three distinctions, *exergasia* is the least difficult to grasp. It is the artistry of proportion used in developing the treatment of commensurate aspects of the subject in the *prose economy* of a work. Inappropriate attention to *exergasia* results in, "either according too much space to unimportant matters, or skimming too nonchalantly over those requiring more thorough treatment" (*On Thuc.* 13). Meijering argues that because Dionysius tends to apply both *diairesis* and *taxis* to the text as a whole, *exergasia* represents economy in the composition of the parts.

Taxis involves order as it concerns appropriate positioning of the sequence of presentation, the distribution and arrangement of each item in its proper place. For Dionysius, good *taxis* arrays narrative sequence and positions argument development in a fashion that creates an appropriate moral and artistic unity. Good *taxis* is conscious management of the artistic unity of the pre-selected arguments or episodes of a narrative. In *On Thucydides*, he offers examples of what he considers flaws in the historian's narrative sequence, but he views the problem primarily as a byproduct of an improper *diairesis*. He summarizes the distinction in this way, "Whereas Thucydides has taken a single subject and divided the whole body into many parts, Herodotus has chosen a number of subjects which are in no way alike and has made them into one harmonious whole" (*Gn. Pomp.* 3).

This eloquently phrased chiastic dictum implies a direct relationship between good *taxis* and good *diairesis*. Here, *diairesis* simply appears to be the accepted term for the principle by which a narrative is partitioned; i.e., its over-arching method of division: "[W]hereas earlier historians divided their accounts either topographically or by means of chronological framework, Thucydides adopts neither of these methods of division" (*On Thuc.* 9). The result of this confusing *diairesis* is general frustration with the *ordering:* "we wander here and there, and have difficulty following the sequence of events described" (9). Thus, the problem of flawed *taxis* is that it comes about as a result of a prior problem of a poor *diairesis*. Dionysius concludes, "It is clear that Thucydides' principle [ὁ κανὼυ] is wrong and ill-suited to history: for

---

[16] Meijering, *Literary and Rhetorical Theories*, 134–62.

no subsequent historian divided up his narrative by summers and winters, but all followed the well-worn roads which lead to clarity" (9). A summary of the relationship between *diairesis, taxis,* and *exergasia* can be found in Figure 1.

Dionysian Use of the Theory of *Prose Oikonomia* as Rhetorical Theory

At this point I want to turn to Dionysius' use of this system in his critique of various Attic orators. I will follow that by demonstrating how he has appropriated the system as the basis of his theory of word arrangement in his major theoretical essay, and then demonstrate how he presents the results in a rhetorical system that he wants to attribute as the implicit Demosthenic rhetoric.

The Theory of *Prose Economy* in Critique of Orators

Bonner has already extensively discussed Dionysius' proclivity to make use of rhetorical systems as the basis of his critique in his comparative method.[17] By the time Dionysius appropriated them as methods in critique, Theophrastus' Virtues of Style system had been codified into primary and ancillary virtues[18] and the Types of Style system was becoming codified as a result of the Asianist-Atticist debate.[19] But it is important to keep in mind that with Dionysius, the term λέξις implies diction apart from word arrangement. Dionysius' version of the Types of Style system was limited to choices in diction and figures of speech, in part, because he wanted to bring greater clarification to the theory of expression.[20] This is why, in the majority of his essays on the orators, he divided his critique into the two areas. In the first part of these essays, he analyzes τὸ λεκτικόν by making comparisons according to distinctions in the Virtues of Style system and his Types of Style system. In the second half of the essays, he analyzes τὸ πραγματικόν primarily according to the precepts of *prose economy,* examining how

---

[17] Bonner, *The Literary Treatises of Dionysius of Halicarnassus,* 15–24.
[18] D. A. Russell, *Criticism in Antiquity,* 137.
[19] Albrecht Dihle, *Greek and Latin Literature of the Roman Empire,* 68–9; see also Kirk Freudenburg, *The Walking Muse,* 39.
[20] Dihle, *Greek and Latin Literature of the Roman Empire,* 257.

well orators were able to *manage* aspects of genre and each of the formal parts of a speech: introduction, narration, etc.[21]

With one exception (which Dionysius notes) he opens each discussion of the orator's handling of subject matter by assessing his skill according to each of the aspects of good *prose economy* (*On Lysias* 15; *On Isoc.* 14; and *On Isa.* 3 and 14). Using *On Lysias* as an example of how he proceeds, he takes up consideration of the genres in which the orator excels (in Lysias' case, forensic). This is followed by an extended section of material in which Dionysius considers how well the orator *manages* (ᾠκονόμηται, *On Lys.* 24) the material partitioned as proem, statement of the case, narration, proof, and peroration (a set of distinctions Dionysius attributes to "Isocrates and his school"; *On Lys.* 16). What becomes quickly apparent is that Dionysius operates in a tradition in which the theory of *prose economy* is the primary system by which proper rhetorical control of arrangement is understood. He treats issues of invention as matters of basic selection in argument, but the quality of an orator's strategy of argument, what amounts to the power of the argument, he treats as a function of good *oikonomia*. I will explore the implications of this in Dionysius' overarching rhetorical theory later in this essay. For now, I simply want to note that at no point does Dionysius treat this rhetorical use of the theory of *prose economy* as something he has imported or invented. His summaries are often so casual that one can only assume that he understands this, as with the other systems he employs, to be common coin among the rhetoricians who comprise his reading audience (cf. *On Din.* 6 and 8). This point becomes apparent when compared to theory Dionysius clearly declares to be new.

The Theory of *Prose Economy* in Word Arrangement

In the proem of *On the Arrangement of Words*, he asserts that the Attic orators obviously "had a system of rules which they practiced and so composed well." He sets the task of the essay to "recover" these principles and proposes three concepts which he maintains are derived from his analysis of Attic practice: the Science of Word Arrangement,

---

[21] This is true for *On Lysias*, *On Isocrates*, and *On Isaeus*. In the fourth of his four extant essays on Attic orators, *On Demosthenes*, Dionysius divides the essay into two aspects of style (selection of words and arrangement of words), indicating that he planned to discuss Demosthenes' handling of subject matter in a separate essay (58).

the Theory of the Two Ends of Composition, and the Types of Composition system. He introduces the first of these with the following definition:

The science of arrangement [τῆς συνθετικῆς ἐπιστήμης] has three functions:

1. to see what combinations produce a total character which is beautiful and agreeable;

2. to know what configuration of each of the elements to be combined will improve the joint effect;

3. to recognize and execute in appropriate fashion [οἰκείως ἐξεργάσθαι] any necessary modification of the original elements—subtraction, addition, or alteration. (6).[22]

He uses the term *exergasia* to describe the third task in the Science of Word Arrangement: This is the editing process, here controlling the proportion of the final period or the equivalent expression of thought. The second task, like that of *taxis*, orders clauses so that the parts of the period or expression of thought are joined into an artistic unity of expression. The first task of *observing* which of the two Ends of Composition will create the overall desired effect, just as with *diairesis*. The effect on the audience will be in view. Here, the sense is that a speaker must weigh in advance the needed effect to be produced (λήψεσθαι) by recognizing how the resources of melody, rhythm, variety and appropriateness (*On Arr.* 11–20) can be marshaled to create an appeal to reason by way of beauty or effect an aesthetic sense of pleasure.

If one considers the overarching structure of the argument of On Arrangement (see Figure 2) it becomes quickly apparent that just as Dionysius used the Theory of the Three Types of Style as the model for his proposal of a Theory of the Three Types of Composition in Chapters 21–24, he has used the theory of *prose economy* as the basis of his proposal of a theory of Word Arrangement in Chapters 6–9.[23] His development of this system, as well as his development of the system of resources that serve the Ends of Arrangement and his Types of Composition system, allowed Dionysius to engage in a far more sophisti-

---

[22] Russell's translation, *Ancient Literary Criticism*.

[23] On Dionysius' Theory of the Ends of Arrangement system and his Types of Composition system see Reid, "Dionysius of Halicarnassus' Theory of Compositional Style and the Theory of Literate Consciousness," 49–55 and Appendices A and B, 63–64.

cated assessment of Demosthenes. These new theories permitted him to demonstrate the comparative superiority of Demosthenes' control of arrangement as well as diction. Once this was fully demonstrated, he felt at liberty to read the formulation of his own theory back on to Demosthenes.

The Theory of *Prose Economy* in Dionysian Rhetorical Theory

The main exposition of what Dionysius claims was the Demosthenic rhetorical theory is found at *On Dem.* 51,

> [Demosthenes] observed that good oratory depends on two factors, selection of subject matter [πραγματικὸν τόπον] and style of delivery [τὸν λεκτικόν], and that these two are each divided into two equal sections, subject matter into preparation [τὴν παρασκευήν] which the early rhetoricians called *invention* [εὕρεσιν] and deployment [τὴν χρῆσιν] of the prepared material which they call *arrangement* [οἰκονομίαν]; and style into choice of words [τὴν ἐκλογὴν], and composition [τὴν σύνθεσιν] of the words chosen. In both of these sections, the second is more important: arrangement [τὸ οἰκονομικὸν] in the case of subject matter and composition [τὸ συνθετικὸν] in the case of style (51).

Outlining the treatment clarifies the nature of his proposed reading of the rhetorical relationships:

I. Factors relevant to Subject matter:

    a. Invention (*heuresis*) as selection of arguments

    b. Arrangement (*oikonomia*) as deployment of prepared material

II. Factors relevant to Style:

    a. Diction (*eklogê*) as selection of words

    b. Composition (*sunthesis*) as deployment of prepared material

Far from the Aristotelian threefold division of invention, arrangement and style, the Dionysian rhetoric treats issues of invention and arrangement as dual tasks in the treatment of one's subject matter and style. In both contexts he argues that factors of selection (*heuresis* and *eklogê*) may precede arrangement in order, but that the second factor (*oikonomia* and *sunthesis*) has far greater "potency" in effecting persuasion.[24] This way of organizing rhetorical theory places far greater emphasis on the affect of the rhetor's stylistic efforts to persuade an audience, which is why Dionysius literally raises "agonistic force" to a place as the fourth means of persuasion in his final statement concerning the significance of his Demosthenic rhetoric: "While it is necessary for the orator to aim at lucidity, vividness, amplification, and good rhythmical composition, above all of these, it is necessary to aim at arousing emotion, evoking character and achieving an appropriate agonistic force of expression, for herein lies the greatest portion of the power of persuasion" (*On Dem.* 58; my translation).[25]

His argument—that potency rests in the task of strategically arranging subject matter and the effect of one's style rather than in the prior steps of selection of arguments and choice of words—is a distinctly Dionysian position, but one that makes sense given the first-century polemic concerning a true civic rhetoric that was being waged over seemingly mundane issues like word order and Types of Style.[26] In effect, Dionysius defined *prose economy* in *On Dem.* 51 as the ability to manage the strategy of arguments previously determined and artistically to structure the result into an agonistically forceful whole. The inventional aspect of structuring the relationship of arguments is separated from the discovery of available arguments, with the latter being reduced to a task of "selection" akin to the selection of appropriate words. It is adroit "arrangement," whether of subject matter (*oikonomia*) or words (*sunthesis*), that is the true "potency" in the Dionysian art of rhetoric. In this sense it may be no mistake that *diairesis* is the inventional aspect of both Dionysius' theory of *prose economy* and Plato's theory of dialectical reasoning.

---

[24] On the Dionysian notion of "potency" see *On the Arrangement of Words* 2.

[25] For the nuance of translating key rhetorical terms see the "Index Dionysiacus" in both Jacobus Van Wyk Cronjé, *Dionysius of Halicarnassus: De Demosthenes: A Critical Appraisal of the Status Quaestionis* and W. Rhys Roberts, *Dionysius of Halicarnassus On Literary Composition*. Both works include an "Index Dionysiacus."

[26] Reid, "Dionysius of Halicarnassus' Theory of Compositional Style and the Theory of Literate Consciousness," 47–9.

We can only wonder whether Hermagoras' conception of *prose economy* similarly problematized this distinction between invention and arrangement that Aristotle had previously worked so hard to separate in the *Rhetoric*. Of course, Hermagoras is primarily known for his advances in the area of invention with a system of questions known as "stasis theory," but the fact that Quintilian credits Hermagoras with formalizing the theory as a system of Arrangement does not mean we should assume the conception originates with Hermagoras. For his part, Dionysius would credit Demosthenes as the perfector of an existing system of arrangement theory, but his critique is already a meta-language interposing itself between actual Attic compositional practice and later theoretical reflection. Clearly, any suggestion that Attic orators had a "system" of anything is anachronistic, since turning theory into systems was the penchant of rhetoricians in the second century BC and not the fourth century. But are we simply to dismiss out of hand the analysis of one of our more careful critics of Attic discourse? D. A. Russell reminds us that it is conservatism in rhetorical teaching over a long period that makes possible the reduction of many of its ideas into "a system."[27] Thus, if we are to see Dionysius' theory as development within an existing tradition of practice, we need to locate some precedent for its precepts. Because we need not be concerned with his ideological interest in promoting the Demosthenic ideal, we are free to look to what Isocrates called his First Principle of composition to find a potential antecedent of what became the theory of *prose economy*.

An Isocratean Antecedent for *Prose Economy* in Composition

According to Gaines, the clearest statement we possess of Isocrates' approach to prose composition is found in a letter *To the Children of Jason*.[28] Isocrates prefaces the statement with the disclaimer that, since others were already teaching his precepts of compositional theory, he hopes that it will not seem infelicitous for him to repeat them as well. He then writes,

> The very first precept I shall present is one of those most often repeated. I am accustomed, that is, to tell

---

[27] D. A. Russell, "The Arts of Prose: The Early Empire," 119.
[28] Robert N. Gaines, "Isocrates, EP. 6.8," 165–170.

> the students in my school of rhetoric that the first question to be considered is—what is the object to be accomplished [διαπρακτέον] by the discourse as a whole and by its parts [τοῖς τοῦ λογου μέρεσι]? And when we have discovered [εὕρωμεν] this and the matter has been accurately determined [διακριβωσώμεθα], I say that we must seek [ξητητέον] the rhetorical elements [τὰς ιδέας] whereby that which we have set out to do [ὑπεθέμεθα] may be elaborated [ἐξεργασθήσεται] and fulfilled [λήψεται τέλος]. And this is the procedure I prescribe with reference to discourse, yet it is a principle [στοιχεῖον] applicable not only to all other matters, but also to your. . . . life [βίον] (8).

In describing his First Principle, Isocrates uses two terms to describe the initial step of rhetorical intellection: *heuresis* and *diakriboô*, that of discovering and of determining the matter. *Diakriboô* is broken down into the tasks of consideration of the discourse as a whole, the relation of its constituent parts, and the way in which these *ideas* are to be elaborated (*exergasia*) and brought to fulfillment.

After stating the First Principle, Isocrates clarifies it by way of an extended analogy from what he considers to be the basic argument for the examined life. First, you determine how to direct your own future and only after these principles have been determined [διορίζω], then and only then, can daily actions be ordered. And, of course, once the plan is enacted, then you can make corrections and adjustments according to expediency (9–10). In other words, Isocrates' counsel involves determining the whole plan, ordering one's actions accordingly, and making adjustments to keep from going astray. Care must be taken to note that Isocrates refers to this as a principle rather than "theory." The notion of theory is a developed conception that has more to do with the Aristotelian literate revolution than Isocratean principles of oratory. But there is good reason to see the Isocratean conception of the tasks of *diakriboô* as part of the early trajectory of what eventually became the theory of prose economy. And like Dionysius, Isocrates' twofold processes of *heuresis* and *diakriboô* seem to involve the task of envisioning the figuration of the moral whole of a discourse. Both tend to view the process of discovery and conceiving the presentation of the argument as processural throughout. These two conceptions of compositional method are compared in Figure 3.

IMPLICATIONS

My thesis is that Dionysius' use of the theory of *prose economy* represents the most important source we possess for tracing a trajectory backward to the recovery of a premodern, prelogical practice of arrangement and disposition as compositional strategies in Attic oratory. Of course de Romilly reminds us that this is the same Dionysius who often expressed shock at the most original qualities of each writer,[29] but valuation of that which is original is part of the gift of an emerging literate age, not the first reaction of an oral age.[30] As a conservative classicist, Dionysius represented the interests in his day of the older order, one that valued the kind of *mimesis* that reified group identity rather than endorsed originality.[31] In less apt hands, and on occasion even in his own hands, his approach turns criticism into little more than a numerical tabulation of technical proficiencies. But Dionysius was not blind to the limitations of such an approach. He always maintained that "experience itself [is] the guide to each of the adjustments" (*On Arr.* 7). Almost a century ago classicist Harry Hubbell began his academic career by arguing that Dionysian rhetoric maintained continuity with central aspects of the Isocratean rhetorical tradition.[32] More recently, D. A. Russell has reaffirmed this notion, rehabilitating the Dionysian rhetoric as a functionally situated, philosophic rhetoric and "a proper moral and social formation for an age of good government. . . . the ideal of Isocrates, 350 years earlier, restated for a larger world."[33]

I have no interest in determining whether Dionysius' critical judgments are correct. That is an aesthetic rather than a rhetorical task. Instead, my interest has been to examine Dionysius' use and adaptation

---

29 Jacqueline de Romilly, *Magic and Rhetoric in Ancient Greece*, 202.

30 In this sense Dionysius was a participant in the increasingly literate Roman society of his day even as he represents a bridge back to the literate revolution that began in 4th century Greece. On his role in this see Robert S. Reid, "When Words Were a Power Loosed," 431–434. For a concise overview of the way in which the Roman rhetorical exigence served to increase the literate aspects of rhetorical theory see Richard Leo Enos, *Roman Rhetoric*, 61–8.

31 Eric A. Havelock, *Preface to Plato*, 157–60.

32 Harry M. Hubbell, *The Influence of Isocrates on Cicero, Dionysius, and Aristides*.

33 Russell, "The Arts of Prose: The Early Empire," 246.

of the theory of *prose economy* that was already part of the existing rhetorical currency among the circle of his peers. Most critics who have examined Dionysius' use of the theory have primarily been concerned with his discussion of method in ancient historiography and their own aesthetic distaste for what is generally referred to as "the theatrical view of history."[34] Because of this resistance to all things rhetorical, critics have been slow to consider the implications of this rhetorical system.[35] However, what becomes quite clear with a consideration of the theory of *prose economy* is that in Dionysius we find an approach to rhetorical reasoning still committed to the poetics of literate compositional style of an older order amidst the furtherance of the literate revolution under the Roman auspices. A conservative by conviction, Dionysius appears to be using and enlarging that tradition of rhetorical theory in which form had yet to be separated from content, in which theories of invention still overlapped with theories of arrangement.

---

[34] Usher, *Dionysius of Halicarnassus: The Critical Essays*, Volume 2, 377 n6.

[35] For example, in his commentary on the essay *On Thucydides*, Pritchett states simply that in Chapters 9–20 Dionysius "is mainly writing as a rhetorician whose preconceptions concerning *diairesis*, *taxis*, and *exergasia* are the direct result of his training and vocation" (*Dionysius of Halicarnassus: On Thucydides*, xxx). Grube expresses some interest, calling it a "new approach," though it is unclear whether by "new" he meant critically neglected or simply original to Dionysius (*The Greek and Roman Critics*, 226; cf. G. M. A. Grube, [1950], "Dionysius of Halicarnassus on Thucydides," 95–110). Bonner offers a summary of the technical criteria of this method and how Dionysius develops them, but has little or no interest in the implications of the principles as method because he considers them as merely another distasteful instance of the way in which Dionysius is "shackled" by the rhetorical apparatus of his era (*The Literary Treatises of Dionysius of Halicarnassus*, 23 and 87–88).

Figure 1. The distinctions of the tasks of *prose economy* as found in Dionysis of Halicarnassus.

	Division (διαίρεσις) On Thuc. 9	Order (τάξις) On Thuc. 10–12	Development (ἐξεργασία) On Thuc. 13–20
Concern	Conceptualizing a treatise as a completed, moral whole, with an appropriate organization or exposition of the subject-matter.	Positioning relative sequence of parts in the progression of an argument or episode; internal order of the parts that make up the presentation.	Controlling the proportion of development at each step; editorial control of the final form.
Indications of Failure	Subject matter unsuitably organized creating a half-finished, or unfinished unresolved sense of a work.	Lack of narrative or organizational continuity; lack of balance in the distribution of ideas in proper sequence.	Either too little space given to important subject matter or too much. Space given to the irrelevant.
Result Achieved	A *Finished* Style of Disposition; argument or narrative as a moral whole.	An orderly presentation of ideas.	Proper Proportion and depth of development.

Figure 2. The following is a schematized summary of the argument of Dionyius of Halicarnassus' *On the Arrangement of Words* as arrayed with the Diairesis appropriate for an epideictic treatise.

> A Introduction—Importance of Prose Arrangement [Chs. 1–5] Dionysius establishes the subject of his treatise on Arrangement and apologetically sets it in the rhetorical context of other approaches to "natural" word arrangement. He argues for the priority of dexterity in word arrangement as more important than word selection.
>
> B Theory of the Three Tasks of the Science of Word Arrangement [Chapters 6–9]—modeled on the Theory of *Prose Economy*. Concerning the threefold Science of

Arrangement: 1) Seeing how to alter forms of words to effect *beauty and pleasure* [Ch. 7]; 2) considering how clauses may best be fitted together in overall relationship to one another; and [Ch. 8]; and 3) editorially tailoring (through addition and modification) the final form in which they are cast [Ch. 9].

C   On the Ends of Arrangement: Aesthetic *Pleasure* [Chs. 11–12]. Concerning the Ends and Resources introduced [Ch. 10-11a]; how to use each of the resources of melody, rhythm, variety and appropriateness to effect *Pleasure* for those hearing as an End.

C'   On the Ends of Arrangement: Inherent *Beauty* [Chs. 13–20]. Concerning how to use each of the resources of melody, rhythm, variety and appropriateness to effect an unreasonably inherent *Beauty* as an End.

B'   Theory of the Three Types of Composition [Chs. 21–24]—modeled on the Theory of the Three Types of Style. Concerning the three different Types of Compositional practices: the Austere Style [Ch. 22], the Polished Style [Ch. 23], and the Well-balanced Style [Ch. 24].

A'   Conclusion: Importance of Prose Arrangement [Chs. 25–26]. Prose that effects the power of poetry without meter is defended; an apologetic for composing according to principles of lyric arrangement defended against naysayers.

Figure 3. A Comparison of the Dispositional Methods of Isocrates and Dionysius.

	The Isocratean First Principle (τό πρώτως στοιχεῖον)	The Dionysian Principle of *Prose Economy* (τό οἰκονομικόν)
First Task	**Division** (διορίξω) • Conceptualizes the effect of a text as a completed moral whole through *heuresis* and *diakriboó*. • Results in a plan for the relation of the whole to the parts.	**Division** (διαίρεσις) • Conceptualizes the effect of a text as a completed moral whole with full exposition of subject-matter. • Results in a plan that makes a unity of the parts.
Second Task	**Structuring the Elements** (τὰς ἰδέας) • Gathers and structures the elements of both rhetorical thought and rhetorical form through figuration. • Necessary to accomplish that "which we have set out to do."	**Order** (τάξις) • Positions parts in relation to one another. • Results in artistic unity.
Third Task	**Development** (ἐξεργασία) • The devlopment of the work so that the treatise can be apprehended in all its proper fullness • Result: Without use text will go astray from plan and fail in its undertakings.	**Development** (ἐξεργασία) • Controls final form of development of the complete discourse. • Results in changes to carry out proper proportioning of parts.

3 The Teaching of the *Progymnasmata* of Pedro Juan Núñez (Valencia 1529–1602)

Ferran Grau Codina

Pedro Juan Núñez devoted his life to teaching philosophy, Greek, and rhetoric at the universities of Valencia (1552–56; 1561–63; 1581–83; 1598–1602), Zaragoza (1557–1561; 1563–67) and Barcelona (1572–1581; 1583–1597), and was closely bound to Antonio Agustín, archbishop of Lérida (1561–1576) and of Tarragona (1577–1586). In this city, Núñez met Andreas Schott in 1585, the Belgian Jesuit who wrote the *Hispaniae Bibliotheca*,[1] and to whom he dedicated his *De Patria Pomponii Melae* and his comments on chapters one and two of book one of the *De Situ Orbis*,[2] as well as the prologue of his edition of Phrinicus *De Vocibus Atticis*.[3] Andreas Schott was the editor of some of Núñez' publications, and probably delivered a copy to the Dutch scholar J. G. Vossius.[4]

---

[1] Schott, A. *Hispaniae Bibliotheca seu de Academiis ac Bibliothecis* (Francofurti, apud Claudium Marnium, 1608).

[2] Pomponii Melae *De situ orbis libri III, cum notis integris Hermolai Barbari, Petri Ioannis Olivarii, Ferdinandi Nunii Pintiani, Petri Ciacconii, Andreae Schotti, Isaaci Vosii et Iacobi Gronovii. Accedunt Petri Ioannis Nunnesii epistola de Patria Pomponii Melae, et adnotata in proemium atque duo priora capita libri I, et Iacobi Perizonii adnotata ad libri I capita septedecim, curante Abrahama Gronovio* (Leiden, 1748).

[3] Phrynichi *epitomae dictionum Atticarum libri III sive Ecloga, a Petro Iohanne Nunnesio Valentino integrate restituta, latine conversa. Eiusdem et Davidis Hoeschelii Aug. notis, in quis et aliorum auctorum loca partim emendantur, partim illustrantur, aucta* (Augusta Vindelicorum, typis Michaelis Manderi, 1601).

[4] Procli *Chrestomathia poetica. Interprete et scholiaste Andrea Schotto Antuerpiensi. Accessere et notae Petri Ioannis Nunnesii Valentini. Item fragmen-*

Núñez studied at the University of Valencia and after his graduation and his doctorate in Arts, went to Paris in 1550 where he heard the lectures of Peter Ramus, as well as A. Turnebus, and J. Carpentarius—opponents of Ramus. He came back to Valencia a year later and published his first book in 1552, the *Institutiones Oratoriae Collectae Methodikvs ex Institutionibus Prioribus Audomari Talaei*, Talon being the inseparable colleague of Ramus.

Núñez was a Hellenist, a Peripatetic philosopher, a rhetorician, and a critical editor, and he published books on all these topics.

Although he always declared himself an Aristotelian philosopher, Núñez changed his views from his initial Ramism, at least on rhetoric, to the Hermogenean tradition. It is difficult to follow the steps of this evolution, because of a lack of publications between 1556 and 1570 *Apposita M.T. Ciceronis Collecta a Petro Ioanne Nunnesio Valentino* (Valencia, 1556 and 1570)—*Epitheta M.T. Ciceronis Collecta a Petro Ioanne Nunnesio Valentino* (Venice, 1570). Perhaps there is a connection between the Ramistic views and the Hermogenean tradition (at least on the concepts of method) and the development of an elaborated elocution.

Núñez published in 1578 his first edition of the *Institutionum Rhetoricarum libri V*,[5] followed by new revised editions in 1585 and 1593. The *Progymnasmata* were also published separately from the *Institutiones* in 1596 following the edition of 1578. Besides, we have in manuscript the *Institutiones Oratioriae ex Variis Scriptoribus ac Praesertim ex Hermogene*, in which Núñez includes *pronuntiatio* as a part of rhetoric, a fact which suggests that Ramism and Hermogenism are not incompatible.[6]

---

tum scriptoris incerti, antea Censorino tributum et cum eius de die natali libro continenter impressum. Nunc correctius et aliquot capitibus ex eiusdem Nunnesii (Hanoviae, typis Wechelianis, apud haeredes Iohannis Aubrii, 1615); cf. K. A. De Meyier, *Codices Vossiani Latini. Descripsit K. A. De Meyier*, pars II codex 120, 263–265.

[5] The title of the first edition is *Institutiones Rhetoricae ex progymnasmatis potissimum Aphthonii atque ex Hermogenis arte dictatae a Petro Ioanne Nunnesio Valentino* (Barcelona, 1578). Cf. J. J. Murphy, *Renaissance Rhetoric: A Short-Title Catalogue of Works on Rhetorical Theory from the Beginning of Printing to A.D. 1700*.

[6] On the rhetorics of P. J. Núñez, see F. Grau, *Las retóricas de Pedro Juan Núñez (ediciones y manuscritos)*.

With regard to the *Progymnasmata*, Núñez attached a great deal of importance to these preliminary exercises as we can see in the printed version. Carefully, Núñez points out how to use these exercises in a major oration and emphasizes the correspondences between each exercise and one of the parts of the speech or a complete speech. So Fable (*Fabula*) refers to *exordium*, Narration (*Narratiuncula*) to *narratio*, Chreia (*Chria*), Proverb (*Sententia*), Refutation (*Refutatiuncula*), and Confirmation (*Confirmatiuncula*) to *confirmatio*, Commonplace (*Locus communis*) to *epilogus*. Encomium (*Laudatio*), Vituperation (*Vituperatio*) and Comparison (*Comparatio*) refer to a whole oration. The remaining *progymnasmata*, Characterization (*Ethopoeia*), Description (*Descriptio*), Thesis (*Thesis*), and Proposal of Law (*Legislatio*) refer to *ornatum*.[7]

The printed *Progymnasmata* of Pedro Juan Núñez are not mere translations of either Hermogenes or Aphthonius. The examples are different, the order is clearer, and chapters are added about how and where to use the *progymnasmata*, illustrated with examples taken from Cicero's speeches. These *Progymnasmata* are included as the first book of his *Rhetoricarum libri V*, because they belong to the Hermogenean corpus, but Núñez tried to integrate them consistently with the other four books, to stress their function in the whole treatise, and their usefulness for composing a text. The *progymnasmata* are preliminary exercises but useful by themselves and also useful in order to compose a speech, a large text. So, this first book of Núñez' Rhetoric ends with a chapter entitled *De Progymnasmatis in Commune* ("On *Progymnasmata* in Common"), where Núñez shows his preference for Aphthonius' rather than for Hermogenes' *Progymnasmata*, because the first one illustrated each exercise with an example. Núñez goes on pointing out the sources where *progymnasmata* are abundantly available; thus, Fables are available in Aesopus, Brabia, and Avienus; narration in Cicero's speech against Verres and in the *Divinatio* against Q. Caecilium. Chreia can be obtained from Plutarch's *dicta et facta memorabilia*, Valerius Maximus, and the current collections of Cicero's proverbs, in allusion, perhaps, to the *Adagia* of Erasmus. Refutations and Confirmations may be gathered from Christian authors who wrote against pagans.

---

[7] An English translation of Aphthonius' *Progymnasmata* is due to Ray Nadeau.

Using the precepts, Núñez advises that neither should all of them be applied in every case, nor do great authors follow them narrowly. Likewise, when students have exercised in every *progymnasma,* they must combine the exercises in order to amplify them. Also, if we want to use the *progymnasmata* in an oration, we have to remove the exordium, and the epilogue from them unless they are an essential part of the *progymnasma*. We must also avoid necessarily applying the *progymnasmata* with all their *topoi* or in the same order in which they are taught.

However, the *Progymnasmata* of Pedro Juan Núñez contained in the manuscript #1185 of the University of Barcelona, and entitled *In Aphtohnii Progymnasmata Dictata Accuratissama et suis Omnibus Numeris Absoluta, Auctore Petro Ioanne Nunnesio,* correspond to Núñez' dictation to his students and seem to be an earlier writing than the printed ones; in fact, they may be the first redaction of Núñez' *Progymnasmata*. The printed book is more accurate, but essentially, the differences are minor: for instance, commonplace (*locus communis*), is more general in the manuscript and develops examples both *in malam,* and *in bonam partem,* as Hermogenes advises. Characterization (*ethopoeia*), is related to the patterns of *epistolae*. So, the *ethopoeia* can be related to a past time, like thanksgiving, or complaining, or to a present time, like congratulation, or consolation, or to a future time, like recommendation, or exhortation.[8]

Nevertheless, we find a great difference in the exercise of praise or encomium, which in the manuscript is developed in a great number of *topoi* and examples, and in the five added concluding chapters: First about "how to amplify *progymnasmata,*" referred to commonplace, and encomium and vituperation, the genre of embellishment, with fourteen *topoi*; second about "how to illustrate narrations"; third on argumentation, referred to the deliberative genres, confirmation and thesis; fourth on epilogues, and fifth on "*pneuma*" or periodic composition.

---

[8] Núñez provides examples of all these kinds of epistles, as we can see in his *De conscribendis epistolis*. Cf. *Formulae illustriores ad epistolas conscribendas* (ms.#152 Biblioteca Nacional de Madrid); *Praecepta ad epistolas contexendas atque illustrandas* (ms.#1185 Biblioteca de la Universidad de Barcelona ff1–20); and *Quaestio de componendis epistolis,* in G. Mayans, ed., *Organum Rhetoricum et Oratorium* (Valencia, 1774).

The key to understanding both the exercise of praise and these concluding chapters is found in another manuscript, the #69 of the Collection of Saint Cugat, preserved in the Archive of the Crown of Aragon ("Arxiu de la Corona d'Aragó") in Barcelona. This text, entitled *Institutiones Rhetoricarum Artium a Doctore Petro Iohanne Nunnesio Valentino Traditae, et ab Eodem a Diversis et Optimis Scriptoribus Collectae*, is dated 1573 and seems to contain a teaching of rhetoric in a practical way prior to Núñez' teaching of the *progymnasmata*, as the first part of rhetoric, or preparatory part for rhetoric.

In this manuscript S. Cugat #69, rhetoric is divided in three genres, first embellishment, composed of praise and vituperation, to which are related the epistolary genres of thanksgiving and congratulation; second, deliberation, composed of persuasion and dissuasion, to which are related petition and consolation; third courtroom speeches, composed of defense and accusation, to which are related complaining and excusing. Besides, Núñez establishes three permanent parts of the speech: Exordium, Confirmation, and Peroration. He excludes Narration because it is not always necessary and it is an amplification of the Proposition which is a part of the Exordium.

Núñez continues analyzing these three parts in each genre and the forms associated with them, and exemplifies exordium with a complete list of the beginnings and endings of the exordiums in Cicero's speeches.

So, after exordiums, he pays attention to confirmation in the deliberative genre, where he deals with argumentation. The chapter on argumentation in the *Progymnasmata* is a résumé of this part. Likewise, he pays attention to confirmation in the genre of embellishment and here, he develops the same *topoi* as in the *Progymnasmata* about praise of persons, cities, and sciences. Finally, Núñez discusses peroration in each genre.

Therefore, the concluding chapters of the manuscript *progymnasmata* are an attempt to combine both *progymnasmata* and commonplaces of argumentation in each genre, relating *progymnasmata* to each of them according to their features, and adding a final chapter on composition from the περὶ εὑρήσεως of Hermogenes.

Now we will examine the contents of some of these chapters in the manuscript #1185, starting with the exercise of Praise, followed by amplification of *progymnasmata*, and ending by argumentation in general.

Praise (*Laudatio*) is the most developed *progymnasma* in the manuscript, as much in the details of the main points, or *topoi* as in the examples. Perhaps Núñez was thinking that this exercise was the most complete, or he is providing his students with the pattern to follow in one of the more practical and useful exercises for their future.[9]

LAUDATIO

Praise is of persons or of other subjects. Persons can be praised from six points: Home Land, Family, Upbringing, Actions, Death, and Sons.

    a) Home Land (*Patria*), which includes People (*Natio*).

    b) Family (*Genus*).

    c) Upbringing (*Educatio*).

    d) Actions (*Res gestae*), are divided into goods of body and goods of soul, which are divided in turn into nature (*indoles*), habits (*mores*), profession (*professio*), and virtues (*virtutes*).

There are also four forms of virtue: prudence, justice, greatness of soul, and self-control. Justice is divided into generosity (*liberalitas*), and proper justice, which is composed of not harming anyone (*nemini nocere*), and giving to each his own (*suum cuique tribuere*).

    d.1) Proper Justice

    d.1.1) To harm no one: We inflict injury because of rage, fear, greed for money, and greed for power (*nocemus propter iram, metum, cupiditatem pecuniae, cupiditatem gloriae/dominandi*).

    d.1.2) To give to each his own:

- To God and divine things. This is religion (*Numa Pompilius*).
- Responsibility to Home Land (*Publius Decius and son*).
- Responsibility to parents (*C. Cotta*).
- Responsibility to teachers (*Rex Alexander*).

---

[9] In fact, a collection of speeches of Núñez' disciples, most of them praises, and two of them in Greek, are preserved in the manuscript #105 in the University of Barcelona.

- Responsibility to older.
- Fidelity: not to refuse any peril arising from virtue (*Scipio Africanus*).

d.2) Generosity: Generosity has to be in the interest of virtue or advantage for the Republic, manifestation of gratitude, magnificence, benevolence whether in general or toward friends.

d.3) Greatness of soul or Fortitude: Patience (*Attilius Regulus*), Constancy (*Metellus Numidicus*), Uniformity of soul in prosperity as in adversity (*Socrates, Lalius*).

d.4) Self-control or Temperance (*Metellus Numidicus*): Continence (*Scipio*), Chastity (*in foeminis, Lucretia*), and Urbanity.

The *laus diuorum* lends itself to the same *topoi* as the *laus personarum*.

LAUS URBIUM

First is praised place, sky, land, sea, country, and neighbour countries.

Sky: If it is exposed to the East, to the West, to the South, or to the North (*Si orientem spectet, si occidentem, si meridiem, si septentrionem*).

Weather: If it is warm, cold or mild (*Si calida sit, si frigida, si temperata*).

Land: If it is fruitful, or unfruitful (*Si ager stirilis non sit, si sterilis*).

Sea: If it is in the middle of the land, in the sea, or near the sea (*Si mediterranea, si in mari sita aut prope mare*).

Country: If it is in the entrance, in the middle, or in the end (*Si in regionis initio, si in medio, si in extremo*).

Neighbour Countries: If they are less famous, more illustrious, more recent, or older (*Si obscuriores, si illustres, si recentior, si vestustior*).

Place: If it is open country, if mountains are around, if it is on a mountain's peak. If there are sources, river, ports, valleys or crossroads, or if it is a fortress (*Si campestris, si montibus ambiatur, si supra montem. Fontes, flumina. Portus, sinus et anceps. Arces*).

After the praise of the geographical conditions, we may praise cities with the following *topoi*:

> First *topos* is from founders (*Primus locus petitur a conditoribus*).
>
> Second from settlers (*Secundus locus a primis colonis*).
>
> Third from age (*Tertius locus ex aetate*).
>
> Fourth from changes (*Quartus locus pertinet ad mutationem*).
>
> Fifth from purposes of foundation (*Quintus locus ex finibus propter quos urbes conditae*).
>
> Sixth from form of state (*Sextus ex statu republicae*).
>
> Seventh from scholarship and art institutions (*Septimus ex studiis litterarum et artium in quibus illa spectantur*).
>
> Eighth from virtues related to public behaviour (*Octavus ex virtutibus quae considerandae sunt publica ratione*).
>
> Ninth from honours (*Nonus ab honoribus*).
>
> Tenth from temples and congregations (*Decimus ex conventibus in quibus expectabatur cui sacri essent*).

LAUS SCIENTARUM

Sciences can be praised through their founders, their practitioners, those who appreciate them, their subjects, their teaching, or transmission, and their utility.

DE RATIONE AMPLIFICANDI PROGYMNASMATA

How to amplify the preliminary exercises of commonplace, praise and vituperation is possible mainly in 14 *topoi*:

> First is available from those who have the most elevated nature, such as Plato who is almost a God of philosophers.
>
> Second from those who have a very good reputation.
>
> Third from idolopoeia, i.e. a characterization of a dead man speaking.
>
> Fourth when we say that something happened for the first time.

Fifth, when we say that something happened only one time.

Sixth, if it is common with few people.

Seventh, by occasion.

Eighth, if it often happened.

Ninth, by gradual increase.

Tenth, from exception of the first, and from previous and consequent.

Eleventh, from relationship to the best or most.

Twelfth, from division, and enumeration.

Fourteenth, when we say that more and better things happened to him.

Núñez avoids naming number thirteen because of superstition. (I guess.)

DE OMNI RATIONE ARGUMENTORUM

The *capita*, or commonplaces of every deliberation, are the same as in the exercise of Thesis: Lawful, Just, Useful, Glorious. And every *topos* can be explained by the circumstances: person, subject, place, time, way, and cause. Then arguments are embellished by one of these points: similarity, example, greater, less, and contrary. We improve argumentation with true and false argument. True arguments are called *enthimemata*. False arguments are if we simulate that what happened, has not happened, or that something happened because of a promise; or we simulate the contrary effect, or we simulate that we have done what has not been done.

I do not know the motives of this development on virtues in the exercise of Praise. It is a manner of classifying actions introducing examples from antiquity, and a detailed guide or exemplum for students' exercises. I think it is why the *topoi* are developed and illustrated in some cases with the praise of the city of Barcelona.

In this way, I think, Núñez gives general rules about amplification, argumentation, and composition, advising and preparing students with particular skills to compose the *progymnasmata*, and an attempt to combine general precepts for argumentation as taught in 1573, with these particular forms of composition which are the *progymnasmata*. When students were exercised in all of them, they had considerable training before embarking on the study of rhetoric.

4 Erasmus's Irenic Rhetorical System

Bohn D. Lattin

For over half a century, historians of rhetoric have considered Erasmus's theory of style to be his only contribution to rhetoric.[1] The appraisal of Erasmus's contribution to rhetoric may be short-sighted. I believe that Erasmus's system of rhetoric has been undervalued because it has been misplaced within the genre of Classical and Renaissance polemical rhetoric. As a pacifist Christian scholar, Erasmus based his conception of rhetoric on a peaceful, collaborative model, a model that may agree better with some contemporary systems of argument.

Erasmus's rhetorical theory was based on his aversion to war and his belief that speech was given to men in order to establish peaceful relationships. War was endemic to Europe during Erasmus's lifetime and a significant portion of his work demonstrated his abhorrence of war. His primary passion was to oppose war and to foster peace and concord among humankind, to "vigorously [raise] my voice against wars."[2]

As a Christian and a pacifist, Erasmus created a system of rhetoric based on the idea that God gave humans the gift of speech as "the chief promoter of friendly relationships."[3] As an educator, Erasmus thought that gentle qualities could be developed in students by training them in the rhetorical practice of *sermo* or the art of conversation.[4] Rather than teaching students the combat tactics of a polemic contest, as did Classical and Renaissance educators, Erasmus taught his students to

---

[1] See the literature review in Bohn Lattin, "The Irenic and Sermonic Rhetorical System of Erasmus," 4–11.

[2] John C. Olin, *Six Essays on Erasmus*, 27.

[3] Erasmus, *The Tongue:* Lingua in the *Collected Works of Erasmus*, Volume 29, 295.

[4] James R. Tracy, *Erasmus: The Growth of a Mind*, 57.

share their thoughts with one another in order to foster *concordia*. He wrote that "God has given us speech for this one purpose, to make the relations of men more pleasant."[5]

The following propositions are offered to support this perspective on the rhetorical thoughts of Erasmus. First, I will review the traditional polemical system of Classical and Renaissance rhetoric. Second, I will suggest that Erasmus's rhetorical theory does not fit the polemical tradition. An examination of his writings on education, theology, and peace reveal Erasmus's rejection of the polemical nature of rhetoric, offering an irenic perspective on the nature of speech. Instead Erasmus offers an irenic perspective on the nature of speech, a perspective partially based on the Ciceronian concept of *sermo* or conversation. Finally, I submit that Erasmus's irenic view of the nature of speech might foreshadow the works of contemporary feminist scholars of argument.

The Polemical Impulse in the Classical and Renaissance Systems of Rhetoric

Classical and Renaissance rhetorical systems developed to suit their respective cultures. These cultures existed in continuous conflict, including armed struggle. From the time of the Greeks through the Renaissance, western culture was predominantly polemical. As a pacifist, Erasmus sought to reject this war-like element of his culture as he saw it manifested in rhetoric.

Classical culture valued fame, which was actively sought after and attained through competitive achievement.[6] Fame could be won in the agora as well as the arena. Isocrates noted that in Athens:

> it is possible to find. . . contests not alone with speed and strength, but of eloquence and wisdom and of all the other arts. . . and for these the greatest prizes.[7]

---

[5] *The Tongue*, 227.

[6] Alvin W. Gouldner, *Enter Plato: Classical Greece and the Origins of Social Theory*, 43–45.

[7] Translated by George Norlin. Isocrates, *Panegyricus*, in Loeb Classical Library, Volume One, 147.

Walter Ong wrote that this quest for *fama* was "typically highly agonistic," involving a struggle between two orators.[8] In *Antidosis*, Isocrates claimed that the Sophists used their oratorical skills:

> in the public assemblies or in private gatherings, contesting each other, making extravagant professions, disputing, reviling each other, omitting nothing in the language of abuse. . . .[9]

The speaker of Classical tradition was "a fighter in a lonely contest."[10]

The vocabulary that described Classical rhetorical theory could have come from a military lexicon.[11] The English word "polemic" was derived from the Greek word "polemos"—war. Up through the eighteenth century the definitions and textual content of rhetorical texts, reveal "an almost exclusive concern for polemical discourse."[12] The rhetorical tradition of the Classical period continued in the formal educational systems of the Medieval dialectic and the Renaissance scholarly polemic.[13] The Renaissance humanists, like the Greeks and Romans, considered a trained orator the ideal citizen. In the tradition of Gorgias, humanists wrote about the heroic dimensions of the orator and his powers of persuasion over the masses.[14] Like their Greek and Roman predecessors, they thought of rhetoric in agonistic terms. To

---

[8] Walter Ong, "Agonistic Structures in Academia," 21.

[9] Translated by George Norlin. Isocrates, *Antidosis*, in Loeb Classical Library, Volume Two, 269.

[10] George A. Kennedy, *Classical Rhetoric and its Christian and Secular Tradition from Ancient to Modern Times*, 10.

[11] According to Kathleen H. Jamieson, Greco-Roman speakers were "armed" with "forceful" "strategies" of argumentation. They would "marshal arguments," "muster" cases, "defend," and "attack." They would "overwhelm," "overpower," "overcome," opponents and audiences. See *Eloquence in an Electronic Age*, 49.

[12] Edward P. J. Corbett, "A New Look at Old Rhetoric," 69.

[13] Ong, "Agonistic Structures," 2.

[14] George of Trebizond advised a man who "hungers for the glory of ruling the republic, let him devote himself to rhetoric." See James Monfasani, "Humanism and Rhetoric," 295. Dave Du Perron praised the power of eloquence when he stated that rhetoric "manages whole assemblies of men . . . shapes their wills." See Marc Fumaroli, "Rhetoric, Politics, and Society," 255. Thomas Elyot and Henry Peachman considered the figures of speech as marshal instruments for the use of invasion and defense. See Brian Vickers "The Power of Persuasion," 421.

I. A. Richards the rhetorical theory of the Classical and Renaissance period "was the theory of the battle of words and has always been itself dominated by the combative impulse."[15]

Erasmus Misclassified

Scholars of rhetoric have misplaced Erasmus in this polemical system arguing that Erasmus did little more than repeat the formulae of the traditional system of Greek and Roman rhetoric.[16] Golden, Berquist, and Coleman, wrote that "Erasmus is quite traditional in his treatment of rhetoric."[17] In a recent article Thomas O. Sloane classified Erasmus within the Classical polemic tradition when he stated that Erasmus's theory of invention was the type of inventive discourse which was found "in forensic oratory."[18] I suggest that while many of the elements of Erasmus's rhetorical system agree with Classical and Renaissance rhetoric, his central philosophy of speech was founded on irenic principles and not on the polemical model of traditional rhetoric.

Erasmus discouraged the use of competitive forms of disputation because he thought that disputes created "strife in the guise of scholarship."[19] He thought that disputes and strife led to quarrels. Erasmus thought of "war as nothing else but a private quarrel extended to others."[20] Instead of teaching students to see themselves as gladiators engaged in a battle of words, Erasmus taught students to be comrades, friends who discussed issues in a colloquy or dialogue.

Erasmus objected to the method of dispute and dialectic used among the Scholastic theologians because it brought forth discord among the brethren.[21] In a letter to his friend Martin Dorp, Erasmus wrote, "What is the purpose of this maze of disputations? How much of it is deadening and destructive by the very fact that it breeds con-

---

[15] Quoted from Jamieson, *Eloquence*, 50.
[16] In *Wit and Rhetoric in the Renaissance*, W. G. Crane stated that while Erasmus made a contribution to English literary wit, he did little more than repeat the formulae of traditional Classical rhetoric. Also in *Desiderious Erasmus*, William H. Woodward suggested that Erasmus's concept of rhetoric was nothing but a reformulation of Classical rhetoric into literary form.
[17] *The Rhetoric of Western Thought* 4th ed., 126.
[18] "Schoolbooks and Rhetoric," 118.
[19] *The Tongue*, 393.
[20] "Dulce Bellum inexpertis," *Adages* in *Collected Works*, 322–323.
[21] J. K. McConica, "Erasmus and the Grammar of Consent," 80.

tention and disagreement."²² Erasmus's protagonist in *The Complaint of Peace* is the goddess of peace. She described her search for fellowship among the scholars, lamenting that they were as war-like as the princes. They engaged in verbal warfare that was:

> not so bloody but just as insane. . . Scholar argues with scholar. . . logicians war with rhetoricians and theologians argue with lawyers. . . the heat of debate mounts from argument to insult, from insult to fisticuffs, and if they don't settle the matter by daggers or spears they take to stabbing with poison pens, tear one another with barbed wit, and attack each other's reputation with the deadly darts of their tongues.²³

Erasmus abhorred the use of disputation as an educational tool. He believed that this form of verbal exchange fostered a student's "insatiable passion for quibbling" where "one quarrel leads to another. . . ."²⁴

The Scholastic theologians and the humanists each used some form of polemical dialectic as the basis of their respective educational systems. Scholastics used argument to educate speculative philosophers and theologians, while humanists employed disputations to train ambassadors.²⁵ Disputation took the form of training for combat. A student was not taught to be objective concerning knowledge, but to take a stand on an issue and attack his opponent's thesis.²⁶ Erasmus felt that the use of disputation fostered contentiousness and therefore was dangerous and destructive.

Erasmus's rhetorical method of education was based on his belief that Jesus Christ was God's *Sermo* to humanity and on Cicero's notion of *sermo*.²⁷ *Sermo* or conversation promoted moral and peaceful instruction. In a letter to Servatius Rogerus, Erasmus wrote of how he

---

²² J. K. McConica, "Erasmus and the Grammar of Consent," 81.

²³ 297.

²⁴ "To John Colet," [October 1499] Letter 108 in *Collected Works*, Volume 1, 203.

²⁵ Tracy, *Erasmus, the Growth of a Mind*, 72.

²⁶ Ong, 2.

²⁷ For an extensive discussion of Erasmus's concept of Jesus as God's *Sermo* consult Marjorie O'Rourke Boyle, *Erasmus on Language and Method in Theology*.

had "improved himself" through the habit of familiar conversation with good men.[28]

Erasmus's theology shaped his concept of rhetoric, allowing it to fill an irenic role in society instead of the polemical role. Erasmus believed that speech was given by God to create peaceful relations among humans, not for the achievement of personal glory.

Erasmus believed that Jesus Christ provided humanity with a model of conduct and speech. He thought that the "scope of learning and eloquence," was to imitate Jesus Christ, the Son of God."[29] He wrote, "The liberal arts, philosophy, and oratory are learned to the end that we may know Christ, that we may celebrate the glory of Christ."[30] He wrote that those who modeled themselves after Christ possessed:

> a heart endowed with chastity, modesty, and charity towards God and their neighbor, breathe forth, as if from a vase of fragrant flowers that pleasant and wholesome odor of chaste and benevolent speech.[31]

Within this paradigm the orator was not a hero who attempted to impose his will upon the masses. Instead, true followers of Christ spoke with a "peaceable, kindly tongue," able to "beseech, console, exhort, confess, and give thanks."[32] Erasmus wrote, "life means more than debate, inspiration is preferred to erudition."[33] As a Christian educator, Erasmus's primary objective was to encourage his students to imitate Christ. He believed that Christ could not be imitated through quarreling.

Erasmus appears to have borrowed Cicero's concept of *sermo* and developed it into an educational and rhetorical system to foster the spiritual or mild qualities in humans.[34] In *De Officiis*, Cicero arranged human discourse into two distinct categories: conversation or *sermo*

---

[28] [8 July 1514] Letter 296 in *Collected Works* Volume 2, 295. Also in Tracy, *Growth*, 77.

[29] Translated by Izora Scott. *Ciceronianus or A Dialogue on the Best Style of Speaking*, 129.

[30] *Ciceronianus*, 129.

[31] *The Tongue*, 360.

[32] *Tongue*, 402.

[33] "Paraclesis," in *Christian Humanism and the Reformation: Selected Writings of Erasmus*, 104.

[34] Erasmus never credited Cicero as his source of *sermo*. As early as 1489, Erasmus did reveal that he had read *De Officiis*. See "To Cornelis Gerard,"

and oratory or *contentio*.³⁵ Cicero distinguished between the two forms of speech by discussing the different ends that can be attained through their respective uses.

Cicero's definition and description of the latter type of oratory clearly places it within the Classical polemical tradition. In reference to *contentio*, Cicero wrote that "there can be no doubt that of the two this debating power (for that is what we mean by eloquence) counts for more toward the attainment of glory . . . ."³⁶ Glory and victory in forensic competition were the goals in this type of discourse.

Cicero wrote that the former type of speech, *sermo*, differed in practice and purpose. He considered the art of conversation to be the form of discourse most useful to philosophers and educators. The purpose of conversation was for "instructing rather than captivating."³⁷ Cicero asserted: "it is not easy to say how far an affable and courteous manner in conversation may go to winning the affections."³⁸ While Cicero used only three or four pages to discuss *sermo*, Erasmus expanded on the concept, using over one hundred sixty pages in his treatise, *The Tongue*.

In "The Art of Learning," Erasmus advised young men to constantly associate themselves with learned men, "whose daily conversation affords so much that is worth knowing, you will learn a great deal. . . ."³⁹ Erasmus's students discussed literature throughout the day. In a letter to one of his former teachers, Cornelis Gerard, Erasmus professed that he preferred to employ the familiar conversational type of communication over that based on *contentio*. He wrote:

> In spite of the very great utility, and to some extent the attractiveness of the kind of. . .[discourse] that deals with struggle and conflict, I must confess, dear Cornelis, that I take much more pleasure in what is called the familiar kind; for while the latter is gentle

---

[1489?] Letter 30 in *Collected Works* Volume 1. 54. A comparison between the two scholars' works on *sermo* reveal a close relationship.

³⁵ *Cicero.* The Loeb Classical Library, Volume 21, 217.
³⁶ Ibid.
³⁷ *Orator*, Volume 5, *Cicero*. The Loeb Classical Library, 353.
³⁸ *De Officiis*, 217.
³⁹ Trans. Craig R. Thompson, *The Colloquies of Erasmus*, 461.

and peaceable, the former frequently verges on ill-will.[40]

Cicero and Erasmus agreed that a conversationalist should possess a moderate temperament. Cicero conceived of sermonic speech in which "there is no anger in it; no hatred, no ferocity, no pathos, no shrewdness; it might be called chaste, pure and modest virgin."[41] Erasmus asserted that all tongues should be honest, sober, modest, decent, careful, mild, peaceable, kindly, able to console.[42] He thought that whoever competed, quarreled, or accused others spoke with the tongue of the devil, the author of discord.[43]

Cicero claimed that great care needed to be taken if a speaker confronted another involved in the discussion. He instructed that reproofs were to be applied without anger or offensive language and that if an issue came into dispute, the correct course of action, even with the bitterest of enemies, was to repress any anger and maintain all dignity.[44]

Erasmus echoed this idea when he wrote that anger was a violent disease of the heart that needed to be met with gentleness. Quoting the Hebrew *Proverbs,* Erasmus wrote that "a soft speech turneth away anger."[45] Erasmus abhorred quarrelsome speeches because they polluted all the pleasantness of concord.[46]

According to Cicero, speakers should avoid dogmatism, stating opinions in an arrogant manner. Erasmus restated that theme when he wrote, ". . .today we see the schools of the philosophers disputing with so many opinions, and all Christians battling to the death with so many conflicting dogmas."[47] He thought that the debates over theological issues created only conceited egos and discord, not the harmony and gentleness that came from imitating Christ as Christians were required to do. Like Cicero, Erasmus believed that those who engaged in conversation should allow for the free exchange of ideas. No one should monopolize the discussion; each "should think it not unfair for

---

[40] [July, 1489?] Letter 27 in *Collected Works,* Volume 1: 49.
[41] *Orator,* 353.
[42] *The Tongue,* 402.
[43] *The Tongue,* 403.
[44] *De Officiis,* 141.
[45] *The Tongue,* 366.
[46] *The Tongue,* 338.
[47] *The Tongue,* 406.

each to have his turn."[48] Cicero advised the participants of a conversation to be considerate of the other members. The time spent on any subject and the degree to which the subject was discussed should be agreeable to all.[49]

Erasmus also disapproved of unrestrained talk. Over fifteen pages of *The Tongue* discuss the evils caused by chatterers, including the following:

> ... God has given us speech for this one purpose, to make the relations of men more pleasant. Chattering makes that very gift which is naturally sweetest when properly employed into a source of misery in life.[50]

Erasmus lamented that persons with an uncontrollable flow of words were often thoughtless of their listeners, topic, and occasion. Erasmus compared drunkenness to talkativeness; both could lead to useless quarreling.[51] Erasmus blamed the disease of loquacity on the instruction of "the dialecticians and rhetoricians and the training methods of the declaimers" who trained these people "to arm their tongues with words, and failed to fill their breasts with moral reasoning."[52]

Summary and Implications

This study is based on the supposition that Erasmus's rhetorical system has been neglected because it has been misclassified. Erasmus's rhetorical system does not fit the traditional forensic mold. Instead of basing his system on *contentio*, Erasmus expanded Cicero's notion of *sermo* into an irenic system of rhetoric that was not based on polemical discourse. Rather than the attainment of glory, the objective of this form of speech was to educate and seek understanding in a peaceful atmosphere.

Erasmus's philosophy of rhetoric agrees more with the contemporary feminist view of argument than with the Classical rhetorical perspective. Feminist scholars have shown an interest in nonconfrontational discourse. For example, Jamieson argues that noncompetitive,

---

[48] *De Officiis*, 137.
[49] *De Officiis*, 139.
[50] 277.
[51] *The Tongue*.
[52] *The Tongue*, 276.

nonadversarial language is inherently feminine in nature.[53] Makua describes the advantage of employing cooperative argumentation.[54] As with *sermo*, the desired end of cooperative argumentation is understanding. Makua's definition of cooperative argumentation appears similar to Erasmus's concept of irenic and sermonic discourse with the view that opposing advocates are colleagues rather than adversaries.[55] Feminist and other scholars interested in cooperative communication may gain insight from Erasmus's thoughts on rhetoric. This article is an attempt to demonstrate that Erasmus's theory of rhetoric is an untapped resource for contemporary scholars.

---

[53] *Eloquence*, 67–89.
[54] Josina M. Makua, *Reasoning and Communication*, 48–50.
[55] *Reasoning and Communication*, 49.

5 Neglected Texts of Olympe de Gouges, Pamphleteer of the French Revolution of 1789

Mary Cecilia Monedas

Overview

Olympe de Gouges, arguably the most prolific producer of women's discourse during the French Revolution of 1789, was a remarkable woman who broke conventions to engage in rhetoric, fully aware that she would forfeit her life in the process. *Les Droits de la Femme* [The Rights of Woman] (1791), in which is found *Déclaration des Droits de la Femme et de la Citoyenne* [Declaration of the Rights of Woman and of the Citizeness], predates Mary Wollstonecraft's *Vindication of the Rights of Woman* (1792). Her other works are virtually unknown in the United States. A notable statistic in French history, Olympe was among the countless who were thought to be silenced forever by the guillotine. For nearly two centuries, her works lay forgotten.

This paper answers basic questions about the woman and her works: Who was Olympe de Gouges? Why are the woman and her work worthy of study? Why have the works been neglected? Which problems exist in making the texts known to the American public? How can this be remedied? Following this background information, two short texts are introduced and discussed.

Who was Olympe de Gouges?

Although she was said to be "no more than a shadow of a name" (Lacour 1900, 4), would-be playwright and pamphleteer Olympe de Gouges is mentioned in old French histories, dictionaries and biographical compilations. Her life reads like fiction. Early book-length biographies by Forestié (1900–1901) and Lacour (1900) were unkind to her, and raise many questions. A beautiful woman, Olympe was labeled a prostitute. Said to be inflated with self-importance, she was alleged to have caused the financial ruin of two men. She was depicted as lonely, frenetic, and demented. In his doctoral dissertation, a "medico-psychological" study of Olympe, Guillois (1904) assessed her condition as "revolutionary hysteria" and "paranoid delirium" a predisposition brought out of its latency by "eras of unrest" (87). How could she have produced *The Rights of Woman?* Yet Decaux (1972) claims that she produced "a thousand and one manuscripts" (488). She was also said to be illiterate. How could an illiterate have written these works? It was alleged that Olympe claimed authorship of works she did not write, and it was rumored that somebody had written them for her. Who would allow her to take credit for their own ideas? If indeed it was Louis-Sébastien Mercier, noted writer of her day, would he have been so generous? True, he was her long-time friend and companion, and perhaps even her lover, who is said to have "tinted" [proofread and probably corrected] her works. But would he give away his work—by the hundreds—even to a lover? He himself was a prolific writer, a member of the *Académie Française,* which set the language standards for France, and he was politically involved. When would he have time?

Decaux (1972) abstracted details from early biographies, unwittingly perpetrating misinformation and negative stereotypes. Rabaut (1978) was particularly pejorative. He called Olympe "that Bovary of the south" who had "nothing more remarkable than her pretentiousness and her loquaciousness." He said, "She lays [as does a hen; i.e. produces] a hotchpotch of works" (57).

Some of the details reported in early biographies were correct; some were not; others were part truth mixed with fiction or hearsay. It is significant to keep in mind that early accounts were colored by prejudice. In eighteenth-century France, outside of noble circles, a woman engaged in writing or speaking in public was automatically labeled a prostitute, even if her virtue was impeccable. The object of disdain and vile insults, she would be publicly ridiculed and jeered, and even attacked physically.

Since the bicentennial of the Revolution, the image of Olympe de Gouges as an eccentric curiosity has begun to change. Thanks to Olivier Blanc's meticulously researched biography (1989), it is possible to sort out much of what has been written. Today Olympe is recognized as a woman of letters, an outstanding proponent of change, with a legitimate place in history. She was an intelligent woman, vibrant and witty, with a passion for life. Recently, she has been the subject of several articles. Her name can be found in books about women and feminists, political science, literature, drama, and even capital punishment.

Brief Biography of Olympe de Gouges

Olympe de Gouges was born Marie Gouze, in 1748, to a bourgeois family in southern France. Her legitimate father was a butcher; but the archives give credence to her claim that she was the illegitimate daughter of the Marquis Le Franc de Pompignan, man of letters (Blanc, 1989). Although she was from a provincial village and an oral culture, she received a better than average education. At sixteen, she married a man she did not love, a "spiritual jailer" (Lacour, 1900), who died shortly after she bore a son. Vowing never to remarry, she called marriage "the tomb of love and trust" (*Droits* [Rights], 1791, p. 16). She created for herself a new identity, and changed her name to Olympe. Adding "de" as a sign of nobility, she became Olympe de Gouges and moved to Paris, where she lived the life of a courtesan. At thirty, she embarked on a career as playwright, attended the grand salons, and sought out writers, philosophers, and actors to learn to write and to improve her speech.

As the Revolution became imminent, she was lured by its appeal. It offered her an opportunity to be heard and to gain fame. In her zeal, she attended political assemblies and women's clubs and she began to write political works. Although the theatre was the primary vehicle for making political statements, she had endured endless difficulties with the *Comédie Française* to have her plays presented. The press offered the next best avenue for disseminating her ideas. Representing no organized group, she used her own money to print and distribute her pamphlets and her placards.

Olympe had something to say about everything: the poor, unwed mothers, the elderly, abandoned children, social assistance, hospitals and public hygiene. She urged women to contribute their jewelry to salvage the depleted national treasury. She spoke out about sensitive political issues, offering to defend King Louis XVI, on trial by his people. Always candid, she warned foreign powers to stop meddling in France's affairs. Through her rhetoric, she challenged the most intimidating politicians of the Terror. In the Assembly, "she competed with the most famous orators" (Prudhomme, as cited in Blanc, 1989, p. 96).

Her activism brought her derision, insults, and threats. She was called "man-woman." Yet she would not be silenced, but continued to circulate her pamphlets and post her messages throughout Paris. Her last placard, urging that citizens have a choice among three forms of government, led to her arrest. From her prison cell, she continued to disseminate her messages and to expose the deplorable prison conditions. After months in prison, she was tried for sedition, but was denied her legal right to the counsel of her attorney. She was told that she had enough wit to defend herself before her judges. The morning after her trial, she was guillotined.

Olympe de Gouges's Texts

A survey of some eighty of Olympe's works quickly dispels any notions of incompetency. She wrote an autobiography, short stories, essays, dramas, novels, addresses, eulogies, petitions, and poetry. She produced pamphlets, placards, plays, and open letters. Her rhetoric addressed Louis XVI, Marie Antoinette, Count Mirabeau, princes, dukes, counts, ambassadors, heads of state, politicians, generals, women, the Comédie Française, writers, and the populace. Subject matter dealt with slavery, the Estates General, the salvation of the country, the collusion of politicians, the revolutionary tribunal, and many others. In her discourse, particularly in her prefaces and postfaces, she often interjected personal asides, such as her troubles with the Comédie Française.

The Importance of Olympe de Gouges and Her Works

The revolutionary discourse of women has been neglected by researchers, as has its role in making possible the progress that women began to make nearly a hundred years later. Rhetoricians have lagged behind historians and those engaged in research in women's studies and feminism. Outram (1987) believes that "once one asks the question of how revolutionary discourse affected a gender rather than a social class, then whole new functions of this language are revealed" (132).

Olympe warrants interest because (1) She was arguably the most active spokeswoman of the French Revolution, embracing numerous causes. (2) She produced a prolific quantity of rhetoric in a variety of genres. (3) Her works offer a wealth of feminine revolutionary rhetoric waiting to be analyzed. (4) As eye-witness testimonies of historical events of her day, they give first-hand information about what women endured because of their rhetorical pursuits. (5) She wrote *The Rights of Woman*, and what appears to be the first social contract between the sexes. (6) A large corpus of her work in printed and manuscript form is preserved in French repositories. (7) She may conceivably be the mother of French feminism, and perhaps of western feminism.

Why the Texts Have Been Neglected

For nearly two-hundred years, Olympe was virtually forgotten, as befit her according to eighteenth-century mentalities. As a bourgeois woman whose behavior was viewed as aberrant, she and her works were dismissed as inconsequential. However, after her execution, Tilly (as cited in Blanc, 1989), "justice of the peace of the revolutionary section" of Paris, asked the feared chief prosecutor Fouquier-Tinville what to do about "the considerable quantity of papers . . . notices, placards . . . every other format . . . hand-written letters and plays written by her" (237). He offered to burn them before witnesses, because he believed it would be "infinitely dangerous" for them to be exposed, because they could "poison the public mind" (237). Perhaps some of her works were destroyed. Some appear to have been "lost"; but a large quantity miraculously survived. Although seditious material normally was burned, her works were neglected. Therein lies their survival. For nearly two centuries, they lay relatively undisturbed, unknown to all but a very few. Today they are preserved in archives all over France.

Problems in Making the Texts Known

Two major problems appear to exist in making the works of Olympe known in the United States: accessibility and dissemination. Because the works are available only in French for the most part, they are not truly accessible to most English-speaking researchers. Consequently, dissemination is limited. To be known, the works must be translated. Of the entire corpus, only two works seem to have been published in English: *The Rights of Woman* and *Last Letter*. Olivier Blanc's biography, the definitive source of information about Olympe and her works, is in French.

Translation for the purpose of analyzing rhetoric is more demanding than translation for the sake of comprehension. It requires mastery of both the original language and English. Selecting the most appropriate word from among several that could convey a similar meaning may depend on subtle nuances to retain images evoked in the original language. Familiarity with the culture, historical events, and biographical details can help to make subtle choices in translation.

Metaphors and idioms often require resorting to equivalent terms in translation; yet equivalency is less than ideal in rhetorical studies because the original images are generally lost. Consequently, metaphors, like idioms, are among the most difficult aspect of translation, requiring a sound command of language.

With respect to analyzing a translation of the original, results can be misleading, particularly in the case of metaphors, which are usually lost in translation. At times, a metaphor in the researcher's language may better express the idea of the original, but in the process it destroys the original image. For instance, the French expression "C'est une autre paire de manches" [That's a different pair of sleeves], is the equivalent of "That's a horse of a different color." Clearly, the original metaphor has vanished.

To bring the texts of Olympe de Gouges to the attention of rhetorical scholars in the United States, it is of primary importance to have translations that are faithful to the originals not only in meaning and imagery, but also in terms of the level of language, without modifications for any shortcomings on the part of the rhetor.

At best, translation is not a passion for many. When intended for rhetorical analysis, it can be tedious and time consuming. Ideally, the one who undertakes the task should be proficient not only in translation, but also in the rhetorical demands imposed on the process of translation, as discussed above. But not every translator is interested in the rhetorical aspect, to say nothing of subject matter. These limitations possibly compound the problems of making the works of Olympe de Gouges known.

Form of the Social Contract of the Man and the Woman

Within *The Rights of Woman* is found *The Declaration of the Rights of Woman and of the Citizeness*. Modeled on the 1789 *Déclaration des Droits de l'homme* [Declaration of the Rights of Man], it was written by Olympe in her outrage because women were not mentioned in the male-oriented document. The 17 articles parallel those of the original. Very similar in content, those of the "citizeness" stress the feminine perspective, the value of women and the need for equality of the sexes.

Buried within *The Rights of Woman,* after the 17 articles and the *Postambule* that follows, is the less well-known *Forme du Contrat Social de l'homme et de la Femme* [Form of the Social Contract of the Man and of the Woman], with which Olympe terminates her brochure. This document within a document, so to speak, has been overshadowed by the *Declaration*. The short *Contract* succinctly states Olympe's views regarding the distribution of personal assets in intimate relationships. The last seven pages of *Rights* support her arguments. Although she urges legal measures against the breach of promise by men, she also stresses providing legal action against any woman "who would have the effrontery" to take advantage of the man by invoking the law following irresponsible behavior on her part (*Droits,* p. 19). Researchers tend to gloss over this important point, which is part of her equal rights creed. Its significance, consistent with her belief in moderation, is that she was neither prejudiced in favor of women, nor inclined to adjust the scales of justice to compensate for the disadvantaged position of women. When she spoke about equality, she meant full equality, giving neither sex the advantage.

Implicit in the *Contract* is Olympe's belief in *union libre* [free love, or cohabitation], which was severely criticized in her era in spite of eighteenth-century moral decadence. Although she does not suggest the exclusion of marriage, she personally rejects the eighteenth-century idea of marriage. Aware that her "form of the conjugal act" might appear "strange" to readers, she foresees that "hypocrites, prudes, the clergy and all the infernal aftermath" will rise against her (*Droits,* p. 18).

Surprisingly, Olympe's *Social Contract,* which was two-hundred years ahead of its time, has been neglected in favor of her *Declaration of the Rights of Woman,* which was a pastiche. Yet it appears to be the first document of its kind to be recorded, presaging twentieth-century pre-nuptial agreements. As such, it would seem to deserve a privileged place in the history of rhetoric.

Last Letter to Her Son

Olympe de Gouges's *Dernière Lettre* [*Last Letter*] (1793), written the night before she was guillotined, is the very last letter she wrote, and the last of her discourse. It was addressed to her son, Pierre Aubry, about whom we know little. Blanc (1989) gives a glimpse of their relationship, which appears to have been rather one-sided. In her letter, Olympe refers to Pierre in endearing terms, though her affection never seemed to be returned. After Pierre learned of his mother's death, he disavowed her. It is not clear if he did so out of disdain, indifference, or an effort to save his own life and his post.

Last Letter is a significant piece of work because it gives us a glimpse into deeply personal aspects of Olympe's life. Moreover, it presents a rare picture of the irrevocable situation in which some activist women of the Revolution found themselves, particularly during the Terror. It vividly depicts the final moments preceding Olympe's execution. The tireless patriot is shown in all her human frailty. Weary, devoid of any kind of aid, in need of medical help for her infected knee, she faces the reality that her pleas remain ignored, and that she misplaced her faith in the justice system. We see her weaken physically and emotionally. As Olympe realizes her error in assuming that the Tribunal would judge her to be innocent, her confidence gives way to disillusionment and disbelief at the iniquity of her judges. She succumbs in resignation to the inevitable. Fully cognizant of her helplessness, Olympe reveals her humanity at her trial as she acknowledges her inadequacy and expresses her love for her son. In a rare display of vulnerability mixed with strength, she says, "I am a woman, I fear death, I dread your torture but I have no confession to make, and it is out of love for my son that I will draw my courage" (Fleury, as cited in Blanc, 1989, p. 177).

Although her last letter does not contain as many images as do some of her other works, particularly scarlet placards such as her addresses to Robespierre or her essay about slavery, it does use vivid metaphors. Olympe's last words about personal possessions at the pawnshop are reminders of the insignificance and triviality of worldly goods in comparison to the loss of one's life.

Alan Sheridan's English translation of Olympe's *Last Letter* (Blanc, 1984/1987) appears to be the only one to have been published. The present version is generally consistent with that of Sheridan, with a few differences of interpretation.

Several observations are worthy of comment. The photocopy of the original letter consists of four pages, the fourth bearing her son's address. The first page of the letter begins without salutation and without a capital letter for the first word of the first line. The second page clearly is a continuation of the first, and the handwriting is more difficult to read.

By the second page, the writer appears to have been in a hurry to complete the letter. Possibly, by the third page, there was considerable pressure, because the letter is even less legible. This page is striking because the writing begins approximately one quarter of the distance down the page, and begins anew what was said in the first line on the first page, "I die my son," with minor variations.

The two paragraphs of the third page appear to be in different handwritings. The writing in the second paragraph seems more consistent with that of the earlier pages, although it appears to have been written more hastily, and there is a sense of urgency in the writing. The first paragraph of the third page is particularly notable. Written in a less steady, or less practiced hand, it contains spelling inconsistencies. Some words are virtually illegible, making translation problematic.

It appears possible that a secretary wrote the first two pages and was in a greater hurry by the second page, because the appointed time for the guillotine was near; and it seems that the second paragraph of page three may also have been written by the same person, in an even greater hurry.

More difficult to explain is why the writing in the first paragraph of the third page looks considerably different from that of the first two pages. It may be that Olympe began her letter with that paragraph. Perhaps because of her writing difficulties, which would slow the process and waste precious time, she asked a secretary to finish the letter, who began afresh on page one. It is said that she had access to secretaries, even in prison. This might explain the repetition of "I die, my dear son" in the first line of page one, and "I die! my son my dear son I die innocent" on page three. The signature, different from the writing on pages one and two, and the second part of page three, most closely resembles the writing of the first paragraph of page three. The signature itself resembles that of other specimens purported to be that of Olympe de Gouges.

Because of the placement of the first paragraph on the last page, it is possible that, rather than being Olympe's intended opening paragraph, it was her personal closing paragraph, in her own writing, as an addition to the previous two pages. Possibly the first paragraph of page three was to emphasize her innocence. The last paragraph, which appears to have been written in the same hand as pages one and two, may possibly have been an afterthought, which Olympe asked her secretary to add in a hurry. It was only hours before Olympe's time to mount the scaffold.

Although the third page appears to express Olympe's thoughts, it would seem open to speculation as to who actually wrote it, where it fits in the organization of the letter, and exactly what the undecipherable words are intended to be. There appears to be no uncertainty as to whose words were written, however.

Summary

This essay has introduced Olympe de Gouges, *femme extraordinaire* of the French Revolution. It has identified early biographies and recent research, particularly that of Olivier Blanc, which has shed light on the woman and her rhetoric. This paper has touched on the range of Olympe's rhetoric, outlined her importance in the history of rhetoric, and enumerated why she and her works are worthy of study. There followed discussion on why these works have been neglected and where they are located. It closed with attention to problems that may be the cause of limiting dissemination of the works and how these problems might be remedied. Two translated works were selected for discussion.

Olympe de Gouges's works are more than women's rhetoric, or political rhetoric. They are women's personal testimonies about the Revolution, whose repercussions are still being felt today. At the same time, the works are first-hand reports of problems that women endured to engage in rhetoric. Introducing these works is a small step toward bringing Olympe de Gouges's works to the attention of the American public. It also contributes to closing the existing gap in women's revolutionary rhetoric.

[The contents of this essay and translated texts have been extracted from "A Rhetorical Analysis of the Revolutionary Discourse of Olympe de Gouges, Phoenix of the French Revolution," the author's dissertation (1996).]

"Form of the Social Contract of
the Man and of the Woman"
by Olympe de Douges
(October 14, 1791)

We N and N, moved by our own will, unite ourselves for the term of our life, and for the duration of our mutual fondness, under the following conditions: We intend & want to put our fortunes in joint estate, reserving for ourselves however the right to separate them in favor of our children, and of those whom we might have through a particular relationship, mutually recognizing that our property belongs directly to our children, from whichever union they issue, and that all indiscriminately have the right to bear the name of the fathers and mothers who have acknowledged them, and we impose subscribing to the law that punishes the abnegation of one's own blood. We commit ourselves as well, in case of separation, to divide our fortune, and to set apart in advance our children's share indicated by the law; and, in the case of a perfect union, the one who should happen to die, would waive half of his properties in favor of his children; and if one should die childless, the survivor would inherit by right, unless the dying [one] had disposed of half of the joint estate in favor of whom he would judge suitable.

"Last Letter of Olympe de Gouges to her Son"
by Olympe de Gouges
(Nov. 2, 1793)

to citizen Degouges
officer general
in the rhine army

I die, my dear son, a victim of my idolatry for the fatherland and for the people* Its enemies under the specious mask of republicanism have led me remorselessly to the scaffold* After five months of captivity I was transferred to a maison de Santé, where I was as free as at home*

I could have escaped. my enemies nor my executioners are unaware of this* but convinced that all the malevolence combined to doom me could not succeed in reproaching me of a single step against the revolution* I myself asked for my judgment* could I have believed that unmuzzled tigers would themselves be judges against the laws* against even that assembled public that soon will reproach them my death* they present me my [bill of] indictment three days before my death* from the moment of the notification of this bill the law gave me the right to see my defenders and all the people I know* all were intercepted* I was as in Secret unable even to succeed in talking to the caretaker. the law also gave me the right to choose my jurats, I was informed of the list at midnight and the next morning at seven o'clock they made me go down to the tribunal sick and weak and lacking the art of speaking in public* like Jean-Jacques as well as for his virtues I felt my total inadequacy* I asked for the defender that I had chosen, I was told that there is none or that he did not want to deal with my case, I asked for another in his absence* I was told that I have enough wit to defend myself—yes, no doubt I had some to spare to defend my innocence which was evident to all those present* I did not put into it what a defender would have put for me* about all the services and benevolent deeds that I rendered to the people* [I have] twenty times I made my executioners turn pale and not knowing how to respond to me with each sentence that characterized my innocence and their insincerity, they pronounced my [confession?] for fear that the people should become aware of an iniquity of which the world has not yet offered an example* farewell my son* I shall be no more when you receive this letter* but leave your situation the injustice toward your mother and the crime that that [sic] was committed against her*

I die! my son my dear son I die innocent. they have veiled [violated?] all the laws for the most [virtuous?] woman of her [century?]. I [give?] you [?] [the tone makes the law?] remember my [preachings?]* I leave your wife's watch as well as the receipt for her jewels at the pawnshop* the jar and the keys to the trunks that [I had] I had sent to [tours?]

olympe degouges [signed]

* indicates spaces without punctuation, as on the original document. Lower case letters have not been altered. Words that are struck out are as they appear on the original manuscript.

6 Samuel P. Newman's *A Practical System of Rhetoric*: The Evolution of a Method

Beth L. Hewett

During the first half of the nineteenth century, American rhetorician Samuel P. Newman (1797–1842), Professor of Rhetoric and Oratory at Bowdoin College in Brunswick, Maine, wrote and published *A Practical System of Rhetoric or the Principles & Rules of Style, Inferred from Examples of Writing* (*APSR*). An 1816 honors graduate of Harvard College and a student at the Andover Theological Seminary, Newman began tutoring at Bowdoin College in 1818. In 1820, he was licensed to preach as a Congregational minister (*Dictionary* 466) and he became Bowdoin's Professor of Latin and Greek. Four years later, Newman was offered a newly established Chair of Rhetoric and Oratory, which he held until 1839 (*National Cyclopedia* 123). Henry Wadsworth Longfellow, who attended Bowdoin with Nathaniel Hawthorne and Franklin Pierce, found Newman to be a fine teacher who encouraged excellence in writing and speaking (Thompson 49–50). Thus, *APSR* was born of an experienced and respected teacher's belief that his students needed a rhetoric textbook that would offer "a regular system of study" and that "furnish[es] such explanations and reasons of the rules of the art [of rhetoric] as are needed" (6). This popular textbook underwent sixty editions and was used in a variety of colleges and institutions through the 1860's. Primarily belletristic, *APSR* reveals Newman's synthesis of contemporary rhetorical theory as it bears on praxis; *i.e.,* teaching thought as a foundation for good writing, general and literary taste, language usage skills, and style.

While Newman's text is distinctive as the first popularly used rhetoric textbook written by an American, it is also distinctive for the level of misunderstanding surrounding its origin and development. In his 1983 dissertation *The Practical Rhetoric of Samuel P. Newman*, Marshall Kremers uses the 1842 edition and states unequivocally that "all sixty editions are the same" (note 2, 9; 28). Nan Johnson, whose *Nineteenth-Century Rhetoric in North America* informs much of current scholarship on the American practice of rhetorical theory in the previous century, offers two first publication dates for *APSR*: 1827 (68) and 1834 (note 6, 267). Unfortunately, both promoting the notion that all sixty editions are exactly alike and confusing the text's first publication date are errors that paint a reductive picture of Newman and his contribution to nineteenth-century American rhetoric.

While both Johnson and Kremers mistakenly date Newman's text, Kremers' error is more problematic. Because his dissertation forms the only full-length treatment of Newman's legacy to American rhetorical history, his misinformation clouds the issues and offers support for the general disdain that many twentieth-century scholars have expressed for Newman's work. Kremers uses the 10th, 1842 edition of the text, stating that although the Bowdoin College library has no extant manuscript and only a few editions of *APSR*, "since all editions are identical," studying any edition from any year "is as good as another" (note 3, 29). Following James Berlin's lead, Kremers believes that Newman "thought of his rhetoric as *the* system, not *a* system" (28). However, evidence to the contrary is not difficult to find.[1] A brief review of the publication history of *APSR* reveals that the frontispiece of both the 3rd (1832) and the 4th (1834) editions proclaim the text to be "enlarged and improved"; the 3rd edition is one of the five versions that Bowdoin College owns.[2]

---

[1] In fact, the titles of the 1st and 4th editions are different. The 4th edition adds the following: *To Which Is Added an Historical Dissertation on English Style*. In early textbooks, the title tends to detail fully what the book claims to do (Schultz 13).

[2] In their Special Collections, the Bowdoin College Library maintains the following editions of *APSR*: 1827, 1st edited by (Portland: Wm. Hyde); 1829, 2nd edited by (Portland: Hyde & Shirley; Andover: Mark Newman); 1832, 3rd ed., "Enlarged and Improved" (Boston: Wm. Hyde); 1835, 5th edited by (Andover: Gould & Newman; New York: H. Griffin); and the 50th, [n.d] edited by (NY: Mark H. Newman & Co.). I have examined copies of the 1827, 1st ed., 215 pages; 1834, 4th ed., "Enlarged and Improved" (Andover: Flagg, Gould, & Newman; Boston: Carter, Hendee & Co.), 303 pages; and 1843, 12th edited by (NY: Mark H. Newman), 311 pages. Although

Using three editions of *APSR* (1st, 1827; 4th, 1834; 12th, 1843), my paper will outline the substantive revisions among and within them, touching on the following four areas: (1) Newman's theoretical expansion from the 1st edition inclusion of Scottish rhetoricians George Campbell and Hugh Blair (1827) to the 4th edition incorporation of Richard Whately's approaches to rhetorical practice (1834); (2) the development of Newman's pedagogical philosophy as represented in his 1830 lecture before the American Institute, from which he extracted the introduction for instructors in subsequent editions (1834, 1843); (3) Newman's movement from using John Pierpont's 1824 *American First Class Book* as *APSR*'s exercise companion (1827) to his own analytical exercises included in subsequent editions (1834, and revised 1843); and (4) the writing and addition of an historical study of English style, spawned from a perceived need for a deeper understanding of stylistic history (1827) and which appears in subsequent editions (as an exercise in the 1834, and as an appendage to the text in the 1843, editions). My analysis of these distinctly different versions of *APSR* reveals Newman to be both a serious scholar and an educatior who recognized and filled a significant gap in available rhetorical teaching materials. In a note to the 4th edition, Newman forecasts three of these four changes and I will use his words as a guide through *APSR*'s complex evolution.[3]

Kremers examines the 1842, 10th edited by of *APSR* (NY: Dayton & Newman), we reasonably can assume that the edition he used is the same as the 1843, 12th edited by since both texts contain 311 pages (note 2, 9) and since Newman died on February 10, 1842, after which presumably there would be no further changes to the text.

[3] The complete text reads:

> In the first chapter of this edition, important alterations and additions have been made. The author has availed himself of suggestions, found in the valuable work of Whately on Rhetoric, which are introduced and illustrated. He has also endeavored to render the Exercise on this Chapter more practically useful.
>
> New paragraphs are also inserted in other parts of the book; but the principal labor in preparing this edition, has been bestowed upon the Exercise on Chapter V, which contains a brief outline of the History of English Style. It is hoped, that this may prove useful to the student, as containing illustrations of the remarks on style found in the text, and also as extending his acquaintance with English literature. In preparing this Outline, a free use has been made of Burnet's "Specimens of Old English Prose Writers."

The "Note to the Fourth Edition" projects significant improvements to the 4th (and possibly to the 3rd) edition of *APSR*. The first is Newman's considered belief that Richard Whately's rhetorical theory should be added to the theories of George Campbell's psychological-epistemological rhetoric and Hugh Blair's belletristic rhetoric. He states: "The author has availed himself of suggestions, found in the valuable work of Whately on Rhetoric, which are introduced and illustrated" in Chapter I entitled, "On Thought as the Foundation of Good Writing" (xii). Newman's links to the New Rhetoric's epistemological assumptions are well-demonstrated by Johnson (1991), Kremers (1983), Berlin (1983), and myself (1995), making a detailed description unnecessary here. His links to Richard Whately's rhetorical philosophy are less-well known, however. Whately's *Elements of Rhetoric*, published in 1828, both endorsed and furthered Campbell's psychological-epistemological trend to its logical end, which included writing a textbook incorporating the theoretical nature of Campbell's beliefs (Ehninger xxviii). In reading Whately, available in an American edition in 1832 (Guthrie 64), Newman found useful and practical ideas for teaching rhetoric to his students.

Whately's contributions to *APSR* include, in Chapter I, Newman's discussion of copiousness in which he suggests that students mistakenly assume that a wide "field of inquiry" will yield more abundant material than a narrowed one. Newman writes: "Experience, however, shews that the reverse is true—that as the field of inquiry is narrowed, questions arise more exciting to the mind, and thoughts are suggested of greater value and interest to the readers" (Whately 38; Newman, 1834, 32; 1843, 33). Another example of Whately's influence can be found in the "Introduction" to *APSR*'s 4th and 12th editions. In *Elements of Rhetoric* Whately suggests that students should create an outline, "a *skeleton* as it is sometimes called, of the substance of what is to be said" (25); Newman offers strikingly similar advice by requiring

---

A syllabus to each chapter in the form of questions, is found among the Exercises. This supplies the place of an index to the book, and may be of some assistance to the student, in apprehending the more difficult parts of the work.

Perhaps some apology may be required for the alterations, made in successive editions of this work. The author has no other, than that he is an instructor in this department of education, and that, in the use of his text-book, he is led to see wherein it may admit of improvement.

students "to exhibit a plan, or skeleton, stating the precise object he has in view, the divisions he proposes to make with reference to this point, and the manner in which he designs to enlarge of each head" (1834, x; 1843, x). Later, in Chapter V, "On Style," Newman directly mentions Whately regarding the need to balance the writing between conciseness and perspicuity (1834, 187; 1843, 190–191).[4] That Newman utilizes Whately in later editions of his text reveals singular proof that he did not, as Kremers believes, consider *APSR* to be *the* definitive system of rhetoric. Newman was open to change on a variety of levels, not the least of which is theory, wherever that change might help him to reach his students and those teachers who would use his text with their own students. Further, Newman's appropriation of Whately's ideas for *APSR* demonstrates that Whately may have been more influential before the mid-century than scholars previously have suspected (Johnson 60).

While the second significant development, that of Newman's pedagogical philosophy, is not forecast by the 4th edition "Note," his two-page Preface to the 1st edition of *APSR* does cue the reader to a gap in instructional theory to which Newman later attends. He writes:

> The complaint is often heard, that the study of Rhetoric is of little practical advantage. Many who have learned its rules, do not become good writers, or good critics; and of those who are able to write well, and to judge correctly of the merit of literary productions, few acknowledge, that they have derived much assistance from the study of this art. (5)

He confirms that his experience as an instructor has "satisfied him that there is ground for this complaint" (5). However, the 1st edition's short Preface, which outlines the major purpose of the book and how teachers might best use it, does not address the questions that Newman raises regarding the "practical advantages" of rhetorical study. These practical advantages obviously concerned the author because, in August 1830, Newman gave a lecture in Boston before the American Institute that addressed not only the "advantages proposed to be at-

---

[4] Curiously, despite his assertion that Newman never revised *APSR*, in his dissertation Kremers notes this particular reference to Whately, stating that "[t]his is the only mention Newman makes of this important work" (note 26, 113).

tained by the study of Rhetoric," but also the "best practical method" by which teachers could acquaint "the young with the philosophy of rhetoric—those whose minds are not accustomed to philosophical investigations, and who are ignorant of those sciences on which the art is founded" (1834, iii).[5] Extractions from his lecture comprise the body of the "Introduction" found in the 4th edition and which may have appeared as early as the 3rd edition (1832).[6]

The "Introduction" opens with a listing of five advantages to studying rhetoric. The first is that one would gain "[s]ome acquaintance with the philosophy of rhetoric"; this "acquaintance" is not heavily stressed because Newman sees his text as an "outlined" study of rhetoric best imparted by "talking lectures," "some general principles plainly stated and well illustrated" (iii, iv). The second advantage to studying rhetoric is the "cultivation of the taste, and in connexion, the exercise of the imagination." Cultivating both general and literary taste, discussed in Chapters II and III, comprises 30% of the text, revealing *APSR*'s belletristic backbone.[7] Obtaining "[s]kill in the use of language" is the third advantage that Newman lists while "[s]kill in literary criticism" is fourth; these advantages are considered in Chapter IV. Finally, from studying rhetoric, one would learn to form a good style—a consideration that Chapter V covers in each edition of the text, but which is expanded to 50% of the text with the addition of an historical examination of English style in the 4th edition.

For the same reasons that Newman delivered his lecture to colleagues in 1830, he abstracted this "Introduction" to assist the teachers who would use *APSR*. Such was a common practice of textbook authors in the early part of the nineteenth century. John Tebbel, author of a 4-volume history of American book publishing, explains that "[a]uthors tried to be helpful to teachers, who were often not well prepared for their jobs . . . . Teaching suggestions were usually a part of

---

[5] By the "young," Newman meant students as young as fourteen years old, which was Longfellow's age as a Bowdoin College freshman (Thompson 24).

[6] Page numbers for citation from the "Introduction" are the same for both the 4th and the 12th editions.

[7] Although Newman's understanding of classical rhetoric certainly is derived from Cicero and Quintilian, *APSR* sidesteps the Neo-Ciceronean concerns that John Quincy Adams promoted when he was the Boylston Professor at Harvard. Newman clearly follows the lead of his former teacher Joseph McKean and, later, that of Edward T. Channing.

textbooks" (549). Newman's suggestions for teachers were particularly apt, striking me as amazingly modern at times. He explains:

> That instruction in this part of rhetoric [i.e., taste and the imagination] is attended with difficulty, no one will deny. The subjects themselves are intricate; hard to be understood, and still harder to explain, especially to those whose minds are immature and unaccustomed to philosophical reasoning. Here, then, is room for much ingenuity in the instructor; and without a skillful effort on his part, the efforts of the pupil will be of little avail. Above all things, let not the mockery of set questions and set answers be practiced, in teaching what pertains to the philosophy of rhetoric. (iv)

And what ingenious teaching methods does Newman suggest to meet these goals? Besides the aforementioned "talking lectures," he encourages exercises to stimulate and develop the imagination (vi), building on the student's natural curiosity regarding the nature of language and the rules governing its use (vii), reading with the student "choice specimens of style" because "[t]o learn how to read, is no easy acquisition" (ix), and private conferences to address student writing "and alone with him freely comment upon its defects and excellences" (xi). Among the writing difficulties that such conferences might treat are "wrong directions," overly labored word choices, and inappropriate attention to figurative language. Of writer's block and imitation, Newman says:

> Sometimes, too, there exists a fastidiousness of taste, which is detrimental. The student is kept from doing any thing because he is unable to do better than he can do. In other instances, there is an injurious propensity to imitation. The student has fixed upon some writer as his model, and servilely copying his master, his own native powers are neglected. Now, in all these instances, the advice of the instructor may be of essential benefit. (xi)

Newman ends his introductory remarks to teachers with what he believes to be the major purpose of rhetorical instruction:

> It should ever be impressed on the student, that, in forming a style, he is to acquire a manner of writing, to some extent, peculiarly his own, and which is to be the index of his modes of thinking—the development of his intellectual traits and feelings. It is the office of the instructor to facilitate the accomplishment of this important end, both by wisely directing the efforts of his pupil, and by removing every obstacle in his way. (xi)

This "Introduction" demonstrates Newman's evolving sensitivity to his purpose as a teacher and to his pupils' developmental tasks as writing students.

Returning now to Newman's "Note" to the 4th edition, we see him forecast the third major development from the 1st to the later editions of *APSR*—that of offering, and then extending, exercises pertinent to those skills he believed that rhetorical study should encourage. Such exercises include analyzing examples of various types of writing and writing "criticism, that may lead them to apply the principles and rules which are stated" (1827, 6). While the 1st edition of *APSR* offers some self-contained exercises, in the "Preface," Newman connects his text to exercises in other books; he explains that he has referred primarily to Pierpont's *American First Class Book* (*First Class*), in use in the Andover Theological Seminary from which he graduated and with which he maintained relations. To complete his suggested exercises, students needed both *APSR* and the *First Class*, in which they found the assigned lesson number.[8] Because Pierpont's *First Class* forms the basis for many of the exercises to which Newman refers his readers, it is useful to review the text briefly.

John Pierpont (1785–1866), a minister at the Hollis-Street Church in Boston and author of *Airs of Palestine*, wrote *First Class* as a reader to be used in the highest levels of public reading and grammar schools of Boston. As of July 18, 1823, the Boston School Committee ordered that this text replace Scott's *Lessons* in the public school system (Frontispiece). Approximately 480 pages long, the *First Class* reader was intended to address the complaint that the city of Boston needed a school reader that was

---

[8] Newman suggests other books that instructors might use, among them Greenwood & Emerson's *Classical Reader* and Frost's *Class Book* (6).

> better adapted, than any English compilation that has yet appeared, to the state of society as it is in this country; and less obnoxious to complaint, on the ground of its national or political character, than it is reasonable to expect that any English compilation would be, among a people whose manners, opinions, literary institutions, and civil government, are so strictly republican as our own. (3)

In other words, Boston wanted a reader with American references from which students might learn about their own literary, cultural, and political history and to which students might aspire in their own writing.[9] Further, Pierpont believed that the "national, moral, and religious sentiments" found in the reading that children are exposed to in their learning impacts "their literary taste [which] is beginning to assume something of the character which it ever afterwards retains" (3). To these ends, Pierpont draws "liberally" from American literature nearly one quarter of the volume's selections in addition to some modern, and "intrinsically" valuable English works (5).[10] *First Class* testifies to Pierpont's beliefs that reading is learned by exposure to examples rather than by rules (7) and that treatises on "Rhetorick, Rules for Reading, and Essays on Elocution" are "almost uniformly, little worn: —an evidence that it is little used; in other words, that it

---

[9] This attention to American literary examples is interesting because Pierpont, by filling a gap in school reader material, quite likely inspired Newman to include American examples in *APSR*. I have speculated that Newman was the first American writer of a rhetoric text to include examples native to America, which I believe to be his most important contribution to nineteenth-century American rhetoric (1995); Newman's reliance on Pierpont for the original 1827 edition of his text reveals that Pierpont's influence may be the root of his use of American exemplum. Of his attention to American literature, Pierpont says: "I have also laid under contribution to the literature of our own country: and this I have done with the view of rendering the book an acceptable offering to the American people, not so much by appealing to their national pride, as by making it more worthy of their approbation, on account of its intrinsic merits" (5).

[10] Selected American authors in *First Class* include Irving, Buckminster, Wirt, Greenwood, Channing, Franklin, Crafts, Webster, Dennie, Bryant, Percival, Huntington, Neal, Hillhouse, and Everett. Pierpont also extracts lessons from contemporary American periodicals: *Idle Man*, *Christian Disciple*, *American Watchman*, and *Monthly Anthology*.

is of little use," leading to his decision to avoid any rules or essays on rhetoric in his reader (6). (Indeed, Pierpont may be one of those skeptics regarding the "practical advantage" of teaching rhetoric to whom Newman refers in his earliest "Preface.") Pierpont notes, as well, that the standard arrangement of literary materials—that of devoting pages and pages to individual lessons, "narrative, didactick, or descriptive," then "dramatick pieces, then examples of eloquence from the senate, the pulpit, and the bar; then making the young literary pilgrim travel over many days' journey of poetry," may be considered good "methodological arrangement, but we shall be sure to make few friends, either among teachers or learners;—among masters who are not displeased with a little variety in their exercises, or among scholars, who must have it" (4). To this end, Pierpont arranges his lessons practically and with variety to capitalize on the "gradually increasing strength" of the young scholar's intellectual capacity; earlier pieces are "plain and easy," while later ones "call for a more mature judgment and a more disciplined taste in reading" (4–5).

Newman uses *First Class* most in writing Chapter I, although he refers to it throughout the book. Examples that he requires his students to abstract and analyze include Law's "Paternal Instruction" (didactic), Channing's "Daily Prayer—Morning" and "Daily Prayer—Evening" (persuasive didactic), Buckminster's "Consideration of the Excuses That Are Offered to Palliate a Neglect of Religion" (argumentative), Adair's "Fortitude of the Indian Character" (narrative), and Irving's "Feelings Excited by a Long Voyage" (descriptive). In addition to these pieces directly from *First Class*, Newman offers many other literary examples, a mix of American and English, as exercises for students; among these are selections from Gray's letters, "Forest Sanctuary," Goldsmith's "Deserted Village," Harvard President Kirkland's writing, and numerous selections from both Irving and Shakespeare (both liberally featured in Pierpont, as well).

The 4th edition of *APSR* changes drastically in this respect; in his "Note," Newman explains that he "has endeavored to render the Exercise on this Chapter more practically useful" (xii). He simplifies his students' tasks by including all of the exercise examples in the one text. He borrows Channing's "Daily Prayer—Evening" but substitutes a morning prayer from Sir Matthew Hale. Likewise, he retains Adair's "Fortitude of the Indian Character," but substitutes different literary essays and short works for those exercises which originally are referenced to Pierpont's *First Class*.[11] The resulting text is far more reader-sensitive.

Newman's "Note" in the 4th edition explains another significant addition—that of a "syllabus to each chapter in the form of questions" located at the end of each chapter's exercises. He explains that these questions serve as "an index to the book, and may be of some assistance to the student, in apprehending the more difficult parts of the work" (xii). Curiously, these useful questions are dropped from the 12th edition.[12] Other changes to the exercises include the following: (1) Newman moves all exercises from the end of each chapter to the

---

[11] Perhaps the most interesting new selection is Mackenzie's "Defense of Literary Studies in Men of Business," representative of argumentation and revealing Newman's awareness that not all of the students who would use his text would be ministers or lawyers. This example lends particular support to my sense that Newman's text was popular for so many years because he was aware of the rising middle class students who would need textbooks speaking to their future aspirations and educational needs (Hewett, 1995). Lucille Schultz discusses similar considerations regarding lower level readers in nineteenth-century general school systems.

[12] Far from offering the "mockery of set questions and set answers" that Newman abhorred, these questions at the end of each chapter's exercises served to guide the student in self-examination of the material and demonstrated a remarkable attention to his reader's study needs. As Tebbel explains, while authors generally tried to assist the teachers who used their books:

> ... there was little in the texts themselves to help students find their way around. A table of contents and an appendix could be found in some books, but they were almost completely missing from the early grammars and geographies, and it was the latter part of the nineteenth century before indexes and references became common. Notes and glossaries were seldom included before 1900, nor was the use of questions at the ends of chapters in wide use. (549)

Newman's texts, each of which have a table of contents in the end of the book, demonstrate a highly sensitive concern for students' instructional needs in learning to write well; his unusual attention to a reader-friendly textbook layout may stem from his long relationship with one of his primary publishers—Mark H. Newman. Although none of the biographical sketches of either Samuel or Mark relate them to each other, both are sons of the third principal of the Phillips Academy, making them brothers. Mark, born in 1805 and graduated from Bowdoin College in 1825 (likely taught by Samuel), started his career in publishing shortly after college. From the second edition of *APSR*, he was a principal publisher in every edition and,

back of the text, giving each chapter its own exercise section. (2) He writes sub-section headings to guide the reader through each chapter; these connect to the questions at the end of the exercises. (3) He expands various explanations of rhetorical terms.[13] (4) Finally, Newman considerably alters the text with additions of new, and deletions of previously used, examples; some examples are relocated to support completely different sections.[14]

Newman's "Note" in the 4th edition anticipates the final major development in his evolving vision for *APSR*. He explains that "the principal labor in preparing this edition, has been bestowed upon the exercise on Chapter V, which contains a brief outline of the History of English Style." He hopes that students will find this history useful "as containing illustrations of the remarks on style found in the text, and also as extending his acquaintance with English literature" (xii).

In each edition, Chapter V, "On Style," begins with Hugh Blair's definition of style as: "'the peculiar manner in which a writer expresses his thoughts by words. It is a picture of the ideas in the mind, and the order in which they exist there'" (156). The substance of this chapter regarding the qualities of good style, the different styles that individuals may display in their writing, and the modes of writing as suited to various occasions remains, while not always verbatim, substantively similar in each edition. Newman's major development for the chapter regards the final subsection, "Directions for Forming a Good Style." The 1st edition offers two specific injunctions: (1) "Be familiar with

---

apparently, the sole publisher from the 12th edition, one year after Samuel's death. About Mark's skill in publishing, Tebbel remarks:

> Coming to New York about 1828, he began to publish textbooks and is sometimes credited with being the first publisher to issue a connected and graded series of spelling and reading books. One of these was Porter's *Reader*, considered at the time to be one of the best of its kind ever published. (333)

Newman followed it with the reading books and spellers of Charles W. Sanders . . . which improved on Porter and gradually took his place. Mark Newman's publishing savvy may have guided Samuel to some of his more useful layout decisions. It is odd, however, that the 12th edition drops the guide questions following each chapter's exercises, detracting from the text's reader-sensitive features.

[13] See, for example, 1st edition page 51 and 4th edition page 60 regarding technical taste, taste of comparison, and philosophical taste.

[14] See, for example, 1st edition page 70 and 4th edition page 82.

the best models of style" (208) and (2) "Compose frequently and with care" (1827, 214). Regarding their presentation, there is no notable change between the 1st, 4th, and 12th editions.

However, Newman apparently decided that his text should incorporate a full assessment of the "best models of style" and, in the 4th edition, his Chapter V exercise becomes a coherent full-length essay offering illustrations of English literature from pre-Renaissance to the Restoration. Acknowledging that he draws freely from Burnet's *Specimens of Old English Prose Writers*, Newman presents segments from such writers as Mandeville, Caxton, More, Wilson, Raleigh, Hooker, Donne, Jonson, Bacon, Hobbes, Milton, Cowley, and Dryden. He illuminates each writer's style with a brief historical background; then he analyzes, classifies, and evaluates each example using the terms that he has introduced in Chapter V. Next, Newman summarizes the major influences and legacies of the writers of each historical age. Finally, the 4th edition concludes the exercise with a series of guiding questions for study and examination purposes.

In the 12th edition, Newman considerably restructures his Chapter V exercise. It becomes a selection of fourteen extensive literary examples, unidentified by title and author and arranged miscellaneously, designed to examine the student's "knowledge and skill" regarding "characteristic traits of different styles" (249). He provides no answer key, thus testing student (and the teacher's) knowledge. In this edition, the historical essay, unchanged in substance, is retitled an "Historical Dissertation on English Style" (266), which is appended to the entire text, rather than to the fifth chapter alone. Although James Berlin regards this discussion as being "without distinction" (38), it's worth does not rest on its generally academic approach. This historical survey makes complete in one text the vision that Newman has for a composition course: theory, practical suggestions, prescriptions, models, exercises, and historical perspective.

What is the relative value to rhetorical history of Samuel P. Newman's evolving method of composition instruction? His "belletristic interpretation of the epistemological rationale" (Johnson 68) is justifiably unpopular today. He did not develop original rhetorical theory, although he did differ in opinion from contemporary theorists when he believed it necessary (Hewett). Newman was, however, a scholar and a teacher—highly respected by both colleagues and students—and one who quite aptly synthesized the theories of those whom he respected.[15] We see Newman's scholarship in his ability to analyze and understand contemporary rhetorical theory. We see his innate sensitivity as a teacher in his ability to distill theory into the first commercially successful American rhetoric textbook.

In the last paragraph of his "Note" to the 4th edition, Newman apologizes for the alterations that he suspects he will make in future editions of *APSR*. He explains: "The author has no other [apology], than that he is an instructor in this department of education, and that, in the use of his text-book, he is led to see wherein it may admit of improvement"(xii). Newman has offered, perhaps for the first time in an American rhetoric text, a full instructional outline for teaching writing. He speaks practically to teachers and offers guided exercises and examination questions. To students, he presents contemporary rhetorical theory, synthesizing it to focus on written discourse, and he guides them through difficult sections in a remarkably reader-sensitive fashion for a nineteenth-century textbook. In sum, *APSR* reveals a method whose evolution is validated by the fact that Newman himself tested his practical system of rhetoric, strengthened it, and re-presented it, "enlarged and improved," to his readers.

On a final note, the evidence in this paper points to a need for a critical edition of *APSR*, a text that (like many nineteenth-century rhetorics) is "at-risk" due to its relative scarcity and the often poor physical condition of available copies. Assuredly, accessing this text in its multiple versions has been difficult for scholars, but examining only one edition has led to both an incomplete and a reductive picture of the rhetorician, his scholarship, and his pedagogy. Because a single edition has become a synecdoche for the writer's entire active relationship with his text, previous research with *APSR* can be considered preliminary at best. A critical edition would enhance future research regarding evolving nineteenth-century methods like Newman's and would assure future generations of scholars access to these valuable materials.

---

[15] Newman's *Elements of Political Economy* (1835), for example, was a well-regarded synthesis of Adam Smith's economic theory (*Dictionary* 467).

7 Visions of the Probable: The Transition from Rhetorical to Mathematical Models of Probability

Terri Palmer

In this paper I will discuss the history of probability mathematics, specifically its beginnings in the mid- to late-seventeenth century. Though this topic may seem to have little to do with the history of rhetoric, I hope to show that there is indeed a connection. To begin, I note that I came to this topic because I, as an undergraduate, studied both mathematics and literature, and in the former role came to know a decent amount about probability mathematics—and, like most Americans in the late twentieth century, associated the term "probability" almost exclusively with mathematics and statistics. Like a lot of undergraduate students of mathematics, I also had fairly little in the way of histories of mathematics. A little research would have shown me that the full-fledged study of probability mathematics began in the mid- to late-seventeenth century, and most histories of the subject begin rather abruptly there.

It wasn't until I began to study the history of rhetoric, however, that I considered the role of reasoning about the probable prior to the seventeenth century. Any student of classical rhetoric, especially of Roman forensic rhetoric, knows of course that rhetoric was one means of estimating probability, that indeed rhetoric was in some ways inextricable from arguments about the probable: whether it was more likely that a particular suspect was innocent or guilty or whether a certain venture was likely to result in a favorable outcome. But by and large this kind of question was limited to the study of rhetoric, since philosophy prior to the seventeenth century dealt much more extensively with universally true statements than with the merely probable (discussions of contingency being the closest many philosophers came to the discussion of uncertain events), and the mathematical tools we take for granted today simply did not exist until that time. Discussions of the probable, where they occurred, usually occurred in literature or in debates in the public sphere.

Given that the term "probability" carries such powerful connotations of the statistical and the mathematical, it's perhaps no surprise that most historians of probability mathematics look for modern probability mathematics' roots in the history of mathematics itself, or, failing that, in the history of logic, or, failing that, in the history of philosophy more generally. Ian Hacking's popular work on the topic, *The Emergence of Probability*, indeed concludes that there was no unified notion of probability in the modern sense prior to the work of a few philosophers and mathematicians in the seventeenth century. He arrives at this conclusion largely because he only looks at the histories of mathematics and logic and, sometimes, philosophy; indeed, he pins the first appearance of a truly modern notion of probability to the final few chapters of the highly influential Port Royal *Logic*. This modern sense of probability he defines as including both aleatory (or statistical) and epistemological aspects—namely, the association of a sense of frequency with a sense of reliability, of belief in the likelihood of a possible event: this understanding of the term "probability" requires that we accept that the same basic operation is in effect when we decide not only whether to bet upon a card game, but upon whether we will, say, survive the next thunderstorm or whether we will be struck dead by lightning. (For Hacking these concepts are intimately tied up with questions of the status of empirical evidence.) Again, let me be clear: Hacking states that not only was there no probability mathematics prior to the mid-seventeenth century, but no unified notion of probability *itself.*

Unfortunately, many or most historians of mathematics have followed Hacking's provocative lead, often simply directing the reader to his work when glossing the history of probability mathematics prior to the mid-seventeenth century. There are a very few exceptions to this. For instance, Daniel Garber and Sandy Zabell in their article, "On the Emergence of Probability," point out the complications in Hacking's neat picture—among them the multitude of references to words indicating notions of probability and notions of the same kind of evidence that Hacking refers to, though Garber and Zabell locate these in a separate field of study, namely that of rhetoric. They point out the similarities between certain passages in classical rhetorical texts and many of the passages Hacking finds so innovative in both the Port Royal *Logic* and in Jakob Bernoulli's *Ars Conjectandi*, which latter work is largely accepted to be the earliest complete "mission statement" of probability mathematics generally (as opposed to the working out of a few given specific problems, as many earlier mathematicians had when describing the likely outcome of a given card game that had been interrupted at a given point).

What I would like to do here is to continue on with this work, for while I think Garber and Zabell's paper points out specific technical errors in Hacking's argument, I believe their argument can be carried still further, for these two early works of mathematical reasoning about probability do not yet wholly resemble modern probability mathematics texts. Indeed, I would like to argue in the next few pages that the *Ars Conjectandi* presents in its theoretical sections a sense of the term "probability" that is highly reminiscent of rhetorical strategies for arguing about probability, and I believe there is sufficient evidence to see this work as being influenced by the rhetorical tradition. As I said, this is a work in progress, and I would like, if I could, to discuss at the end of this paper some of the questions I am dealing with in the process of writing a longer work on the subject.

I am looking at both the Port Royal *Logic* and the *Ars Conjectandi* by Jakob Bernoulli. In the *Ars Conjectandi,* Bernoulli proved a weak version of the law of large numbers, which is the law of probability mathematics that states, roughly, that the larger your sample size, the more likely you are to come to a stable value for a probability that will allow you to make reliable predictions. In simpler terms, this means that the more examples you collect of a trend, the more accurate your future predictions about that trend will be (i.e., it is better to poll a thousand people than one hundred). Bernoulli's work was important in that it laid a strong mathematical foundation for the future study of probability mathematics, particularly in the *Pars Quarta* of the *Ars Conjectandi*.

However, Bernoulli was laying the foundations of his theory, and so before he reached the stage of proposing mathematical terms, he stated his theories about probability in non-mathematical terms. So

Bernoulli begins the fourth part of the *Art of Conjecturing* with a discussion of the terms "certainty" and "contingency"—but also with a discussion of the merely possible, the morally certain, and luck, both good and bad. He then goes on to state

> *The art of conjecturing* . . . is defined by us to be the art of measuring as exactly as possible the probabilities of things with this end in mind: that in our decisions or actions we may always be able to choose or to follow what has been perceived as being superior, more advantageous, safer, or better considered; in this alone lies all the wisdom of the philosopher and all the discretion of the statesman. (Bernoulli, 13)

He then goes on to discuss the ways in which probabilities must be judged, namely by both the weight and the number of proofs, which he divides into two categories: the intrinsic, or artificial, or the extrinsic, non-artificial. By the artificial proofs he means those "taken from places relating to the thing's cause, effect, subject, accessory, or sign, or relating to any other circumstance which seems to have any connection whatsoever with proving the thing," and by the non-artificial he means those that are derived from the authority and testimony of men (14). He then goes on to demonstrate what he means: Titius is found dead on the road and Maevius is accused of the crime. Why? First, Maevius was known to hate Titius, which is identified by Bernoulli as a proof for cause; second, upon questioning, Maevius turned pale and answered apprehensively (which Bernoulli identifies as a proof for effect); third, a blood-stained sword was found in Maevius's house (a sign); fourth, on the same day that Titius was murdered, Maevius was seen traveling on that same road (circumstance of place and time); and fifth, a witness, Gaius, alleges that he had intervened in a dispute between Maevius and Titius the day before the murder (testimony).

From there Bernoulli goes on to "set forth some general rules or axioms which simple thought is wont to dictate to any man of sound mind, and which are also continually observed by more judicious men in the experience of civil life" (15). These axioms are as follows:

1. There must not be a place for conjectures in things about which one may attain complete certainty.

2. It is not enough to weigh one or another proof, but everything must be sought out which can come within our realm of knowl-

edge and which appears to have any connection at all with proving the thing.

3. One must attend not only to those things which serve to prove the thing, but also to all those things which can be adduced to prove the opposite of the thing, so that after both sides are weighed, it will be clear which of them has more weight.

4. Remote and general proofs are sufficient for judging about general events; but for forming conjectures about specific events, more closely related and special proofs must be added, if only they can be obtained.

5. In uncertain and dubious matters, our actions should be suspended until more light has come to bear upon the matter; but if the occasion allows no delay of action, the choice that must be made from two alternatives is that which seems more suitable, safer, wiser, or more probable, although neither choice is positively suitable, safe, wise, or probable.

6. That which can be useful on some occasion and harmful on no occasion is to be preferred to that which is useful on no occasion and harmful on no occasion.

7. One must not decide about the value of human actions from their outcomes.

8. In our judgments we must beware lest we attribute to things more than is fitting to attribute, lest we consider something which is more probable than other things to be absolutely certain, and lest we foist this more probable thing upon other people as something absolutely certain.

9. Because it is still rarely possible to obtain total certainty, necessity and use desire that what is merely morally certain be regarded as absolutely certain. (15–22)

Further, though I do not have the space here to describe all the examples given by Bernoulli to explicate these axioms, roughly half of his examples are stochastic (i.e., having to do with frequency, as in the combinatoric mathematics of dice games) and the other half are of civil affairs. One such example is associated with number 3: is a man who has not been seen in his homeland for many years presumably dead? Bernoulli says that the proofs in the affirmative are that no one has been able to reach him, that men who wander the earth are likely to run into more dangers than those who stay at home (death by shipwreck, war, highwaymen, etc.), that he has been so long absent that he would by now be very old and thus unlikely to have survived in the best of circumstances, and that he would have written by now because he knew an inheritance awaited him at home. Proofs to the negative, Bernoulli says, are the following: the man was lazy, hated to write, and was contemptuous of his friends; he might have been kidnapped and thus unable to write or his letters might have been lost in transit, and thus his silence may not imply his death; and, finally, many people have been absent long times and yet returned.

The final discussion that Bernoulli engages in before he turns to setting up mathematical equations based upon these presuppositions is the difference between different kinds of proof—among them, truths which necessarily exist and indicate something contingently; truths which exist contingently but indicate something necessarily, and, finally, those proofs which exist contingently and indicate something contingently. Bernoulli also distinguishes between pure and mixed proofs, as he puts it, where pure proofs are those "which in certain cases prove the thing in such a way that in other cases they prove nothing positively," and mixed those "which in some cases prove the thing in such a way that in other cases they prove the opposite of the thing" (23–24). Bernoulli clarifies these confusing terms by describing the case of Gracchus, who was amidst a crowd of men who were seen (according to the trusty testimony of worthy men) near a man who was stabbed. The criminal wore a black cloak; if Gracchus wore a black cloak but so did three other men in the crowd, then the proof is mixed, for it might show that Gracchus committed the crime—or it might show that one of the three other men did. However, if Gracchus turned pale upon questioning, that is a pure proof: for while Gracchus might turn pale for many reasons, one of them (his guilty conscience) might point to his guilt, the others cannot prove his innocence (i.e., he might have turned pale due to illness but have stabbed the man anyway). Bernoulli later notes too that some further proofs might eliminate all doubt, however. For instance, if the murderer was a red-headed man in a black cloak and Gracchus was the only black-cloaked man in the crowd with red hair, then surely Gracchus is guilty (provided the witnesses are trustworthy). In other words, some combinations of proofs are irrefutable, while some are merely highly suggestive (though Bernoulli notes that one must be careful about how one decides whether something constitutes one or many proofs—for instance, in the above example, Gracchus' entire appearance is important, not just his cloak or his red hair.

I would like at this point to discuss ways in which Bernoulli's procedure up to the very point where he introduces actual mathematical equations are highly reminiscent of the method of reasoning proposed in rhetorical handbooks.

First, again, Bernoulli is interested here in not only the situations we now think of as those suitable for mathematical treatment but also those kinds of situations we no longer consider so suitable, or at least not in precise terms; as I said, about half his cases are examples of disputes in civil law and the other half are stochastic examples. These former examples are, as Garber and Zabell note, strikingly similar to passages from the *Ad Herennium,* Cicero's *De Inventione*, and Quintilian's *Institutio Oratoria*. The kinds of proofs Bernoulli gives in these cases are very much like the kinds of proofs given in rhetorical handbooks, furthermore.

Specifically, and second, Bernoulli relies upon the artificial and inartificial proofs (which Garber and Zabell do not discuss): internal or artificial proofs—those which must be crafted from the evidence at hand—and external or non-artificial—those which are given, usually in the form of testimony—were seen extensively in the rhetorics of Aristotle (where they were called the artistic or non-artistic proofs), Cicero, and Quintilian.

Third, I would like to note that Bernoulli's procedure for arriving at the probably true consists of a series of heuristics. To estimate probabilities using Bernoulli's method, one does not formulate universally true statements, as was common in most philosophical works prior to this time; one rather weighs the evidence at hand and decides whether the circumstances of the particular case outweigh generally true statements (i.e., it may be that our absent friend was simply too lazy to write—we must know the pertinent circumstances). This is a strange echo of such precepts as Thomas Wilson's, who stated that rhetoric dealt with the particular case as opposed to the universally true, which was the realm of logic. Further, Bernoulli's procedure involves piling up positive proofs and weighing them against contrary proofs, a highly rhetorical procedure. Bernoulli's real innovation was suggesting that numbers be involved (in the case of Gracchus, if the murderer wore a black cloak and Gracchus is one of four men wearing such a cloak, then the chances that he is the murderer, based on that fact alone, are one in four—but these odds may be modified by other circumstances).

Fourth, this is not merely a series of suggestions about the factuality of a case, but rather a series of suggestions for choosing the best course of action (see particularly axioms 5, 6, 7, and 9). One is reminded that one of the goals of the rhetor is to urge a given course of action.

Fifth, the very outline of these kinds of axioms follows a rather rhetorical pattern. These are commonplaces, more or less, heuristics for deciding outcomes, and in the text, as I have noted, they are followed by a variety of examples, as was common practice in rhetorical handbooks.

Sixth, and finally, Bernoulli's discussion of proof that I discussed last appears to have a great deal in common with rhetorical notions of proof—namely, that some proofs are conclusive and some are not (see especially Quintilian's discussion of signs).

It is clear from Bernoulli's examples and his correspondence with Leibniz that he was interested in legal examples. However, the widely used Roman canon law, which Leibniz in particular has been shown (by Lorraine Daston) to have used in his own studies of probability, has its roots in the Roman rhetorical tradition. Further, as I have noted above, there are certainly formal similarities between Bernoulli's work (at the level of terminology and kind of example, as Garber and Zabell point out) and the work of Roman rhetoricians. However, I think there is a similarity at a more general level, at the level of approach to the evidence in a given case. I refer here to a quotation by Cicero from *De Inventione* which seems to me to encapsulate many of these traits, including all those I have discussed in conjunction with Bernoulli's work:

> Furthermore, the mind will more easily come upon "inventions" if one examines frequently and carefully one's own narrative of the events and that of the opponent, and eliciting any clues that each part may afford, ponders why, with what intent and with what hope of success each thing was done; why it was done in this way rather than in that; why by this man rather than by that; why with no helper or why with this

> one; why no one knew about it, or why some one did, and why it was this one who did; why another act was not performed earlier; why this was done in immediate connexion with the event, and this other thing after the event; whether this was done intentionally or followed as a natural consequence of the event; whether what he said is consistent with the events or with itself; whether this is a sign of this or of that, or both of this and of that and of which the more; what was done that ought not to have been done, or what was left undone that ought to have been done. When the mind studies so attentively every part of the whole affair, then the topics mentioned above which are stored up will come forth of their own accord; and then sometimes from one, sometimes from a combination of topics definite arguments will be produced, part of which will be classed as probable and part as irrefutable. (Cicero, II.xiii.45–46)

I would like to note here, too, that Hacking's argument regarding the history of the term and concept "probability"—namely, that it arose in a recognizably modern form only in the seventeenth century—makes sense provided one only looks to the history of mathematics, the natural sciences, and logic for its history. This is true because none of these disciplines, prior to the seventeenth century, dealt widely or systematically with the topic of probability (though there were exceptions; for instance, Galileo relied fairly heavily on reasoning about the probable in his scientific work). However, it would be in error to say that no one did, for rhetoricians for two thousand years had been reasoning about the probable and making arguments based upon such evaluations, whether or not logicians and mathematicians had. Given the formal similarities—as well as what I would argue are less formal similarities, but similarities in styles of reasoning about the probable—it seems reasonable to suggest that this work was influenced in some way by works of rhetoric. At the very least, this work was influenced directly by legal works, which stem from a history of Roman rhetorical works. I would like, eventually, to make the argument that this work was influenced more directly still, but that must await closer examination of the Latin.

The question then arises: even if this is the case, even if some influence can be shown, so what? This question matters because I initially came to this topic asking not only the question, "Where did probability mathematics come from?" but also "Where did rhetoric go?" As is often discussed, rhetoric after the Renaissance went into a long decline, in that it was not held in as much esteem by influential thinkers, no matter how widely it continued to be taught in the schools and in handbooks written for general audiences. Much of this decline has been attributed to the influence of Ramus (who attributed many of the functions of rhetoric to dialectic, which he conflated with logic). I would like to suggest here, too, that part of this decline may be due to the rise of probability mathematics as a tool for public policy-making—for certainly probability mathematicians saw it that way, and there was a great movement in the eighteenth and nineteenth centuries to cast every possible decision in terms of numerical data (as has been discussed in various books that have come out in the past five to ten years). But probability mathematics and, later, statistics have come to hold great use for opinion-makers. Indeed, as I have said above, the mathematical and statistical sciences are often considered to be the only truly reliable means of estimating the likelihood of an event's occurrence. So, on the one hand, I think this study could shed light on a particular way that some of rhetoric's functions as an art were absorbed by other disciplines.

However, more than that, I think such a study could also contribute to our understanding of the rhetorics of science and contemporary public policy-making. One of the ways that the "hard" sciences and mathematics are presented as being more reliable than the so-called "soft" sciences and the humanities is through the use of the claim that the kind of quantitative evidence that hard sciences and mathematics rely on is fundamentally different from the kind of evidence used by qualitative studies. Rhetoricians of science often claim that quantifiable data always requires qualitative judgments, that a scientist always makes his or her observations from a necessarily subjective and limited position. I believe that such a study as I have introduced here would further the work of the rhetoric of science by clarifying the transition from one understanding of evidence and its proper uses to another understanding, namely our understanding today of the term "evidence," in which all things can and perhaps should be subject to numerical evaluation. If the origins of the mathematical tools we use today in making such judgments can be shown to be intimately tied to the history of rhetoric, then it seems that the claim that the quantifiable is inherently qualitative would thereby be strengthened.

8 A Rhetorical Liturgy: Ephesians I and the Problem of Race Relations in the Early Christian Church

Gary S. Selby

In its earliest years, the Christian church faced few problems as difficult or as threatening to its future as that of the hostility between Jewish and Gentile converts to the movement. Both groups clearly brought to their experience of Christianity the longstanding antagonism and suspicion which had characterized their relations in the ancient world. To Greek society the customs and beliefs of the Jews were strange and, ironically, perceived as irreligious, and their rejection of Greek culture caused them to be viewed as misanthropic.[1] Consequently, Jews in the ancient world were often met with suspicion and disdain, attitudes which are reflected in numerous writings of the period. For example, Cicero on several occasions derided the Jewish religion as a *superstitio barbara*,[2] and Horace, the great Roman satirist, ridiculed the Jews for such things as their zealous efforts to proselytize, their superstitious beliefs, and their strange customs of Sabbath-keeping and circumcision.[3] Perhaps most derisive was Tacitus' account of the origins of the Jewish people, which accused Moses, their founder, of introducing "new religious practices, quite opposed to those of all religions. The

---

[1] For example, as early as the fifth century BCE, the Greek historian Hecataeus asserts that Moses, the leader of the Jews, "initiated a form of life encouraging seclusion from humankind and hatred of aliens." Cited in V. Tcherikover, *Hellenistic Civilization and the Jews*, 360–61.

[2] *Pro Flac.* 28, 67.

[3] *Serm.* 1.4.143; 1.5.100; 1.4.70.

Jews regard as profane all that we hold sacred; on the other hand, they permit all that we abhor."[4]

As might be expected, such antisemitism was met with equally hostile attitudes by many Jews toward the "uncircumcised pagans." These attitudes are reflected, for example, in such popular non-canonical Jewish writings as the *Wisdom of Solomon*, where the long-awaited Messiah becomes God's instrument of punishment upon the Gentiles, destroying "the godless nations with the word of his mouth" (17:17).[5] Similar Jewish attitudes can be found in the New Testament as well, for example, in Jesus' depiction of a Greek woman's request that he heal her daughter as throwing "the children's bread to their dogs" (Mk. 7:27), in the request of James and John that Jesus allow them to call down fire from heaven upon a Samaritan village which refuses them hospitality (Luke 9:51–56), and in Peter's hesitance even to enter the home of—much less preach to—Cornelius, a Gentile who desires to know the Gospel (Acts 10–11).

Within this climate of longstanding prejudice and animosity, then, the writers of the New Testament faced the Herculean task of uniting the members of these traditionally hostile racial groups, newly converted to Christianity, into one new movement—the Christian church. Indeed, New Testament writers persistently find themselves called upon to address the Jew-Gentile problem.[6] Their commitment to this vision of one united church, transcending racial boundaries, presented

---

[4] *Ann.* 5.4. See also W. Wiefel, "The Jewish Community in Rome ." For an account of how these attitudes were later crystallized in Roman law, see A. Linder, *The Jews in Roman Imperial Legislation*.

[5] See also *1 Enoch*, where, in frequently depicted judgment scenes, God destroys the enemies of the Jews (38:4–5; 46:4–8; 48:8–10; 62:1–16; 63:1–12). These attitudes are also reflected in a number of places in the Hebrew Bible. See, for example, the book of Isaiah's parody of pagan religion (44:9–20; 46:1–13), its predictions of the fall of Babylon (47:1–15), and its graphic descriptions of God's punishment of Israel's traditional enemies (63:1–6; cf. 34:1–17): "I trampled down peoples in my anger, I crushed them in my wrath, and I poured out their lifeblood on the earth." See also Ezek. 38–39; Dan. 1–5; Joel 3; Nahum; and Ezra 9–10. It should be noted, however, that although not a dominant voice, other writings represent a more gracious view toward the Gentiles. For discussion, see D. S. Russell, *The Method and Message of Jewish Apocalyptic*, 297–303.

[6] See, for example, Acts 8:4–40; 10–11; 21:20–25; Romans 1:16–4:25; 7:1–25; 9–11; 14:1–15:13; 1 Corinthians 1:18–25; 8:1–11:1; 2 Corinthians 8–9; Gal. 2:1–4:7; and Phil. 3:2–4. For a discussion of how this emphasis is

them with a difficult rhetorical dilemma: How does one overcome longstanding racial hostility? How does one even gain a hearing in order to address the issue? One particularly creative response to this pressing issue can be found in the blessing with which the epistle to the Ephesians begins (1:3–14).

The epistle to the Ephesians is clearly dominated by concerns for unity between Jews and Gentiles in the Christian church.[7] As John Pohill commented, the key to the epistle "is to be found in the theme of unity which runs throughout . . . of Jew and Greek bound together into one body in Jesus Christ."[8] For all his concern with fostering racial harmony, however, the author[9] does not at first address the issue explicitly. Instead, he begins the epistle by offering a carefully composed liturgy, an extended, formulaic expression of praise to God. As I shall argue, this liturgy plays a central role in the overall rhetorical design

---

particularly reflected in Romans, see Jeffrey Crafton, "Paul's Rhetorical Vision and the Purpose of Romans: Towards a New Understanding," 317–39.

[7] This concern for unity is reflected in the writer's description of the work of Christ as the bringing together of Jew and Gentile into "one new man" (2:11–22); in his assertion that God's "mystery," long hidden but now revealed, was to make the Gentiles "fellow-heirs with Israel," as well as in the prayer which follows, that the Christians be "rooted in love" (3:14–21); and in the epistle's petition (4:1–16), which focuses explicitly on unity in the church. For discussion, see John Pohill, "An Introduction to Ephesians," *Review and Expositor* 76 (1977): 477; Jack T. Sanders, "Hymnic Elements in Ephesians 1–3," *Zeitschrift fur die neutestamentliche Wissenschaft* 51 (1965): 230; Carl B. Hoch, "The Significance of the SYN-Compounds for Jew-Gentile Relations in the Body of Christ," *Journal of the Evangelical Theological Society* 25 (1982): 175–83; Calvin J. Roetzel, "Jewish Christian-Gentile Christian Relations: A Discussion of Ephesians 2:15A," 81–89; Andrew T. Lincoln, *Ephesians* (Dallas: Word, 1990), lxxiii–lxxxiii; and Edna Mouton, "The Communicative Power of the Epistle to the Ephesians," 290–91.

[8] "Introduction to Ephesians," 477.

[9] For discussions of the authorship of Ephesians, see E. K. Harrison, *Introduction to the New Testament*, 331–39; and P. Feine, J. Behm, and W. Kummel, *Introduction to the New Testament*, 248–58. As Lincoln points out, the consensus view among New Testament scholars is that Ephesians was written by a later follower of Paul, who wrote in Paul's name and "was responsible for the portrait of Paul that can be constructed from the letter by the reader" (*Ephesians*, lxii). He notes, however, that a sizable minority of scholars still hold to Pauline authorship, many of whom include the possibility that the letter was in some way edited by a secretary.

of the epistle. For it invites the audience to celebrate a constellation of values, among them a value toward which the author expects antagonism and resistance—that of racial unity in the church. In this way, the author exploits a traditional form for rhetorical purposes, along the lines suggested in the writings of Kenneth Burke. The blessing of Eph. 1 thus provides an important insight into the conception of rhetoric held by early Christian writers.

Kenneth Burke and Rhetorical Form

Kenneth Burke's understanding of form arises from his view of the human mind, which he conceives of as possessing certain "potentialities of appreciation"[10] for various processes of arrangement or development within an artistic work. These "innate forms of the mind" enable an audience to appreciate such things as crescendo, balance, repetition, disclosure, reversal, contradiction, expansion, magnification, and series.[11] He argues, for example, that the formality of beginnings and endings, "such procedures as the greeting of the New Year, the ceremony of laying cornerstones, the 'housewarming,' the funeral, all indicate that the human mind is prone to feel beginnings and endings as such."[12] Consequently, for Burke, artistic form is no mere embellishment to content. Much more, it readily awakens

> an attitude of collaborative expectancy in us. For instance, imagine a passage built about a set of oppositions ("we do this, but they on the other hand do that; we stay here, but they go there; we look up, but they look down," etc.). Once you grasp the trend of the form, it invites participation regardless of the subject matter. Formally, you will find yourself swinging

---

[10] Kenneth Burke, *Counter-Statement*, 46. See also, 48–49.

[11] *Counter-Statement*, 46–47. Burke conceives of the mind's appreciation for crescendo, for example, in this way: "If we wish to indicate a gradual rise to a crisis, and speak of this as a climax, or a crescendo, we are talking in intellectualistic terms of a mechanism which can often be highly emotive. There is in reality no such thing as a crescendo. What does exist is a multiplicity of individual artworks each of which may be arranged as a whole, or in some parts, in a manner which we distinguish as climactic. And there is also in the human brain the potentiality for reacting favorably to such a climactic arrangement . . ." (45).

[12] *Counter-Statement*, 139.

along with the succession of antitheses, even though you may not agree with the proposition being presented in this form.[13]

"Participation" in the form invites assent to the content of that form or, at least, "prepares for assent to the matter identified with it."[14] Thus, for Burke, the potential of poetic discourse to engage an audience, to invite symbolic participation by means of artistic form, explains its power to move or persuade an audience.[15]

The blessing of Eph. 1 reflects just such a conception of the nature of rhetorical form. As a liturgical text, it has a complex structure which conveys a clearly discernible line of thought reflecting the epistle's overall rhetorical aim of uniting Jewish and Gentile believers into one Christian community. Indeed, a careful examination of the blessing suggests the author's intention to invite his audience to "participate in the form" of the discourse in hopes that, as Burke suggested, they will give their assent to its content.

The Structure of the Ephesian Blessing

At first reading, even in translation, Ephesians 1:3–14 appears to the modern reader to be an almost hopelessly tangled mass of participial phrases and relative clauses thrown together in haphazard fashion.[16] A

---

[13] Kenneth Burke, *A Rhetoric of Motives* (Berkeley: University Press, 1969), 58.

[14] *A Rhetoric of Motives*, 58.

[15] Burke's conception of the power of the artistic act to bring the audience into "participation" with the act underlies the distinction he makes between the audience's watching a performance and the audience's experiencing the act (*Counter-Statement*, 59–60; cf. 145). Thus he writes, "It is the suspense of certain forces gathering to produce a certain result. We know that it will be snapped—there is thus no ignorance of the outcome. *Our satisfaction arises from our participation in the process, from the fact that the beginnings of the dialogue lead us to feel the logic of its close*" (*Counter-Statement*, 145, italics mine).

[16] Indeed, the structure of this passage has presented an enduring problem for NT scholars, who have offered an assortment of possibilities, many based on the assumption that the passage is a quotation of an early Christian hymn. Their efforts, however, have fostered a confusion which led Sanders to declare that "every attempt to provide a strophic structure for Eph. 1:3–14 fails," to dismiss the notion that this text is a quotation of an early Christian

closer look, however, reveals it to be a carefully constructed liturgical discourse, modeled after the traditional Jewish *berakah,* or blessing. As Andrew T. Lincoln observes,

> Repetition and redundance are the essence of liturgy and here the repetition of certain words and phrases, the repeated genitives, and the collection of synonyms not only have the effect of intensifying the force of the concepts involved, but also serve to provide the sentence with a certain rhythm. In addition, the succession of long syllables in a number of places periodically slows down the flow of words so that a chant-like effect is produced as the eulogy is spoken.[17]

The blessing begins with an expression of praise in vv. 3–4, "Blessed be the God and Father of our Lord Jesus Christ," and the reason for that praise, the fact that God "has blessed us with every spiritual blessing," specifically, "having chosen us from the foundation of the world . . . to be holy and blameless in his sight." This basic content is then amplified in the remainder of the blessing in two distinct, parallel units of thought which are structured, as Dibelius, Kasemann and others noted,[18] around the prepositional phrases "in love" and "in all wisdom and insight," as shown in the following translation:

OPENING

> (3) Blessed be the God and Father of our Lord Jesus Christ, who has blessed us with every spiritual blessing in the heavenly places in Christ, (4) for he chose us from the foundation of the world to be holy and blameless in his presence;

---

hymn, and to assert—an overstatement in my view—that "formal elements in 1:3–14 cannot even with a minor degree of precision be related to the subject matter" ("Hymnic Elements in Ephesians 1–3," 225, 227). For other discussions, including historical surveys, see Markus Barth, *Ephesians,* 97ff.; Peter T. O'Brien, "Ephesians I: An Unusual Introduction to a New Testament Letter," 504–16; J. Cambier, "La Benediction d'Eph. 1:3–14," 58–104; and Lincoln, *Ephesians,* 11–19.

[17] Lincoln, *Ephesians,* 12. For discussions of this form, see Barth, *Ephesians,* 97–98; "Hymnic Elements in Ephesians 1–3," and O'Brien, "Ephesians I."

[18] Cited in "Hymnic Elements in Ephesians 1–3," 225.

BODY

A1 In love
  (5) having predestined us for adoption unto him through Jesus Christ

A2 according to the good pleasure of his will
  (6) unto the glory of his grace which he lavished on us in the one he loves

A3 (7) in whom we have redemption through his blood, the forgiveness of sins according to the riches of his grace (8) which he caused to overflow unto us;

B1 In all wisdom and insight
  (9) having made known to us the mystery of his will

B2 according to his good pleasure which he displayed in him
  (10) unto the working of his plan in the fullness of time, to bring all things together in Christ
    both things in heaven
    and things on earth,

B3a in him (11) in whom we were chosen, having been predestined according to the plan of him who works in all things according to the purpose of his will, (12) in order that we might be for the praise of his glory, we who were the first to believe in Christ,

B3b (13) in whom you also [were chosen], who heard the word of truth, the gospel of our salvation, in whom having believed, you were sealed with the promised Holy Spirit,

CONCLUSION

  (14) who is the guarantee of our inheritance, unto the redemption of our possession, unto the praise of his glory.

Schematized in this way, one can readily observe an almost line-by-line parallel structure built into the text, achieved grammatically and syntactically, as well as by the writer's lexical choices. The sequence of phrases in stanza A, "in love," "according to the good pleasure of his will," and "in whom we have redemption," are grammatically and syntactically parallel to the sequence in stanza B: "in all wisdom and insight," "according to his good pleasure," and "in whom we were chosen/in whom you also were chosen." The phrases "having predestined us" and "unto the glory of his grace" in stanza A are similarly parallel to the phrases "having made known to us" and "unto the working of his plan" in stanza B. Finally, within stanza B, part 3, a structurally parallel relationship exists between the phrases "in whom we also were chosen" and "in whom you also were chosen."[19]

The blessing of Eph. 1, then, is a highly structured ceremonial or ritual expression of praise to God which can be divided in this way:

Opening: states the basic content concerning our having been chosen by God ("Blessed be . . . in his sight")

Body: develops the basic content, in two structurally parallel stanzas, each consisting of three well-defined thought units ("In love . . . Holy Spirit")

Conclusion: recalls the concept of "chosenness" introduced in the opening and developed in the body ("who is the guarantee of our inheritance. . ."), and closes with a final, formulaic expression of praise ("unto the praise of his glory")

Within this structure, moreover, the author uses traditional formulaic, possibly hymnic, thought and phraseology, much of which is likely familiar to his audience. What is the purpose behind this liturgical language and intricate structure? That purpose, I believe, is a rhetorical one: to create for an audience, through language, a symbolic experience of unity and to reinforce the values centered on unity which will be explicitly taught later in the epistle.

---

[19] Because of the parallel structure between the opening clauses of vv. 11 and 13 ("in whom we were chosen," and "in whom you also"), and because of the absence of the verb in the latter, I am treating the phrase "in whom you also" (v. 13) as an elliptical expression for which the verb "were chosen" can be supplied. As Blass and Debrunner point out, ellipsis in the New Testament commonly takes a form in which "the repetition of a grammatical element is left to be supplied." For discussion of ellipsis in the New Testament, see F. Blass and A. Debrunner, *A Greek Grammar of the New Testament and Other Early Christian Literature*, 253–55.

The Blessing's Rhetorical Function

On the most general level, the blessing accords with what classical theorists said of epideictic rhetoric. As Aristotle conceived it, the purpose of epideictic rhetoric was the praise or blame of the values addressed by the rhetor or the persons or deeds held up as examples of those values.[20] On this basis, Chaim Perelman and Lucie Olbrechts-Tyteca observe, epideictic rhetoric "has significance and importance for argument because it strengthens the disposition toward action by increasing adherence to the values it lauds."[21] In epideictic rhetoric, they continue, "The speaker tries to establish a sense of communion centered around particular values recognized by the audience."[22] On the most general level, this explains the function of the blessing, as an attempt of the author to create a sense of community simply by using a form of discourse through which a congregation would worship God. His consistent use of the first person plural pronoun to describe both himself and his audience constitutes rhetorically, out of both, one congregation united in praise: "We praise God for what God has done for us." The author invites the audience to praise God, moreover, for the blessings in which they have participated together, namely, God's love, grace, redemption, and election—shared experiences which, by implication, overshadow whatever barriers might separate them. Further, among those values which are held up for the audience to praise is the unity to which God has brought them. In this way, simply by virtue of its being epideictic rhetoric, the blessing creates out of the diverse members of the audience one community united in praise and it reinforces adherence to the values it holds up as worthy of praise.

More specifically, along the lines suggested by Burke, the author uses artistic form in the body of the blessing to move the audience toward assent to its content. In part A, he invites the audience to praise God for the richness of his love, expressed in his act of having predestined "us" for "adoption unto Him." This was accomplished "according to the pleasure of his will" through the outpouring of "his grace," resulting in "our redemption through his blood" and "the forgiveness of sins." Using language and concepts with which his audience was no doubt familiar, the author thus engages them in praise for the acts of God which constituted the "core" of their Christian experience and

---

[20] *Rhet.* 1.9.
[21] C. Perelman and L. Olbrechts-Tyteca, *The New Rhetoric*, 50.
[22] *New Rhetoric*, 51.

for which they no doubt felt genuinely thankful. This content is then connected, by means of the parallel grammatical and syntactical structure, with the ideas in part B of the body—ideas to which the audience was resistant. Along the lines Burke suggested, the blessing's form invites the audience's "collaboration" with its content.

In part B, the author invites the audience to praise God for his wisdom and insight, demonstrated in the revealing of "the mystery of his will," again according to his good pleasure. This will of God, long a mystery but now made known, was "to bring all things together in Christ, both things in heaven and things on earth." In this way, the audience praises God for the ultimate, cosmic unity toward which, in the fullness of time, God is taking all things. Having praised God for this ultimate, cosmic unity, they are then led to praise God for the concrete expression of that unity in their own experience. That concrete expression of cosmic unity, of course, is the bringing together of "we who were the first to believe"—that is, Jewish Christians, with "you also . . . who heard the word of truth"—that is, Gentile Christians.

By means of this complex structure, then, the blessing begins by leading the audience to praise God for the elements of their Christian experience with which they are both comfortable and familiar, and then moves them to continue praising God for that which they are reluctant to accept—the fact that from traditionally hostile races they now form one new community. All of this is accomplished, finally, in a form which readily invites participation and assent, the traditional *berekah*, so that in effect, the audience ends up praising God for the values which later they will be explicitly urged to accept. Having symbolically enacted their unity through their participation in the blessing of Eph. 1, the audience is thus prepared to accept the more explicit doctrinal exposition and moral exhortation centered on Christian unity which follow.

Conclusion

This analysis suggests that the author of Ephesians and—to the extent that this epistle represents early Christian rhetoric, the early Christian writers—possessed a sophisticated understanding of the nature of persuasion which included at least three important elements. First, the author possesses an acute sensitivity to the constraints of his rhetorical situation. He appears to appreciate the nature of racial hostility—that it is driven by irrational beliefs and deeply-held values which, at best, are extremely difficult to change, and against which explicit, logical argumentation may be ineffective. Indeed, the author appears to anticipate initial resistance on the part of his audience to any direct treatment of their need to accept each other, and in response, creates a text which deals with the issue indirectly.

Second, the blessing shows the author's appreciation for liturgy as a potent rhetorical form. Certainly, the early Christians' religious heritage would have led them to emphasize the need for discursive expressions of worship. This text, however, demonstrates more than just an appreciation for poetic expressions of praise to God, for it deliberately invites the audience to praise God for the very things to which the author anticipates his audience will be resistant. Further, it invites a symbolic enactment of, or participation in, the values of racial harmony which, the author hopes, will replace the suspicion and hostility which now characterize relationships in the Ephesian church. In other words, the author hopes that by celebrating these values through a liturgy—in Burke's words, through their participation "in the form of the discourse"—the audience will actually come to possess those values. In this way, the Ephesian blessing suggests the author's sense of what liturgy as a rhetorical form might be expected to accomplish in an audience.

Finally, on a still broader level, one wonders if this use of the liturgical form does not indicate an implicit "theory" of character development and change—an understanding that these are not achieved exclusively or even primarily through conveying doctrinal information or argument. Rather, the early Christian writers understood, or at least sensed, that they could most affect their audiences' deeply-held values and attitudes by creating, through language and form, these symbolic, celebratory experiences. They sensed that change at so deep a level is not accomplished merely by explanation or argument, but rather, by creating liturgical discourse—expressions of praise, worship, and prayer—through which their audiences would symbolically enact the very values the authors most wished to instill.

9 "Danced through Every Labyrinth of the Law": Benjamin Austin on Rhetoric as Virtue and Vice in Early American Legal Practice

Sean Patrick O'Rourke

This paper was originally presented as the author's Presidential address to the American Society for the History of Rhetoric in November of 1997. The author wishes to thank Jim Ely for his help with the literature on anti-lawyer sentiment, as well as the reference staff of the Jean and Alexander Heard Library at Vanderbilt University.

Historians of rhetoric, like historians of any other art, often find ourselves toting the historical baggage of the craft we study. Unwittingly, perhaps, and despite the delicate two-step we dance between detachment and intervention, the twin canons of historiography,[1] all too often we find ourselves saddled with the legacy of rhetoric's rap sheet. This is all the more true in the United States, for here most historians of rhetoric are also, like those we study, teachers of public speaking, argumentation, composition, homiletics, trial practice, and the like. Imbued as we are, then, with both historical perspective and contemporary practice, we may well consider ourselves all too familiar with the criticism of rhetoric.

And yet, attending to the critiques of rhetoric pays no small reward. By studying the attacks of Plato, Philodemus, Sprat, Locke,

---

[1] On intervention and detachment as canons of historiography, see in particular, G. Edward White, *Intervention and Detachment* 3–72. For my sense of these tensions see my review of White's work in *American Journal of Legal History*.

Kant, Croce, and the like we gain entre to the cultural milieu of the time and place of their origin. We are also able to grasp the continuities and changes that such critiques undergo as they appear and reappear in different eras and in different circumstances. And, by studying attacks on rhetoric, we are better able to grasp the fate of the art as it is held up to different standards, manifested in different practices or, to paraphrase Brian Vickers, bludgeoned by different sticks.[2]

We have not, however, studied the attacks on rhetoric in the early American republic, roughly 1787–1828. As a result, our understanding of rhetoric in the period remains incomplete, as does our sense of rhetoric's critics. In what follows I begin an inquiry into the problem by examining the critique of legal rhetoric found in Benjamin Austin's *Observations on the Pernicious Practice of the Law* (1786/1814). The article's first section identifies several key questions arising out of the cultural life of the young republic. The second section takes note of the larger shape of Austin's project, then attends to what he has to say about rhetoric, ostensibly the lawyer's vice but, as we will see, also the lawyer's virtue. In the final section I sketch a few tentative conclusions regarding forensic rhetoric in the period.

I

Early republican culture gives rise to two sets of questions. The first is related to the nature of the rhetorical models and precepts that dominated the culture and the republican ideology that undergirded it.

The period of the early republic witnessed the composition and publication of two of the most important American rhetorics, those of John Quincy Adams[3] and John Witherspoon,[4] lectures on rhetoric by William Smith at the College of Philadelphia,[5] essays on oratory by

---

[2] Brian Vickers, "Territorial Disputes: Philosophy *versus* Rhetoric," 251.

[3] John Quincy Adams, *Lectures on Rhetoric and Oratory*.

[4] The most accessible version of the "Lectures on Eloquence" today is Thomas Miller, ed., *The Selected Writings of John Witherspoon*, 231–318. Miller reports that the lectures were written in 1768, published in 1801, and widely distributed in the 1810 edition of Witherspoon's *Works*.

[5] William Smith's "The Substance of a Course of Lectures on Rhetoric; Read in the College of Philadelphia," are student notes taken by Jasper Yeates in 1760 now housed in the University of Pennsylvania Archives. They have been published by Dennis Barone in his "An Introduction to William Smith and Rhetoric at the College of Philadelphia," 111–60.

William Wirt[6] and Francis Gilmer,[7] publication of E. B. Williston's massive *Eloquence of the United States*,[8] and an anonymous volume on *American Oratory*,[9] as well as numerous periodical essays on oratory and rhetoric.[10] Indeed, the period was often referred to by later critics as the "Golden Age" of American oratory for, true to its republican ideology, the period witnessed large-scale oratorical debates over matters central to the formation and maintenance of the American experiment.[11] For many the era marked, like other periods of intense cultural transformation, important developments in rhetoric.[12]

Recent work on the rhetoric of the period has called attention to the prominence of classical, especially Ciceronian, rhetorical precepts and oratorical models. Gregory Clark and Michael Halloran note the orator's central position in republican culture, and argue that the orator's chief task, "to articulate a public moral consensus and bring it to bear on particular issues," was undertaken through forms that were

---

[6] See, e.g., the essays attributed to Wirt in *The Letters of the British Spy*, *The Rainbow; First Series* and *The Old Bachelor*. Wirt also wrote "On Forensic Eloquence" for the *Richmond Enquirer* in November of 1804. For a survey of Wirt's contributions, see Judy Hample, "William Wirt's Familiar Essays: Criticism of Virginia Oratory," 25–41 and Jay B. Hubbell, "William Wirt and the Familiar Essay in Virginia," 136–52.

[7] Gilmer's *Sketches of American Orators* was published anonymously. Gilmer later added to his sketches and published them (with other materials) under his name as *Sketches, Essays, and Translations*.

[8] E. B. Williston, editor, *Eloquence of the United States*, 5 volumes.

[9] *American Oratory, Or, Selections from the Speeches of Eminent Americans*. The compiler is described as "A member of the Philadelphia Bar."

[10] The periodic literature on rhetoric and oratory in the period is enormous. For a sense of this material see Stephen Chambers and G. P. Mohrmann, "Rhetoric in Some American Periodicals, 1815–1850," 111–20.

[11] Edward G. Parker, *The Golden Age of American Oratory*; Barnet Baskerville, *The People's Voice*, 32–87. But see also, Owen Dudley Edwards, "American Oratory," 453–56.

[12] Rufus Choate attributes the remarkable rhetorical activity of the time to the revolutionary nature of the discourse. See his "The Eloquence of Revolutionary Periods," 1:439–63. Edward G. Parker credits the orators of the period and the "budding and blooming of American nationality." See Parker, 1.

"more or less classical."[13] Stephen Botein[14] and Linda Kerber[15] bear witness to the Ciceronian influence on lawyers of the time, and Robert Ferguson and James Farrell emphasize the extent to which Ciceronian standards of eloquence permeated the forensic oratory of the period.[16]

The questions are then raised, is Austin concerned with rhetoric generally or with its misuse? What might Austin's criticism of legal rhetoric tell us about the Ciceronian standards of the time? To what extent does Austin's attack seek to undermine and subvert the Ciceronian ideals of republican culture? And, on a somewhat more specific note, does Austin shed any light on the question of whether Ciceronian precepts and models were, as Farrell and Ferguson argue, well-suited or, as John Quincy Adams suggested, poorly suited to early American legal practice?[17]

A second set of questions is raised not by the nature of the period's rhetoric but by the nature of the criticism of the period's rhetoric. In the early American republic rhetoric was criticized as an instrument of that most controversial profession, the law. And while we know that forensic rhetoric has, over the course of the discipline's long history, often served as a focal point for those distressed by the practice of rhetoric, more often than not the use of lawyers as negative exemplars has come as part of a larger attack on rhetoric *per se*. In the early American republic the emphasis seems to be reversed: The larger attack is on the lawyer *per se*; the criticism of his rhetorical practice is but one part of that larger attack. Anti-lawyer sentiment is a familiar theme in American legal history. It manifested itself in colonial times, when law books

---

[13] Gregory Clark and S. Michael Halloran, "Introduction: Transformations of Public Discourse in Nineteenth-Century America," in Clark and Halloran, eds., *Oratorical Culture in Nineteenth-Century America*, 24–25.

[14] Stephen Botein, "Cicero as Role Model for Early American Lawyers," 313–21.

[15] Linda K. Kerber, "Salvaging the Classical Tradition," 95–134.

[16] See Robert A. Ferguson, *Law and Letters in American Culture*, 69; James M. Farrell, "*Pro Militibus Oratio*: John Adams's Imitation of Cicero in the Boston Massacre Trial," 233–49 (dealing with a slightly earlier period but one which still embraces the concerns Austin addresses). On oratory at the bar see also G. Edward White and Gerald Gunther, *History of the Supreme Court of the United States, Volumes III & IV,* 203: "Oratory was high art; listening to lengthy speeches was an established social and intellectual activity."

[17] See Adams, I: 293.

and well-trained lawyers were few, in the revolutionary era, when Tory lawyers were held to be grand impediments to colonial rights, and in the Federalist and Jeffersonian periods, when anti-lawyer sentiment was part of the struggle between federalists and republicans for control of the judicial machinery.[18]

In this context Austin (1752–1820) published, under the pseudonym "Honestus," his *Observations on the Pernicious Practice of the Law*. A northern Republican and vocal anti-federalist, Austin first published the work as ten essays in the Boston *Independent Chronicle* over several months of the spring and early summer of 1786. He re-published them at the request of "many respectable citizens" in 1814,[19] and finally came out with a corrected edition in 1819. This book version contained, in addition to the ten original essays, a prefatory address and an essay on the "Rights of Juries as Judges of Law and Evidence."[20]

The work was, according to Richard Ellis, the clearest example of the anti-lawyer sentiment produced in the period.[21] It certainly evoked strong responses at the time, drawing the wrath of John Quincy Adams, who called it a "despicable" book, and the praise of those who felt they had suffered at the hands of the legal profession.[22] The work engendered a lively debate, for Austin spent quite a bit of time rebutting and answering the many responses to his original essays and, over the years between their original publication in 1786 and their first re-publication in 1814, they "retained," the author writes, "a peculiar celebrity."[23] Yet never, to my knowledge, has Austin's *Observations* (or any other anti-lawyer tracts for that matter) been read for what it can tell us about the state of rhetoric at the time.[24]

---

[18] In addition to Austin, see, e.g., [Jesse Higgins], *Sampson Against the Philistines*.

[19] Honestus [Benjamin Austin], *Observations on the Pernicious Practice of the Law*. The quoted material is from the revised edition (*infra*, note 20, at 3).

[20] Honestus [Benjamin Austin], *Observations on the Pernicious Practice of the Law*. Although the work has been reprinted in the *American Journal of Legal History*, all citations below are to the 1819 revised edition.

[21] Richard Ellis, *The Jeffersonian Crisis*, 113.

[22] Ellis, 114–15.

[23] Austin, 3.

[24] On the effect of anti-lawyer rhetoric, compare Charles Warren, *A History of the American Bar*, 212–33 (arguing that the American Revolution left the bar devastated and subject to tremendously damaging anti-lawyer senti-

Hence the second set of questions: How does Austin's critique of lawyers' rhetoric participate in the more general anti-lawyer arguments of his time? What, according to Austin, is the proper relationship between the advocate and the law? Finally, in what direction does this study of Austin's critique point students of early American rhetoric?

II

Austin is at pains to note that the "study of the law is highly honourable," and that the law "is a science, on which the permanent interest of the community essentially depends."[25] This is especially true in republican governments, where "the rights of the citizens are founded on one uniform system of jurisprudence."[26] His views, therefore, are "not intended to reflect on [lawyers] in their particular character, as many individuals among them are gentlemen of high esteem and confidence."[27]

His concern, rather, is the "multiplicity of evils" he sees in "the many pernicious practices of the profession of the law."[28] His list of evils is extensive.

First, Austin argues that current practice represents an enormous waste of time. He speaks of the "long tedious Court process"[29] and the many "unreasonable delays and illegal charges."[30] Austin describes the procedure in a memorable passage where he relates the typical conduct of an action at commercial law:

> [W]e have become so inconsiderate as to place such causes in the hands of lawyers, who in general are unacquainted with the customs of merchants, &c.

---

ment) to Dennis R. Nolan, "The Effect of the Revolution on the Bar," 969–90 (concluding that Warren's thesis is not upheld by the Maryland experience and questioning Warren's historiography). On anti-lawyer sentiment generally see also, Maxwell Bloomfield, *American Lawyers in a Changing Society, 1776–1876* 1–58; Bloomfield, "Lawyers and Public Criticism," 269–77; and Gerald W. Gawalt, "Sources of Anti-Lawyer Sentiment in Massachusetts, 1740–1840," 283–307.

[25] Austin, 3.
[26] Austin, 3–4.
[27] Austin, 7.
[28] Austin, 7.
[29] Austin, 8.
[30] Austin, 4.

and after the parties have danced through every labyrinth of the law, are at last obliged to leave their cause to a rule of court, and to have it settled by the very men who should have determined it in the first instance.[31]

Second, the system and practice of law results in tremendous loss of money. Austin writes of litigants being deprived of "disproportionate amounts of income" on a single dispute, the loss coming in part from the long delays perpetrated by lawyers. "Every man," Austin urges, should "have his cause decided without the imposition of enormous Court charges, and lawyers' fees."[32] This harm affects debtors terribly, who, he writes, "languish in prison, [and] whose misfortunes are increased by Court charges."[33] Austin appeals not only to the poor but also to those in the various strata of society by showing how all are harmed by the excessive costs associated with the conduct of an action at law. He notes satirically how the client must "dance attendance" for many days while his lawyer lives the good life at the client's expense, and he emphasizes the financial toll a suit takes on the client and his family. In suits involving between six shillings and ten pounds, Austin asserts, entire estates are lost.

A third evil of the present system is the threat of an empire of lawyers. Honestus argues that the state is "threatened to fall under the rule of lawyers," a nation, then, of men not laws. Austin paints a dark visage of a nation where estates are mortgaged to lawyers in payment for services rendered, the results of legal actions are fixed by a "Star Chamber"-like collusion of bench and bar, and lawyers control the populace by controlling the machinery of justice and legislation.[34]

Finally, the evils of the present system leave clients deprived of the full advantage of the law, the poor placed at a disadvantage before the law, and citizens of the commonwealth left with neither rights nor remedies. Justice, then, "and every principle of equity," which should be the chief aims of the law, are lost. As Austin concludes, "Legal impositions are the worst species of tyranny," and when common citizens

---

[31] Austin, 13.
[32] Austin, 10.
[33] Austin, 11.
[34] Austin, 28–29.

"cannot appeal with safety to the laws of their country, they have become absolute slaves."[35]

To reduce or eliminate these evils, Austin proposes a five-part plan. The majority of cases would be turned over to referees. British laws would be eliminated. Parties to an action would argue the cases themselves, "personally or in writing," to juries. For the reticent, Austin would allow "a friend" to appear on the party's behalf. Finally, the legislature would appoint an "Advocate-General" to represent all criminal defendants and to serve as the counterpart of the Attorney-General, who prosecutes.[36]

This plan is less radical than Austin's proposal of 1786 which, stopping just short of Shakespeare, was to "abolish" the lawyers.[37] Austin backed away from this option only when he realized that his scheme required judges, and judges required some training in the practice of law.

Why limit lawyers so severely? Because, Austin asserts, a good deal of the present evils are a result of their pernicious rhetorical practices. It is here that we learn the most about rhetoric.

Austin first establishes the standards of legal practice, standards derived, as he puts it, from the finest authorities:

> The beautiful portrait drawn by Quintilian of the character of a Lawyer comes fully within his idea of the dignity attached to the profession.—He lays it down as a fundamental principle, "that eloquence should not be separated from *integrity;* without this, *eloquence,* which is the most beautiful gift, that nature can bestow on man, and by which she has distinguished him in a particular manner from other living creatures, would prove a fatal present to him.—If it is used to oppress innocence, and pervert truth, it is a weapon of the most destructive nature.—Justice and truth only have a right to the assistance of his voice, guilt has no title to it."[38]

---

[35] Austin, 11.

[36] Austin, 25–26. The idea of an "Advocate-General," while not original to Austin, is highly innovative for his day. It is the early precursor to today's office of the public defender.

[37] Austin, 4–5.

[38] Austin, 5.

Later he states explicitly the sources of the standards he applies and the method by which he judges contemporary lawyers when he writes,

> The author had no other object in the following numbers, than to distinguish, *between the pernicious practice of certain individuals within the Bar, and the purity which ought to constitute a Court of Justice.* He has strictly followed the sacred Doctrines of QUINTILIAN and CICERO, on the duties of a Lawyer, and he defies any man to show a sentiment in the following numbers, which does not correspond with the rules laid down by those learned and philanthropic Civilians.[39]

To make his "authorities" modern, and to make his use of them in contemporary American society legitimate, Austin adds George Washington to his cadre of standard bearers. He is then able to conclude that, because he "can plead such *authorities*," readers must agree that "if HONESTUS is wrong, Quintilian, Cicero and Washington are equally erroneous."[40]

The standards, then, are that lawyers should serve justice, equity, truth, and their clients; that they should have few or no interests beyond these; that eloquence must always be joined with integrity, which assumes an adherence to the principles just mentioned; and that lawyers must always promote innocence and reveal guilt, certainly not the reverse.

Austin's authorities are in fact the two chief icons of republican rhetoric, Cicero and Quintilian, and he embraces a somewhat idealized Ciceronian standard of eloquence. Far from condemning rhetoric, Austin promotes it. He distinguishes good rhetoric from bad and, in this way, offers a model of forensic excellence.

That most of his contemporaries fail to measure up to the Ciceronian standard is clear. In Austin's eyes, their vices are numerous.

First, they are motivated more by self-interest and financial remuneration than by the principles of justice, equity, or truth. Austin characterizes the lawyer as one who, "in consideration of his fee, may be influenced to pervert the general principles of the law," as one "under a bias to misconstrue the laws," or to "warp the laws to answer his own

---

[39] Austin, 5.
[40] Austin, 5.

particular purposes."[41] They are "mercenary troops . . . hired to support any cause for the consideration of a large reward."[42]

The financial motive prompts them, Austin believes, to make of the law "a strange mystery."[43] They do so in two ways. The first is by securing positions in the legislature so that they can promulgate a greater number of laws, all for the purpose of creating an infinite variety of interpretations, meanings, and readings to be exploited in court. As Austin puts it, lawyers are men who "make laws," and then "live upon the practice of them." The lawyers make laws "so indefinite in their construction, as to allow of many plausible objections against them in their future practice."[44] The legislative method of mystifying the law pales, however, when compared to the second method, which is to import the intricacies of the British common law and its attendant forms of pleading. By far "the greatest part of" the mystery of the law, Austin claims, is "owing to the introduction of British authorities."[45] The British system of special pleadings introduces a great "variety of sophistry" into the American system, which in turn produces an ever greater "intricacy" in American law. "[L]awyers are crying up the intricacy of the law," Austin asserts, "and by hard words, in all their judiciary proceedings, they amuse the people, (like Romish priests in matters of religion) by vehemently asserting, that without abstruse and special pleadings, the laws could not be executed."[46]

Austin also indicts the art of rhetorical interpretation, long held to be central to the inventional repertoire of the lawyer. Lawyers employ the "tricks" of rhetorical interpretation in matters of law and fact to extend legal proceedings and thereby increase profits:

> I observe, that this "variety of views" is the slough of the law; and the greatest part of those "views" arise merely from the sophistry introduced by lawyers; for the more divisions, subdivisions, distinctions, and vague indefinite ideas that are introduced into any controversy, the better for them. In short, the whole bundle of perplexities originate from the metaphysi-

---

[41] Austin, 21.
[42] Austin, 21.
[43] Austin, 22.
[44] Austin, 12.
[45] Austin, 22.
[46] Austin, 22.

cal pleadings of this "order," they being studious to show a cause in as many shades as fancy can picture it; and very often the most simple cases are thrown into such a "variety of views," as to become a jumble of intricacies. But the principal part of this parade is mere pageantry of profession, calculated to perplex the Jury, and deceive the wondering crowd.[47]

Such techniques fail to live up to the ideals of Ciceronian eloquence. Austin urges that "[t]he ostentatious display of *technical formalities* in a court of Law" do not bear scrutiny against the Ciceronian standard. Indeed, they were "ludicrously described by Cicero in his plea for L. Murena before Roman Judges." "If," Austin concludes, "*Cicero was wrong*, I must only modestly plead, that his sentiments and my own are analogous."[48]

Lawyers succeed in extending and delaying proceedings by a variety of sophistic "tricks." Austin is never fully clear on how lawyers achieve the effects he attributes to them, but he is convinced nonetheless that they successfully "puzzle the jury" and "bewilder the judge." They do so by practicing, in Austin's words, a form of "sophistry": By admitting more than mere evidence and law; by supplying "false glosses" and subterfuge; by endeavoring to perplex and embarrass every judicial proceeding; by cloaking themselves in the "sacredness of the law"; by rendering intricate even the most simple principles of law; by "finesse" and "gross impositions"; by "chicanery"; by a "parade of tedious pleadings"; by, in short, practicing "the greatest art to delay every process."[49]

III

We are now in a position to suggest a few tentative answers to the questions posed at the outset.

---

[47] Austin, 41–42.

[48] Austin, 33.

[49] All ten of Austin's original essays, as well as the prefatory address and the essay on juries, are replete with his terms of sophistic art. I have attempted to capture some of the bolder statements to provide the reader a sense of Austin's language. To cite directly to any given page, however, appears unnecessary.

Austin does not condemn rhetoric so much as the *misuse* of rhetoric. The *Observations* are essentially a series of contrasts between good and bad rhetoric, the Ciceronian ideals of the past versus the dominant practices of the present. The criticism of legal practice is on ethical grounds: Rhetoric is bad when it perverts truth, circumvents justice, prolongs hardship, and misrepresents or mistreats the parties in dispute. As such, the criticism serves two functions. First, it reasserts or reconfirms the standards of eloquence and argument in republican culture. Rhetoric must be animated by and respond to republican ideals of civic virtue, whether that rhetoric is found in the legislature, the pulpit, or the courtroom. Second, Austin's criticism serves as a form of cultural critique. The misuse of rhetoric, Austin makes clear, represents a fundamental danger to the infant and fragile republic. We must keep in mind here the great fear of failure that animated much of the discourse of the era. Austin's generation often saw itself as fighting history itself, for republics old and new had all, they believed, ended in failure.[50] Austin's critique is not merely of the law as a profession but rather of legal rhetoric as indicative of the health of the republic in general.

That said, Austin's *Observations* also seem to suggest that the early republic may mark a high point of Ciceronian rhetoric in the art's long history. Austin does not question, as did Plato, Kant, and Croce, rhetoric's place at the center of civic or aesthetic life. Like many others, Austin assumes an intimate connection between rhetoric and what came to be called the "Higher Law," a term used to refer to a loose amalgam of justice, equity, divine law, and, later, the principles embedded in the federal Constitution.[51] He also emphasizes the importance of integrity and truth, certainly rhetorical standards present in Quintilian, if not Cicero, and finds them well-suited to early American legal practice. And, in keeping with the Ciceronian spirit of early

---

[50] On the fear that the republic would fail, see, e.g., Joseph Story's letter to Samuel P. P. Fay, 18 February 1834, in W. W. Story, ed., *Miscellaneous Writings of Joseph Story*, 3 volumes. II: 154. See also Gerald T. Dunne, *Justice Joseph Story and the Rise of the Supreme Court*, 338, and Ronald F. Reid, *American Rhetorical Discourse*, 2nd edition, 185.

[51] For the period's sense of the "higher law," see William Hosmer, *The Higher Law*. On the higher law and the Constitution, see Edward S. Corwin, "The 'Higher Law' Background of American Constitutional Law," 365–409. On the higher law as a rhetorical construct, see Sean Patrick O'Rourke, "Cultivating the 'Higher Law' in American Jurisprudence." 33–43.

American republicanism, Austin stresses the vital connection between oratorical display and civic virtue.

While the *Observations* may well mark a high point of Ciceronian rhetoric, Austin departs from the Ciceronianism of his day on two crucial points. His repeated admonitions against extended argument, tinged as they are with a suspicion of persuasion, stand in direct opposition to the Ciceronian commitment to *controversia*, the old notion of debating both sides of the question, of arguing *in utramque partem*. *Controversia* is, one recent critic has opined, "a rhetorical stance predicated on the assumption that controversy engenders doubt, and doubt begets possibilities for argument."[52] Austin's repeated appeals for mere statements of the facts (as opposed, one assumes, to extended argument) and for parties simply to tell their stories unadorned with rhetorical flourishes distinguishes his position from the prevailing Ciceronianism.

So too does his argument against the use of professional advocates. Critics of rhetoric have long questioned the hiring of professional pleaders in cases at law. Austin falls, it would seem, into a line of thinking that dates back at least to the tension between the jurisconsults and the advocates of the Roman Republic, where jurisconsults saw advocates as "contemptible creatures,"[53] and sought to remove the "noisome weed of rhetoric"[54] from the law, while advocates "demeaned the jurisconsults as persons who wished to practice in the law courts but lacked the natural endowments for oratory."[55] Austin participates in this historical debate by severely limiting the role of the advocate and by stressing the heightened ethical standards to which the advocate must be held. In this way the *Observations* seek to redress what Austin perceives as an imbalance between law and advocacy.[56]

---

[52] O'Rourke, 37. On *controversia* as characteristic of Ciceronian rhetoric see Thomas O. Sloane, "Reinventing *inventio*," 461–73; Sloane, *On the Contrary*; Thomas M. Conley, *Rhetoric in the European Tradition*, 36–37.

[53] Anthony M. Honore, *Tribonian*, 31.

[54] Fritz Schulz, *History of Roman Legal Science*, 71–72.

[55] Bruce A. Kimball, "Legal Education, Liberal Education, and the Trivial *Artes*," 189–90.

[56] Bruce W. Frier, in his *The Rise of the Roman Jurists: Studies in Cicero's Pro Caecino*, 266, has argued that the movement toward legal security in the late [Roman] Republic did not seek to subject rhetorical advocacy to the dominance of legal science; rather, it aimed to redress the balance between the two disciplines within the judicial system or (more precisely) to recon-

Finally, and in closing, I would only note that further study of anti-lawyer tracts and the courtroom oratory of the period is warranted. If, as Austin suggests, legal rhetoric was both central to early republican society and replete with subterfuge and delay, then an investigation of anti-lawyer tracts and courtroom oratory would appear essential to a deeper understanding of republican culture and its ethical underpinnings. Such inquiry will also broaden and extend our nascent knowledge of the rhetoric of the period and, to the extent that it affords us a better grasp of the fate of the art, clarify our historical perspective and enrich our contemporary practices.

---

struct the balance on a new and far more sophisticated plane. By the time he published the revised edition of the Honestus essays in 1819, Austin seems to have viewed his project in a similar way. By that time Austin was no longer devoted to the abolition of the legal profession so much as he was to its restraint and reform.

10 The Human Genome Project: Novel Approaches, Probable Reasoning, and the Advancement of Science

Charlotte A. Robidoux

Though no one has ever seen deoxyribonucleic acid (DNA) with the naked eye or without the assistance of specialized techniques such as X-ray diffraction (used by Rosalind Franklin and then by James Watson and Francis Crick in the 1950's), this submicroscopic molecule engenders deliberations of epic proportions (along with hundreds of millions of dollars per year). Why? Because the genetic inscription comprising the double helix within our chromosomes directs the entire process of life, the function of every cell in the human body. Moreover, an understanding of genes and their protein-coding mechanisms yields insight into genetic disease. In 1990, roughly forty years after Watson and Crick discovered the structure of DNA, the Human Genome Project (HGP) began its 15-year study to create a series of chromosomal maps that will describe the composition of the DNA molecule within each human chromosome at increasingly refined resolutions. The definitive genomic map will spell out the precise sequence of the 3 billion base pairs or nucleotides constituting human DNA. Ultimately, the HGP intends to locate the 50,000 to 100,000 genes spanning our chromosomes and then harness that genetic information for the benefit of biology and medicine, a necessary outcome for continued funding. Of course, the hope implicit in deciphering the code cannot lay claim to foolproof and/or immediate medical treatments. Every genetic breakthrough gives rise to some other unknown and to some unforeseen consequence and controversy:

> Serious difficulties arise from the relative ease with which information on DNA sequences can be acquired, when adequate knowledge of its correct interpretation is lacking. . . . The ground is shifting almost from week to week. Physicians need to recognize the limitations of the new information and the commercial pressures behind the speed with which preliminary scientific data are being turned into tests.[1]

Commenting on the discovery of the breast cancer gene, Francis Collins, HGP director, recognizes the extent of this problem: "[A]t present there are insufficient data to guide the surgeon or oncologist. Clinical research is urgently needed to address . . . uncertainties."[2] Nevertheless, Collins, who continues to promote the hopeful frontiers of molecular genetics, has issued an appeal for what he calls a "genome attitude," a belief system that will usher in "Genome II": "In the long run, genetic discoveries will surely lead to opportunities for treatment, which in turn will reduce the dilemmas surrounding genetic testing."[3]

Given this unstable terrain that typifies a science in its early stages, how do scientists arrive at truth? How do they "carry out" science with such inconclusive data? Especially when uncertainties persist in every aspect of research? When strict proof is not possible because no one can directly observe DNA nucleotide sequences? Scientists seem to rely on dialectic and rhetoric as interim instruments of knowledge when engaged in controversy. More specifically, as scientists interpret, evaluate, and debate the truth claims of emerging data, they use formal deliberation, or dialectic, to remove uncertainty, as James L. Kinneavy makes clear in his *A Theory of Discourse* (esp. 88). And rhetorical figures—as dialectical tools that depict similarities and differences about "genetic reality," much as the DNA clones—provide scientists with conceptual frameworks for testing out hypotheses and probing at truth. Analogy and metaphor, as seen with the term genetic "map," describe and locate biochemical processes. For instance, some experiments attempt to "fingerprint," "tag," and "digest" copies of DNA;

---

[1] R. Hubbard and R.C. Lewontin, "Pitfalls of Genetic Testing," 1192–1193.

[2] Francis S. Collins, "BRCA—Lots of Mutations, Lots of Dilemmas," 186–188.

[3] Francis S. Collins, "Sequencing the Human Genome," 35–53.

to establish "landmarks," "labels," and "probes" on polymerized genetic terrain; and to find various ways "to walk across the surface of a gene" in an effort to construct various maps. Researchers even identify cloning inaccuracies as a kind of genetic "infidelity" that occurs when clones are unfaithful to the DNA from which they were derived.[4] Geneticist Thomas Fogle sees the double edge of rhetorical strategies:

> Metaphors can provide powerful imagery for encapsulating the abstractions of theory. Carefully chosen imagery can effectively communicate a difficult concept; poorly chosen imagery can create ambiguous meaning or erroneous understanding... What is discovered at the molecular level, and what is distilled for public consumption as the fundamental structure of that information, do not coincide.[5]

With and without metaphoric assistance, the general public confronts the rhetoric of biomedical issues almost daily in newspapers, magazines, and on television. Insofar as a range of discursive media greatly influence scientific and public opinion, communication plays an important role in the world of biotechnology. Given the complicated nature of human genetics, if communication goes unmanaged, education will occur by default. Exploring more precisely how communication functions in biotechnology could yield insight into the communicative barriers noted by Collins: "[A]lthough people can be educated . . . doing so is difficult because of the complexity of the information to be communicated, the lack of incentives on the part of some providers to teach people about the information, and the lack of motivation on the part of consumers to learn it."[6]

In this essay, I examine the dialectical and rhetorical aspects of the HGP through an Aristotelian lens, studying the assumptions and opinions that consistently anchor scientific and public arguments.[7] In

---

[4] Ilya M. Chumakov, *et al.*, "A YAC Contig Map of the Human Genome," 175–183.

[5] Thomas Fogle, "Information Metaphors and the Human Genome Project," *Perspectives in Biology and Medicine*, 38 (1995): 535–546.

[6] Mark S. Guyer and Francis S. Collins, "How is the Human Genome Project Doing, and What Have We Learned So Far?" 10841–10847.

[7] Though I argue that rhetoric and dialectic emerge in scientific discourse, I do not assume that modern scientific investigations are operating out of an Aristotelian framework. It is not my objective in this paper to

accordance with Aristotle's conception of the instruments of knowledge, I examine how rhetoric and dialectic function in scientific discourse, particularly how rhetorical figures, such as analogy and metaphor, are used as dialectical tools in formal scientific discourse. Following my brief discussion of dialectic and rhetoric and their relationship to science, I focus the first part of my analysis on scientific arguments from noted journals in which assumptions, metaphors, and analogies function as epistemological catalysts to guide and support research practices.[8] In the second part of my presentation, I examine

compare ancient and modern scientific methods. Thus, when I use the term science, I am simply referring to well corroborated and generally accepted knowledge, a broad definition that could serve ancients and moderns equally well. Furthermore, in examining formal scientific discourse, I am not attempting to classify scientific discourse as a specific kind of "reference discourse" as described by Kinneavy, who in Chapter 3 provides a meticulous discussion of scientific methodologies and discourse types: "Indeed, one of the differentiations of one science from another is the unique methodology of investigation by which each particular science analyzes and evaluates some aspect of reality . . . [S]cientific discourse consists in a consideration of one facet of an object and the making of certain kinds of assertions (descriptive, narrative, classificatory, and evaluative) about this facet. These two characteristics, however, are certainly not enough to isolate scientific discourse from other discourse. Therefore, "reference" can be best understood as comprising scientific, informative, and exploratory discourse." Instead, I examine specific instances in which scientists use rhetoric and dialectic—consciously or unconsciously—as necessary tools for scientific inquiry.

[8] In her pioneering work *Shakespeare's Use of the Arts of Language,* Sister Miriam Joseph Rauh is credited with demonstrating how figures of speech not only adorn prose but also create meaning. With respect to scientific arguments, in "Figures of Speech in the Rhetoric of Science and Technology," S. Michael Halloran and Annette Norris Bradford examine the role of rhetorical figures in the "formulation and communication of scientific ideas." In particular, they refer to the schemes that enhance "the comprehensibility of scientific and technical prose" and the tropes that provide "heuristic power" in scientific discourse. They comment on the tropes employed to describe the structure of DNA (a zipper-like molecule) and the coding process (a communicative enterprise). Their purpose is "to undermine the pedagogical tradition that simply rejects the use of figures in writing about science"—not to examine precisely how figures as dialectical tools structure scientific arguments, frame presentations when findings are made public, and shape the essence of public opinion. See S. Michael Halloran and Annette Norris Bradford, "Figures of Speech in the Rhetoric of Science and Technology," 179–192.

rhetorical strategies used in the public realm in popular discourse and in a lecture given by Francis Collins to medical school professors and students.

Instruments of Knowledge: Demonstration, Dialectic, and Rhetoric

Aristotle's *Organon* provides a comprehensive understanding of the various instruments of knowledge, outlining the differences among certain proof (science in the strict sense), dialectic, and rhetoric.[9] Book I of the *Posterior Analytics* tells us that the knowledge claims of science come from 1) universal principles from what is self-evident, 2) understanding the causes of phenomena, and 3) sense experience. Necessary principles are materially correct and are often the basis for deduction—syllogistic reasoning or formal demonstration. Sense experience, on the other hand, lends itself to induction, a reasoning from particulars that allows us to abstract and discern universals (81b). Generally in science, researchers accept demonstrable propositions and reject those that lack proof. Universal propositions that are commensurable will always be convertible, revealing a one-to-one relationship between a subject and a predicate: $S = P$ is the same as $P = S$. In other words, when we say that DNA consists of three components—sugar, a phosphate group, and four nitrogenous bases[10]—then the reverse must also be true. But when certainty is not possible, dialectic can become useful to experts grappling with generally accepted premises—informed opinion—in their pursuit of truth. Aristotle's *Topics* describes dialectic as a rigorous examination of a subject or issue, one that explores contrary positions and can guide us to universals.[11] Dialectic's counterpart is rhetoric, which we can distinguish by the proofs used to gain adherence to a

---

[9] In *Aristotle: Selected Works*, Hippocrates G. Apostle and Lloyd P. Gerson provide a concise compilation of the works of Aristotle.

[10] Lynn Jorde, John Carey, and Raymond White, *Medical Genetics*, 134.

[11] Specifically, Aristotle states in the *Topics*: [I]f we can go over the difficulties on both sides of a[n] . . . issue in a science we can detect more easily what is true and what is false about each side. In addition, it is useful for the first [presuppositions] leading to the principles of each science. [E]ach of these principles must be discussed by means of generally accepted opinions. [T]his [kind of discussion] is . . . most appropriate to dialectic, for dialectic, being exploratory, is the path to the principles of every inquiry" (Book I, 100b, 101b, 104b).

position (rather than to find truth). Although reason is paramount in Aristotelian rhetoric, appeals to emotion (*pathos*) and character (*ethos*) also serve important functions, namely, to move an audience.[12]

In both dialectic and rhetoric, deduction and induction will structure arguments in the form of enthymemes (abbreviated syllogisms that depend upon an audience's adherence to certain opinions and values) and examples respectively.[13] However, in these arenas, because propositions are indefinite or inconvertible—i.e., the fact that S = P does not guarantee that the opposite is true—comparison and analogy are the next best means to demonstration. These counterparts to scientific propositional analysis, then, rest on assumption and opinion about matters that are uncertain. Since a one-to-one relationship does not exist between subject and predicate, claims based on uncertainty can accommodate numerous definitional comparisons (even when S = P, S may also = Q and R)—what Aristotle described as topical reasoning. In scientific investigation, the *topoi*, as inventional strategies, attempt to define the essential nature of phenomena through an examination of parts, wholes, contraries, causes, as well as comparison through metaphor and analogy.[14]

Throughout the course of genetic research, we see a similar investigative process—one that passes from rhetoric and dialectic to certainty. Ever since Gregor Mendel "first described [the] 'hereditary' elements" he observed while conducting his famous garden pea experiments in 1865,[15] modern genetics has been a recombination of knowledge, with

---

[12] In the *Rhetoric*, we learn that "Rhetoric then may be defined as the faculty of discovering the possible means of persuasion in reference to any subject . . . The function of rhetoric . . . is to deal with things about which we deliberate . . . about things which seem to admit of issuing in two ways" (1355b, 1357b).

[13] Aristotle also explains "[E]nthymemes . . . are the body of proof . . . [P]roof is a sort of demonstration, since we are most strongly convinced when we suppose anything to have been demonstrated; that rhetorical demonstration is an enthymeme, which, generally speaking, is the strongest of rhetorical proofs" (*Rhetoric* 1354b–1355a).

[14] Edward P.J. Corbett refers to the position advanced by Sister Miriam Joseph Rauh that figures of speech can be used to invent ideas and find lines of argument; metaphor, for instance, uses the topic of comparison or similarity to describe phenomena. See *Classical Rhetoric for the Modern Student*, 40–46, 424.

[15] Robert Cook-Deegan, *The Gene Wars*, 10.

certainty informing uncertainty (and the reverse). Although Mendel could not see DNA, he was able to arrive at a theory of inheritance by reasoning from specific effects he observed (traits that were inherited) to their apparent causes (heritable substances). Another geneticist who used provisional data to draw conclusions was Edmond B. Wilson; he "deduced that the gene for color blindness must lie on the X chromosome," given that "fathers did not pass it on to sons, and it was rare among women."[16] Watson and Crick also made inferences about the structure of DNA and published these findings before they had conclusive evidence:

> To get anywhere at all, we had to make assumptions. At the moment of writing, detailed interpretation of the X-ray photographs. . .has not been completed, and until this is done, no structure can be considered proved.[17]

Inasmuch as probability seems destined to punctuate all aspects of the HGP, research methods that incorporate comparative analyses—both metaphorical and analogical modes of reasoning—are necessary for drawing conclusions about phenomena not yet seen (even with the assistance of advanced technological instruments). The predominant metaphor, of course, pertains to mapping the surface of human chromosomes, a comparison that dates back to 1911 and grew out of research initiatives designed to *locate* genes (31): "Physical maps consist of ordered, overlapping cloned fragments of genomic DNA covering each chromosome."[18] Scientists use the term map as a way to represent chromosomal territory. Since the primary and most efficient way to study DNA is to make clones or replicas of the chromosomal surface, the resulting data are only as accurate as the clones synthesized—an important consideration especially if specific genetic regions are "uncloneable."[19] To describe the nature of the chromosomal surface in strict scientific propositions—$S = P$, or the map *is* the chromosome—would be incorrect. Until the surface of chromosomes is ren-

---

[16] *The Gene Wars*, 30.

[17] F.H.C. Crick, "The Structure of Hereditary Material," 82–88. See also S. Michael Halloran, "The Birth of Molecular Biology," 70–83.

[18] Chumakov, *Nature: The Genome Directory*, 175.

[19] Charles R. Cantor and Cassandra L. Smith, "Perspectives on the Human Genome Project," 7.

dered exactly, emerging or interim data will lead to assumptions and comparative analyses about chromosomal reconstructions or maps. Metaphors specific to the HGP thus include those of location and sensation, which provide access to unseen conditions and characteristics; each metaphoric variation (as a "linguistic seeing-eye dog") provides an analytical foundation for scientific research. Given the pressure to find treatments for genetic diseases, "early" stages of uncertainty will extend well into the future—and with it dialectic and rhetoric, reasoning strategies that can accommodate or contend with "vigorous and creative scientific efforts" needed for "continuous. . .improvements in technology."[20]

As seen above, common metaphoric comparisons connected to this map-making enterprise include techniques that fingerprint, tag, digest, mark, label, probe, and walk on human DNA. One way that scientists make estimates about landmarks is by attaching a florescent tag to a probe—a DNA clone with a known sequence—that will find unknown base pairs on a DNA fragment or clone with a complementary nucleotide sequence. This tagging terminology reflects the tentative nature of the data gleaned. One group of researchers refers to these tagged sites or locations as addresses.[21] Another approach called "shotgun sequencing" relies on probability rather than perfect knowledge, seeking the assistance of experimental redundancy to make the experiment "pure."[22] Researchers, once again, are wary of the "infidelities" of unfaithful clones.[23] Below, I demonstrate how these comparisons guide argument, prompting researchers toward specific inductive or deductive strategies that seem likely to yield necessary propositions.

THE REALM OF SCIENCE

A Genetic Tour Guide

To understand technical discussions about maps requires familiarity with basic principles of genetics and an understanding of mapping

---

[20] Francis S. Collins, "Ahead of Schedule and Under Budget," 10821–10823.

[21] Thomas J. Hudson, et al. "An STS-Based Map of the Human Genome," 1945–1954.

[22] Mark S. Guyer and Francis S. Collins, "How is the Human Genome Project Doing," 10841–10847.

[23] Chumakov, *Nature: The Genome Directory*, 175.

strategies.[24] Insight into all biological activity rests on knowing the essence of DNA—its chemical composition, overall structure, and cellular function. The nucleus of each human cell holds 46 chromosomes (23 from each parent), which contain all the genetic information needed to sustain life. Each chromosome consists of one elongated molecule of DNA, a tightly wound helix consisting of the four nucleotide bases, adenine (A), guanine (G), cytosine (C), and thymine (T), that bind together as base pairs—A with T, and C with G. The order or sequence of the 3 billion of base pairs that constitute the human genome differentiates us from other organisms and from each other. Interspersed throughout the DNA are genes or functional sites of the molecule (10,000 to 100,000 nucleotides long). Genes contain segments called exons that code for proteins plus noncoding units called introns. Before the code can direct protein synthesis, ribonucleic acid (RNA, a close relative of DNA) is needed to reproduce DNA. An RNA polymerase molecule transcribes the DNA that makes up the gene, organizing and assembling the RNA nucleotides that correspond to the DNA template; the resulting molecule is called messenger RNA (mRNA), which adjusts itself for travel, splicing together the exon units (that will exit the nucleus) and cutting out intron units. Once outside the nucleus, ribosomes (rRNA) and transfer RNA (tRNA) interpret the mRNA code as triplets, called codons, which can then be translated into the amino acids chains that become proteins. Cloning methods use transcribed mRNA—the molecules that "express" genetic information—as a DNA substitute that can generate cDNA clones—named as such because the copy corresponds to the DNA prototype and is "complementary to mRNA."[25]

Mapping strategies attempt to flesh out a big picture of this biochemical process, finding the exact position of the genes on chromosomes. Genetic linkage maps determine the likelihood that certain genes are *linked* and so will be inherited together. Linkage maps rely on approaches that identify and track polymorphisms, regions that are highly variable, unstable, and prone to mutations.[26] Physical

---

[24] For a general and readable introduction to the HGP, see *Exon, Introns, and Talking Genes: The Science Behind the Human Genome Project and Medical Genetics*.

[25] Arthur L. Beaudet and Andrea Ballabio, "Molecular Genetics and Medicine," 350.

[26] National Research Council, *Mapping and Sequencing the Human Genome*, 20.

maps chart actual biochemical distances, that is, nucleotide sequences thought to exist between genes and "landmarks" along a chromosome.[27] The difficulty lies in developing reliable cloning methods to discover the exact order of base pairs. Some physical maps that describe distances are more refined than others. Low resolution (or top-down) mapping provides an aerial view of distance, assembling large pieces of cloned DNA for a snapshot of the terrain. High resolution (or bottom-up) mapping provides a close-up view of distance—piecing together small overlapping clones for a more detailed genetic rendering. Both approaches yield inaccuracies. Just as bad sectors on a computer disk make data inaccessible, some genomic regions—called junk DNA—are indecipherable, preventing the evolution of a "perfect map."[28]

Mapping as a Basis for Argument

In my consideration of scientific arguments, a primary source for my analysis comes from *Nature: The Genome Directory*,[29] one of the most comprehensive summaries of HGP data since the research began. Moreover, this text, published in 1995, has relevance because it has prompted an ongoing dialogue among experts around the world about the validity of the results presented. Accordingly, we can isolate some of the operating assumptions being debated. Often, the articles reveal an interplay of deduction and induction, as assumptions give rise to and result from experiments. The first article I examine by Adams, *et al.*,[30] considers complementary DNA sequences (cDNAs), the cloning method referred to above—a controversial method that focuses on the functional protein-coding regions of DNA that represent actual genes.[31] Another article by Chumakov, *et al.*, considers an equally controversial low-resolution cloning strategy known as Yeast Artificial Chromosomes (YACs), which are used to construct a more comprehensive physical map. Other material I examine, Hudson, *et al.*,[32] responds to the findings presented in these articles. A comparison of these arguments reveals that the articles dense with rhetorical

---

[27] *Mapping and Sequencing the Human Genome*, 37.
[28] *Biotechnology and Human Genetic Predisposition to Disease*, 7.
[29] *Nature: The Genome Directory*, 377 Supp. (1995).
[30] Adams, *et al.*, *Nature: The Genome Directory*, 3–7.
[31] Peter Goodfellow, "A Big Book of the Human Genome," 285–286.
[32] *Science*, 1945–1954.

and dialectical strategies seem to gain greater currency than those employing "straight" scientific discussions.

Let the Mapping Begin

Because "the ultimate physical map" will depict the "complete DNA sequence of the entire genome,"[33] many scientists, like Adams, *et al.*, have been shifting their research efforts from mapping landmarks to the partial sequencing of cDNA clones—in spite of the purist argument that "intuitively" this "simplistic philosophy . . . feels wrong"[34]: "Ever since Sydney Brenner first argued for a programme to sequence random complementary DNA clones to identify genes, this approach has been surrounded by dissension, and the name 'expressed sequence tags' [ESTs] . . . is almost synonymous with controversy."[35] The push to sequence DNA continues because sequencing signals the advent of second stage research, which holds further promise for understanding the causes of genetic disease. Sequencing serves as leverage for increased funding. In "Initial Assessment of Human Gene Diversity and Expression Patterns Based on 83 Million Nucleotides of cDNA Sequence," Adams, *et al.*, promote what is termed a "cost-effective argument,"[36] arguing that even the partial sequencing of clones—referred to above as "expressed sequence tags" (ESTs)—will "provide a rapid identification of expressed genes [and] greatly speed the search for disease genes."

Those who are skeptical of the new technology can find more reason to be so when studying how probable reasoning is passed off as certainty. Observe the enthymemic[37] nature of the statement above about speed, which links the rapid identification of (partial) genes with a quick search for disease genes. If we represent this statement as complete syllogism, the middle term's reliance on EST (suppressed in the

---

[33] *Mapping and Sequencing the Human Genome*, 6.

[34] Goodfellow, *Nature*, 285.

[35] *Nature*, 3–17.

[36] *Nature*, 3–17.

[37] Scholarship on the enthymeme is vast, but some of the classic discussions include: Lloyd F. Bitzer's "Aristotle's Enthymeme Revisited," 399–408; John T. Gage's "A General Theory of the Enthymeme for Advanced Composition," 161–178; Lawrence D. Green, "Enthymemic Invention and Structural Predication," 623–634; James H. McBurney, "The Place of the Enthymeme in Rhetorical Theory," 49–74; Jeffrey Walker, "The Body of Persuasion: A Theory of the Enthymeme," 46–65.

enthymemic form) does not induce assent: *ESTs provide a rapid identification of expressed genes. Disease genes can be found using ESTs. Disease genes can be found rapidly.* The Adams group has not proved anything about disease genes and ESTs; the enthymemic inference relies on the values of an audience that has much to gain from speedy research. The inference embodies an emotional proof. This toggling between science and probable reasoning typifies many of these HGP discussions.

Looking at the Adams research more closely, we see persuasive strategies operating throughout. Because controversy underlies their major premise, the Adams group must incorporate sound and convincing evidence into their minor premise by demonstrating the efficacy of EST methods. Many proofs throughout the article appeal to *ethos*, highlighting the researchers' credibility and the reliability of the data:

> Large-scale sequencing demands attention to the quality of materials and to accurate performance of each step in the process, both to provide sequence data of the highest possible quality and to detect or avoid problems. At each step of the EST methodology, both in the laboratory and during sequence analysis, a quality control and evaluation procedure was developed to assess the EST data. . . . The objective was to assure at each step that the material produced was of sufficient quality . . . or purity . . . to provide a high level of confidence that a high proportion of the sequencing reactions would produce useable data. Checks of the accuracy of ESTs and the EST assemblies . . . served to define confidence values for interpreting database matches.[38]

The researchers also find it necessary to make an even more direct appeal to expertise: "[A]n EST or THC was determined to match a database sequence based on an evaluation of the alignment by an *experienced* [my emphasis] scientist."[39]

To further offset the high degree of uncertainty underlying their approach, the authors arrive at inferences and conclusions gradually, establishing agreement through self-evident statements initially so

---

[38] Adams, *Nature: The Genome Directory*, 4.
[39] *Nature: The Genome Directory*, 10.

that controversial claims and interpretations will seem less dubious to the audience: "It is inherently difficult to calculate the proportion of human genes matched by the ESTs described here because neither of the two fundamental variables—the number of genes and the number of genes matched by ESTs—are known with any certainty."[40] A technical explanation follows, listing percentages that show the uncertainty. The paragraph, however, ends enthymemically with a third-person-plural, all-inclusive approach that induces the audience to reason thus: "We can assume, however, that some undetected redundancy does exist, and that as many as half of the human genes have been matched by the ESTs described here."[41] Even though no evidence supports this conclusion, the authors assume that the audience will tolerate the missing premise perhaps because the "numbers" accounting for imprecision are consistent with "good" science. Truncated logic persists when the authors endorse their research as an indisputable "discovery," describing the partial sequences they have identified as new genes: "Mapping these new genes will be of enormous value . . . to medical genetics. . . . [T]he dataset presented here doubtless contains hundreds to thousands of disease genes."[42] Although their research has not yet proven that partial sequences equal new genes, the Adams group relies on the expectations of the audience, just as the enthymeme pertaining to speed did above. In both cases, "EST"—a metaphoric variation of the term "tag"—exerts its rhetorical power as an acronym for new genes.

In another section of their discussion, because their main premise is based on opinion, not fact, the authors can use dialectic to invert an accepted belief about certain problems associated with repetitive data. Most scientists believe that numerous entries of identical clones in a cDNA database could skew results: "abundant transcripts will be sequenced multiple times, producing no new information, and rare transcripts will be missed."[43] The Adams group argues dialectically, however, revealing that this "deficiency" is actually beneficial: "We have taken advantage of the inherent redundancy of cDNA sampling to build assemblies of ESTs, essentially treating the expressed portion of the genome [the varying data that come from duplicate cDNAs] as

---

[40] *Nature: The Genome Directory*, 15.
[41] *Nature: The Genome Directory*, 15.
[42] *Nature: The Genome Directory*, 15.
[43] Goodfellow, *Nature*, 285.

a shotgun sequence assembly project."[44] The here accredited "shotgun" approach—referred to above as an example of metaphor—analyzes random snapshots of a target region, finds the overlapping regions, and then sequences that target region.[45] The Adams group argues that these clones cannot be considered redundant if in fact they yield new data—genetic regions called "tentative human consensus sequences (THCs): "The process of assembling THCs served to identify ESTs from the same gene to reduce redundancy."[46] This argument uses metaphoric elements to completely reverse the premise that redundancy is an inevitable flaw in cDNA libraries.

The rhetorical and dialectical strategies used by the Adams group help to advance their controversial hypothesis. Many in science and in the public world are eager to accept evidence suggesting that an expedient hunt for genes is possible. The outcome for science is profitability (in *Business Week,* Craig Venter, a co-author of the Adams article, is portrayed as striking it rich[47]). Public investors benefit with cures for disease, not just financially but also medically. Though their research practices violate "canonical science," according to some, the Adams group makes the most of probable reasoning and the power to persuade.

Mapping the Human Genome: A Glimpse into the Next Generation

"A YAC Contig Map of the Human Genome," another argument in the *Genome Directory* that rests on opinion, promotes the YAC (yeast artificial chromosome) method for large-scale physical mapping.[48] This technology, which employs yeast cells to reproduce or clone human DNA, is particularly enticing because YAC cells can accommodate and clone large DNA fragments. Recall, however, that maps attempting "complete" coverage will have a lower resolution. Another problem with YAC is that unstable regions within the clone will reorganize and misrepresent the DNA surface—a case of genetic infidelity, as we saw

---

[44] Adams, *Nature: The Genome Directory,* 4.
[45] *Proceedings in National Academic Science,* 10843.
[46] Adams, *Nature: The Genome Directory,* 7.
[47] John Carey, "Gene Therapy: Promises, Promises," 75.
[48] Chumakov, *Nature: The Genome Directory,* 175.

above.[49] In this article, Chumakov, *et al.*, present follow-up data to a preliminary map that depicts the entire genome. Their "second generation map," so termed metaphorically, is a transitional draft comprised of YAC contigs (overlapping clones) covering only 75% of the genome: "YAC-based physical maps are important intermediates in producing a 'sequence-ready' physical map."[50]

When confronting the problems associated with YAC research, the Chumakov group's use of rhetoric and dialectic is minimal, unlike the Adams group. Observe how the following deduction bypasses the rhetorical opportunity to highlight research about a map of complete coverage; instead, the passages cited below emphasize many challenges to the research:

> Given the size of the mammalian genomes, physical mapping of the entire human genome requires using clones with extremely large inserts. . . . YACs are currently the only cloning system capable of propagating such large DNA fragments. . . . YACs have been crucial tools in cloning disease genes based on their chromosomal location. YACs are invaluable for the purpose of covering such large regions, although their utility for detailed genomic analysis is somewhat limited by problems of infidelity.[51]

At times, the authors are so tentative in making claims about their research, noting every possible pitfall, that they almost persuade the readers to dismiss their findings—to conclude that their results have little significance:

> Inferring the actual proportion of the physical length of the genome covered is not entirely straightforward. The proportion of the genetic length covered (66%) may overestimate the actual proportion covered because it neglects the physical distances. . . . But it

---

[49] *Nature: The Genome Directory*. See also *Science*, 1945. For information on the World Wide Web, see Human Genome Management Information System (HGMIS), U.S. Department of Energy, Office of Energy Research and the National Center for Biotechnology Information (NCBI), National Institutes of Health (NIH).

[50] *Nature: The Genome Directory*, 175.

[51] *Nature: The Genome Directory*, 175.

may underestimate the coverage because the density of YACs appears to be sparsest in the telemetric regions. . . .[52]

Admittedly, the researchers are wary of conducting "bad science"; however, they could have placed greater rhetorical emphasis on specific positive findings—no matter how small—averting some of the criticism that came from other scientists responding to their work, as we see below.

In "An STS-Based Map of the Human Genome," the Hudson group responds to the Chumakov findings in an issue of *Science*—only three months after the *Genome Directory* was published:

> An international collaboration [Chumakov] . . . has also produced a clone-based physical map estimated to cover up to 75% of the genome in overlapping YAC clones. . . . The map is clone-based rather than STS-based. . . . The map does not provide a scaffold for sequencing the human genome. The YAC clones themselves are not suitable for sequencing.[53]

The Hudson group used a technique called sequence-tagged sites (STSs), an approach that coins yet another metaphor. These researchers argue that the STS technique is extremely reliable, especially in its ability to compensate for YAC deficiencies, thoroughly deciphering a specific genetic region with a high degree of certainty: "STSs have rapidly gained acceptances as the markers of choice for map construction."[54] Because this technique teases out error, the researchers have been able to secure a map covering 94% of the genome.

In reference to the six percent deficiency and any other possible inaccuracies, the Hudson group argues rhetorically, using the metaphor of a "street address" as a basis for reasoning:

> To facilitate screening, we used a . . . library . . . divided into 33 "blocks". . . . For each block, we prepared . . . a pooling system based on row, plate, and column address of each clone. . . . For blocks with a single positive YAC, the row, column, and plate sub-

---

[52] *Nature: The Genome Directory*, 183.
[53] Hudson, *Science*, 1946.
[54] *Proceedings in National Academic Science*, 10841.

> pools should specify the precise address of the YAC ("definite addresses"). . . . [I]f . . . dimensions did not yield a positive result, partial information was obtained ("incomplete addresses"). Incomplete addresses were not used in initial map assembly but were used at the final stages to detect connections between nearby loci. Definite addresses composed 88% of the total hits.[55]

Even though the researchers allude to error, they identify "error" as incomplete information. In addition, they use the metaphor of a street address as a strategy to clarify and convince the audience that the error factor was controlled effectively and purged from their results. In concluding remarks, the Hudson group, like Adams, handles doubt enthymemically, inviting readers to dismiss their shortcomings:

> [I]n the STS map . . . the loci may be significantly misplaced in the maps . . . [T]he local order in the map must be regarded as uncertain. There will surely be many errors requiring attention and correction . . .The current map falls short in terms of marker density and local order, but neither shortcoming poses a serious obstacle for initiating large-scale sequencing now.[56]

Just as the Adams group prompted inference with little or no proof, so does the Hudson team rely on *pathos*, emphasizing sequencing, funding, and ultimate scientific success.

THE PUBLIC REALM

GENETIC RESEARCH AND PUBLIC OPINION

To the extent that persuasive strategies permeate specific scientific discussions, rhetoric and dialectic also determine what the public knows about the HGP. Researchers like Francis Collins work tirelessly to keep the public informed—to provide "incentives" for "providers to teach" and "motivation" for "consumers to learn" about the HGP.[57]

---

[55] Hudson, *Science*, 1946.
[56] Hudson, *Science*, 1953.
[57] *Proceedings in National Academic Science*, 10846.

Excerpts below include a speech published in *Vital Speeches* (titled "Genomics"),[58] a press release published by Merck,[59] and a magazine article in *Business Week,* which indicate the range of discourse available to the public. In "Genomics," George Poste demonstrates mature dialectical thinking:

> Modern science remains a powerful force for human progress and we must not surrender this mission. Solutions must be agreed on with the full recognition that there are no absolutes. . . . One thing is for certain. Deciding how to incorporate new genetic data into medical, social and legal policies is by far the largest long-term challenge posed by the genome project.[60]

The message in *Vital Speeches* influences correctly; quite often, though, the message can overstate the truth. In the Merck press release, it seems obvious that this company has provided substantial funding for genetic research. Possible gene therapies are highlighted: "[R]esearchers will find new ways to understand gene expression, which will lead ultimately to new therapies for diseases as yet unconquered." The enthymematic reasoning in this statement resembles that of Adams and Hudson, linking gene expression with therapies for disease. Once again, the middle term that would generate conviction is missing. Admittedly, the link between understanding and conquering disease is overconfident, obscuring the fact that private industry has much to gain from investments in biotechnology. But the uninformed public might not observe the faulty reasoning.

Genetic research has been promoted similarly in popular business magazines. In *Business Week,* for instance, Craig Venter, the scientist who conducted research with the Adams group, is valorized for his money-making ability. The data that Venter supplies the journalist for the article on cDNAs and ESTs is at times distorted. That is, the author describes cDNAs as "sturdier DNA copies," a questionable state-

---

[58] George Poste, "Genomics," 165–169.

[59] This 1995 press release, "First Installment of Merck Gene Index Data Released to Public Databases: Cooperative Effort Promises to Speed Scientific Understanding of the Human Genome," was accessible on the World Wide Web through an NCBI link.

[60] "Genomics." *Vital Speeches of the Day,* 169.

ment given the many cloning inaccuracies that can occur.[61] To portray Venter's method as highly effective and cost-efficient, the writer seems to support shortcut research: "To speed things even more, he read just part of the DNA, since each interesting fragment could later be used to fish out the whole gene. The approach cut the cost of sequencing an unknown gene from an estimated $50,000 using older methods to roughly $20.[62] Once again, the "spin" (trimmed with a useful fishing metaphor) ignores the issue of error, along with an important detail: a "tag" is not a gene. Other metaphors further reflect bias: "But, as he says, 'cells are smarter than scientists.' To create necessary proteins, cells ignore the junk [DNA] and copy the DNA of important genes into a related molecule."[63]

Given that distortion surrounds the release of genetic findings to the public, Collins wants to educate the medical community for a correct understanding of gene therapies. He relies, therefore, on metaphor to elucidate complex medical concepts and to provide motivation for life-saving discoveries. In a speech at George Washington University, Collins argued that systematic research, which requires ongoing funding, is the only means to making progress with genetic disease.[64] He began by comparing a cell to the universe. Zeroing in on a chromosomal surface is like a galactic journey that moves from the outer reaches of the universe down to a specific spot in a city park. The comparison allowed Collins to demonstrate the need for systematic research, given the difficulty involved in conducting successful genetic experiments. To travel such genetic distances requires planning and precision, if money is to be used wisely. Exposing the enthymemes within his metaphoric illustration, we find the following assumptions:

- We need funding for systematic research.
- Systematic research will make us productive and lead to cures.
- Productivity is a sign of our success.
- Success warrants further funding.

---

[61] *Business Week*, 75.
[62] *Business Week*, 75.
[63] *Business Week*, 75.
[64] Francis S. Collins, "The Human Genome Project," The George Washington University, 23 February 1996.

This deductive chain enables Collins to shift attention from establishing agreement to identifying degrees of acceptance: "The community is no longer arguing whether the HGP is a good idea but is now debating the most effective ways to reap its rewards."[65]

In a recent article published in the medical journal *Hospital Practice,* Collins summarizes the essence of current genetic research so that medical professionals and researchers can understand its importance. He validates the concerns of his audience by acknowledging the frustrations that physicians and scientists might face:

> Such knowledge provides glimmers of therapies, including a group of RAS inhibitors now being tested against colon cancer. So far, however, the knowledge has not led to a new generation of therapeutic breakthroughs. The time line is unforgivingly linear. Hence, for many diseases, we will be living, for the next decade or more, in an uncomfortable interval in which sophisticated diagnostic tests are not yet matched by potent interventions.[66]

Having acknowledged these challenges, he launches a pseudo-advertising campaign and appeals to his audience by invoking the metaphor of pioneers:

> The appetite for sequence data will be accompanied by one for improved sequencing technology . . . . The future of gene hunting will include increasing emphasis on polygenic . . . disorders . . . . Such an era is rapidly approaching. Indeed, one can readily imagine the investigation of intracellular tapestries using clones from the existing cDNA library. Such explorations are not among the explicit goals of the Human Genome Project. They are for Genome II—and for biomedical researchers with a genome attitude.[67]

Whether Collins is correct in his long-term approach continues to be the source of great debate. Still, the public needs to be informed. It is incumbent on the scientists and medical professionals to use communication effectively—in technical debates and in public presentations—to send the correct message, especially considering that the public receives generous amounts of misinformation. The public, too,

---

[65] *Proceedings in National Academic Science,* 10843.
[66] *Hospital Practice,* 49.
[67] *Hospital Practice,* 53.

must become aware of the ways in which discourse practices can both obscure and promote understanding. When a research initiative like the HGP relies on language, rather than science to puzzle out and present problems, we need to understand how ideas, issues, and questions are subject to the shaping power of the very people who present them.

11 Let's Re-Enact Rhetoric's History

John C. Adams

INTRODUCTION

There are numerous texts where rhetoric's idea is spelled out in terms that celebrate its power and significance—from Gorgias' "Encomium of Helen" to seventeenth-century Harvard's Ramist commencement theses, and beyond. There is also a literature that sets out rhetoric's vices. Like its other it attempts to establish rhetoric's place in the hierarchy of approaches to life and learning. The narratives celebrating and vituperating rhetoric call upon listeners and readers to believe them, to adopt them, and to channel their experiences of the cultural category they name through the accounts of rhetoric's place proffered by their authors.

However, since rhetoric *is* (if it *is* anything at all) a cultural category, no particular idea of rhetoric is necessary, although some narratives of rhetoric's idea claim they are descriptions of what people naturally do. But what people naturally do may be *second* nature—their linguistic values-in-action that mark the tacit or normal idea of rhetoric in their community of speakers—habitual ways of rhetorically speaking that may be formed through the conscious or unconscious practice of *imitatio*.

This essay proposes a way of studying the history of rhetoric from comparative and experiential perspectives through the practice of *imitatio*. It affords one with a way of supplementing one's understanding of different ideas of rhetoric by putting them into practice—by literally re-enacting rhetoric's history. In addition, it affords one with a way of assessing or reassessing one's *own* idea of rhetoric from a practical standpoint. It puts one's practice of rhetoric on a level with one's theory of rhetoric as an index of its value and as an inducement to adopt its idea. For example, imaginatively creating and delivering a speech by imitating Plato's idea of rhetoric as he articulates it in *Phaedrus* may actually change one's idea of rhetoric as its imitation may afford one a quality of insight into its value that one could not obtain simply by reading and discussing the dialogue.

The Body

When most people think of values they think of the orders of the good they mobilize consciously or unconsciously when faced with objects of choice, or when engaged in gauging something's worth. Values are applied (or emerge) in specific cases for purposes of locating what's being judged in the context of the good. They are often projected or affected toward artifacts or actions, or both, in attempts to understand their aesthetic, ethical, practical, and moral significance—four contexts of the good that are far from independent and which may, in fact, be substituted for each other in life's play, conflict with each other in one's deliberations with others and even one's self, or combine in some deeply cultured blend of protean priorities.

But the story of any set of values can never be adequately told if it poses itself as a description, and not as an inducement. For the very idea of value cannot be comprehended without the charge of its concept of the good flowing forth from its image. In addition, as rhetoricians have known for a long time (probably from rhetoric's birth when someone couldn't do *it* alone or feel *it* alone, cried/ bleated/ grunted/ moaned/ out for help, and got it), these descriptions are hortatory insofar as they call upon us to pay attention at all to anything at all when we can always be paying attention to something else, or to nothing at all. Moreover, descriptions always inevitably float their depictions on pieces and parts as far as the part we play as objective recorders is partial—we can't know it all because we're not know-it-alls in our piecemeal, perspectival lurch through life. What we know is a part that has parts that we cannot know, but nevertheless we must get up and go, give reasons, take chances, place bets, act, dance, sing, speak.

But there's always the question of firstness—it's the grand implication of the rhetoric science project or the movement of thought motioning toward rhetoric's epistemic significance—where inducements to cooperate (rhetoric's wards and neighborhoods) create fixations that function as knowledge, and as far as they do, that is, as far as we are willing to act on them, they ARE. But where's the foundation for what's first or does what is first need no foundation—Atlas stands with the world, or I should say, Hermes stands with the word, on his shoulders, but what is Atlas/Hermes standing on? And is there an infinite set of Atlases/Hermeses, or a circular strand of alternating World/Word-Atlas/Hermes beads strung out on a string of faith? But where does one's faith in the rightness of one's idea of rhetoric come from?

In the late twentieth century, when Atlas has shrugged and Hermes has flown, rhetorical words—the *logoi* toys—are falling, floating, bouncing but still moving in the flux of life's complexities toward the same ends they always have—to induce—to induce to murder or to love or to buy or to sell or to open or to close or to hit or to miss or to some other binary twirl of some dialectical *dissoi logoi*—*either/or-oi*—the only thing that's changed are the words of the story. But the story of word's place does not end where it says it does, because it starts from somewhere and that place is the story's FORE-WORD—the clasp that enables closure of its circular hermeneutic—in its reading *from* its first place. In fact, the foreword may be so cleverly worked into rhetoric's strand so as to disappear into the pages of the book of word's philosophy one has in one's hand when one is trying to understand its mysteries. As the maxim says: "Art is that which best conceals art."

But a change or revision of the foreword surely sets in motion a conversion as one reorients one's sense of word's place—of rhetoric's place—in one's approach to life and learning. That is, wherever they come from, and however they go, one's beliefs about what speech can do and can't do, and why and how it can or can't, set the tone of one's life in the world of one's utterances which *is* the world of connection/rejection—the place of not being or being alone. Accordingly, one's linguistic values may be first, and rhetoric's place in the book of speech is foreworded in the stories told of its possibilities—where possibility itself is the ultimate term of the foreword—an important place—a circular space where we may spin a world wide web that sets the limits of the world's width with wishes and fears, hopes, cheers and jeers traversing the years we live through and beyond in the memories we spawn by doing the deed of speaking. Speaking is indeed a deed—we do it—it is a way of being.

Forewords to rhetoric's book are words about words that reflexively set in their speaking the speaking of speaking's speech. And what is the shape of speech's speech—it is the non-scientific prescript that settles faith in word's worth at its hearing. It is the ultimate soliloquy.

Nevertheless these stories—these forewords—may fail to fixate, and instead, initiate the ethnographer's distant response: "My, how deeply cultured this local knowledge is." Or the ethnocentrist's response: "Ah, get the hell out of here!" as she or he derides the speech of speech's place spoken from an alien quarter. For example, reviewing the history of rhetoric and pausing at the elocutionary place—the response to *its* foreword (to its speech about speech) may be put in terms so alien from the desires of elocutionists—yes my friends and enemies there WERE PEOPLE who called themselves ELOCUTIONISTS—that ridicule of its first assumptions seems appropriate, but a chance is lost—a possibility is foreclosed by derision—rhetoric's history is deframed.

Why don't *I* believe in elocution's tenets? Why did THEY (those OTHERS) believe? As far as ways of speaking and listening are ways of being, what would it be 'like' (let's go with an *epoche* as a minimal gesture toward a community of interests that is good and dead in the late twentieth century) to BE an elocutionist—what quality of life is tied to or implied by its commitments? Can't "quality of life" be a criterion for accepting or rejecting the plot line of rhetoric's place it sets forward as its foreword? And where does its past plausibility fit in the history of ideas—if it *was* plausible, how come it *isn't* plausible to virtually all late twentieth century students of rhetoric (show me where it's currently being taught as *the* way into eloquence)? Can it become plausible again? That is, may we ever hope to re-enact its ethos and gather together under its wide tenets as culturally sensitive listeners, at the minimum, to the discourses of its bearers?

Let's examine a central self-reference from Fulton and Trueblood's *Practical Elements of Elocution*, where persuasion and eloquence remain, but once again (and again and again) the way to get them—the foreword—is differently framed. Again, let's settle in on the question—what is it like to BE an elocutionist. Let's read:

> Eloquence is the art of spiritual reproduction, rather than of spiritual transportation. It is measured by the success of the speaker in making his thought and feeling and will become incarnate in other lives. (421)

This is heady stuff—this "spiritual reproduction." In the late twentieth century, where, in the hearer/reader response story of discourse's so-called effect, the hearer/reader has complete autonomy to "picnic" as she or he wishes on the text, the very idea of eloquence in these elocutionists' view entails the complete opposite. Now, where do we go from here?

If it was the elocutionists' desire to more or less become re-incarnated in listeners' lives, one would have to think that this is what listeners desired too—that the relationship between speakers and listeners was built off a sweep away/swept away model of eloquence. It harks backs to the images of rushing fluid caught in the idea of fluency—and even the literal translation of the deeply technical term "rhetoric" from its origins in an ethic of flowing where the rhetor's voice is heard as a kind of honey-sweet torrent—where hearing is like tasting and tasting's taste is instant.

But how do we re-capture the elocutionist's ethic of desire longing to be re-possessed by some other's speech as Fulton and Trueblood's speech about speech speaks of "spiritual reproduction"? What is spiritual reproduction if it isn't some kind of birth-thing carrying the image to its ends—where the soul is a womb—or one's "life" is a womb as far as it's one's "life" is where the incarnation of the other's/speaker's "thought and feeling and will" is reproduced. Incarnation is a lofty goal/desire. There must have been a lot of rhetorical failure during the period—but when success hit, it hit big.

Fulton and Trueblood's *Practical Elements of Elocution* was first published in 1893—but the text on incarnation may have been added as late as 1903, for it is a part of an appendix attached to the 1903 edition entitled "Truth, Personality, and Art in Oratory" authored by James W. Bashford B.D., Ph.D., and President of the Ohio Wesleyan University. Clearly, Christian interests are appended here. But what does all this mean? It means that any speech uttered under the terms of *Practical Elements of Elocution*'s "contract"—where listeners and speaker collude in the construction of the speech's meaning—there's great potential for people attempting to account for what happened in the terms of "spiritual reproduction." They would be likely to think also that the linguistic values appended by Bashford (as they learned them and believed them) are not specific to their time and place and cultural interests, but that any piece of rhetoric could be read/heard off Bashford's order of the good—his linguistic values. But there's still more.

Is it possible that we, converted/unconverted students of rhetoric and its naturally biased history can ever become fond of Bashford's appendix—not bash it—but embrace it as better-suited to our lives' purposes and their achievement than some other deeply cultured rationale of the suasory? These rationales of the suasory are all about the same ends—they all paraphrase each other in the terms resonant with their means—but the means—the means may mean more than the ends—the *rationale* of the suasory clearly means means that mean more than the ends as far as the ends don't begin without the means' meaning which is laden with motive as what's 'before,' as first in the order of action—as a second *thought* after the hoped-for ends, but still *means* performed toward ends providing the tone of their action's hopes to achieve the ends they move toward achieving. If this seems too convoluted try this: An act of speech production/reception in Bashford's appendix takes one down a different vein than I.A. Richards' *Philosophy of Rhetoric* where words interinanimate each other in some kind of ecological all-at-onceness that is plausible on examples. *For example,* the difference between the meanings of one word in two statements: "Hello!" and "Hello nitwit!" where "Hello" means something different in both cases because of what doesn't and does come after it. But what kind of examples can Bashford give—he can't give examples because he's talking/writing about qualities of experience that can only be referenced to one's own experiences, or less significantly, to earwitness accounts that claim some event happened and that's how everybody understood/experienced it. What he has written is not about literal properties of texts that can be seen in print. Elocution's game is played on the field of delivery with the body and the voice.

But let's get back to desire. If one desires to have an "elocutionary" experience, one just might have one. Where does the desire for an elocutionary experience come from—of course—it comes from elocution's FORE-WORD—the pretext that sets out the "imagine this" and engages you for a moment in contemplating the benefits of change—a change in perspective and the quality of one's experience. Clearly, Bashford and, say, the Communist Lenin would be angling in differently on the same discourse as a matter of preference as they listened to or read the following (which may or may not be rhetorical):

I walk through the valley of the shadow of death.
The Lord is my shepherd.

"So what?" you think. This is what—the very idea of a difference of some kind in the hearing/reading—whether mine, yours, Bashford's or Lenin's—the very idea that we'll never know how 'others' may hear it is settled itself on a FORE-WORD whose pivotal terms are "we'll never know" and which unknowingly set a block or barrier because they fail to figure the worth of what can't be known—of imagination—in the setting of one's interpretation of some other's possible interpretation—where engaging the "as if" in full recognition of "it's not" may eke out a line of plausibility stretching one's consciousness to the point of being raised in a new sense of something's possibilities—some text's possibilities—some new/old idea of rhetoric's possibilities—to answer some questions one could not otherwise even address.

There are many examples in the literatures of religious conversion where all of a sudden the same old/ancient/archaic words take on new meanings—where hearers/readers are astonished by their impact. There are all sorts of glib pronouncements one may make in one's attempts to account for these qualities of experience—where the same suddenly becomes different. But what makes, or can make, the difference? Can it be a change in one's idea of word itself—one's linguistic values—one's beliefs about what speech can and can't do and how it does or does not do it?

Conclusion

In my own life's quest for new meaning, I continue to study rhetoric. In my studies there have been episodes of adjustment and re-adjustment as I learned more about rhetoric—well maybe not more, but different. When a different idea of rhetoric takes in my head it takes me some place I could not otherwise be. For example, when I first taught Erasmus' *Copia*, I practiced it. My students practiced it. Together, through its oral practice, we learned far more about *copia* than we ever could have if we had simply read Erasmus analytically and left it at that. Among other things, we learned that *copia* is a way of coping—of unlocking one's creative potential and ability to encompass a problem or concept more fully as each different way of saying the same thing enables one to understand the same thing differently—putting it in other words crafts facets or lenses which enable different points of view. There's more to *copia* than this, but this is what we learned through its practice. Our practice supplemented our ideas of Erasmus' idea of *copia* and enabled us to alter to some degree our *own* ideas of rhetoric—its place and potential to enrich our lives.

Now, as I go on about my studies of rhetoric at each turn in the historical road as I read I find myself entering in—taking as seriously as I possibly can the stories I read—from Isocrates' *Antidosis*, to Omer Talon's *Rhetorica*, to Fulton and Trueblood's *Practical Elements of Elocution*. But that's not all.

I am convinced that stories of rhetoric set life-changing possibilities. If one has no story of rhetoric, one is like a person who has never thought about love, or hunger or any of life's pressing urgencies. And I'm not simply saying that *stories* set life-changing possibilities. I'm saying the stories of *speech's place* in our lives set us on the way to our lives as far as acts of speaking and listening are ways of being that pose our prospects for being not-alone—for being social and more.

A powerful way of teaching rhetoric's history should engage re-enacting rhetoric's history—of feeling its play in the body and the voice under the array of answers to the question "What is rhetoric and how do we make it?" A part of the answer should engage the question "What would it be like to BE a Platonist—to wear Mr. P's toga, walk his walk & talk his talk—to go-a to the *stoa*—to be an Aristotelian, a Ciceronian, an Augustinian or a Quintilianian, or for that matter, a Perelmaninian or a Derridadadidian?"

Of course we'll never *really* know what it was like to walk through the snow in Francis Bacon's boots—his handmade swash bucklers. But if we can't put our bodies into history and feel rhetoric's play at a period, then we've spun a tale of rhetoric's past that places it in an abstract analytic position—as if its *idea* is more important than its *practice* and that experimenting with practice under a range of rationales is not relevant to learning about its idea and its history. But it is—and it always can be.

The idea of *imitatio* draws a more or less magic circle around rhetoric's history—*imitatio*'s history is a part of rhetoric's history and the reflexiveness of its prospects is enacted through the reflectiveness of its desire to enter into a stream of practice—to practice like some fargone virtuoso, but within the tradition that made the virtuoso's performance possible in the first place. It has faith in a human's ability to imitate more than imitation in a practice tending toward perfecting something more than an echo, but at least part echo nevertheless, nevertheless, never less, but more. *Imitatio* explicitly acknowledges bodily rhetoric—rhetoric's possession of some-body in practice feeling its play on desire's desire to be liked by, or be like, some other. But not simply some other's idea, but some other—some *ethos*—some-body in action—some body being speaking or listening here or there—some place different from a library or a study's chair.

This quality of *imitatio*, for the sake of learning rhetoric's history, or revising one's idea of its idea, must be practiced in public. It must be before—be *for*—some gathered group set on trying it out on an outing where together stander and bystanders—speaker and listeners—attempt to conjure past sensibilities by auditing and by mounting the rostrum, the platform, the stage, the hustings in full recognition that even the idea of rhetoric's appropriate site shifts with its shifting idea to cultured venues that themselves must be imagined and re-enacted by all present for the re-enactment of one bit of rhetoric's history. At any rate, it's "magic time" when the curtain rises and the players engage an ethic as much as they can and are willing to bend to what they cannot know—it's time for the history of rhetoric show!

So, in conclusion, let's practice: let's imitate (in the good sense) some theory's play—let's re-enact a little piece of rhetoric's history—let's go back to Fulton and Trueblood. As you read the excerpt printed below, try and act like the readers/listeners of 1909 eager to learn an idea of eloquence—an art of spiritual reproduction strongly identified with elocution. I suggest you get up and read the excerpt aloud and follow its instructions:

> (a) First Position Right. (Fig. 24. [see Appendix]) In this position the right foot is placed about one-half its length in advance of the heel of the left, so that a straight line projected through and parallel with the right foot must strike the heel of the left. The feet are at an angle of about 75 degrees with each other. The right foot is at an angle of about 37 degrees, and the left at about 38 degrees, with the line FF projected in front of the body; the little swaying movements of the body to right and left may cause this line to vary about 15 degrees, as indicated by the short arc in Fig. 24, without changing the position of the feet.
>
> While the weight of the body is placed chiefly upon the left foot, as explained by Dr. Austin, we would insist the preponderance of weight be given to the *ball* of the left foot as indicated by the shading in Fig. 1. This distribution of weight and angles gives an easy

graceful bearing to the lower limbs, and secures the harmonic poise of the entire body.

The significance of the First Position Right is that of mentality, self-poised and under control. It is used in narration, description, didactic thought, and in the gentle emotions, —and not swayed by strong emotion or passion; hence our classification of this position as Mental. (388–89)

This is not a speculative stab—this is the rhetorical canon of delivery delivering its points self-evidently—"Read my feet!" says *Practical Elements of Elocution.*

Of course, the excerpt you read is a small part of elocution's course of studies, but it serves as a reminder: there *were* people who strongly identified with its movement of thought, who screened their reception of rhetoric, and engaged its practice, through the terms of its pronouncements. If one cannot find some strand of empathy to tie to its boatload of promises, one may be just as much adrift on a rhetorical sea as in the know and on the right course. There's no way to know for sure. But there were generations who bought this image—who floated out onto life's waters between its gunwales.

It's not enough to ask at what price they bought elocution's bill of goods; we must also ask what price we pay for not doing likewise. This is a good question to ask. And generally it seems to me it is best asked *after* we've tried on some alien idea of rhetoric's tenets—by embodying its hopes in a performance of its desires in accord with its FOREWORD—as back to the past we go through the practice of *imitatio*.

As actors susceptible to being changed by roles we play in the play of rhetoric's history, we may clarify our ideas of alien rhetorics by painstakingly practicing the "others" own tenets. Likewise, one may change one's idea of rhetoric and in so-doing alter one's course through life. In sum, there's a fairly significant difference between being an Aristotelian delicately sniffing out the available means of persuasion and being a Fultonean Truebloodean solidly and self consciously setting one's feet "at an angle of about 75 degrees with each other." It's the difference between using an in-born mental faculty souped-up by classical *techne* and expecting to make one's thought, feeling and will "incarnate in the lives of others." But what does one name this "difference," and finally, what difference does it actually make? The only way to answer the question, it seems to me, is to practice different ideas of rhetoric and find out for yourself.

Appendix I

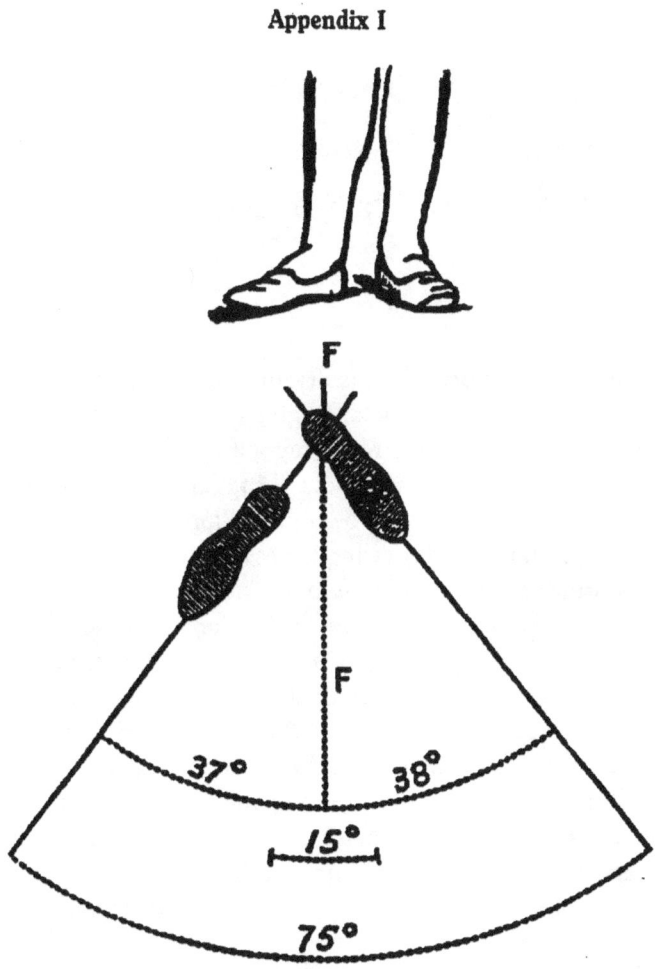

Figure 24. First Position Right

12 Leading Lady or Bit Part: The Role of the History of Rhetoric in Communication Education

Glen McClish

To those of us who study the history of eloquence, Dame Rhetoric is—in the manner of many of our aging rock stars—still alive and well. In fact, one might go so far as to say that, as the twentieth century slouches to a close, the old gal is flourishing, and her colorful history continues to preoccupy us. Our own professional meetings, journals, and monographs buzz with pressing issues and controversies. Were the Sophists postmodern ironists, protofeminists, elitist cultural conservatives, or sage empiricists? Just how egalitarian is Aristotle's conception of public deliberation, and what is the true relationship between rhetoric and democracy? Was Ramus the great villain of our tradition, or was he a kind but misunderstood fellow who loved dogs, children, and *inventio,* even if he did not quite know how to classify them? Were the eighteenth-century Scottish rhetoricians advocates of the Roman tradition, imitation French aesthetes, masters of the Enlightenment, or merely oat-eating aristocratic wanna-be's? These questions and many others drive ambitious research programs for rhetoric faculty and graduate students alike.

In addition to producing a flurry of primary research on specific issues concerning the history of rhetoric, we have recently brought out several broadly defined revisionist projects such as Victor Vitanza's *Negation, Subjectivity, and the History of Rhetoric* and *Writing Histories of Rhetoric,* Andrea Lunsford's *Reclaiming Rhetorica: Women in the Rhetorical Tradition,* and Takis Poulakos's *Rethinking the History of Rhetoric: Multidisciplinary Essays on the Rhetorical Tradition.* Closer to the classroom, our people have in the last decade published a series of new textbooks for teaching the history of rhetoric to undergraduate and beginning graduate students. Patricia Bizzell and Bruce Herzberg's *The Rhetorical Tradition: Rhetoric from Classical Times Through the Present*, Thomas Conley's *Rhetoric and the European Tradition*, James Herrick's *The History and Theory of Rhetoric*, and, most recently, Craig Smith's *Rhetoric and Human Consciousness* have helped us bring the message to the rhetoricians of the next generation. As scholars and as teachers, we are doing what we can to demonstrate the pithy truth of last year's ASHR preconference theme—"the centrality of rhetoric."

Yes, in our own spheres of influence, Dame Rhetoric's role is assured, and we are better situated than ever to celebrate her part in the world of letters. What concerns me here, however, is not our realm at all, but the more expansive domain of our institutional host, the National Communication Association, that massive organization that, through acts of generosity or benign neglect, sanctions our preconferences and provides the spaces in which we gather. I wonder about the role rhetoric's history plays in the rooms beyond our friendly, but largely neglected, enclaves. In particular, I am curious about the status of rhetorical education—the specific topic of this year's preconference—among those folks interested in the theoretical state of our greater discipline. How are *they* teaching the history of rhetoric to their students? What part, if any, does our lady perform in *their* dramas? With these questions in mind, I will explore the place of traditional rhetoric in the textbooks dedicated to communication theory. To accommodate the space requirements of this study, I have chosen eight representative textbooks to examine: Stephen Littlejohn's *Theories of Human Communication*, James Anderson's *Communication Theory: Epistemological Foundations*, Julia Wood's *Communication Theories in Action: An Introduction*, John Cragan and Donald Shields's *Understanding Communication Theory*, Jo Liska and Gary Cronkhite's *An Ecological Perspective on Human Communication Theory*, Rob Anderson and Veronica Ross's *Questions of Communication: A Practical Guide to Theory*, Em Griffin's *A First Look at Communication Theory*, and James Neuliep's *Human Communication Theory: Applications and Case Studies*. For those rhetoricians who reside in English—rather than communication—departments, reading on may seem a bit like participating in a counseling session for someone else's extremely dysfunctional family. Do not forget, though, that your own domestic sphere could benefit from therapy, if of a different kind. Perhaps another rhetorical context will constitute an intervention of sorts for your *domus*.

From our standpoint, of course, the history of rhetoric *is* the history of communication theory. It is our leading players—the Sophists, Plato, Aristotle, Isocrates, Cicero, Quintilian, St. Augustine, Erasmus, and the like—who establish the fundamental questions central to communication. We would admit the importance of other figures, but we believe we have identified the heart of the matter. We do not exactly expect communication-theory textbooks to proclaim this message verbatim, but we hope they will offer some kind of friendly paraphrase.

Not surprisingly, all eight texts selected for this study include at least some mention of twentieth-century rhetorical theorists and their near relations. For example, the dramatistic pentad of Kenneth Burke is at least mentioned in all but Anderson's text, and Walter Fisher's narrative paradigm makes its way into every book but Neuliep's and Liska and Cronkhite's. When it comes to the history of rhetoric, though, and the nuts-and-bolts story of public eloquence in the Western tradition, the picture is less predictable. Let us now turn to a careful examination of the texts, book by book.

I begin with the industry standard, Stephen Littlejohn's *Theories of Human Communication*, which was originally published in the seventies and has reached its sixth edition this year. Meticulous and thorough, Littlejohn's book was the first in the field, and it has shaped all the others. I daresay that many of the scholars currently writing about the history of rhetoric were brought up on it. Despite its authoritative reputation, though, *Theories of Human Communication* has virtually no interest in the history of our discipline. Those familiar with the book will not be surprised to discover that the term "rhetoric" is not listed in the index. "Rhetorical sensitivity," Rod Hart and Don Burk's term for "the tendency to adapt messages to audiences" (103), appears; and if one investigates this concept, the notion of the "rhetorical reflector" is encountered (103–04), as well as the "RHETSEN," the instrument that Hart and his colleagues developed to measure rhetorical sensitivity empirically (104). Furthermore, the rhetorically inquisitive reader will discover the phrase "rhetorical vision," Ernest Bormann's label for those stories that "structure our sense of reality in areas that we cannot experience directly but can only know by symbolic reproduction" (167).

But surely he has not utterly ignored *Rhetorica,* in all of her glory and complexity. In fact, his opening chapter alludes to the history of rhetoric as a kind of ancient ancestor of communication, but he cannot quite articulate the word "rhetoric" itself, and he skips ahead to recent times with breathtaking speed: "Although communication has been studied since antiquity, it became an especially important topic of concern in the twentieth century. One author referred to this development as a 'revolutionary discovery' . . ." (4). The author to whom Littlejohn refers is none other than Barnett Pearce, who—despite his accomplishments in the theory of coordinated management of meaning and the area of dispute resolution—is hardly an expert on the history of our discipline. There is a note accompanying the first sentence I have quoted, which refers the reader to several publications not known for their insight into or emphasis on classical rhetoric, including John Stewart's *Language as Articulate Contact* and an essay written by Pearce and Karen Foss entitled "The Historical Context of Communication as Science." Empirically oriented, Littlejohn has no inclination to include the story we want told.

The same sort of erasure is observable in Anderson's *Communication Theory.* This challenging, intellectually sophisticated text, which is explicitly designed for "graduate students and their faculty colleagues" (3), is built upon a fundamental epistemological dichotomy between empiricism and hermeneutics that, however erudite and insightful, entirely overlooks the history of rhetoric. Like Littlejohn's index, Anderson's excludes the term "rhetoric." Once again, "rhetorical sensitivity" is featured (205–08), as is a brief discussion of contemporary developments in rhetorical analyses of science (193–94), but there is no coverage of our tradition.

Even more frustrating, perhaps, is Julia Wood's *Communication Theories in Action.* Wood, who has written many textbooks, including a thoughtful, accessible account of the relationship between communication and gender, shares Littlejohn's and Anderson's neglect of the longstanding history of rhetoric, but lacks their general thoroughness and rigor in the areas of inquiry she does feature. Her only mention of classical rhetoric comes when, in her opening chapter, she seeks to outline the breadth of the communication field. She remarks, "More than 2,000 years ago, when the study of communication began, the field focused almost exclusively on public communication. Aristotle, a famous Greek philosopher, believed effective public speaking was essential to a citizen's participation in civic affairs. He taught his students how to develop and present persuasive speeches to influence public and political life" (20–21). With that summary, she abandons the subject for the rest of the book. I find the passage particularly problematic because it is followed by a nearly two-page discussion of *intrapersonal* communication, a subject that—to my mind—hardly compares in importance to the history of rhetoric. A bit later, Wood includes a brief mention of rhetorical critics, who "study important communication events" and show an interest in "discovering and teaching principles of effective public speaking" (25), but the discussion lacks historical context. No sense of rhetoric's ancient and venerable role in communication theory can be gleaned from this book.

Like Littlejohn, Anderson, and Woods, John Cragan and Donald Shields, authors of *Understanding Communication Theory*, introduce their topic with virtually no mention of what we would call the rhetorical tradition. Once they establish their preliminary methodology and begin to examine individual theories in detail, though, they demonstrate more interest in the history of our discipline. The second major topic presented in the book is "rational argument theory," affectionately abbreviated as "RAT." According to Cragan and Shields, RAT's roots "grew in the fertile soils of rhetoric, dialectic, and logic in ancient Greece" (67). They go on to discuss Aristotle's three means of proof, as well as "the dialectical arena," which they aptly label "the counterpart of rhetoric" (68). It is gratifying to discover an explicitly classical origin for RAT, and it is pleasing to observe the presence of Perelman and Olbrechts-Tyteca's work throughout the treatment. It is a bit surprising, though, that the subject of stasis can be discussed without explicit mention of the classical tradition developed by Hermagoras, Cicero, Hermogenes, and others (77). Historians of rhetoric may also be disappointed that Richard Whately's name is not mentioned in the coverage of "presumption" and "burden of proof" (77–78).

The second major sighting of traditional rhetoric takes place in the ninth chapter, titled "Public Speaking and Organizational Communication Context Theories." Here, Cragan and Shields begin a presentation of eight theories with a unit on Neo-Aristotelian theory, which they quickly dub "NAT." Gratefully, we see mention of the Sophists, Plato, Cicero, Quintilian, John Quincy Adams, and someone named John Whately, who looks suspiciously like a figure we know as Richard. Considering the necessarily broad scope of this book, the authors make a genuine effort to present and contextualize several key components of the Aristotelian tradition. Nonetheless, it is unnerving to see how easily Cragan and Shields complement the ancient position with detailed explanations of recent scholarship. Eager to test and refine Neo-Aristotelian ideas empirically, they create a misleading synchronism. The likes of James McCroskey and Robert Bostrom appear all too soon for my taste. It is my nostalgic wish that we could have had a bit more Aristotle before we move to the neo variety.

Like Cragan and Shields, Liska and Cronkhite incorporate at least some material from the history of rhetoric into *An Ecological Perspective on Human Communication Theory*. I appreciate their assertion that "the disciplines of law and communication find their roots in the writings of the ancient Greeks and Romans" (78), and I am grateful for their effort to provide coverage of Plato, Aristotle, Cicero, Isocrates, the Sophists, St. Augustine, Campbell, and Whately. However, their treatment of the history of rhetoric is rather quirky and—in several places—misleading. For example, their discussion of Isocrates *follows* the summary of Cicero, thus confusing chronology (82). Since there is no biographical information provided, the uninitiated reader will probably assume that Isocrates was a Roman. Furthermore, although this section of the text is labeled "Isocrates," it has just as much to say about the rhetoric of Cicero and Quintilian as their Greek predecessor. Liska and Cronkhite's synopsis of Plato is not preceded by any discussion of the Sophists, which means that his attack on rhetoric is presented without its proper context (79–80). Even more problematic, their section labeled "Sophists"—which, like their piece on Isocrates, follows discussion of Cicero—features not the influential teachers of the Greek tradition such as Gorgias, Prodicus, Thrasymachus, and Protagoras, but the Roman rhetoric of the Second Sophistic (82–83). Furthermore, this section spends more time discussing the exploits of "modern-day sophists" or "image-makers" such as Bank One, Anita Hill, and Ronald Reagan than the specific characteristics of Roman discourse. Their discussions of Medieval and Renaissance rhetoric fail to mention a single historical figure by name (84–85). The principal source for this section is Nancy Harper's 1979 book *Human Communication Theory: The History of a Paradigm,* hardly a standard reference for the rhetoric of these periods. Liska and Cronkhite's emphasis on biological and environmental issues is intriguing, but their coverage of the rhetorical tradition is unreliable and frustrating.

One of the most basic treatments of communication theory is Rob Anderson and Veronica Ross's *Questions of Communication*. This text, which is designed to answer ten fundamental queries about communication, includes questions that make traditional rhetoricians nervous such as "When Have We Communicated?" and "What's Inside My Head When We Communicate, and Why Do I Need to Know?" With the eighth question, though—"How Are People Persuaded through Rhetoric?"—Anderson and Ross launch into more welcome territory. After some general discussion of the terms "mind" and "persuasion," they turn their gaze backward in time: "Classical rhetoric in Western civilization has had a long and influential history. Even early theoretical assertions from persons such as Aristotle, Plato, and Isocrates . . . have themselves been so persuasive that they are still studied intensively by scholars" (208). Drawing on the *Rhetoric*, the *Gorgias*, and the *Antidosis*, Anderson and Ross embark on a thoughtful—if brief—discussion of ancient approaches to rhetoric. Readers are introduced to the epideictic, deliberative, and judicial forms of oratory; artistic and inartistic proofs; *ethos*, *pathos*, and *logos*; Quintilian's notion of "a good man, speaking well"; and rhetorical examples and enthymemes (208–15). Although, like Cragan and Shields, Anderson and Ross seek to update classical concepts with modern empirical research, the former principles, rather than the latter studies, seem to shape and dominate the discussion. Furthermore, the final chapter of the book—which takes up the question "When is the Effective Choice the Ethical Choice?"—includes a section entitled "Aristotle's Ethic of Virtues," which quotes directly from the *Rhetoric* and the *Nicomachean Ethics* (268–69). Anderson and Ross have done us good.

Another relatively elementary text is Em Griffin's *A First Look at Communication Theory*, which is currently in its third edition. Griffin's first three chapters establish a basic framework for theorizing about communication, and the next thirty-two present one theory at a time, from Shannon and Weaver's information theory to Cheris Kramarae's work on muted groups. On the whole, I find his three-chapter introduction promising, but also a bit frustrating. Griffin establishes communication theory as a sort of dialectic, an ongoing tension or tug-of-war between scientists and humanists. On the positive side, he—unlike many of his fellow textbook writers—gives humanists (which include rhetoricians) equal billing with their empiricist competitors. The problem lies with his second chapter, which provides an inappropriately short history of communication theory. Although the treatment dutifully balances the work of rhetoricians and social scientists, Griffin chooses to begin not in ancient Greece or even in the Enlightenment, but in 1914, with the founding of the organization that eventually became the sponsor of the American Society for the History of Rhetoric, the National Communication Association. Thus, his stream of communication history lacks what we would consider its most vital source.

Nonetheless, the book entirely redeems itself when Griffin takes up the specific theories he classifies as "public rhetoric." The introduction to this cluster of chapters includes a three-page synopsis of the history of rhetoric, from Plato through several twentieth-century figures (299–301). Griffin touches upon the work of the usual Greek and Roman suspects, but he also mentions rhetoricians not often included in such summaries such as St. Paul, Francis Bacon, and Peter Ramus. The first chapter in the section on public rhetoric constitutes the most thorough treatment of Aristotle's *Rhetoric* I have encountered in communication-theory textbooks (302–11). Although his introductory remarks are unnecessarily hard on the Sophists (302), Griffin goes on to emphasize probability, the tripartite classification of speeches, the three modes of rhetorical proof, the enthymeme and rhetorical example, the canons of rhetoric, the *topoi*, and the theory of metaphor. His "Critique" of the *Rhetoric* touches on the potential ambiguities concerning *pathos*, then concludes with the following assessment: "Despite the shortcomings and perplexities of this work, it remains a foundational text of our discipline—a starting point for scientists and humanists alike" (310). By deeming Aristotle worthy of his own chapter, and by granting him "foundational" status, Griffin lends particular credence to the rhetorical tradition.

But the story does not end here. The fourth edition, which is scheduled to come out late in 1999, will be revised to reflect more accurately the centrality of traditional rhetoric to communication theory. In the new text, the second chapter—which originally included a rather myopic view of our discipline—has been entirely restructured. Building on the work of communication theorist Robert Craig, the upcoming version consists of concise descriptions of seven key traditions that form the foundation of twentieth-century communication theory. The third of these seven, "the rhetorical tradition," outlines the Greco-Roman approach to conceptualizing and teaching oratory. In this way, classical rhetoric resumes its rightful place at the heart of the discipline. It must vie for attention with other traditions such as the socio-psychological, the cybernetic, the semiotic, and the critical, but at least it competes on equal terms.

There is a rather personal coda to this story—I have advanced knowledge of Griffin's revisions because I have served as a consultant on the project. We began corresponding after I taught his book several years ago, and as a result of our communication, I have had the opportunity to lend a hand in revision. An empiricist by training, Griffin has made use of my interest in rhetoric. Although I cannot claim credit for the virtues of *A First Look at Communication Theory,* my efforts have helped to portray the history of rhetoric's role more effectively.

The final book featured in this analysis is Neuliep's *Human Communication Theory.* Neuliep, who places more sustained emphasis on application than any of the other authors, structures his text around four basic approaches to theory. The first of the four, rhetorical theory, is allotted a generous seventy-six pages, forty-two of which are dedicated to rhetoric prior to the twentieth century. He begins his discussion of the history of rhetoric with this welcome assertion: "At the heart of the communication discipline is the study of classical rhetoric and at the heart of that study is public speaking" (67). Systematically, he works through the Greek origins of the art of rhetoric, including useful treatments of Corax and Tisias, Protagoras, Gorgias, Isocrates, Prodicus, and Thrasymachus (69–73). His discussion of Plato includes thorough analyses of the *Apology,* the *Gorgias,* and the *Phaedrus* (74–79). Thoughtful coverage of Aristotle, Cicero, Quintilian, and St. Augustine rounds out the section on classical rhetoric (79–101). Particularly noteworthy is Neuliep's extensive "Neo-Aristotelian" case study, in which he applies classical rhetorical principles to Mario Cuomo's keynote speech at the 1984 Democratic National Convention (83–94). His discussion of the Middle Ages, the Renaissance, and the Neoclassical rhetorics of Campbell, Blair, and Whately are relatively terse, but its presence itself is commendable (101–05). Although Neuliep's own scholarship is empirical, his text is the most friendly to the history of rhetoric of those I have examined.

The implications of this discussion are straightforward, but significant. Communication-theory textbooks often neglect, minimize, skew, or misrepresent the rhetorical tradition. Although there is sustained interest in the rhetorical theorists of the second half of the twentieth century, those figures whose contributions fall before the empirical revolution in communication study tend to fare less well. Nonetheless, there is certainly a range of coverage among the possible choices, and some books serve our cause more effectively than others. For the good of our collective enterprise, I encourage you to familiarize yourself with this body of textbooks so that you can help your departmental colleagues make informed selections. Offer to deliver guest lectures in their courses in an effort to bring alive the vibrant connection between the kind of work you do and the theories they present as central to the overall discipline. If you are so inclined, you may even cultivate relationships with the authors of these books. With your help, for example, a communication-theory textbook writer or two could break from the Aristotelian bias I have documented here. It would be invigorating to see an occasional shift in emphasis to the Isocratean-Ciceronian line of rhetorical theory that, according to scholars such as Thomas Sloane, may be more central to the development of civic discourse than the *Rhetoric*. I believe that some of my most satisfying hours as a rhetorician have been spent helping other scholars with their writing, and my consultation with Em Griffin is no exception.

And while I am confessing, I will admit that the antithesis that comprises my title is, no doubt, a false dilemma. Dame Rhetoric may never be expected to dominate the stage in the communication-theory class, but that does not mean that she must be relegated to a walk-on part, either. Instead, I would like her cast as best actress in a *supporting* role. You and I can help her reestablish her venerable foundation.

13 *Encomium on Helen* as Advertisement: Political Life According to Gorgias the Barbarian

Michael William Pfau

Introduction

Gorgias stands prominently at the eve of the rhetorical tradition. Unfortunately, we have few sources from which to determine the character of Gorgias's art of persuasion. This situation invites contemporary students of rhetoric—even those sharing the barbarians' ignorance of Greek—to carefully examine Gorgias's surviving work in order to learn as much as possible about this important figure. In this paper I provide a reading of Gorgias's *Encomium on Helen* that attempts to approach the text from a subtly different angle than most previous readings. John Poulakos, in his essay "Gorgias' *Encomium on Helen* and the Defense of Rhetoric," categorizes previous readings of Helen into two main categories. One group, Poulakos argues, reads the speech as a "model" speech; while the other group reads the speech as a "'pretext' for Gorgias' real purpose"—which Poulakos argues was to defend his art of rhetoric.[1]

Poulakos's argument is worth briefly reviewing because I share several of the assumptions of his position. To Poulakos, Gorgias's *Encomium* is a defense of rhetoric in which Gorgias uses myth and metaphor in order to "artfully avoid being explicit for political reasons."[2] Gorgias was aware, Poulakos explains, that many powerful forces in Athenian society were suspicious of rhetoric's destabilizing potential.

---

[1] John Poulakos, "Gorgias' *Encomium on Helen* and the Defense of Rhetoric," 1–16.

[2] Poulakos, "Gorgias' *Encomium*," 2–7.

As a result, he continues, Gorgias was compelled to conceal his defense of rhetoric with mythological allusions: "Gorgias' discourse must have seemed perfectly harmless and non-threatening to the forces of the establishment, which tend to take things literally, anyway. Thus, Gorgias's wish to defend rhetoric without antagonizing a powerful status quo, and thereby endangering himself, is fulfilled."[3] Poulakos's more specific claim that Gorgias intended to defend his art of rhetoric in the speech is discredited by Schiappa's observation that no art of rhetoric yet existed at the time the *Encomium* was written (let alone a generally accepted dichotomy between philosophy and rhetoric). Schiappa correctly places Gorgias in a "predisciplinary" historical context, in which neither the later conceptualizations of rhetoric, philosophy and logos, nor the genres (such as epideictic in which the *Encomium* is usually categorized) had yet been developed. Schiappa interprets the *Encomium* as one of the "earliest surviving extended discussions of logos and certainly the most sophisticated of the time," yet admits that Gorgias's texts "like anyone else's—potentially can serve multiple functions."[4] Nevertheless, I agree with Poulakos's more general assertion that the *Encomium* is a pretext for a position that he felt compelled to hide behind an allegorical veil. To address Schiappa's "predisciplinary" observation, however, I examine the interface between Gorgias's *Encomium* and the Athenian political culture in general (rather than a particular rhetorical or philosophical outlook). If I am correct, Gorgias's *Encomium* allegorically represents his characterization of political life in Athens, a characterization which, in denying the conventional democratic Athenian view of politics as the realm of freedom and choice, is decidedly that of a barbarian.[5]

My interpretation of the *Encomium* begins with two common assumptions about the piece. The first assumption is that it amounted to

---

[3] Poulakos, "Gorgias' *Encomium*," 7.

[4] Edward Schiappa, "Gorgias's Helen Revisited," 314, 310, 319, 312.

[5] My use of the term "barbarian" deserves further explanation and clarification. While the term was generally applied to non-Greeks it was also employed by Athenians from time to time to refer to other Greeks who were not of Athenian blood. For the use of the term barbarian in reference to non-Athenians (in terms of the "not a citizen by birth *topos*"), see Josiah Ober, *Mass and Elite*, 269–71. In this respect Gorgias is a barbarian twice over. Not only was he not a native Athenian; as I shall argue, his aristocratic rhetorical doctrine was also quite contrary to democratic Athenian political culture. In sum, both his birth and rhetorical doctrine marked him as an outsider.

a sort of ancient "advertisement" directed toward prospective students. As Segal writes, the *Encomium* "may have served as a kind of formal profession of the aims and methods of his art, a kind of advertisement."[6] The second assumption is even less controversial—that Gorgias's discussion of the effect that persuasion might have had on Helen's choice is intended to indicate the power of persuasion and its potential effect on an audience (in the speech, represented by Helen). From the character of the speech as "advertisement," and its construction of Helen as "audience," I will proceed to make a speculative leap—Gorgias, I suggest, may have intended to convey in his *Encomium* a sort of model of Athenian politics (and perhaps politics in general). I will contend that the *Encomium*'s Helen represents democratic citizens acting in their deliberative capacity, and the four forces which Gorgias speculates may have influenced her actions (the gods, violence, persuasion and love) represent a delineation of the forces affecting political life in general. Among these influences, persuasion is included as one influence denying the capacity for choice—persuasion, along with violence, love and the gods is portrayed as compelling action. In this respect, Gorgias's view of political life is that of a barbarian, one who does not share the Greek—and especially Athenian—reverence for language and its capacity to reveal the best course of action in a democratic state. The conventional democratic Athenian view—exemplified in both Attic orations as well as the doctrines of Isocrates, Protagoras and Aristotle—held the capacity to speak as a defining characteristic of human beings. Speech, so the argument went, allowed humans the capacity to live in political communities because it enabled deliberation about the just and the expedient. Most importantly, speech allowed human beings, both as individuals and collectives, to choose consciously among alternative courses of action.[7] My reading of the

---

[6] Charles P. Segal, "Gorgias and the Psychology of Logos," 102.

[7] Corroboration of this view may be found in the doctrinal statements of teachers of rhetoric as well as in the speeches of Athenian practitioners of rhetoric. See Plato, *Protagoras*. Translated by W.K.C. Guthrie, in *Plato: The Collected Dialogues*, ed. E. Hamilton, H. Cairns, 318–20 (320d–323d); also Isocrates, *Antidosis*, in *Isocrates II*. Translated by George Norlin, 327–9; Aristotle, *The Politics*, translated by C. Lord, 37 (1253a1: 1–20). Ober (*Mass and Elite*, 75–6, 165) draws similar conclusions about Athenian political ideology, observing both the importance Athenians attached to their capacity to choose among alternative courses of action through political debate, as well as the faith the *demos* had in its own deliberative wisdom and ability.

Encomium, then, suggests that its power as an "advertisement" lay in its allegorical portrayal of Athenian politics; a portrayal which implied that those learning persuasion would possess a tremendous power—equal to divine will, violent force, or erotic love—to compel fellow citizens toward their will.

Conventional Athenian Views of Politics as Agency

Before I proceed to examine the *Encomium* itself, it is essential to first examine the conventional Athenian view of democratic politics. Perhaps the most eloquent spokesperson of Athenian political life, Hannah Arendt, provides a useful starting point. Arendt portrays the realm of political life as one of freedom, in which actors may be liberated from the components of life related to mere necessity: "The realm of the *polis* . . . was the sphere of freedom, and if there was a relationship between these two spheres, it was a matter of course that the mastering of the necessities of life in the household was the condition for freedom of the *polis*." According to Arendt, political life was considered by the Greeks to represent an arena in which actors were free to choose courses of action, rather than responding to the dictates of necessity that had dominated life before political societies: "What all the Greek philosophers, no matter how opposed to *polis* life, took for granted is that freedom is exclusively located in the political realm, that necessity is primarily a prepolitical phenomenon, characteristic of the private household organization."[8] Arendt's view, of course, is a synthesis of a variety of fourth-century sources (especially Aristotle's dichotomy between household and *polis*), many of whom either were not born or had not yet begun to write at the time that Gorgias composed his *Encomium*. To address this potential criticism (and insulate myself from Schiappa's criticism of Poulakos), I will examine two further sources that corroborate Arendt's basic portrayal of Greek (and particularly Athenian) political life.

In Thucydides's *History of the Peloponnesian War,* we find assumptions about Greek and Athenian political life similar to those put forward by Arendt. In Arendt's scheme, politics was the realm of freedom. Such freedom allowed political actors the opportunity of exercising their capacity for agency—freely choosing among alternative choices in the course of deliberation with fellow citizens. Thucydides's

---

[8] Hannah Arendt, *The Human Condition,* 30–1.

History clearly illustrates the importance of deliberation and choice in Greece, and especially Athens. Thucydides's extensive reporting of deliberative speeches in his *History* seems to indicate the importance that he assigned to such activities as the determinants of action. Thucydides felt that an account of the process by which agents determined their course of action was indispensable to writing a history of these actions and events. Indeed, the Athenian penchant for deliberation was posited by Pericles as a decisive advantage in the war with Sparta: "they have no central deliberative authority to produce quick decisive action."[9] Thucydides, in fact, contended that the revolutionary character of the later Peloponnesian War eclipsed the Greek predilection to determine courses of action by debate and argument with a destructive factional dogmatism.[10]

Josiah Ober's comprehensive review of a wide array of Attic orations provides a characterization of Athenian political culture similar to that suggested by Arendt and Thucydides. According to Ober, the fifth century BCE saw the creation of an Athenian "state in which public debate over real alternatives preceded genuine decision making by the masses ... for the Athenians, democracy and equality became central organizing principles of the social and political order."[11] Such institutions, however, coexisted alongside a predominantly egalitarian and democratic ideology that understood the *demos* not just as the genuine decision makers of Athens, but (for the most part) as wise and able decision makers.[12] In sum, the conventional view of Athenian democracy envisioned citizens who faced choices together, and arrived at courses of action, in a manner that displayed their capacity for collective agency. In terms of the argument of this essay, Athenian political

---

[9] Thucydides, *History of the Peloponnesian War* Translated by R. Warner, 120 (I:141). Thucydides reports many deliberative events, both within particular political communities such as Athens and Sparta (The Debate at Sparta, 72–87, I: 66–88, the Mytilenean debate, 212–23, III: 36–50), and the pan-Hellenic debates among city-states (the dispute over Corcyra, 53–67, I: 31–55, the Melian dialogue, 400–08, V: 84–116).

[10] Thucydides, *History*, 242–45 (III: 82–4).

[11] Ober, *Mass and Elite*, 75–6.

[12] Ober, *Mass and Elite*, 161–5, 313. Ober acknowledges that the *demos* invariably relied upon the superior knowledge and eloquence (derived from leisure) of political orators in order to articulate and frame the issues. Nevertheless, the *demos* did not voluntarily surrender its decision-making capacity to the elites.

culture provides an essential point of reference from which to examine Gorgias's views on politics and persuasion.

The *Encomium* as the Eclipse of Agency: A Barbarian's View of Politics

Having made a case as to the character of the conventional view of democratic politics in ancient Greece (and Athens in particular), I now return to Gorgias's speech. To establish the *Encomium* as an allegorical portrayal of Athenian politics that denies democratic political actors the capacity to freely choose among alternate courses of action, I must establish several points. First, I must establish that the forces influencing Helen's decision in the *Encomium* are plausibly read as a sort of delineation of the various factors potentially influencing political action, of which persuasive speech is only one. Ancient listeners could certainly recognize the various roles the gods, force, persuasion and love might play in the *polis*. Second, having established that these forces were intended to portray influences affecting political life, I will argue that Helen's role in the allegory is that of political audience which is compelled to take a certain course of action. In this respect, persuasive speech is one among several influential factors in politics that deny the possibility of individual or collective agency. Finally, I will contrast the way in which Gorgias positions persuasion as one of several factors denying collective agency to the more conventional democratic Athenian perspective.

The four factors influencing Helen in the *Encomium* were readily understood by Gorgias's contemporaries as a delineation of factors affecting political life. I will examine each in turn, providing examples of the influence of the gods, violence, persuasion and love upon *polis* life. The first, fate of the gods, is fairly straightforward. All *poleis* had their own particular gods which provided a mystical bond reinforcing the political, and good citizens were expected to show a certain degree of piety as well as make the appropriate religious sacrifices. Lack of piety might conceivably result in punishment from the gods (a common occurrence in Homeric epics), or, more likely, from the state. The trial of Socrates is perhaps the most notable example of the political importance of the gods, and the dangers of charges of impiety.[13] In

---

[13] Plato, the *Apology*, in *Euthyphro, Apology, Crito*. Translated by F. J. Church, esp., 31–4.

any event, the gods were certainly a resource available for justifying certain courses of political action, or condemning political opponents. The second type of influence on Helen, violence (or force) was without doubt a very familiar influence on political life. Whether tyrants were putting people to death, or democratic and aristocratic factions fomenting coups and revolutions, violence and force were very common political realities in the turbulent city-states. Thrasymachus's definition of justice as the right of the stronger reflected a clear recognition of the role of force in politics.[14] The third factor, persuasion, is most obviously recognizable as a potential political influence. As Arendt, Ober and Thucydides suggest, persuasion was considered an essential tool in the democratic political process, one that made the realm of politics one of freedom and not necessity. The last possible influence on Helen, love or passion, is certainly less straightforwardly political than the previous three, though it could play an important role in the *polis*. The political bond of loyalty among Spartan soldiers was thought to be strengthened by the love and passion they shared for each other. Such passions were said to have functioned politically in Athens as well. According to Xenophon, one reason for the popularity and political influence of Alcibiades in Athens, and Hellas in general, was the *eros* he was able to inspire in both men and women:

> Alcibiades . . . was courted because of his good looks by many women of rank, and . . . pampered by many influential men and held in honor by the people, and enjoyed an easily won supremacy.[15]

In any event, love and passion could plausibly be recognized as having an influence on political affairs insofar as they could serve to tie men together in bonds of friendship more carnal and compelling than mere loyalty. In sum, the political implications of all four of these influences were likely recognizable by Gorgias's audience(s).

If these four forces are plausibly read as the stuff of politics, it is a fairly easy transition to understand Helen as an allegorical representation of political audience subject to these forces. Helen's initial choice—whether or not to go to Troy—is analogous to the kind of situation in which deliberative political groups found themselves. The

---

[14] Plato, *The Republic*. Translated by A. Bloom, 15 (338c).

[15] Xenophon, *Conversations of Socrates*. Translated by H. Tredennick & R. Waterfield, 77.

Athenian democracy clearly conceived of itself in this way. Citizens gathered together in order to choose courses of action for the *polis* in which they lived. Collective choices, according to the conventional view, were made through the deliberative use of speech to weigh alternatives. That Helen was said to have made an individual choice, while political audiences made collective choices, need not detract from my argument. As Segal writes, "For Gorgias, however, the psyche is the common denominator in both the collective and the individual [persuasive] situations...."[16] With only a slight stretch of the imagination, one may read Helen's initial position in the *Encomium*, in which she is faced with a choice (though a *private* one), as analogous to that of citizens within political audiences.

It is well known, however, that Gorgias's portrayal of the manner in which Helen's decision is made denies her the capacity to truly choose among alternatives. Each of the hypothetical forces Gorgias suggests may have influenced Helen's decision is well outside her capacity for choice. If she was influenced in her decision by the gods, clearly she had no choice: "For it is impossible to forestall divine proposals by human disposals."[17] If, on the other hand, violent force was the reason she went to Troy, Helen was not an agent, "she was the victim."[18] Similarly, if Helen was smitten by Alexander, she also did not choose freely: "If ... the eye of Helen, charmed by Alexander's beauty, gave to her soul excitement and amorous incitement, what wonder? How could one who was weaker, repel and expel him who, being divine, had power divine?"[19] Finally, if Helen was indeed persuaded, it was not persuasion in the sense of speech leading to free and reasoned choice. Rather, Gorgias portrays persuasion as being akin to witchcraft in its power to compel action: "the power of song in association with the belief of the soul captures and enraptures and translates the soul with witchery."[20] In sum, Gorgias's defense of Helen relies on the assumption that one of these forces (or a combination of them) compelled her course of action, and that in neither case did she choose of her own free will: "If, however, it was against her will, the culpable should not be

---

[16] Segal, "Gorgias and the Psychology of Logos," 108.

[17] Gorgias, *Encomium on Helen*, in *Isocrates III*. Translated by Larue van Hook, 56.

[18] Gorgias, *Encomium on Helen*, 56.

[19] Gorgias, *Encomium on Helen*, 57.

[20] Gorgias, *Encomium on Helen*, 57.

exculpated."[21] Indeed, Gorgias concludes that Helen did not go to Troy of her own free will no matter which force influenced her: "How, then, is it fair to blame Helen who, whether by love captivated, or by word persuaded, or by violence dominated, or by divine necessity subjugated, did what she did, and is completely absolved from blame?"[22] Helen is blameless precisely because she never really had a choice. As most readings of the *Encomium* conclude, Helen is portrayed as subject to powerful forces beyond her control, thereby denying her the capacity for choice usually considered a prerequisite for blame.

If one accepts the notion that the *Encomium* may have been an oblique reference to politics, the fact that persuasion is noted as just one of the forces is significant. Such a placement of persuasion implies that it is but one of many forces of necessity compelling political actors. Placement of persuasion as but another force of necessity certainly suggests that Gorgias did not partake of the conventional Athenian view of democratic politics. Persuasion was understood by the more democratically-minded Greeks as an essential component of deliberation, a capacity that enabled political actors to transcend mere necessity and achieve a degree of freedom based on their ability to freely choose among alternatives. Violence was considered to epitomize necessity, and to be subject to it was the lot of a slave, not a free citizen:

> force and violence are justified in this sphere [the household] because they are the only means to justify necessity . . . and to become free . . . is the prepolitical act of liberating oneself from the necessity of life for the freedom of the world. This freedom is the essential of what the Greeks called felicity, *eudaimonia*, which was an objective status depending first of all on health and wealth. To be poor or to be ill in health meant to be subject to physical necessity, and to be a slave meant to be subject, in addition, to man-made violence.[23]

Xenophon confirms Arendt's dichotomization of force (necessity) and persuasion (freedom) in his relation of Alcibiades's question to Pericles: "And what is violence and lawlessness, Pericles? Isn't it when the stron-

---

[21] Gorgias, *Encomium on Helen*, 56.
[22] Gorgias, *Encomium on Helen*, 57.
[23] Arendt, *The Human Condition*, 31.

ger party compels the weaker to do what he wants by force instead of persuasion?"[24] Gorgias's placement of persuasive speech along with forces of necessity, especially violence, as a denial of agency, was most certainly the act of one who did not share the Greek reverence for language and its capacity to allow citizens to freely choose their own destiny in political societies. In this respect, the scheme of political life, which I suggest the *Encomium on Helen* allegorically represents, is decidedly that of a barbarian in the original sense—one who was neither Greek nor Athenian and therefore did not share a belief in the potentially liberating aspects of political speech.

OTHER CORROBORATIONS OF GORGIAS AS BARBARIAN

Evidence that Gorgias possessed a "barbaric" view of politics may also be found in other sources. Isocrates provided one piece of corroborative evidence in his observation that Gorgias, moving from place to place, neither became attached to any particular city-state; nor did he ever pay taxes or provide for public benefits in any of the city-states in which he lived and taught.[25] Plato also provided several pieces of the puzzle. In the *Philebus*, Plato made Protarchus say "I often heard Gorgias say that the art of rhetoric differs from all other arts. Under its influence all things are willingly but not forcibly made slaves."[26] Not only does this account of the power of persuasive speech agree with the account in the *Encomium*, it also confirms my argument that Gorgias possessed a "barbaric" understanding of politics. No conventionally-minded Athenian would have subjected himself to persuasion had he believed he was at risk of becoming willingly enslaved. For this very reason, Gorgias would not be so foolish as to voice his barbaric conception of persuasion and politics in public. Indeed, in public, Gorgias showed the appropriate contempt for barbarians. In his speech at the Olympic games he is said to have "denounced the barbarians." Gorgias also emphasized the difference between Greek and barbarian in his *Defense on Behalf of Palamedes*.[27] As these passages suggest, Gorgias was a master of

---

[24] Xenophon, *Conversations*, 81.

[25] Isocrates on Gorgias (a selection of fragments on Gorgias, translated by G. Kennedy), in *The Older Sophists*, edited by R.K. Sprague. 37.

[26] Plato on Gorgias (*Philebus* 58a), in *The Older Sophists*, 39.

[27] 35. Philostratus on Gorgias, *Epistle* 73, in *The Older Sophists*, 41; also Gorgias, *Defense on Behalf of Palamedes*, in *The Older Sophists*, 56.

dissimulation. These passages also support my earlier claim that the *Encomium*'s simultaneously barbaric and aristocratic portrait of politics would necessarily be hidden behind an allegorical veil.

The Platonic dialogue *Gorgias* provides additional evidence of Gorgias's barbaric conception of politics and persuasion, as well as his wise determination to keep these views well hidden. Plato's dialogues, of course, must be used carefully, for Gorgias himself denied that Plato's portrayal of him was accurate: "It is said that also Gorgias himself, having read the dialogue which bears his name, said to his friends, 'How well Plato knows how to satirize!'"[28] With this caution in mind, I will use the *Gorgias* in only a very general sense. Callicles was the first interlocutor to suggest that Socrates was able to make Gorgias appear foolish precisely because Gorgias was unwilling to admit to his unconventional, or barbaric, views of politics and persuasive speech:

> ... when Gorgias was questioned by you as to whether, when anyone came to him desiring to learn rhetoric but without a knowledge of justice, Gorgias grew ashamed and said he would teach him, complying with conventional morality, because people might grow indignant if he said he wouldn't; and it was through this very admission that he was forced to contradict himself....[29]

Only Callicles was bold (or foolish) enough to ignore the value of convention, asserting that the originators of the "laws and conventions are the weak, the majority.... But my opinion is that nature herself reveals it to be only just ... that the better man should lord it over his inferior ... the true state of affairs, not only in other animals, but also in whole states and communities ... the stronger shall rule and have advantage over his inferior."[30] Callicles, though surely lacking Gorgias's prudence, appears to provide good evidence that there was much that Gorgias was unwilling to say due to the authority of democratic conventions. Callicles may also provide an example of the type of person toward whom the *Encomium* as advertisement may have been directed.

---

[28] 15a. Athenaeus on Gorgias, in *The Older Sophists*, 37.

[29] Plato, *The Gorgias*. Translated by W. C. Hembold, 50 (482c).

[30] Plato, *The Gorgias*, 51–2 (483).

Conclusion: Intended Recipients of the *Encomium*'s "True" Meaning as Advertisement

One aspect of my reading of the *Encomium* that may seem paradoxical is its attitude toward the persuasive power of speech. If we assume Helen to represent a political audience, then the *Encomium* clearly suggests that decisions in the political realm, far from being characterized by the human capacity for reason and choice, are subject to a variety of forces (love, the gods, force and persuasion) that virtually compel outcomes. If the *Encomium* presents a vision of persuasion in which the possibility of individual or collective choice is eclipsed, what is the use of speech, and why would one wish to learn the art of persuasive speech? To understand what room is left for agency (and who exercises it) in this barbaric conception of politics, we must first take a brief look at Gorgian epistemology. Richard Leo Enos, Bruce Gronbeck and Laszlo Versenyi all explore the relationship which Gorgias perceived between language and knowledge. All of these authors assume that Gorgias's epistemology denied the possibility of true knowledge.[31] For Gronbeck, Gorgias's conclusion that true knowledge is impossible led to the "tragedy of knowledge." Because one cannot truly know, it becomes impossible to choose among opposite courses of action, both of which have support in decent arguments (the *dissoi logoi*). Deception, therefore, in the form of operating upon the emotions in order to make one side appear stronger, is necessary in order to make any choice at all.[32] To Enos, Gorgias's rhetorical theory of deception is clearly spelled out in the *Encomium*: "the power of persuasion resides in its ability to conjure up and excite feelings and attitudes associated with past experiences."[33] To Versenyi, the *Encomium on Helen* is also important, for it serves as a "pretext to argue that logos 'might have nothing to do with knowledge, intellect, reason, but move in an altogether different realm.'"[34]

---

[31] Laszlo Versenyi, *Socratic Humanism,* 44–5 (cited in Poulakos, "Gorgias' *Encomium,*" 4); Bruce Gronbeck, "Gorgias on Rhetoric and Poetic: a Rehabilitation," 27–38; Richard Leo Enos, "The Epistemology of Gorgias' Rhetoric," 35–51.

[32] Gronbeck, "Gorgias on Rhetoric," 32–6.

[33] Enos, "Epistemology of Gorgias' Rhetoric," 48–9.

[34] Poulakos ("Gorgias' *Encomium,*" 45) quoting Versenyi, *Socratic Humanism,* 45.

Gorgian epistemology, then, appears to deny the possibility of knowledge (making deception necessary), as well as agency in the conventional sense of Athenian democratic practice. The citizens in the assembly lack both the ability to acquire knowledge through discussion about public issues, as well as the capacity to freely choose among alternatives. Citizen deliberation, in other words, is driven by something other than a capacity for speech allowing knowledge and choice. If I am correct in my interpretation of the *Encomium*, it presents a vision of politics in which the gifted and ambitious—the aristocrats—are the only citizens capable of freely choosing their actions. As an unidentified ancient writer put it "as Gorgias says . . . 'the deceiver is more justly esteemed than the nondeceiver . . . .' The deceiver is more justly esteemed because he succeeds in what he intends . . . ."[35] In this respect, Gorgias's *Encomium* as allegorically-veiled advertisement for the power of persuasion sends a clear message to those listeners able to read between the lines. Politics, Gorgias implies, is not as you have been taught to believe. The common people do not truly choose their course of action based on persuasion, reason and deliberation. Rather, the best men, those who are most persuasive, are able to compel certain outcomes according to their will. Audience (especially the *demos*), like Helen, lacks agency, and is subject to many compelling forces, foremost among them, persuasion. In this respect, only the persuader possesses agency. This type of agency, however, is based not on a capacity for knowledge through reason, but a will to power. Clearly, such an advertisement would be found offensive by many conventionally-minded Athenians, insofar as it converts the realm of the political from one of freedom to one of slavery; and denies the democratic assumption that all citizens exercise a form of agency in public deliberations.[36] For this reason, I argue, Gorgias's "barbaric" view of politics and persuasion could only be advertised if concealed behind an allegorical veil. One can easily imagine that the clever and ambitious aristocrats able to transcend a literal reading (or listening) of the *Encomium* would be mightily tempted to employ Gorgias as an instructor.

---

[35] Fragment from unidentified authors, "On the Fame of the Athenians," translated by G. Kennedy, in *The Older Sophists*, 65.

[36] Ober emphasizes the extent to which the *demos* recognized the potential dangers of deceptive orators and resented the possibility that well-trained orators could deceive. After all, an ability to deceive the masses suggested the superiority of the rhetor. In general, the *demos* is said to have held public speakers fairly closely to the tenets of democratic ideology. *Mass and Elite*, 166–9, 315.

14 Upholding the Values of the Community: Normative Psychology in Aristotle's *Rhetoric*

Ulrike Zinn Jaeckel

George A. Kennedy suspects that Aristotle's treatment of the emotions in Book 2 of the *Rhetoric* may "have originated in some other context and have been only partially adapted to the specific needs of a speaker." As he points out, most of "the examples given are not drawn from rhetorical situations" (122). Yet even if we grant that many passages are not directly applicable to the three genres—deliberative, forensic, epideictic—of ancient rhetoric, we can make a case that the famous chapters on the emotions and on character traits of the audience are well adapted to the needs of the *Rhetoric*: they closely reflect and help maintain the ideology and values of the Athenian *polis*, the community in which rhetoric happened.

As a foreign-born resident of Athens, Aristotle knew Athenian democracy and the role of rhetoric in its ongoing operations from observation, not from active participation.[1] In fact, Thomas Conley maintains that Aristotle was "an outsider who exhibited little interest in the problems of Athens itself" (20). However, he was familiar with political and rhetorical goings-on in the city where he lived for decades. Paul Brandes, for example, speculates that Aristotle frequently attended the law courts to "establish what contemporary practice was" (203 n.7). Certainly the *Rhetoric* must be understood in the context of rhetorical practice in Athens, such as it is described by Josiah Ober in his *Mass and Elite in Democratic Athens* and by Ober and Barry

---

[1] On September 28, 1998, the H-Rhetor list featured a brief discussion concerning Aristotle's civic status in Athens. Carol Poster reminded readers that "Aristotle was a metic."

Strauss in "Drama, Political Rhetoric, and the Discourse of Athenian Democracy."

Taking into account the probable reasons leading to the preservation of the corpus that has come down to us, Ober analyzes the ideological content and probable rhetorical effects of the extant speeches of Greek orators. He demonstrates that *isegoria*, the right of every Athenian citizen to deliver a speech from the speaker's platform (the *bema*), although extolled as a principle, in practice was limited to the elite group of well-trained politicians called *rhetors*. In examining the ideology working in and through ancient writings, Ober makes an important distinction between elite/elite and elite/mass discourse (43; Ober and Strauss 238). While, according to Ober, "most ancient texts were written by elites, specifically for an elite readership" (43), his point that Greek orations were elite/mass texts highlights the role of audience adaptation in the composition of speeches. Since the audience acted as decision maker, elite speakers had to project an *ethos*—glossed by Ober as *ideology*—that showed their identification with the audience's values. Those Athenian citizens who did not belong to the elite but who were the audiences for the speeches of the *rhetors* constituted what Ober calls the *mass*. Through their votes and verdicts they made the decisions called for in Athenian political and juridical life, but—lacking formal training in rhetoric—they were not usually expected to seize the speaking role and to define rhetorical situations.[2] If we keep in mind that women, foreign residents, slaves (and children, of course) did not form a part of that mass, we realize how exclusive and esoteric rhetoric and rhetorical training were in democratic Athens. In Ober's terms, Aristotle's *Rhetoric* is an elite/elite text that provides a theory for how to construct elite/mass speeches.

Traditionally, such considerations have not shaped scholars' readings of Aristotle's treatment of the audience. Rather, the relationship between speaker and audience in the *Rhetoric* has been seen in psychological terms. Indeed, Aristotle is celebrated for having laid the foundations for the "science of human psychology" (Corbett 24), and for providing "the earliest systematic discussion of human psychology" (Kennedy 122). According to Cooper, "the *Rhetoric* of Aristotle is a

---

[2] Note that Aristotle identifies the Athenian audience as "such listeners as are not able to see many things all together or to reason from a distant starting point" (1.2.12) and elsewhere refers to the "incapacity of the hearer" (3.1.5).

practical psychology" (xvii), "a searching study of the audience" (xx). Admittedly, Aristotle's treatment of the relationship between speaker and audience in the chapters on the emotions (as temporary states of mind, 2.2–11) and on the *ethos* (as character, a basic and relatively enduring state of mind, 2.12–17)[3] of the audience is psychological. However, Aristotle's psychology was embedded in the cultural context of his reflections on rhetoric. His remarks are addressed to potential *rhetors* who are to apply them in addressing jurors in the courts, participants in the Athenian assemblies, even slaves; that is, as a specimen of elite/elite discourse, the *Rhetoric* provides tools for the assertion of speakers' authority. It is shot through with references to the social order in Athens, which Aristotle did not question but took for granted. Perhaps, if the modern term psychology is to be applied to Aristotle's treatment of the emotions, it would be more appropriate to speak of his psychology as a social psychology. Indeed, Friedrich Solmsen uses this term in his 1942 article on Aristotle and the rhetorical tradition (282).

For, far from being irrational urges, the emotions described by Aristotle are largely determined by the relative social positions of those who arouse and those who experience them, as Kennedy adumbrates when he remarks that the emotions "arise in large part from perception of what is publicly due to or from oneself at a given time" (124). For example, in his treatment of the emotions of anger and calmness, Aristotle remarks that anger is provoked by a perceived slight (*oligoría*) to a person's dignity. Such slights, or as Kennedy translates, belittling, can take three forms: contempt, spite, insult. All three imply that the person receiving the slight is inferior to the person inflicting it. Thus it is especially galling to receive a slight from a person inferior in rank; for "inferiors have no right to belittle" (2.2.18).[4] They may have no right, but, for example, in the case of giving insult, they engage in *oligoría* because "they think they themselves become more superior by ill-treating others" (2.2.5).[5] Anger as such is an emotion, a psychological

---

[3] Grimaldi (2.6; 2.183–189) exhaustively discusses the relationship of the *ethos* of the speaker to the *ethos* of the audience.

[4] Unless otherwise noted, I shall cite book, chapter, and paragraph as given in Kennedy's translation of the *Rhetoric* (*Aristotle, on Rhetoric*).

[5] Aristotle here cites Achilleus's anger against Agamemnon, who treated him "like a dishonored vagrant" (2.2.6). This example is confusing because neither hero is clearly inferior to the other. According to Kennedy, Grimaldi sees Agamemnon, the commander of the Greek army at Troy, as superior and

state, but its causes are heavily determined by a person's position in the social order. In fact, as Kennedy emphasizes (124, n.8), in Aristotle's scheme a person will not feel anger against another (socially equal or superior) person who metes out a deserved rebuke or punishment, "for anger does not arise against justice" (2.3.15). Furthermore, the rhetor can induce audiences to cease being angry by making them "regard those with whom they are angry as either persons to be feared or worthy of respect" (2.3.17). That is, social rank determines who is entitled to be angry with whom.

In fact, one could argue that Aristotle provides a normative definition of anger as the response a higher-ranking man owes it to himself to feel when insulted by an inferior. This kind of anger Aristotle terms *orgé*. There is no reason to suppose that he was not aware of the anger experienced by inferiors against superiors, even when a rebuke or punishment is deserved. When he mentions a slave's anger at being punished by his master, he uses the verb *aganaktein* (2.3.15).[6] But in the *Rhetoric* the emphasis is less on emotions as private feelings than on, as one could term it, emotions that count in the eyes of others—count as badges of rank. Most of the numerous examples that Aristotle provides contain references to social position.

For instance, when discussing calmness,[7] Aristotle mentions the punishment of slaves: an owner ceases to be angry and becomes calm when a slave admits to wrongdoing and accepts punishment meekly (2.3.5). Aristotle must have known that owners could very well remain angry, regardless of how the slave took the punishment, but he stipulates that they should not. Another emotion, shame, is defined as "a sort of pain and agitation concerning the class of evils . . . that seems to bring a person into disrespect" (2.6.2). Among these evils are not only

---

concludes from this example that Aristotle allows for anger against superiors. In contrast, Kennedy argues that Achilleus is superior to Agamemnon "in fighting, in fame, and in birth." And he adds, "The point is that the angry person regards one who insults him as an inferior and that one who insults is trying to assert superiority" (126, n. 14).

[6] Translated as "to be indignant" by Kennedy; the dictionary by Liddell Scott Jones provides "to be irritated, vexed, angry."

[7] On the translation of *praotes* and *praünsis,* see Kennedy 130. Since the emotions treated by Aristotle are temporary states, a welling up and subsiding of an emotion, neither calmness nor mildness is a good translation. There is no English word to denote calming down or becoming mild and well-disposed as a process.

vices, such as cowardice, but also the failure to "share" in the "fine things" enjoyed by "one's equals," such as education (2.6.12). Thus shame results from having lost the approbation of one's peers. Pity is felt for someone who does not deserve a suffering that one fears for oneself or one of his own (2.8.2). Aristotle explicitly states that people "pity those like themselves in age, in character, in habits, in rank, in birth" (2.8.13). One can extrapolate that, for example, ugliness (2.8.10) is an evil to be pitied in a peer, not in a slave. Although "chance [*tykhe*] is the cause" of afflictions such as ugliness, they seem to be more appropriate for slaves than for masters. Similarly, "no good person[8] would be distressed when parricides and bloodthirsty murderers meet punishment" because the punishment is deserved (2.9.4). That someone might be distressed by the sheer cruelty of a punishment, be it deserved or not, does not interest Aristotle here. Clearly, the emotions he describes in the *Rhetoric* are not simply "gut reactions," but learned, culturally conditioned responses. For example, the young are said to be "inclined to pity, because of supposing [that] everybody is good or better than the average; for they measure their neighbors by their own innocence, with the result that they suppose them to be suffering unworthily" (2.12.15); that is, young men often pity incorrectly and have to learn to pity only those who deserve to be pitied. As Solmsen's contemporary, the anthropologist Ralph Linton put it in his classic *The Cultural Background of Personality,*

> social pressure keeps the developing behaviors of the individual within the limits set by his society's culture patterns and insures that his emergent habits will be such as to make his behavior predictable in terms of his position within the society. It also insures that these habits will be of a sort congruous with the habits established in other members of the society through the same mechanisms. (92–93)

This anthropological point of view is anticipated in the *Rhetoric.*[9]

---

[8] By translating *chrestos* as "good person," Kennedy veils that Aristotle is only thinking of men.

[9] I am quoting Linton because his version of social psychology is comparable to Aristotle's in the sense that both assume a stable individual that exhibits enduring identifiable traits. For an overview of more recent social psychological theories of emotion see Smith-Lovin. As Vivien Burr points out, modern social constructionist views deny the existence of an independent, coherent self as the seat of emotions; rather, they focus on relations *between* in-

Again, Aristotle is quite explicit about the importance of rank when he discusses righteous indignation (*to nemesān*), that is, the "being distressed at the evidence of unworthy success" (2.9.7). As he explains,

> since what is long established seems close to nature, necessarily people are indignant at those having the same advantage if they have recently gotten it and do well because of it; for the newly rich cause more annoyance than those wealthy a long time and by inheritance. (2.9.9)

And so for public office and other good things: the old rich "seem to have what belongs to them, the former not." Furthermore, "[it is] also [a source of indignation] for a lesser person to dispute with a greater one, especially those engaged in the same activity" (2.9.11). Similarly, envy seems to be a learned response, for according to Aristotle, people do not envy "those they or others regard as inferior or much superior" (2.10.5).[10]

Repeatedly, we are told that "good" men are the ones who feel the emotions described here, and we can conclude that the rhetor appealing to the audience's emotions has to cast the audience as good men, or present a defendant as a good man. The rhetor is able to do so because the correct emotional response can be learned. For, as William Fortenbaugh has shown, Aristotle assumes an "involvement of cognition in emotional response" (12): each emotion is caused by a thought or belief (anger by the belief that one has been insulted, fear by the thought of impending evil) and is thus "intelligent behavior open to reasoned persuasion" (*Aristotle* 17). This observation suggests that it is possible for the rhetor to change the audience's emotional responses by changing their beliefs. In other words, "emotional appeal" does not mean that emotions are stirred up through manipulation or enchantment (as suggested, for example, by Gorgias) but that they are called forth or modified by influencing the audience's thought processes. This is

---

dividuals and thus see emotions and what used to be called "personality" as fluid events that are effects of discourse (22, 34, 58).

[10] On the role of these attitudes in the social context of what he calls the "agonistic society" of Athens, see Cohen: "Individuals, then, conduct their social relations with an eye to the normative expectations of others, expectations largely centered upon rivalry for the acquisition of honor and the avoidance of shame" (65).

possible because, according to Fortenbaugh, Aristotle assumes a bipartite soul that has a logical and an alogical half, the latter being the seat of the emotions. The alogical half cannot reason on its own but can follow reasoning presented to it, and it needs to be trained to obey the reasoning of good men.

Citing the *Politics*, Fortenbaugh shows how Aristotle assigns people to positions in the social order according to their capacity for reasoning. Children (to be understood as the male offspring of the elite) must obey their elders because the logical half of their souls is not yet developed. Women should obey their husbands because their logical half is too weak to prevail over the alogical half. Slaves have to obey their masters because they lack the logical component altogether. Only "men of mature intellect" are destined to be rulers. As Fortenbaugh remarks, "Aristotle accepted Plato's demand that a difference in role be tied to a relevant difference in nature or capacity . . . and at the same time defended the *status quo* of much of Greek society" (*Aristotle* 50).[11]

Thus, even the most clearly psychological chapters of the *Rhetoric* incorporate what we would call sociological observations: the emotions as reactions to the actions of others are heavily colored by the relative social positions of the people interacting in a situation. In fact, Aristotle seems to suggest that emotions can be appropriate or inappropriate to different social positions. Even more striking is what we would now call the sociological component of Aristotle's treatment of character (*ethos*). Birth, wealth, and power are presented as gifts of *tykhe*, blind fortune (2.12.2; 2.15.1). That these qualities are manmade, in Vico's sense, is not conceivable to Aristotle. In the case of good birth, he wrestles with the biological component of the concept (speaking of "harvest" and "stock"), but apart from that, *tykhe* has to stand in for an unexplained realm of forces shaping human relationships. The attitudes (*ethos*) associated with birth, wealth and power, although they are influenced by factors such as age, are those of people who know themselves or strive to be superior: ambition and contempt are inspired by good birth; insolence and arrogance, by wealth; earnestness and dignity, by power.

---

[11] This insight does not prevent Fortenbaugh from claiming that, "when Aristotle says that slaves do not possess the deliberative capacity, he is not drawing a conclusion based upon the menial role of slaves. Rather he is indicating why slaves have the role they do" (59). But, clearly, Aristotle used his psychology to undergird his ideology.

Whereas Aristotle presented the emotions as they should be experienced rather than as they probably were often experienced by the Athenians, in his treatment of character he furnishes an unflattering portrait of the ruling class. Yet here also he suggests that education is needed to develop the correct attitude. When he compares the newly rich to those with old wealth, he remarks that the newly rich "lack education in the use of wealth" (2.16.4).[12] In other words, a person has to be socialized into a position of birth, wealth, and power—the corresponding attitude, at least the correct attitude, is not an automatic corollary of the position. Although he treats only good birth, wealth, and power explicitly, Aristotle points out that "their opposites" (2.12.2) are also gifts of fortune, and his readers are to extrapolate the characters of the disadvantaged from his remarks on those of the privileged.

To sum up, Aristotle's psychology specifies the emotional responses expected of the best members of the Athenian citizenry. These idealized emotional responses could serve the rhetor in a double function: on the one hand he could cast the audience of his fellow citizens as a group that participated in the elite's characteristics; on the other, he could present individuals (such as defendants in trials) as fulfilling or violating these norms. That the audience was vitally necessary to the political process and, as Lloyd Bitzer has argued, actively collaborated with the speaker in the joint production of enthymemes, does not alter what Ober calls the elite/mass relationship between speaker and audience in this rhetoric. A closer examination of Aristotle's so-called psychology shows it to be a social, even normative, psychology. As such it supported a rhetorical theory and practice that grew out of and maintained the ideology of *isegoria* and the self-image of the audience as citizens entitled to full membership in the *polis*. At the same time, it reinforced the division between elite and mass—and thus upheld both the hidden and the professed values of the Athenian political community.

---

[12] In this case, Cooper's translation is to be preferred to that of Freese and Kennedy, who both add the phrase "use of" to their translation of *apaideusía ploútou* ("non-education of wealth"). What Freese glosses as "they have not been educated to the use of wealth" and Kennedy as "to lack education in the use of wealth," Cooper simply renders as "to lack training in wealth." Cooper's translation does not add the restrictive turn of those of Freese and Kennedy. Aristotle's term is more broadly suggestive than training in the *use* of wealth: training in wealth encompasses the attitudes and habits associated with wealth, not only the actual use (in the sense of administrating and spending) made of one's riches.

15 Enacting the Roman Republic: Reading Pliny's Panegyric Rhetorically

Davis W. Houck

"Praise and deliberations are part of a common species in that what one might propose in deliberation becomes encomia when the form of expression is changed."

—Aristotle, *Rhetoric*, 1367b35

Rarely is it the case among ancient historians and rhetoricians that so little has been written about so much. The "much" is in reference to Gaius Plinius Caecilius Secundus's (Pliny the Younger's) loquacious *gratiarum actio*, or panegyric, to Emperor Trajan. "Little" refers to the dearth of scholarship devoted to the text: George Kennedy, Richard Bruere and Betty Radice are the only contemporary scholars, writing in English, who have paused long enough to make more than a passing reference.[1] Moreover, given that Pliny's panegyric is the only complete surviving oration spanning a period of approximately 150 years—a period bridging Republic with Empire—one might logically conclude that its contents would be thoroughly investigated.

Such a conclusion, though, clearly fails to account for scholarly justifications for ignoring the text. Radice complains that the speech is "indispensable but unreadable, and only a historian's sense of duty towards his sources can make him keep on until the last, ninety-fifth

---

[1] George Kennedy, *The Art of Rhetoric in the Roman World*, 526–48; Richard T. Bruere, "Tacitus and Pliny's *Panegyricus*," 161–79; Betty Radice, "Pliny and the *Panegyricus*," 166–72.

chapter."[2] Caplan characterizes the speech as "dull and dry."[3] Kennedy adds that the speech is "tiresome in the extreme."[4] In like fashion, Syme notes that "the speech is a strange and blended product, heavily loaded with poetical ornaments," and it "has done no good to the reputation of the author or the taste of the age."[5] Gomberini similarly concludes, "Indeed, its length and wealth of rhetorical devices, the repeated additions of detail, the use of often specious arguments . . . have caused readers to shun the work . . . ."[6] To acquiesce to such "justifications," though, is akin to a biblical hermeneut bypassing the book of "Revelations" because its imagery is too confusing and enigmatic. In the case of Pliny's panegyric, the text is not mere "vaporous claptrap."[7] What, then, is consequential about this document? Unlike others who have argued that the text's significance lies *only* in its antecedents, I contend that the text's antecedents serve as a starting point for criticism and interpretation. To date, historians and critics have emasculated the text of its status as rhetoric; the text's potential persuasiveness is sacrificed to the god of influence, thereby privileging discursive origins and not socio-political action.[8] As Sabine MacCormack notes, the speech has been treated principally as literature and only secondarily as rhetoric.[9] But to confine ourselves to making claims of textual influence and/or aesthetic value discounts the importance of the panegyric's rhetorical content—a content characterized by a series of rhetorical enactments. Specifically, I argue that the text's ostensibly epideictic modes of address often function reflexively to reinscribe the Roman Republic; praise for the emperor, in other words, functions not only as a guide to future public policy but also as a performance of that policy in the present. Though I will attempt to identify influences on Pliny, such influences are important rhetorically only to the extent that they shed light on Pliny's political agenda. Such an agenda, as I will illustrate,

---

[2] Radice, "Pliny and the *Panegyricus*," 169.
[3] Harry Caplan, *Of Eloquence*, 37.
[4] Kennedy, *The Art of Rhetoric in the Roman World*, 546.
[5] Ronald Syme, *Tacitus*, 114.
[6] Federico Gomberini, *Stylistic Theory and Practice*, 377.
[7] Julian Bennett, *Trajan Optimus Princeps*, 63.
[8] Bruere, for example, gets so involved in Tacitus's influence on Pliny via philological analysis that he largely ignores the text's status as oratory. He concludes simply that the theme of the panegyric "is the contrast between Trajan and the satanic Domitian," 162.
[9] Sabine MacCormack, "Latin Prose Panegyrics," 150.

is only partially hinted at by Pliny in his letter to Vibius Severus.[10] To facilitate a rhetorical reading of the Panegyric, I will proceed by: (1) providing a brief look at the historical context of the speech; (2) detailing an overlooked influence on the speech; (3) offering a reading of the text informed in part by Quintilian's "good man" theory of rhetoric; and (4) offering concluding remarks.

Rhetoric in the Early Empire

Many contemporary historians and rhetoricians are univocal in their claims that free speech and eloquence "died with the death of the Republic."[11] This view prevails despite the fact that no single complete speech text survives from the first century A.D.! Such a conclusion represents the epitome of question-begging: how can eloquence in particular and speech in general be judged in the absence of oratory? It would appear that modern scholars are guilty of appropriating a first century A.D. "literary" genre—that of decline. As Caplan comments, "especially in the first century it was a pious convention among Romans to glorify the good old times."[12] To be more historically specific, "fictive voices" such as Maternus and Messalla and "real voices" such as Longinus, Persius, Juvenal, and Pliny the Elder all lament the decline of Roman eloquence.[13]

Perhaps none is more specific in isolating the causes for the decline than Tacitus's Maternus—a figure, Kennedy argues, who represents the historian's "real" views on oratory.[14] He concludes that "great and renowned eloquence is the offspring of license," that eloquence does not obtain from stable governmental structures.[15] Eloquence was also a victim in the law courts during the first century A.D. given the many restrictions, the impromptu format, and the small crowds.[16]

---

[10] The letter I am here referring to is 3.18. *The Letters of the Younger Pliny*, translated by Betty Radice, 104–105.

[11] Caplan, *Of Eloquence*, 27; see also, MacCormack, "Latin Prose Panegyrics," 148.

[12] Caplan, *Of Eloquence*, 176; see also Kennedy, *The Art of Rhetoric in the Roman World*, 448.

[13] Caplan, *Of Eloquence*, 180–86.

[14] Kennedy, *The Art of Rhetoric in the Roman World*, 518.

[15] Tacitus, *Agricola, Germany and Dialogue on Orators*, translated by Herbert W. Benario, 129.

[16] *Agricola, Germany and Dialogue on Orators*, 127–28.

Aside from these structural variables, Maternus targets what would later become a late twentieth-century political *topos*: family values. He argues, for example, "that eloquence and other arts have declined from that ancient renown not because of the incapacity of men, but because of the laziness of the young, the lack of concern of their parents, the ignorance of professors, and the disregard of old practices."[17] The last two causes Maternus mentions refer to a "new" type of rhetorical teaching known as *declamatio*, in which students spoke on "unreal" situations and issues.[18]

Despite the purported qualitative and quantitative decline of oratory in the late first century A.D., its study occupied the center of Imperial Roman education.[19] Suetonius, in fact, notes during Vespasian's reign, the establishment of "a regular salary of a hundred thousand sesterces for Latin and Greek teachers of rhetoric."[20] Suetonius gives us few clues regarding the extent to which freedom of speech and eloquence prospered during the early years of Flavian rule; however, under Domitian's reign it appears that freedom of speech was under assault: Aelius Lamia, Mettius Pompusianus, Sallustius Lucullus, Junius Rusticus, and Flavius Sabinus all were executed owing to matters of public, private, and even written speech.[21] Additionally, Domitian banished all philosophers from Rome and Italy in 93 A.D.[22] Pliny, too, recounts Domitian's assault on freedom of speech: "We too were spectators in the Senate, but in a Senate which was apprehensive and dumb since it was dangerous to voice a genuine opinion and pitiable to express a forced one."[23]

---

[17] Agricola, *Germany and Dialogue on Orators*, 117.

[18] Declamation was not a new type of teaching; it had been a part of Roman society since the mid-50s B.C. See Janet Fairweather, *Seneca the Elder*, 104–31; see also Lewis A. Sussman, *The Elder Seneca*, 16ff.

[19] Prentice A. Meador, Jr., "Quintilian and the *Institutio Oratoria*," 151; see also, Stanley F. Bonner, *Education in Antiquity*, 65–89, 250–73; H.I. Marrou, *A History of Education in Antiquity* Translated by George Lamb, 244, 284–89.

[20] Suetonius, *The Lives of the Caesars, Volume Two*, translated by J.C. Rolfe, 311.

[21] *The Lives of the Caesars, Volume Two*, 361, 363.

[22] *The Lives of the Caesars, Volume Two*, 361; see also, Tacitus, *Agricola*, 26.

[23] Pliny, *Letters*, (8.14), 220–21; Radice claims that "freedom of speech was impossible" during Domitian's reign, "Pliny and the *Panegyricus*," 169.

After Nerva succeeded Domitian in September of 96, though, "a new freedom of speech" was alive "in the person of a new type of ruler."[24] Pliny would later proclaim, "Away, then, with expressions formerly prompted by fear: I will have none of them. The sufferings of the past are over: let us then have done with the words that belong to them."[25] Thus, it was under much less onerous conditions that Pliny delivered his panegyric to Trajan for appointing him *consul suffectus* from September to October.[26]

THE PANEGYRIC AND ITS SOURCES

Pliny delivered his panegyric before the Senate on 1 September 100.[27] What survives in the present is not the speech as delivered that day, but a much longer version since Pliny "thought it [his] proper duty as a loyal citizen to give the same subject a fuller and more elaborate treatment in a written version."[28] Pliny's "loyalty" though, has been interpreted by some as simply a desire to reach a broader audience given that September and October were vacation months for the Senate.[29] Unfortunately, Pliny does not indicate which material was orally delivered and which was later appended or edited.

On an initial reading, the reader is struck by both the length of the speech and by the multifarious topics covered. Praise for Trajan is not limited to heroic efforts in war specifically or character attributes generally; rather, Pliny ranges across a great variety of topics, beginning with Trajan's adoption by Nerva and concluding with the honorable actions of the Emperor's wife and sister. In between lies such "non-epideictic" *topoi* as tax policy, the restoration of property and estates, the security of wills, and the recounting of an Egyptian drought. How, then, are we

---

[24] Radice, "Pliny and the *Panegyricus*," 169.

[25] Pliny, *Letters and Panegyricus, Volume Two*, translated by Betty Radice, 325. All future references to Pliny's panegyric will be noted parenthetically within the text.

[26] The custom of newly appointed consuls thanking the emperor was established under Octavian/Augustus; see MacCormack, "Latin Prose Panegyrics," 149.

[27] For the standard Latin text of the speech see, "*Panegyricus Plini Secundi dictus Traiano Imp*," in *XII Panegyrici Latini*, edited by R.A.B. Mynors, 1–81.

[28] Pliny, *Letters*, (3.18), 104.

[29] Radice, "Pliny and the *Panegyricus*," 166.

to "make sense" of our initial reading? Or, is the text so fragmented and diffuse as to render critical commentary a series of non-sequiturs?

Fortunately, Pliny provides us with a possible interpretive key in his letter to Severus. Regarding his motives for his speech, Pliny notes, "I hoped in the first place to encourage our Emperor in his virtues by a sincere tribute, and, secondly, to show his successors what path to follow to win the same renown, not by offering instruction but by setting his example before them."[30] In a word, Pliny acknowledges the "deliberative" strain of his message; his words are "no idle flattery in conventional form"; politics, in addition to praise, is Pliny's stated intent.[31]

Given Pliny's fairly overt intent, one is surprised by some of the claims made of both Pliny and the panegyric. Lundy and Thompson, for example, conclude that Pliny viewed speechmaking more as an art form than a practical tool; moreover, they argue that Pliny reflected a political situation in which deliberative oratory was prevented altogether and epideictic rhetoric was confined to praising the emperor.[32] Somewhat shockingly, they judge Pliny to be unconcerned with the canon of invention.[33] Along similar lines, Caplan claims that Pliny's panegyric was empty of ideas insofar as form predetermined content.[34]

While Radice is not guilty of the egregious dismissal of the panegyric, she leaves her "political" characterization of the speech at the level of "skilful [sic] propaganda, a subtle blend of fact and 'wishful thinking,' a tactful way of telling Trajan what his grateful subjects would have him become."[35] By focusing exclusively on Pliny's disclosure to Severus, though, Radice also falls victim to Pliny's "skillful propaganda," thereby leaving the "political" contents of the text largely unexplored. Such contents function both as a means to persuade and as a performative gesture of Republican virtue.

---

[30] Pliny, *Letters*, (3.18), 104.

[31] Radice, "Pliny and the *Panegyricus*," 167.

[32] Susan Ruth Lundy and Wayne N. Thompson, "Pliny, A Neglected Roman Rhetorician," 412, 413.

[33] "Pliny, A Neglected Roman Rhetorician," 413.

[34] Caplan, *Of Eloquence*, 39.

[35] Radice, "Pliny and the *Panegyricus*," 168.

ENACTING THE ROMAN REPUBLIC

Pliny's deliberative clue to the reader, as confided to Severus, must be further developed if it is to have any hermeneutic salience.[36] Such salience is to be found with his rhetorical tutor, Quintilian.[37] Pliny's fusion of Aristotelian rhetorical categories takes us directly to Quintilian's *Institutio Oratoria*. In his chapter on panegyrics, Quintilian notes, "panegyric is akin to deliberative oratory inasmuch as the same things are usually praised in the former as are advised in the latter."[38] While such a claim perhaps renders Pliny's motives a bit more explicable, it offers little else. Quintilian's main contribution to rhetorical theory, however, the "ideal speaker," or the "good man speaking well" ("*vir bonus, dicendi peritus*"), may aid our interpretive efforts.[39]

Quintilian's good man is a distinctly classical concept. More important for my purpose is the political program associated with the good man—a program allied with the Roman Republic. As Meador notes, Quintilian's version of the good man "suggests his strong desire to revitalize the ideal of eloquence that had played such a significant role in the history of Greco-Roman civilization."[40] To paraphrase, Quintilian's good man is the "orator-philosopher-statesman" characteristic of Athenian Democracy and the Roman Republic.[41] Quintilian's good man is not a man of the Roman Empire: orator-philosopher-statesmen become largely obsolete in the age of emperors. Thus, "Quintilian's attempts to infuse into his students a fresh moral purpose" in order to "guide the affairs of state" is a categorical rejection of the "decaying culture"—a culture inimical to speech, eloquence, and the good man.[42]

---

[36] For a similar emphasis on Pliny's use of deliberative rhetoric, albeit in epistolary form, see Rodney Farnsworth, "Contextualizing the Pliny/Trajan Letters," 29–46.

[37] Despite being Pliny's rhetorical tutor, scholars have ignored Quintilian's potential influence on the panegyric.

[38] Quintilian, *Institutio Oratoria, Volume One*, translated by H.E. Butler (Cambridge: Harvard University Press, 1963), 479.

[39] It should be noted that Quintilian's "good man speaking well" was not original with him; rather, the "good man skilled in speaking" is directly traceable to Cato the Elder; see Alan E. Astin, *Cato the Censor*, 153–54.

[40] Meador, "Quintilian and the *Institutio Oratoria*," 172.

[41] "Quintilian and the *Institutio Oratoria*," 173.

[42] "Quintilian and the *Institutio Oratoria*," 173.

What are the attributes of the good man? Quintilian delineates them in Book Twelve, Chapter One of the *Institutio Oratoria*. They include: respect for public opinion (xii 1.12), integrity (xii 1.16), fortitude (xii 1.17), eloquence (xii 1.21), bravery (xii 1.23), honor (xii 1.24), responsibility (xii 1.26), knowledge (xii 1.25), sincerity (xii 1.29), sense of duty (xii 1.29), common sense (xii 1.30), virtue (xii 1.31), and justice (xii 1.35). Pliny, interestingly enough, praises Trajan for possessing these very attributes.[43] Moreover, as for Quintilian's four qualities that most commend the rhetor, Trajan possesses each one to varying degrees: benevolence, courtesy, kindliness, and moderation.[44] At this point the skeptic might object, noting that an alignment of categories does not warrant the claim that Trajan is Quintilian's good man. And, even if he happens to resemble the ideal orator, so what?

The answer to this "so what" question leads us back to the panegyric. We must not forget that Quintilian's good man is ideally situated within the Republic. As such, if Quintilian's influence on Pliny is extended, might we not expect a rhetorical emphasis on a return to the glory days of Republican Rome? It would seem so given Quintilian's fairly overt classicism.

The text does not disappoint; Pliny repeatedly mentions and even advocates a return to the Republic. His references to the Republic are organized temporally—from present to future. One of the first references to the Republic occurs in Chapter 44: "The rewards of virtue are now the same under an emperor as they were in times of liberty" (419). In Chapter 57, Pliny attempts to persuade Trajan to hold the consulship for a third time. He states, "There was a republic then, you say to summon them; but surely there is still a Republic to call on you, as well as a Senate, and the consulate itself" (457). In Chapter 69, Pliny discusses "the descendants of liberty" and praises Trajan who "revives

---

[43] What follows are the good man's attributes and where they occur in the panegyric: bravery (361, 453); common sense (353); honor (361, 375); integrity (421); justice (395, 405, 459, 507); knowledge (359); respect for public opinion (347, 425); responsibility (369); sense of duty (331, 345); sincerity (349); virtue (324, 457). While fortitude and eloquence are not explicitly praised by Pliny, the former is implied in his discussion of Trajan's bravery and courage; Trajan is praised for the latter insofar as the political climate he has fostered engenders eloquence.

[44] Trajan is praised for each of these qualities on the following pages: benevolence (459); courtesy (459); kindliness (369, 459); and moderation (327, 329, 331, 343, 359, 361, 363, 429, 437, 447, 449, 459, 473, 509, 519).

and cherishes and promotes to the service of the state . . . any remnant of an ancient house" (487). In each of these passages, Pliny implicitly and explicitly redefines the political climate of the present by recourse to the Republican past.

In Chapters 78 and 93, though, Pliny situates the Republic in the future, thereby making an important "deliberative" transition.[45] In the former chapter Pliny states, "We know that your intention is to set up liberty in our midst again. What distinction should find more favour with you, what title should you bear more often than that which was the first creation of liberty restored?" (507). While still referencing the future, Pliny makes the deliberative transition explicit in Chapter 93: maintenance of the Republic will depend on his colleagues in the Senate. "So far as rests with our prince," states Pliny, "the consuls are free to fill their role as they did before the days of emperors. Is there any proper return we can make you, to match all you have done for us? Only perhaps by . . . playing an active part in public affairs to show we believe that the republic still exists" (541). Note the epideictic/deliberative pivot: by praising Trajan for appropriating the past in the present, Pliny urges his peers to instantiate Republican principles in the future. The Republic will exist only to the extent that Pliny and his collective "we" play "an active part" in "enacting" the Republic; in other words, the Republic's existence in both the present and the future is contingent on embodying the principles for which the Republic stands.[46]

Perhaps the most important principle to be enacted or embodied, on Pliny's account, is the act of speech. The very act of public speaking reifies the Republic even as it praises this form of government. Such an enactment might not surprise us, though, given oratory's privileged status in both the Roman Republic and in Quintilian's rhetorical cosmology.

---

[45] Both Aristotle and Quintilian situate deliberative speaking as being concerned with the future.

[46] "Enactment," as conceptualized by rhetoricians, is an embodiment and performance of that which the speaker recommends to his/her audience; the speaker represents the views that s/he is advancing. Pliny, in fact, references the concept of enactment by referring to Trajan as "a living example of their [the liberal arts's] precepts," 427. For a more detailed exposition on rhetorical enactment, see Karlyn Kohrs Campbell and Kathleen Hall Jamieson, "Form and Genre in Rhetorical Criticism: An Introduction," 9–10. For a recent critical application of enactment, see Angela G. Ray, "'In My Own Hand,'" 387–405.

How does enactment manifest itself in the speech? It works on a global as well as a more localized level. Regarding the former, the totality of Pliny's panegyric is a very powerful enactment of the Republic; the sheer prolixity of the speech calls attention to the act of speaking. Pliny enacts the Republican virtue of freedom of speech by simply speaking at such great lengths. Pliny, in fact, alludes to this global enactment in Chapter 67: "in making use of the freedom he [Trajan] granted we are acting only in obedience to him" (481). To speak is simply to obey. The fact that Pliny speaks at length reflects his own deep (obsequious?) allegiance to Trajan.

Enactment, however, is not so facile a rhetorical concept as to be recognizable at an exclusively global or macroscopic level; rather, Pliny engages in several localized rhetorical enactments that call attention to the act of speaking. Each enactment, moreover, represents a necessary step in Rome's return to the "days of old."

From the outset, Pliny calls attention to oratory. He notes that "An open tribute to our Emperor demands a new form, now that the wording of our private talk has changed. Times are different, and our speeches must show this" (325). A significant part of Pliny's "show" or "new form" is the excess of his laudation and its overtly deliberative elements; praise is not restricted to Trajan's character, but is extended to matters of law and imperial politics. By invoking deliberative themes in an "epideictic" address, Pliny enacts the formal features he urges; form and content become inseparable.

Speaking also functions as an enactment of confidence since Pliny claims to feel "no danger" that his remarks will be misinterpreted by Trajan (329). Similarly, Pliny is "not afraid of seeming long winded" in his praises since he has "much to offer . . ." (377). Later in the speech, Pliny claims that the "greatest glory" available to Trajan is "the fact that in expressing our thanks we have nothing to omit or conceal" (451). Pliny's remarks on speaking and its relationship with danger, being afraid, and concealment is, as Bruere has noted, a direct commentary on Domitian's reign.[47] To speak freely, therefore, is to both publicly resist—albeit posthumously—Domitian's tyranny, and to reinscribe the empire with Republican virtues. As Pliny notes,

> you tell us to express ourselves openly, and we shall do so, for our previous hesitation was due to . . . fear

---

[47] Bruere, "Tacitus and Pliny's *Panegyricus*," 162.

and apprehension, and the lamentable caution born of our perils which bade us turn eyes and ears and minds from our country, from that republic which was utterly destroyed. Today we can . . . open our lips long sealed by servitude, loosen our tongues which were bound to silence by so many evils. (479)

Speaking enacts hope instead of fear, confidence instead of apprehension, and freedom instead of caution.

As suggested by the preceding remarks, to speak is to enact collective social purification. Not only has Trajan's rule allowed Roman speakers "to criticize bad rulers with impunity," but it has served a purgative function: "to avenge ourselves daily on the evil emperors of the past." Public speaking in this context is analogous to social baptism; by speaking Pliny attempts to rectify, if not purify, the past. Pliny is not engaging in historical revisionism; rather, he enacts historical redemption. Finally, to speak is also to enact a Republican future since in the past "only the speeches of the emperors were made safe for all time . . . . Today these [acclamations to the Emperor] have been sent out into the world . . ." (501–503). Because Pliny's speech will be "made safe for all time," "future princes . . . will learn to distinguish between true acclamation and false, and owe it to you [Trajan] that they can no longer be deceived" (501). The immortality of his praise will function to preserve the Republic to which Pliny hopes to return. In so doing, of course, Pliny hopes to attain "the literary [rhetorical] immortality he so desired."[48]

Conclusion

Several concluding remarks on Pliny's *opus* are in order. First, an initial critical step in understanding the panegyric is to treat the speech as rhetoric, not literature—a step that only with this essay has been taken. Second, treating the speech as rhetoric necessitates looking to Pliny's tutor Quintilian and his system of rhetoric. Third, claims of influence are not postulated in order to find origins. While origins are important, they emasculate rhetoric of its rhetoricity—as its ability to do work in the socio-political realm. Through my appropriation of Quintilian's good man and its political antecedents, I have restored the text's status as rhetoric. More important than mere restoration is

---

[48] Bruere, "Tacitus and Pliny's *Panegyricus*," 176.

interpretation. I hope to have illustrated the extent to which Pliny's panegyric functions deliberatively to reinscribe Republican Rome under Trajan's reign. Pliny's repeated enactments of a critical Republican virtue (public speech) is his primary persuasive vehicle. Lastly, though Bruere emphasizes the close friendship between Tacitus and Pliny, Pliny directly challenges Tacitus's (Maternus's) view that eloquence thrives only in chaos. The panegyric is a lengthy attempt to disprove such a thesis.[49]

---

[49] George Kennedy would appear to agree with my contention; see *The Art of Rhetoric in the Roman World*, 548.

16 Hrotsvit, Strong Voice of Gandersheim

Janet B. Davis

Hrotsvit, a tenth-century Saxon canoness, is a little better known in Germany than she is in the English-speaking world. *Britannica Online* calls her "the first German woman poet" (1998). Even so, her relative obscurity is astonishing, given that her corpus includes eight sacred legends in verse, six dramas in rhymed prose, two historical poems, three prose prefaces, several dedications, and a poem that summarizes *The Revelation of St. John*. Besides being the first German woman poet, she is the first known post-classical playwright of either sex, and her historical poems were arguably of political significance to the ruling Ottonian dynasty of the Holy Roman Empire.

In the preface Hrotsvit wrote to her plays, she made the following statement, which suggests the way in which her whole body of work called into question and challenged a set of cultural assumptions about gender and personal worth:

> ... victoria probatur gloriosior, praesertim cum feminea fragilitas vinceret et virilis robur confusioni subiacaret. *Praefatio II:* 5 (ed. Strecker 1930)
>
> [... victory proves especially glorious whenever womanly frailty wins and masculine strength is thrown into confusion.] (1)[1]

---

[1] Translations are by the author, except where a published translation is cited. I am grateful to Becky Harrison and David Christiansen of Truman State University for their help. Thanks are also due to Natalie Alexander, Mike Ashcraft, Julia DeLancey, Martha Edwards, Christine Harker, Sara Orel and Steve Reschly for helpful comments on my writing.

In what follows, I argue that Hrotsvit's education, especially in rhetoric, empowered her to become what she called herself, a "strong voice."

A Convent Education

Even nine hundred years after her active career, Hrotsvit's work so contradicted the conventional narrative about women's rhetoric that in 1867 a German scholar, Joseph Aschbach, published a paper arguing it was all a forgery by Conradus Celtis, the humanist scholar who had rediscovered and published her manuscript in 1501. Aschbach's view was still being given some credence as late as 1945 (Zeydel 1946).

Such presumptions had some basis in the scarce evidence for either women's education or rhetorical activity by women in the Middle Ages. However, Jourdain (1888) has reviewed the scanty records concerning women's education to show that, within the context of Christianity, some pedagogy had been offered to some women as early as the lifetime of St. Jerome (374–420), who wrote instructive letters to Paula, Gaudentia, Laeta and Marcella. In about 510 the bishop of Arles founded a convent with the intent that "the nuns learn their letters [*omnes litteras discant*]." In the sixth century, St. Radegonde was "an habitual reader [who] exhorted her companions to follow her example, and instructed them herself" (Jourdain 468).

By the time of Charlemagne, "a group of girls mingled with Charlemagne's sons as students in the palace school, where Alcuin taught them the basic elements of grammar using Priscian and Donatus, some bits of rhetoric and logic using Cassiodorus and Boethius . . . [and] some notions about arithmetic, geometry and astronomy." An edict by the bishop of Soissons at the end of the ninth century forbade mixing girls and boys in the parish schools, "proof," as Jourdain claims, "that girls were already attending school alongside boys" (473).

So the emergence of a playwright who was a woman was not perhaps so surprising, given her circumstances. Hrotsvit lived almost exactly one millennium ago and probably died around 1000 (Haight 1965; Dronke 1984). She was a canoness living under the Benedictine rule, which is characterized by a balanced daily routine of prayer, manual labor and study that is regulated in great detail. A medieval Benedictine house served as a liturgical and educational center for the region in which it was located. Hrotsvit's home community, at Gandersheim in Saxony, had been founded about a hundred years before her birth as a convent housing both nuns and canonesses. The canonesses differed from the nuns in that they took vows of obedience and chastity, but not of poverty. Therefore they could own property, buy books and writing materials, receive guests, and even (with permission) travel. The vocation of canoness must have seemed more appealing than an arranged marriage to many women from wealthy families; these indeed seem to have been the women who formed the community at Gandersheim. Hrotsvit was on terms of close friendship with her abbess (a niece of the Holy Roman Emperor) and with the Emperor's brother, Chancellor Bruno, so Wilson (1989) follows Dronke (1984) in assuming she came from a family that enjoyed rank and privilege.

To write what she did when she did, Hrotsvit needed the following tools: a fluent and correct command of Latin; familiarity with the rules of Latin prosody; familiarity with the plays of Terence; access to sources of apocryphal materials (for the plays and legends) and to documents (for the historical poems); and a broad general knowledge of academic subjects such as harmony and mathematics. There is reason to suppose she found these tools, as well as a community whose members were willing to serve as both performers and audience, within the walls of the convent at Gandersheim.

If we accept the evidence that some women, especially nuns, were offered education similar to boys' in northern Europe under the Holy Roman Empire, the question arises of what subjects and texts such an education might include. Unfortunately, the rule of St. Benedict, in other respects so detailed in its prescriptiveness, is silent on required reading other than Scripture; details of the educational program were left to the discretion of the abbess or abbot.

Laistner (1957) has made a study of library catalogues to produce a list of what can be called "standard works" commonly found in monastic houses (such as those at St. Gall, Tours, and Treves) around 900. For the subjects of the trivium (grammar, rhetoric and dialectic) they include Latin grammars by Donatus, Priscian, Virgilius Maro and Isidore. Alcuin's *De Rhetorica* was widely available as an introductory work on rhetoric, with the *De Inventione* of Cicero for more advanced students. *Rhetorica ad Herennium* and Cicero's *De Oratore* are also mentioned in catalogues, though less frequently than *De Inventione*. For instruction in dialectic, Alcuin's *De Dialectica* served as an introductory text, with the commentaries of Boethius for more advanced students. Laistner comments that "on the subjects of the quadrivium [arithmetic, geometry, music and astronomy] . . . few fresh works were composed" (218). Most libraries contained compilations, bulky volumes that might include calendars and tables for establishing the dates of religious festivals, manuals on arithmetic and (less frequently) geometry, Isidore's *Etymologies* and *De Natura Rerum*, Bede's *De Temporum Ratione*, Aratus's *Phaenomena*, treatises on music and a glossary.

These are all texts likely to have been available in the library at Gandersheim, where Hrotsvit learned her Latin characterized by fluency and variety, and developed her idiosyncratic prosody, including the rhyming prose used in the plays (Polheim 1925). Medieval Latin is the language systematized by Priscian and Donatus. Some rhyming prose already appears in the works of Boethius. One is on yet firmer ground in claiming that Hrotsvit read apocryphal works and the plays of Terence in the convent, since she mentions them specifically. She writes of finding sources "that I collected here within the walls of our convent at Gandersheim," as follows:

> Si . . . quaedam huius operis . . . sumpta sint ex apocrifis, non est crimen . . . quia quando huius stamen seriei coeperam ordiri, ignoravi dubia esse, in quibus disposui laborare. At ubi recognovi, pessumdare detrectavi, quia, quod videtur falsitas, forsan probabitur esse veritas. *Praefatio I:* 13–16.

> [If . . . some of this work . . . is taken from uncanonical sources, it is not a crime . . . because when I began to weave the text of this series I was unaware that the materials I had decided to work with were questionable. And when I did become aware, I refused to abandon them, because what seems false will perhaps prove to be the truth.]

Throughout the plays, allusions and references offer internal evidence of Hrotsvit's familiarity with the seven liberal arts of an education in the humanities. Two striking examples bear witness to encounters with textbooks on music and on mathematics. In *Pafnutius*, the play's hero is shown instructing his pupils in harmony in a lengthy scene extending through several speeches, of which this is the first:

> PAFNUTIUS: Prima dicitur diatesero, quasi ex quattuor, et possidet proportionem epitritam sive

sesquitertiam. Seconda diapente, quia constat ex quinque, et est in ratione emiolei sive sesqualteri. Tertia diapason; haec fit in duplo perficiturque sonitibus octo. *Pafnutius* I: 14

[PAFNUTIUS: The first [interval] is called a fourth, as it were four tones, and is in the proportion of four to three, or four thirds. The second is a fifth, consisting of fives [tones], and in the mode of one-and-a-half. The third is the octave . . . .]

In *Sapientia*, the mother of three virgin martyrs is asked by the Emperor Hadrian how old her children are. Instead of answering him directly, she asks them, "Daughters, do you want me to wear this stupid man out with mathematical argument?" and proceeds to express their ages in abstruse formulas covering two pages of text, of which this is a sample:

SAPIENTIA: Omnis namque numerus inminitus dicitur, cuius partes coniunctae minorem illo numero, cuius partes sunt, summae quantitatem reddunt: ut VIII; est autem medietas IIII, pars quarta II, pars octava I: quae in unum redactae septem reddunt. Similiter denarius habet dimidiam partem V, quintam autem II, decimam vero I: quae simul copulatae VIII colligunt. *Sapientia III*:13–15.

[SAPIENTIA: Every number is said to be undiminished if its fractions when added together yield a sum that is smaller than the number. For example, 8. Its half is 4, its quarter is 2, and its eighth is 1; adding them together gives the result 7. Similarly the quantity ten has the half 5, the fifth 2, and the tenth 1. Put them together and they add up to 8.]

These displays of erudition are unusual for a playwright whose hallmark is brief scenes and rapid action. They appear to be set pieces that rehearse and review textbook material on academic subjects. But the plays do more than parade their author's credentials; they also present a distinctive point of view about human relationships.

Hrotsvit's Works

At first, Hrotsvit wrote within and for her convent community, and in so doing broke much new ground: first, because she addressed women as a rational audience; second, because her body of work is innovative in both form and content; third, and perhaps most significantly, because her writings repeatedly show frailty (*fragilitas*) as morally and pragmatically superior to strength (*robur*) (*Praefatio II:* 5), thus consistently disrupting conventional assumptions.

It was rare in the tenth century to take an audience of women seriously. The way in which people thought about human physiology was grounded in theories ascribed to Hippocrates, a Greek physician who practiced and wrote in the sixth century B.C.E and held that male and female bodies were constituted in fundamentally different ways. Hippocratic theory functioned as science-based justification for women's limited role in society. Because women menstruate, the elements of blood, phlegm, yellow bile and black bile are not well balanced in their bodies; the proportion of blood is never stable. According to this theory, the healthy blood flow which in men is upward, nourishing the heart and mind, streams downward to the pelvic region in women. The composition of their parts is geared to reproduction; they are not physically equipped to be fully rational agents. Writing more than a century after Hippocrates, Aristotle placed greater emphasis on the amount of heat in male and female bodies. Because men are able to "concoct" white-hot semen, they are shown to have hotter and drier bodies.

Christianity easily appropriated these ancient physiological theories because they "dovetailed neatly" with the biblical story of Adam and Eve (Filipczak 1997). Before the Fall, the two existing human bodies were both in perfect health; after it their punishment included a constant tendency to disorder. However, Adam's sin in eating the proffered apple was less, so men's disorders typically involved the excess of yellow bile—men are choleric, they tend toward anger and violence, but they are still hot and dry. Since Eve initiated the first sin, her punishment was more severe: she and all her female descendants are condemned to inhabit cold, moist, phlegmatic bodies that make them weak, slow, and stupid.

Given this background, one sees why women had lower status in general, and especially as audience, in antiquity and the Middle Ages. Though emotionally susceptible to the appeals of poems and music, they were not thought to have the physical capacity to be rational. So, of the very few women we know of as writing in late antiquity or the Middle Ages, Egeria (*c.* 380) kept a journal of a pilgrimage, and Dhuoda (*c.* 850) wrote a manual of etiquette for her absent teenage son, but Hrotsvit has no known female predecessor as a conscious creator of works intended to give moral instruction, even though Wilson (1998:3) places her "entirely within the mainstream of the didactic hagiographic *exemplum*'s tradition."

The fact that a specific type of hagiographic tradition existed reinforces internal evidence suggesting she wrote the sacred legends first, perhaps starting not many years after entering the convent. In the preface to the legends she describes herself as having worked on them when "not yet of mature age, nor proficient in knowledge" (I.1.20–21). The first book (the legends) is dedicated to Gerberga, the abbess of Gandersheim, who is acknowledged as a teacher along with "the very wise and kind Mistress Rikkardis." The dedication invites Gerberga to correct the verses and then, perhaps, to read them for pleasure when tired after work.

A letter addressed to patrons that precedes the second book (the dramas) suggests it was circulated to a wider audience. Hrotsvit expresses gratitude to learned people who, though much more knowledgeable than she, "have thought this little work by an ordinary little woman worthy of admiration and . . . have praised me with fraternal affection, judging me to possess some little knowledge of the arts whose subtlety far outstrips my womanly talent" (II.2.3–4). It seems, therefore, that by the time the dramas were in finished form the manuscript was being circulated to other religious houses, including monasteries, and to critics Hrotsvit respected, including men.

Probably later still, when her name was known among a scholarly elite, she was commissioned to write two verse chronicles for a wider, courtly audience. Nagel (1965:60) proposes both the abbess Gerberga and William, Bishop of Mainz, as sponsors who gave direction to her historical-political works. One was an historical account of the convent at Gandersheim from its foundation in 856. The other was a celebratory epic reviewing the achievements of the Emperor Otto I and his son, Otto II. In her preface to the *Gesta Ottonis*, Hrotsvit draws attention to, but does not apologize for, the fact that being a cloistered woman had limited her experience of the world and specifically of warfare.

From the progression outlined above, it seems clear that Hrotsvit's reputation was founded on the legends and dramas she offered initially to an audience of women. In the preface to the legends, she tells of working alone, almost in secret (*"clam cunctis et quasi furtim"*), drawing her material from sources found within the convent at Gandersheim; then of referring to several authors about whom Gerberga instructed her (although Hrotsvit takes full responsibility herself for what she has written). She explicitly names her teachers in the convent as her first audience. It is worth noting that, under Benedictine rule, the members of the religious community were read to during mealtimes. The legends are in narrative form, yet they contain many speeches in *oratio recta*. It was not perhaps so big a step to move from writing legends that could be read aloud to writing plays for members of the community to read and perform together.

Whether the plays were performed is a question that has been vigorously debated. Aschbach's charge of forgery was credible because it had long been thought there was no drama—no "theater"—in western Europe in the tenth century. Theater arts in general were held to have been "completely and finally suppressed" by the Roman Catholic Church through bans issued at the Trullan Synod in 692 (Butler 1960:2–6). The plays of Plautus, Terence, and Seneca were doubly condemned because of their scandalous and often bawdy themes. While mystery and miracle plays started appearing in the eleventh century, the only trace of sanctioned drama other than Hrotsvit's in the tenth is a reference (in rules written by a bishop of Winchester) to dramatized reading during the Easter liturgy of the gospel account of the discovery of the empty tomb.[2]

There is an explanation, advanced by Sprague and others (1955; Butler 1960; Pollack 1990) for the radical nature of this apparent flouting of church discipline by a Benedictine canoness. Though it was censured by the western church, theater seems to have flourished under the Orthodox regime in Byzantium.[3] Two female members of the Ot-

---

[2] This would have been called a *Quem quaeritis* (Whom do you seek?) dialogue. Contemporary churches in the U.S. continue this tradition of responsive readings of the Resurrection account by clergy and congregation during the Easter liturgy.

[3] The failure of the Iconoclasts to maintain control over the eastern church in the ninth and tenth centuries "provided the occasion for the reestablishment at the heart of imperial institutions of the Greek cultural heritage" (Conley 1990, 65).

tonian royal family had close ties to Byzantium, and both of them frequented the convent at Gandersheim: the wife of Otto I, Adelheid of Burgundy, was acquainted with the East through long residence in Italy; and she arranged a marriage between her son, Otto II, and Theophano, a sister of the Macedonian Emperor Basil II. A later chronicler of the convent at Gandersheim (Bodo, cited by Magnin, 1845) reports that Adelheid retired there to spend the last years of her life, and that Sophia, a daughter of Theophano and Otto II, became a member of its religious community. It is not unreasonable, therefore, to suggest that Hrotsvit heard in the convent about the staging of religious dramas in Eastern churches, and ventured to write in Latin what she knew was being performed elsewhere in Greek.

The Byzantine connection also helps to explain why the content of four of the legends and all six of the plays is based on apocryphal materials, which were, like classical drama, accepted in the East but not by Rome. The apocryphal subjects for legends include the birth of the Virgin Mary, the conversion of Theophilus, and the lives of Saint Basil and Saint Dionysius. The plays are about the conversion of Gallicanus, a general under the Emperor Constantine; the martyrdom of three virgins, Agape, Chionia, and Irene, at the hands of a persecutor under the Emperor Diocletian; the miraculous love story of Calimachus; the fall into harlotry and subsequent salvation of a woman named Mary; the repentance and salvation of the courtesan Thais; and another three-virgin martyrdom, this time of the daughters of a woman named Sapientia, under the Emperor Hadrian. All these stories were extra-canonical for the Western church, but were well known and read in the East.

Hrotsvit evidently became aware that her sources were rejected by her church, but she used them nonetheless. At the beginning of her first preface (to the verse legends), she acknowledges there could be some objection to making use of apocryphal sources. That, however, "is not a crime of arrogant wilfulness but a mistake resulting from ignorance" (*Praefatio* 1.1). That she was also well aware of the suspect status of drama, and sought to justify her playwriting, is shown in her second preface (to the plays), as follows:

> Plures inveniuntur catholici, cuius nos penitus expurgare nequimus facti, qui pro cultioris facundia sermonis gentilium vanitatem librorum utilitati praeferunt sacrarum scripturarum. Sunt etiam alii, sac-

ris inhaerentes paginis, qui licet alia gentilium spernant, Terentii tamen fingmenta frequentius lectitant et, dum dulcedine sermonis delectantur, nefarandum notitia rerum maculantur. Unde ego, Clamor Validus Gandeshemensis, non recusavi illum imitari dictando, dum alii colunt legendo, quo eodem dictationis genere, quo turpia lascivarum incesta feminarum recitabantur, laudabilis sacrarum castimonia virginum iuxta mei facultatem ingenioli celebraretur. (*Praefatio II*.1, ed. Strecker: 113)

[Many Catholics are found doing something for which we cannot entirely forgive ourselves, because they prefer vain pagan books (for the elegance of the more cultivated language) to the practicality of sacred scriptures. And there are others who, though loyal to the sacred pages, and although they reject other pagan works, still too often keep reading the fictions of Terence; and while they take pleasure in the sweetness of his language, they are defiled by the exposure to things that are illicit. For that reason I, the Strong Voice of Gandersheim, have not declined to imitate him while others revere (Terence) by reading him; and in the same kind of discourse in which the lewd wrongdoing of loose women used to be described, the laudable chastity of virgins may be celebrated through the exercise of my tiny talent.]

The argument runs as follows: we Catholics know we should not be reading Terence, yet we continue to do so because his plays are well written and reading them is a pleasure. Rather than persist in guilty pleasure, I have written plays using language to entertain, as Terence did, but celebrating themes appropriate to the religious life. The use of self-deprecation ("my tiny talent") is a move Hrotsvit made in the first preface with the reference to "mistake resulting from ignorance." Such formalized modesty was a practiced element in Christian rhetoric known as *humilitas;* Hrotsvit used it often. The passage in which she calls herself the Strong Voice of Gandersheim offers probably more accurate insight into the vigor of her self-esteem. It appears to be legitimate Latinization of the two elements of her Saxon name (*hruot* = voice, *suid* = strong) (Grimm, cited in Wilson 1998).[4]

Hrotsvit's commitment to using the literary tools of pagan Terence for the praise of Christian virtue, announced in the second preface quoted above, is a strategy of appropriation that can be observed throughout her work. Several examples illustrate the way in which characters who would usually be cast as "victims" in classical drama turn the tables on their oppressors by rejecting sexual overtures, asserting verbal defiance, and refusing to be swayed by threats or physical force, thereby seizing and retaining moral authority.

For instance, in the play *Calimachus*, this is how Drusiana, a faithful wife, responds to her lovesick admirer Calimachus when he ventures to praise her beauty:

> Lenocinia tua parvi pendo, tuique lasciviam fastidio, sed te ipsum penitus sperno. (*Calimachus*, 3)

> [I despise your pimping, I scorn your lewdness, and I totally reject *you*.]

And in the sacred legend *Pelagius*, a beautiful boy, Pelagius, fends off the attentions of the Moor Abdrahemen thus:[5]

> Non decet ergo virum Christi baptismate lotum/
> Sobria barbarico complexu subdere colla. (*Pelagius*, 243–4)

> [It is not decent for a man baptized a Christian to bend his chaste neck to a barbarian embrace.]

In a world in which physical force was the paradigm of strength and authority, Hrotsvit offered graphic descriptions of violence, both

---

[4] The Germanic languages were still vernaculars in the tenth century, and a brief review of the bibliography will illustrate the difficulties that result from uncertain orthography in manuscripts. Today the name is spelled at least seven different ways (Hrosvitha, Hroswitha, Hrotsvit, Hrotsvitha, Hrotswitha, Rosvita, Roswitha). She may have been named after an abbess of the community who had died in about 890.

[5] The legend *Pelagius* is based on an eyewitness account of a martyrdom that took place in Cordova, Spain, in 943. The Moslem ruler involved is identified as Abdel-Rahman III (Magnin 1845).

physical and psychological. But the intended victims always deride the threats, for example:

> Simphronius inquid: . . . Sed si mea ne praecepta sequaris/ Ultra non parco, sed vim iustam faciendo/ Mando, sub obscenae latebris claudier aedis,/ in qua criminibus turpes gaudent mulieres/ Et faciam pollutarum sociam meretricum . . . ." At sacra virgo, minis nimium trepidans super istis/ Audacter mox praefecto dedit ista responsa:/ Si tu namque scires hunc, quem colo, verum/ Illiusque potestatem sine fine vigentem/ . . . Talia verba tuo nolles profundere rostro/ . . . Spero delicti numquam maculis violari/ carnis spurcitias fragilis sed vincere cunctas.
>
> [*Agnes,* 186–205 in *Hrotsvithae Opera* ed. P. de Winterfeld, 1902:58.]

> [Simphronius said . . . "If you do not follow my orders, I will not spare you but will apply just force: I will have you shut up in the shadows of a house of ill repute, in which loose women enjoy wrongdoing, and make you live with filthy whores . . . . " To which the holy virgin, not shaken by these threats, at once boldly answered the prefect: "If you knew the true God I worship, and his power . . . you would not want to spew such words from your mouth . . . I hope never to be soiled by the smirch of sin, and to overcome all debaucheries of the fragile flesh."]

Thus, in Hrotsvit's plays and legends, characters such as young girls, chaste wives and attractive boys, who were typically sexual prey in classical drama, assert the power that gendered assumptions attribute to them, and use it to claim moral authority.

Hrotsvit addressed women as a rational audience, she knowingly defied edicts of the Roman Catholic church in her choices of literary form and content, and she subverted gendered assumptions of the world she lived in. To challenge that world, she had to show she was in command of a full range of its discourse. Her rhetorical education gave her the resources and the language that she needed, so that her audience—like the leading citizens of Cordova who came to visit the martyr Pelagius in his dungeon—"heard words embellished with the honey of rhetoric" (*Pelagius* 201, tr. Wilson 1998:34).

17 Classical and Christian Conflicts in Keckermann's *De rhetoricae ecclesiasticae utilitate*

Jameela Lares

This article concerns rhetoric in sixteenth- and seventeenth-century Europe, and specifically, how the Reformation and Counter-Reformation affected the production of preaching manuals. Although all of the *artes praedicandi* produced by these two movements reflect the revival of classical rhetoric, they often differ sharply in terms of how they make use of that rhetoric. Those sermon theorists who were loyal to Rome often employed classical rhetoric without any sense of disjunction between sacred and profane. Protestant theorists, on the other hand, were particularly dedicated to Scripture as a model of discourse, which meant that for them the use of classical rhetoric needed to be explained and ratified in terms of Scripture. They thus held up the preaching models of Christ, Paul, and acceptable early patristic commentary, particularly that of St. Augustine.

My discussion here is divided into three parts. First I will describe how theorists on both sides of the confessional divide were influenced by classical rhetoric. I will then show briefly how these manuals differed. Finally, I will examine the preaching manual or *ars praedicandi* of the Protestant scholar Bartholomew Keckermann, his *De rhetoricae ecclesiasticae utilitate* of 1600.

All sermon theory in sixteenth- and seventeenth-century Europe was heavily influenced by the revival of classical rhetoric. The arrangement of the sermon, for example, differed little from Rome to Heidelberg to Geneva. Whereas medieval homiletics had arranged sermons in terms of logical categories, such as the triune branching of the *Arbor Picta* described by Otto Dieter or the elaborate divisions of Robert of

Basevorn, Renaissance homiletics universally based the sermon on the classical oration, with some version of the *proemium, narratio, divisio* or *propositio, confirmatio, confutatio,* and *peroratio*.¹ The classical oration was as handy in the Renaissance as the five-paragraph essay is today.

But whereas all religious confessions made use of some form of the classical oration at the arrangement stage, confessional differences dictated different inventional categories, and indeed, different attitudes toward the ends to which rhetoric could be used. Protestants tended to be more shy of using classical rhetoric than were Roman Catholics. We can look, for instance, at the work of the Protestant Andreas Gerhard Hyperius, who was recognized in the last century as the "first proper theoretician of the evangelical sermon."² Hyperius devotes a brief, early section of his text to an overview of classical rhetoric since, as he says, "oratory and preaching have many things in common, as Augustine . . . has copiously shown."³ In this early section, Hyperius mentions such things as the five parts of oratory, the three levels of style, and the means of stylistic variation. He also agrees in a later section that the preacher may employ all the types of *amplificatio*—i.e., multi-part ar-

---

¹ Otto A. Dieter, *"Arbor Picta*: The Medieval Tree of Preaching," 123–144, reports on the Munich codex 23865 (Bayerische Staatsbibliothek); Robert of Basevorn, *Forma praedicandi*, translated by Leopold Krul, 114–215. Gerald R. Owst notes that "Tracts by Englishmen on the formal art of preaching, on dilating and dividing the sermon, are so numerous from the second half of the thirteenth century onward, that the practice might almost be looked upon as a speciality of the pulpits." "Sermon-Making, or the Theory and Practice of Sacred Eloquence," in *Preaching in Medieval England: An Introduction to Sermon Manuscripts of the Period c. 1350–1450* (Cambridge: Cambridge University Press, 1926), 309–359, 314. See also Th.-M. Charland, *Artes praedicandi: contributions à l'histoire de la rhétorique au moyen âge*, Publications de l'Institut d'Etudes Medievales d'Ottowa, no. 7 (Paris: 1936).

² Yngve Brilioth, *A Brief History of Preaching*. Translated by Karl E. Mattson., 125.

³ "Plurima vero esse concionatori cum oratore communia, diffuse Augustinus [de doctrina Christiana lib. 4.] demonstravit." Andreas Gerardus Hyperius, *De formandis concionibus sacris, seu de interpretatione scripturarum populari* (1553; Marburg, 1562), I:4, 14r. The 1562 Marburg is 7.3 in the bibliography of Gerhard Krause, *Andreas Gerhard Hyperius: Leben, Bilder, Schriften*, 136. All translations are mine unless otherwise noted.

guments, enthymemes and other artificial proofs, emotional appeals, schemes, tropes, and so forth—that rhetoric supplies.[4]

Hyperius even begins his text with a comparison between the narrow methods of the schools and the bountiful rhetoric of those who want to preach in church, a comparison which suggests the characterization, attributed to Zeno, of logic as a closed fist and rhetoric as an open palm.[5] Overall, however, Hyperius insists that classical rhetoric cannot be adopted uncritically for use in Christian speaking and writing, and he betrays the same uneasiness about rhetoric which earlier troubled Augustine in his *De Doctrina Christiana*. Augustine said:

> I must thwart the expectation of those readers who think that I shall give the rules of rhetoric here which I learned and taught in the secular schools. And I admonish them not to expect such rules from me, not that they have no utility, but because, if they have any, it should be sought elsewhere.[6]

Indeed, much like Augustine, Hyperius refers to "the rhetoricians" as if they are finally outsiders. He adds these authorities in at the beginning and makes occasional reference to them, and he does urge the preacher to consider time, place and persons throughout the text, but he always insists that adequate rhetorical practice can be derived

---

[4] "Quidquid verò ad perspicuè docendum, vel etiam ad movendum conducit, id omne concionator, tanque maximè necessariam suppellectilem sibi comparabit. Itaque et argumentationes tripartitas, quinquepartitas, enthymemata: deinde schemata atque tropos: ad haec artificium amplificandi, movendique affectus, & quicquid tandem huius est ordinisà rhetoribus benè dicendi magistris traditum, sciet ad se pertinere. Caeterum de argumentationum formulis, de schematibus ac tropis animus non est quicquam dicere, quando in eorum duntaxat gratiam nos ista congerimus quibus illa omnia iam probè nota esse arbitramur." Hyperius, *De formandis concionibus sacris*, 58v.

[5] "[Logic] is exercised within the narrow walls of the schools; [rhetoric] takes place in spacious temples. [Logic] is concisely tied to philosophical solitude and smacks of criticism; [rhetoric] is expansive, free, and effusive; indeed, oratory rejoices in light and open space." ("Illa exercetur intra scholarum angustos parietes: haec in spaciosis templis locum obtinet. Illa concisa & adstricta est philosophicam solitudinem, seu crititatemque redolens: ista expansa, libera, & effusa, necnon oratoria luce & quasi foro gaudens.") Hyperius, *De formandis concionibus sacris*, I:1, 1r–v.

[6] Augustine, *On Christian Doctrine*. Translated by D.W. Robertson. IV.i, 118.

from the Scriptures themselves, or at least ratified there. St. Paul is the preacher most held up for emulation. The Danish Protestant sermon theorist Niels Hemmingsen likewise insists on scriptural models in his preaching manual, citing Christ's own examples in preaching and "the tradition of Paul."[7]

By contrast, Erasmus's *Ecclesiastes* (1535), a vast, messy, but comprehensive treatment of Catholic homiletics, employs classical rhetoric without apology.[8] Books II and III treat extensively the technical aspects of pulpit rhetoric, especially the sermon form and the minutiae associated with each division thereof. Erasmus's classicism is extended and explicit. He takes his major headings from such works as Aristotle's *Rhetoric*, Cicero's *De oratore*, the anonymous *Ad Herennium*, and Quintilian's *De institutione oratoria*. He discusses sacred oratory in terms of judicial, legislative and encomiastical types (ASD V.4:268–274), of the duties to teach, delight and move (274–278), and of the five canons of oratory, that is, invention, disposition, style, memory, and delivery (279–280).

Erasmus is just as tied to classical rhetoric in details as he is in overall design. He discusses, for instance, artificial and inartificial proofs in the same terms as the classical theorists. Artificial proofs are to be derived from the circumstances of person and matter or cause. Of these, the personal circumstances are identical to those listed for encomia by Quintilian: descent, birth, country, sex, age, education, bodily condition, fortune, place, character, studies, passions, promises and acts, emotion, counsel, and name.[9] By contrast, Hyperius generally provides no classical formulae for sermons other than the oration form.

---

[7] Niels Hemmingsen, *The Preacher*, 1555; translated by John Horsfal, 1574, edited by R.C. Alston in Scolar Press facsimile no. 325 (Menston: Scolar Press, 1972), 17.

[8] Desiderius Erasmus, *Ecclesiastes, sive concionator evangelicus*, edited by Jacques Chomarat, in *Opera Omnia Desiderii Erasmi Roterodami* ("ASD"), ord. V, vols. 4–5.

[9] ASD V.4:372–388. The personal attributes are *genus, natio, patria, sexus, aetas, educatio, habitus corporis personae, fortuna, conditio, animi natura, studia, adfectatio, antefacta* and *antedicta, commotio,* and *nomen*. As editor Jacques Chomarat points out (373, n. 129–131), this is the same list in the same order as in *Institutes* V:10.24–31. Cf. Quintilian, *Institutio Oratoria*, translated by H. E. Butler. II: 214–219.

The later works of the Counter-Reformation are no less classical. St. Charles Borromeo's *Instructiones praedicationis verbi Dei* of 1575 followed the five-fold canon of invention, arrangement, style, memory, and delivery, as did the influential, "fully classical" preaching manuals of Luis de Granada and Cardinal Valerius.[10] Valerius followed Aristotle's *Rhetoric* closely, and Luis de Granada relies heavily on Cicero and Quintilian. Valerius has three categories of preaching to match Aristotle's three categories of oratory, and he makes *ethos, logos, pathos*, enthymeme, and example his five means of proof.[11] By contrast, Protestant inventional categories are derived from Scripture itself, and thus Melanchthon proposed in *De officiis concionatoris* (1529) the "didactic" sermon for teaching doctrine and the "adhortative" sermon for urging that such doctrine be accepted.[12] Hyperius later derived the *usus quintuplex* or five-fold use of the Protestant sermon—doctrine, reproof, correction, instruction, and comfort—from two different scriptural texts rather than from the inventional categories of classical authors.[13]

Thus Catholics and Protestants alike made use of classical rhetoric in their sermons yet differed sharply as to how they did so. Catholic sermon theorists saw less disjunction between the types of discourse represented by classical and scriptural texts, whereas the Reformers' dedication to Scripture as a model of discourse impelled them to ratify any use of classical rhetoric in terms of Scripture and Christian commentary. One interesting case in point is the work of Bartholomew Keckermann (d. 1609), who made extensive use of classical authorities,

---

[10] Joseph M. Connors, "Saint Charles Borromeo in Homiletic Tradition," 13–14.

[11] Joseph M. Connors, "Homiletic Theory in the Late Sixteenth Century," 318. Connors also notes that although Valerius proposed the same three *genera dicendi* as Aristotle, he found the judicial to have little scope.

[12] "From out of the duties of the preacher the types of preaching may be easily gathered. These are three: teaching, *epitrepticum* for believing, *paraeneticum* for urging morals." ("Ex officiis concionatoris facile quot sint genera concionum colligi potest. Sunt enim haec tria: didacticum, epitrepticum, quod ad credendum, paraeneticum, quod ad mores hortatur.") *De officiis concionatoris* (1529), in *Supplementa Melanchthoniana*, edited by Paul Drews and Ferdinand Cohrs, 5 volumes, II:5–6.

[13] The verses are II Timothy 3:16 and Romans 15:4. For a discussion of the importance of Hyperius to Reformed homiletics, see my "Milton in the Context of Reformation *Artes praedicandi*," *Milton and the Preaching Arts*, 48–95.

but not without heavy reference to similar concerns in Scripture itself and in the early church fathers, most notably Augustine.

Keckermann was a German Calvinist scholar of the late sixteenth and early seventeenth centuries. He taught at the Collegium Sapientium—a theological academy at Heidelberg—and then as professor of philosophy at the Academic Gymnasium in his hometown of Gdansk. His output was extensive and important. According to Joseph S. Freedman, who has written a number of heavily researched articles on the subject of Protestant learning in Renaissance Europe, Keckermann's publications were encyclopedic in scope. He wrote on theology, metaphysics, physics, mathematics, ethics, family life and politics, logic, rhetoric, Hebrew grammar, and history. Moreover, Keckermann published these works at a time when European universities and schools were heavily committed to teaching a broad group of academic disciplines, and thus Keckermann's publications were put to use as textbooks. Commentaries were produced on his works for three decades following his early death in 1609, the most popular commentary going through ten editions.[14] He was also an apparently likeable man who inspired loyalty among students and printers; he was even cited by his own teacher, Clemens Timpler, more times than that teacher cited any other post-1500 author.[15]

Keckermann's preaching manual, *Rhetoricae ecclesiasticae sive artis formandi et habendi conciones sacras libri duo* (1600), is a comprehensive discussion of the preacher's task even though it is relatively short, only 66 folio columns long in the particular edition I examined at Trinity College Dublin Library.[16] (By comparison, Erasmus's *Ecclesiastes* ac-

---

[14] Joseph S. Freedman, "The Career and Writings of Bartholomew Keckermann (d. 1609)," 307– 308, 311. I am indebted to Professor Freedman for additional helpful research suggestions.

[15] Joseph S. Freedman, *European Academic Philosophy in the Late Sixteenth and Early Seventeenth Centuries: The Life, Significance, and Philosophy of Clemens Timpler (1563/4–1624)*, 123–4, 142. Freedman also notes, however, that Timpler—apparently a difficult person—openly criticized Keckermann after his death (156).

[16] *Rhetoricae ecclesiasticae sive artis formandi et habendi conciones sacras libri duo* (1600) in *Operum omnium quae extant* (Geneva, [Coloniae Allobrogum], 1614), 2 vols., Trinity College Dublin library shelf mark L.a.1., 2[nd volume]. *Rhetoricae ecclesiasticae*, separately numbered in two folio columns per page, appears at the end of the second volume. Including its *princeps* of 1600, *Rhetoricae ecclesiasticae* as a separately printed text went through

counts for two amply annotated volumes in the new Amsterdam edition.) In the Trinity College Dublin edition of Keckermann's work, thirty folio columns are devoted to invention, arrangement, and style, and an additional four columns to delivery. Keckermann does not discuss memory, even though he indicates that the sermon should be "firmly in mind"; he may have disapproved of preaching from memory rather than notes.[17]

Of the other four canons of rhetoric, Keckermann concentrates most heavily on invention, which he divides into a thorough understanding of the scriptural text being preached, dividing the text, explaining its individual terms, amplifying its meaning, and applying the lessons derived from the text to the hearers. (The seven-column section on amplification is itself particularly amplified, accounting for more than one-tenth of the total text.) He then moves into disposition, insisting that the sermon only has three parts, an *exordium*, the *tractatio intermedia*, and an epilogue or *peroratio*. He also insists that the sermon be kept short—no more than an hour. His section on style (*exornatio*) is but three columns long, touching on simplicity, perspicuity, *copia*, efficacy (that is, propriety and evident signification of the terms), and selected tropes and figures: metaphor, *exclamatio, interrogatio, apostrophe, compellatio, obsecratio, adjuratio, compellatio conscientia, optatio, admiratio, prosopopeia, sermocinatio, sustenatio*. His section on delivery is likewise short, at four columns. Throughout, Keckermann's method is to define terms, state general propositions, and then discuss them.

---

five editions in twenty years. All editions were printed in Hanau by the Antonius printing house, the 1600, 1604, and 1606 editions by William Antonius, and those of 1616 and 1619 by William's son Peter. Freedman, "The Career and Writings of Bartholomew Keckermann (d. 1609)," 341. For the importance of the Antonius printing house to European Protestantism, see especially Josef Benzing, *Die Hanauer Erstdrucker Wilhelm und Peter Antonius (1593–1625), Archiv für Geschichte des Buchwesens* 21:4–6.

[17] "To preach is to act: thus the sermon, so to speak, is *actio*. This presupposes that the sermon is firmly formed in the mind. What things are in the voice are none other than signs of those things first conceived in the mind." ("Concionari est agere: hinc concionatio, ut sic dicam, actio est: haec praesupponit ipsius concionis factam in mente firmam formationem: quae enim sunt in voce, nil sunt aliud quam signa eorum, quae mente prius concipiuntur," col. 40).

In spite of its classical debts, Keckermann's system of ecclesiastical rhetoric is distinct from his secular one. His *Systema rhetoricae*, published in 1609, the year of his death, concerns itself with discourse directed to practical affairs of this world, and notably to ethics, economics (household management) and politics.[18] By contrast, his earlier *Rhetoricae ecclesiasticae* urges in its preface the superiority of the preacher's task, which is to preach a message which flesh cannot understand. So difficult it is, he says, to lead deficient humans to salvation that the work is nearly superhuman (3–4). Such a protestation of preaching's importance is a common enough *topos* in preaching manuals—in Erasmus's it fills the entire first book—but there are far fewer comments on its marked difference from human communication. At the very least, Keckermann describes two different kinds of discourse.

Indeed, Keckermann's preaching manual makes constant reference to Scripture and Christian commentary even while it makes heavy use of classical rhetoric. For instance, Keckermann was a noted Aristotelian, and he does refer to Aristotle at critical moments. He cites Aristotle as his authority for his shortened version of the classical oration form (*exordium*, *tractatio intermedia*, and *peroratio*) because, he says, "just so Aristotle divides the whole economy of the oration."[19] But one might expect Keckermann to make heavier use of Aristotle than he does. Barely has he begun his discussion of invention when he devotes two chapters—six folio columns in my edition—to discussing *affections*, that is, appropriate passions to be raised by the preacher, but he does so without heavy reference to Aristotle.

Passions, of course, are the central concern of the second book of Aristotle's *Rhetoric*, and they also are a central focus for Keckermann, who says "let invention . . . excite admiration by the moving of affections."[20] Yet his authorities for his two chapters on general and special advice on moving the passions are mostly Christian authors, recent and

---

[18] Joseph S. Freedman, "The Career and Writings of Bartholomew Keckermann (d. 1609)," 320, 344. See also the discussion of this text in the standard biography of Keckermann, W. H. van Zuylen, *Bartholomäus Keckermann: Sein Leben und Wirken*, 33.

[19] "Sic et ipse Aristoteles dividit totam orationis oeconomiam. 3. Rhet. cap. 1 & De re Poetica cap. 7" (33).

[20] "Inventio sit . . . qua admirationem excitet in affectuum commotione" (12). See also Van Zuylen, *Bartholomäus Keckermann: Sein Leben und Wirken*, 32–36.

ancient: St. Paul's epistles to Timothy and Titus, Augustine, Gregory Nazianzen, Gregory the Great, Chrysostom, St. Bernard, Beza, Calvin, and another German preaching theorist named Bucholerus (15–22). He does cite Aristotle four times in these sections on passions, often in a "see-also" capacity, but he cites Rudolf Agricola five times. One reason for his citation of Christian authorities is that the passions to be moved are so particular to the preaching task: shame, contrition, and repentance; hatred of Satan, sin, and all vice; the love of God, one's neighbor, and all virtue; the fear of God and terror of punishment and judgment; consolation, joy, patience, and hope; mercy and compassion toward the poor and afflicted. These are not typically the passions which are listed in classical rhetorics.

If there is any section almost entirely given over to classical authorities, it is Keckermann's section on delivery. There he makes almost exclusive reference to Cicero and Demosthenes, the two giants of classical oratory, in his advice on proper voice and gesture. On the other hand, there was little concern in the Renaissance for voice and gesture, so those two concerns typically received little contemporary attention. Keckermann's section on delivery is one of the shortest in the text, yet even here Keckermann insists that a preacher has a privilege that no classical orator could count on—he is not liable to be interrupted (41); he has the position of magistrate rather than that of advocate.

In addition to his main discussions on forming and delivering sermons, Keckermann includes an additional section on how and what materials the preacher should study, also a common *topos* of the sermon manual. This section is devoted almost exclusively to Scripture and the early church fathers. It even urges the preacher to read those Scriptures that best model preaching: Isaiah and Jeremiah in the Old Testament, and St. Paul in the New (44). Among the church fathers, Keckermann predictably favors those deemed by Reformers to be most pure—that is, most Protestant—Chrysostom, Basil, and Gregory Nazianzen among the Greeks, and Cyprian, Augustine, Jerome, Ambrose, and Bernard among the Latins. Keckermann cautions against much use at all of Scholastics. Of these, he only recommends Aquinas and Bonaventure, and then only judiciously (45).

Overall, then, Keckermann's approach to the preaching task follows the pattern I had earlier described for the typical Protestant preaching manual. Although he makes use of classical rhetoric, he is careful to ratify that use by citing relevant Christian authority. I am not suggesting that there was no range of acceptance or rejection of human authority among Protestants, nor for that matter that Roman Catholic use of classical rhetoric was monolithic, but I am arguing that the two groups represent different approaches to rhetoric and that Keckermann reflects that difference.[21]

But such an argument should make sense in terms of how homiletics developed in the Latin West. According to such historians of rhetoric as James J. Murphy and Thomas M. Conley, Augustine's stress in *De Doctrina Christiana* on imitation rather than precept foreclosed any systematic European development of theoretical homiletics until the golden shower of the late Middle Ages.[22] Since Protestants tended to claim that most of the Middle Ages were spiritually corrupt, and especially those later years which incidentally produced a coherent system—or systems—of homiletics, Protestantism should logically have developed its own system of homiletics, skipping back in time to the Scriptures themselves, to Augustine, and to other acceptable fathers of late antiquity, rather than to the more recent, but therefore more suspect, authors of the late medieval *artes praedicandi*. Because of these factors, the late development of homiletics in Western Europe should have encouraged a separate development of homiletics along confessional lines. And this separate development is what we do find in Keckermann.

---

[21] Richard A. Muller has described Keckermann's syllogistic arguments for accepting the benefits of philosophy as a God-given faculty. "*Vera Philosophia cum sacra Theologia nusquam pugnat:* Keckermann on Philosophy, Theology, and the Problem of Double Truth," 343–366.

[22] James J. Murphy, *Rhetoric in the Middle Ages*, 275–276; Murphy, "Introduction," *Three Medieval Rhetorical Arts*, xvii–xxi; Thomas M. Conley, *Rhetoric in the European Tradition*, 95–97.

18 Rethinking the History of African-American Self-Help Rhetoric: From Abolition to Civil Rights and Beyond

Jacqueline Bacon

Self-help rhetoric—which promotes moral improvement through education, economic self-sufficiency, and religious commitment—is an important genre of African-American discourse. A few examples will demonstrate that this form of persuasion has been fundamental to activist causes and to struggles for freedom, equality, and civil rights. In his 1855 autobiography, *My Bondage and My Freedom*, Frederick Douglass connects the moral status of free African Americans to abolition, noting that "one of the best means of emancipating the slaves of the south is to improve and elevate the character of the free colored people of the north."[1] Speaking more than one hundred years later at the founding rally of the Organization for Afro-American Unity in 1964, Malcolm X proposes that self-help principles are central to fostering African-American independence. He quotes from the group's goals: "We must create meaningful, creative, useful activities for those who were led astray down the avenues of vice. . . . We must be a good example to our children and teach them to always be ready to accept the responsibilities that are necessary for building good communities. . . ."[2] In a speech given two years later to the graduating class at Howard University, Adam Clayton Powell, Jr., asserts that "black power" depends upon abiding religious faith: "[O]ur faith in God must

---

[1] *My Bondage and My Freedom*, in *Autobiographies*, edited by Henry Louis Gates, Jr. (New York: Library of America, 1994), 398.
[2] *By Any Means Necessary*, 2nd ed. (New York: Pathfinder, 1992), 51–52.

never falter. We must sustain that faith which helps us to cast off the leprosy of self-shame in our black skins.... We must have the faith to build mighty black universities, black businesses, and elect black men as governors, mayors and senators."[3]

Although these examples demonstrate the broad activist potential of a discourse of moral uplift, historians—with some notable exceptions—often overlook the significance of the connections between self-help and activism in African-American discourse. For example, scholars of the antebellum period perpetuate a false dilemma by proposing that African-American leaders chose *either* to highlight moral reform *or* to promote action, resistance, and even militancy in the fight against slavery. As a result, analyses of the self-help rhetoric of antebellum African-American leaders usually separate it from abolitionist and other activist texts and represent it as primarily focused on self-improvement and adaptation to white America's values rather than on societal change.[4] The implication that antebellum rhetoric of moral uplift is necessarily conservative, individualistic, or nonconfrontational connects to misconceptions about the self-help rhetoric of other periods as well. Contemporary African-American self-help rhetoric, for example, is often mistakenly associated only with conservative leaders.

---

[3] "Can There Any Good Thing Come Out of Nazareth?" 1033.

[4] For examples of this conventional perspective, see Frederick Cooper, "To Elevate the Race: The Social Thought of Black Leaders," 604–25; Monroe Fordham, *Major Themes in Northern Black Religious Thought, 1800–1860*, 33–56; Kwando M. Kinshasa, *Emigration vs. Assimilation*, 45–62. Exceptions to this tendency include the following studies which relate the antebellum crusade for moral uplift among African Americans and the abolition cause: Benjamin Quarles, *Black Abolitionists*; Peter P. Hinks, *To Awaken My Afflicted Brethren*, 1997; James Oliver Horton, *Free People of Color*, 1993; James Oliver Horton and Lois E. Horton, *In Hope of Liberty*, 1997. In a related vein, recent studies establish that antislavery activity among antebellum African Americans can be found within churches, the temperance movement, literary and educational societies, and organizations devoted to moral improvement; see Anne M. Boylan, "Benevolence and Antislavery Activity Among African American Women in New York and Boston, 1820–1840," 128–29; Paula Giddings, *When and Where I Enter*, 49; Carol V. R. George, "Widening the Circle," 79; Roy E. Finkenbine, "Boston's Black Churches," 169–89. On the use of self-help rhetoric by twentieth-century activists such as the Black Muslims and W. E. B. Du Bois, see August Meier and Elliott Rudwick, *From Plantation to Ghetto*, 120; William Jordan, "'The Damnable Dilemma,'" 1564.

Not surprisingly, then, we lack rhetorical analyses of the activist and even militant messages contained within African-American self-help rhetoric.

In what follows, I challenge this bifurcation between self-help and activism and suggest an alternate history of African-American self-help rhetoric. I feature the discourse of four historical moments: (1) the 1820s and 1830s; (2) the beginning of the twentieth century; (3) the 1960s Civil Rights era; and (4) the late twentieth century—in other words, our present time. My analysis undermines common perceptions about self-help rhetoric, demonstrating that messages of moral reform serve to empower audience members to fight for rights; that self-help rhetoric need not be focused on accommodation to white America; that an emphasis on moral regeneration need not elevate the individual over the community; and that there is a militant potential contained within the advocacy of moral advancement, particularly educational achievement. My investigation also reveals that, although African-American leaders' philosophical perspectives and concerns may vary within a particular time period and evolve over time, self-help rhetoric is a flexible and enduring genre that can serve a variety of social and political agendas. Finally, I suggest that a close examination of this genre allows us to resist either/or perspectives of African-American rhetoric and activism, both of the past and in contemporary society.

The quotations with which I began suggest that African-American abolitionists believed that moral uplift among free African Americans would lessen the prejudices that buttressed slavery. Although this premise may seem problematic, ostensibly placing the burden for reducing oppression on African Americans, it serves an important rhetorical function. These messages of moral reform exhort free African-American audience members to identify with slaves and to connect their behavior and actions to slaves' oppression. This effort to create a sense of identification based on the ways audience members define themselves is important for all rhetors, as Kenneth Burke proposes,[5] but it has particular resonance for those from disenfranchised groups. John Waite Bowers and Donovan Ochs maintain that appeals to solidarity create a sense of cohesiveness within groups that are excluded from society's decision-making processes.[6] This feeling of connection

---

[5] *A Rhetoric of Motives*, 19–29.
[6] *The Rhetoric of Agitation and Control*, 20.

would activate the antislavery sentiments of free African Americans in the North, exhorting them to act against slavery in spite of their marginalized position in society and assigning them a fundamental role in the antislavery crusade.

To create the feeling of solidarity between slave and free, antebellum African-American self-help rhetoric often features sharp criticism of the morals and behavior of audience members. Consider, for example, an excerpt from abolitionist and reformer William Whipper's 1828 address to the Colored Reading Society of Philadelphia, an organization devoted to lending books and promoting intellectual inquiry. "[T]here is an indifference in ourselves relative to emancipating our brethren from universal thralldom," Whipper asserts, proposing that a "strict attention to education" in the free African-American community would affect slavery. Whipper does not claim, though, that individual efforts for advancement are sufficient to undermine the institution. His critique encompasses all African Americans who do not feel connected to slaves, including those who have elevated themselves while ignoring the plight of others: "Those who enjoy liberty, and have accumulated considerable property are satisfied with their situation, and will not meddle with the cause; while the middle class are too busy in procuring the necessaries of life to alter their course. And the lower class remain regardless of themselves or their brethren, who are existing in a state of ignorance and under the debasing influence of slavery and wicked men."[7] The premise of Whipper's self-help message is not that comfort, respectability, or acceptance into white society will themselves end prejudice or slavery. Nonetheless, through self-elevation one attains the means, the position, and the responsibility to fight the oppression of others.

The harshness of this message may seem troubling at first glance, particularly Whipper's strong reproof of the "lower class," who, he says, "reflect disgrace on those who enjoy a more retired life and civil society."[8] At least in part, he appears to blame the victim of oppression for the racism of society. Yet Whipper's comments can also be viewed as part of a rhetorical strategy designed to evoke group coherence among African Americans. Bowers and Ochs assert that members of marginalized groups often create solidarity through strategies of "polariza-

---

[7] *An Address Delivered in Wesley Church on the Evening of June 12, Before the Colored Reading Society of Philadelphia, for Moral Improvement*, 115–16.

[8] *An Address Delivered in Wesley Church*, 116.

tion"—based on an either/or choice distinguishing the "committed" from the "uncommitted." Because a rhetor who relies on bifurcation needs to create a strong emotional response to bring the uncommitted into the fold, Bowers and Ochs explain, harsh language may be requisite.[9] Whipper's strong critique demands that his audience view society in bifurcated terms—as divided into those who are on the side of the slave and those who are not. To choose to be in the former class demands not only self-improvement and participation in society but also a commitment to fight for others.[10]

In his militant and controversial 1829 *Appeal to the Coloured Citizens of the World*, David Walker also appears to hold African Americans at least partially responsible for ending racism. "You have to prove to the Americans and the world, that we are MEN, and not *brutes*, as we have been represented," Walker counsels. Yet he, like Whipper, does not advocate moral uplift for its own sake, but as a way to fight against slavery. His text, he remarks, is directed to "[m]en of colour, who are also of sense" because their "more ignorant brethren are not able to penetrate its value." These enlightened readers, though, must not neglect the elevation of all African Americans. They have an obligation to "rescue" others as well as themselves "from degradation," Walker asserts, particularly by promoting "education and religion." Walker explicitly links this responsibility to slavery:

> [G]o to work and enlighten your brethren! ... Do any of you say that you and your family are free and happy, and what have you to do with the wretched slaves and other people? ... If any of you wish to know how FREE you are, let one of you start and go through the southern and western States of this country, and unless you travel as a slave to a white man ... or have your free papers, (which if you are not careful they will get from you) if they do not take you up and put you in jail, and if you cannot give good evi-

---

[9] *Rhetoric of Agitation*, 26–27.

[10] It is notable that leaders such as Whipper, whose social agenda cannot be categorized in terms of an either/or choice between self-help and activism, feature language that relies on another bifurcation—in the terms of the Civil Rights Movement, "Which side are you on?" It is not, then, that these activists do not create either/or choices in their rhetoric, but that they do not divide moral improvement from agitation.

> dence of your freedom, sell you into eternal slavery, I am not a living man . . . . And yet some of you have the hardihood to say that you are free and happy! . . . [Y]our full glory and happiness . . . shall never be fully consummated, but with the *entire emancipation of your enslaved brethren all over the world.* You may therefore, go to work and do what you can to rescue, or join in with tyrants to oppress them and yourselves . . . .[11]

Walker connects moral improvement to political awareness, and—like Whipper—he offers a striking either/or choice between commitment and disregard.

The deployment of self-help themes can be a powerful argument on behalf of racial pride. In a speech commemorating the abolition of slavery in New York on July 4, 1827, William Hamilton exhorts young African Americans to demonstrate that they are unworthy of oppression not because he privileges the views of white America, but because it is a matter of racial honor:

> White men say you are not capable of the study of what may be called abstruse literature, and that you are deficient in moral character. I feel, I know, that these assertions are false as hell. Yet I do know, you are sunk into the deepest frivolity and lethargy that any people can be sunk. Oh Heavens! that I could rouse you . . . . Youth of my people, I look to you. Shall this degrading charge stand unrepelled by contrary facts? Oh! that I could enflame you with proper ambition. Your honour, your character, your happiness, your well-being, all, all are at stake . . . .

---

[11] *David Walker's Appeal, in Four Articles; Together with a Preamble, to the Coloured Citizens of the World, But in Particular, and Very Expressly, to Those of the United States of America,* 28–30. Scholars, as Hinks notes, tend to overlook Walker's advocacy of moral improvement in this text, to "[identify] him and his *Appeal* exclusively with a call for violent resistance and some form of racial separatism," and to suggest that Walker's thought was atypical of most African-American leaders of his time (*To Awaken,* 108–09). My analysis reinforces Hinks's view that these perceptions are inaccurate.

As his choice of the word "enflame" suggests, Hamilton has no desire for his audience to adopt a conciliatory posture toward white society. Indeed, he informs them that elevating themselves will be an act of defiance: "[Whites] do not wish you to be equal with them—much less superior. Therefore, in all advancements they assist in . . . they will take care that you do not rise above mediocrity."[12]

This latter quotation implies an even more radical argument of moral reformers of this period, one with militant potential. If whites deny African Americans avenues for self-improvement, it must be because they fear the results. Self-help—particularly the central component of education—has the militant potential to free the oppressed. This theme is central to David Walker's *Appeal*, in which he establishes that if ignorance is a tool of the oppressor, education is a defiant act of freedom and self-assertion. Walker takes this argument to an explicitly militant conclusion:

> [F]or coloured people to acquire learning in this country, makes tyrants quake and tremble on their sandy foundation . . . . Do you suppose one man of good sense and learning would submit himself, his father, mother, wife, and children, to be slaves . . . ? No! no! he would cut his devilish throat from ear to ear, and well do slave-holders know it. The bare name of educating the coloured people, scares our cruel oppressors almost to death.[13]

Walker's implication is clear. Education is a militant act and violent antislavery action—even slave rebellion—is a natural consequence of intellectual advancement.

Maria Stewart also emphasizes the aggressive and empowering aspects of elevation in an 1833 speech at the African Masonic Hall in Boston. "[K]nowledge is power," she asserts, asking, "is it blindness of mind, or stupidity of soul, or the want of education that has caused

---

[12] *An Oration Delivered in the African Zion Church, on the Fourth of July, 1827,* 102–03. Hamilton's quote—like those of Walker and Stewart that I feature below—demonstrates the inaccuracy of Frederick Cooper's claims that antebellum "black leaders did not face the fact that most whites, far from welcoming black intellectual improvement, would work to prevent it" ("To Elevate," 613).

[13] *David Walker's Appeal*, 31–32.

our men who are 60 or 70 years of age, never to let their voices be heard, nor their hands be raised in behalf of their color? Or has it been for fear of offending the whites? . . . Shall the chains of ignorance forever confine them? Shall the insipid appellation of 'clever negroes,' or 'good creatures,' any longer content them?" Like her mentor Walker, Stewart adopts an impassioned tone when she makes clear the implications of African Americans' intellectual advancement:

> Talk, without effort, is nothing; you are abundantly capable, gentlemen, of making yourselves men of distinction; and this gross neglect, on your part, causes my blood to boil within me. . . .
>
> . . . Most of our color have been taught to stand in fear of the white man from their earliest infancy. . . . But give the man of color an equal opportunity with the white from the cradle to manhood, and from manhood to the grave, and you would discover the dignified statesman, the man of science, and the philosopher. But there is no such opportunity for the sons of Africa, and I fear that our powerful ones are fully determined that there never shall be. . . . O ye sons of Africa, when will your voices be heard in our legislative halls, in defiance of your enemies, contending for equal rights and liberty?[14]

Education, Stewart suggests, represents for African Americans both freedom—a freedom that white America fears—and defiance of those who would keep them enslaved.

The common perception of African-American rhetoric of the 1890s and early twentieth century associates self-improvement with the accommodationist message of, for example, Booker T. Washington. Yet my historical reevaluation provides a context for considering how self-help rhetoric functions in the discourse of those who strongly critique America, call for fundamental change, and advocate racial pride and often racial independence. Speaking in 1909 at the National Negro Conference in New York City—a meeting that led to the formation

---

[14] *Maria W. Stewart, America's First Black Woman Political Writer: Essays and Speeches*, 57–59. On Walker's influence on Stewart, see Richardson's introduction, 5–19.

of the NAACP a year later—the activist W. E. B. Du Bois maintains that those who seek political power do not neglect self-help principles. In fact, a comprehensive view of moral reform that includes more than merely economic advancement is fundamental to the agenda of those who believe in "frank agitation" for the ballot:

> It is untrue that any appreciable number of black men today forget or slur over the tremendous importance of economic uplift among Negroes.... But [the] problem of work and property is no simple thing....
>
> We ... believe in vocational training, but we also believe that the vocation of a man in a modern civilized land includes not only the technique of his actual work but intelligent comprehension of his elementary duties as a father, citizen, and maker of public opinion, as a possible voter, a conserver of the public health, an intelligent follower of moral customs, and one who can at least appreciate if not partake something of the higher spiritual life of the world.[15]

Like his abolitionist forebears, Du Bois does not separate his activist agenda from an emphasis on moral advancement.

In the rhetoric of the civil rights movement, as well, activists marshal self-help rhetoric to argue for significant change in American society. In a speech at Lincoln University in 1961, Martin Luther King, Jr., maintains that achieving the "American dream" involves both "creative protest" and a focus on moral elevation:

> If we are to implement the American dream we must get rid of the notion once and for all that there are superior and inferior races. This means that members of minority groups must make it clear that they can use their resources even under adverse circumstances. We must make full and constructive use of the freedom we already possess. We must not use our oppression as an excuse for mediocrity and laziness. For history

---

[15] "Politics and Industry," in *Voice of Black America*, 675. For an extended discussion of Du Bois's deployment of tactics associated with both "accommodation" and "protest," see William Jordan, "Damnable Dilemma."

>has proven that inner determination can often break
>through the outer shackles of circumstance.[16]

Self-help principles in King's view are not accommodationist, but are part of a transformative view of society. Malcolm X, the leader most often portrayed in popular culture as King's polar opposite, shares with King a commitment to moral reform as part of his activism. His famous speech "The Ballot or the Bullet" may not generally be characterized as self-help rhetoric, but his definition of black nationalism is replete with its general themes. "The social philosophy of black nationalism," he explains, "only means that we have to get together and remove the evils, the vices, alcoholism, drug addiction, and other evils that are destroying the moral fiber of our community. We ourselves have to lift the level of our community . . . ."[17]

The message that self-help can be critical of society, radical, and even militant is also relevant to contemporary African-American discourse. As Cornel West notes, the African-American leaders advocating moral reform who gain the most attention from the media are conservatives such as Shelby Steele or Stanley Crouch. In the public consciousness, self-help thus becomes synonymous with the elimination of affirmative action and welfare and with a focus on primarily "individualistic" solutions to racial problems. Yet messages of moral uplift, West remarks, are not exclusively conservative, but are also marshaled by reformers such as Jesse Jackson who demonstrate that self-help can be part of a larger agenda that includes protest against existing institutions and both community-based and governmental programs to fight oppression. West himself advocates such an approach, arguing, "[E]ven effective jobs programs do not fully address the cultural decay and moral disintegration of poor black communities. Like America itself, these communities are in need of cultural revitalization and moral regeneration."[18]

Two contemporary examples demonstrate this deployment of self-help themes by those who, in contrast to conservatives, argue for institutional and political change as well as moral transformation in American society. In an address to the Congressional Black Caucus in 1987, Children's Defense Fund founder Marion Wright Edelman argues for programs that will help prevent early pregnancy, focus attention on

---

[16] "The American Dream," in *Voice of Black America*, 937–38.
[17] "The Ballot or the Bullet," in *Voice of Black America*, 997.
[18] *Race Matters*, 49–59.

education and stable family life, provide "constructive alternatives" to crime and drugs, and foster self-esteem in at-risk children. Self-help messages are central to this agenda:

> Tell our children they're not going to jive their way up the career ladder. They've got to work their way up—hard and continuously . . . . Tell them to do their homework, pay attention to detail, and take care and pride in their work . . . . Tell them to be reliable, to stick with something until they finish . . . . And tell them to take the initiative in creating their own opportunities. They can't wait around for other people to discover them or do them a favor.[19]

Societal and governmental programs are not antithetical to moral transformation in Edelman's view; they are fundamentally related to it. Speaking in 1994 at commencement exercises at the predominantly African-American North Carolina Central University in Durham, Vernon Jordan similarly advocates societal and individual change to address "the really tough problems that face us all." Self-help, social programs, and political activity are fundamental to addressing contemporary questions, Jordan argues, telling his audience to emphasize education; promote family stability; support job training; "look to the White House, the State House, and City Hall for policies that create opportunities"; and "fight for those policies" through the "electoral process."[20]

In his connection of "opportunities" and "responsibilities," Jordan recalls Frederick Douglass's words: "Men may not get all they pay for in this world, but they must certainly pay for all they get."[21] It is significant that Jordan acknowledges the historical precedent for a view that combines self-help and moral renewal with a focus on community regeneration and political activism. Rethinking the history of African-American self-help rhetoric reveals that leaders have challenged either/or choices between morality and societal change, between the individual and the community. And this activity can be useful in reframing contemporary concerns that have often been posed in either/or terms. As Cornel West remarks, "neither black liberals nor the new

---

[19] "Educating the Black Child: Our Past and Our Future," 113.
[20] "The Struggle is Not Over," 123.
[21] "The Struggle is Not Over," 123.

black conservatives" provide comprehensive solutions for the problems that face African Americans today. West locates a middle ground in religious and educational institutions that can help "affirm the humanity of black people, accent their capacities and potentialities, and foster the character and excellence requisite for productive citizenship." These organizations and their rhetoric, he maintains, ideally influence not only individuals but the very institutional framework of American society.[22] Given the way the media portray contemporary debates in bifurcated terms, this multifaceted perspective often appears elusive. Yet the rhetoric of activists from Douglass to Malcolm X, from Maria Stewart to Marion Wright Edelman, suggests that radical self-help rhetoric can free leaders from either/or choices. This rich discourse has the potential to challenge Americans—on both an individual and societal level—to face their shortcomings, to transform society, to fight oppression, and to empower people to truly enjoy liberty.

---

[22] *Race Matters*, 58.

19 Historical Continuity and the Politics/Rhetoric of Democracy: Solonian Reforms and the Council of 400

Davis W. Houck

Few areas in classical scholarship are more contested than the life and reforms of Solon, the early sixth-century Athenian reformer. As Gallant notes, "The number of articles, chapters, and books written about them [Solon's reforms] is legion."[1] Why Solon? Many historians trace ancient Athens' democratic antecedents directly to Solon. As such, he is a seminal, if not the seminal, figure in Greek antiquity. Given this "Founding Father" status, Solon's early sixth-century reforms involving the cancellation of debt (the *Seisachtheia*), the substitution of wealth for noble birth as criterion for holding the archonship, and thetic membership in the Assembly (the *ekklesia*), to name a few, have been the source of much scholarly speculation and debate.

Perhaps the most hotly debated Solonian "reform," however, is the mysterious Council of Four Hundred. The debate stems not only from the lack of historical evidence surrounding the Solonian *boulê*, but also the council's ostensibly democratic nature. Several scholars have asserted that because the Council of Four Hundred functioned as a *probouleutic boulê*, this "proves" Solon's democratic intent. As DeLaix claims, "*probouleusis* was in large part the basis for Athenian democracy in the fifth and fourth centuries B.C."[2] Similarly, Day and Chambers argue that since a large *probouleutic boulê* was an "eminently dem-

---

[1] T. W. Gallant, "Agricultural Systems, Land Tenure, and the Reforms of Solon," 111.
[2] Roger Alain DeLaix, *Probouleusis at Athens*, 145.

ocratic body," then "Solon could be considered the founder of Athenian democracy."[3] In like manner, Stockton refers to the *probouleutic boulê* as "the lynch pin of democracy."[4] Not only was such a council a necessary concomitant of democracy, but Woodhead refers to Solon's *boulê* as providing "the key to the functioning of the Athenian government."[5]

As evidenced by each of these historians, the historical stakes for the existence of a Solonian Council of Four Hundred are extremely high; the very foundations of democracy are at stake! It is here that methodological choices explicitly intersect with the writing of history; moreover, these choices greatly influence what historical account gets written. In this sense, as Carole Blair among others notes, historical writing is shot through with rhetoricity: "historiographical stances . . . contain embedded, but typically unacknowledged, presuppositions about history and/or rhetoric." Such unacknowledged assumptions have "culminated in partial historical accounts that mask their own partiality."[6]

Equally important as the historical stakes in the existence of a Solonian *boulê* are the rhetorical ones. If, as so many classical historians and rhetoricians contend, rhetoric and its full flowering in 5th century BCE Athens owes its institutional existence to democracy, then the Solonian reforms should be carefully interrogated. Perhaps more important for this study, the historiographical assumptions underlying the treatment of those reforms should also be carefully interrogated.

The intersections among history, method and rhetoric serve as my point of interest in this essay. My purpose is to explore an extremely important historiographical assumption in several modern historical accounts supporting Solon's creation of the Council of Four Hundred. By using one side of the debate on this pivotal issue as exemplar, I will illustrate some of the problems with historical claims of continuity—claims embedded deep in the tradition of history writing. Importantly, by focusing solely on the historiographical assumption of the "pro-Solon" side, I am not trying to prove them wrong; rather, I am attempting to expose the assumption on which their claims are

---

[3] James Day and Mortimer Chambers, *Aristotle's History of Athenian Democracy*, 86.

[4] David Stockton, *The Classical Athenian Democracy*, 94.

[5] A. G. Woodhead, "Isagoria and the Council of 500," 135, n17.

[6] Carole Blair, "Contested Histories of Rhetoric," 403.

premised—something which Finley notes, "Historians . . . are reluctant to analyze."⁷ In so doing, I will demonstrate the extent to which historical writing is greatly influenced by a methodological choice that many historians have long ignored. I will proceed by: (1) examining the ancient sources for evidence of a Solonian Council of Four Hundred; (2) delineating the modern arguments supporting a Solonian council; (3) sketching the contemporary arguments rejecting a Solonian council; (4) examining the historiographical assumption of the "pro-Solonian" side and its rhetorical importance to history writing; and (5) offering a brief conclusion.

THE ANCIENT SOURCES

The ancient sources explicitly attributing a *probouleutic* council to Solon are limited to two textual accounts: Aristotle's *Athenaion Politeia* and Plutarch's *Lives*—both of which are fraught with problems of historical reliability.⁸ In the former book, Aristotle makes explicit mention of a Solonian Council of Four Hundred in only one rather brief passage: "Solon instituted a council of four hundred, one hundred from each tribe."⁹ Aristotle implies the existence of this same council in two other passages. In *AP* 21.3, he states that Cleisthenes "made the council a body of five hundred instead of four hundred."¹⁰ And in *AP* 31.1, in which Aristotle details the constitution of the Oligarchs, he states that "The committee drew up that constitution for the future, and the following for the immediate crisis. There should be a council of four hundred in accordance with tradition."¹¹ Plutarch, on the other hand, explicitly mentions a Solonian council in only one passage:

> But he [Solon] saw that the people were swollen with self-assurance through the cancellation of debts. So he established a second Council, selecting 100 men from each tribe (there were four tribes), whom he in-

---

⁷ M. I. Finley, *Ancient History*, 1.

⁸ For a discussion of the historicity of each book see P. J. Rhodes, "Introduction," in *The Athenian Constitution*, 9–35; Arthur Hugh Clough, "Introduction," in *The Lives of the Noble Grecians and Romans*, translated by John Dryden, rev. Arthur Hugh Clough, ix–xxiv.

⁹ Aristotle, *The Athenian Constitution*, 49.

¹⁰ Aristotle, *The Athenian Constitution*, 63–64.

¹¹ Aristotle, *The Athenian Constitution*, 76.

structed to deliberate in advance of the people and not to allow any matter to be brought to the Assembly without its having been deliberated on in advance.[12]

Plutarch not only confirms Aristotle's account in the *AP*, but he adds that this council functioned as a *proboulêutic* body. Owing to these two references, modern scholars have waged a heated debate as to the historical validity of a Solonian *boulê*. It is to this debate that I now turn.

The Modern Debate

Many scholars have argued for the historical validity of a Solonian *boulê*. Importantly, though their "types" of evidence differ, each historian assumes historical continuity between Solon and Cleisthenes since no mention is made of a *proboulêutic boulê* from Solon's reforms in 594/3 until Cleisthenes' "creation" of a Council of Five Hundred in the late sixth century. Stanton aptly notes this assumption of continuity: "Even the function . . . which Plutarch attributes to the Council may be a sheer guess based on knowledge of the function of the Council of Five Hundred instituted by Kleisthenes."[13]

Two contemporary ancient historians have devoted book-length monographs to the Athenian *Boulê*. While Rhodes' *The Athenian Boulê* and DeLaix's *Proboulêusis at Athens* are concerned primarily with the functioning of the council after the Cleisthenic reforms, both authors do suggest that it had its origins with Solon. Rhodes' evidence rests with his willingness to accept Aristotle's and Plutarch's accounts. Aside from purely textual grounds, Rhodes argues that because the Council of the Areopagus would continue to be dominated by aristocrats, a "second council makes sense" since it could provide political balance.[14] Rhodes concludes that, other than its organizational structure, Cleisthenes' *boulê* "remained as Solon had established it, simply a *proboulêutic* body," thereby asserting historical continuity between the two councils.

---

[12] Quoted in G. R. Stanton, *Athenian Politics c. 800–500 B.C.*, 74.

[13] Stanton, *Athenian Politics*, 75.

[14] P. J. Rhodes, *The Athenian Boulê*, 208. Rhodes' argument of "balance" is no doubt informed by Plutarch's mention of the two councils acting together as an "anchor" to ensure political stability in Athens; see Stanton, *Athenian Politics*, 74.

DeLaix does not blindly accept Aristotle's and Plutarch's statements, but offers a more detailed argument than Rhodes. He argues that Solon was simply responding to the need for a council given Athens' new commercial interests with other city-states and the emergence of a newly rich class.[15] Thus a parliamentary body was needed to facilitate matters pertaining to Athenian economic interests. Though DeLaix does not doubt the historicity of a Solonian *boulê*, the sources for its *probouleutic* function are nearly "impossible to ascertain."[16] Borrowing from Andrewes, though, DeLaix implies that a *probouleutic* council had its roots in the seventh-century Spartan *gerousia*.[17] Despite DeLaix's reservations about a *probouleutic* council—"there is little evidence for *probouleusis* at Athens during the following century [the sixth-century]"—he nonetheless claims that Cleisthenes simply re-organized Solon's Council of Four Hundred.[18]

Several other ancient historians have offered slightly different iterations than Rhodes and DeLaix; however, historical continuity is their fundamental "proof" for a Solonian *boulê*. Importantly, historical continuity is not maintained exclusively between Solon's Council of Four Hundred and Cleisthenes' Council of Five Hundred; rather, some ancient historians, based largely on epigraphical evidence, also assume historical and political continuity between Solon and Cleisthenes via Chios. For example, Forrest argues that a sixth-century stele found in Chios provides parallel proof for a Solonian *boulê* in Athens.[19] His argument, of course, rests on the assumption that Chian and Athenian

---

[15] DeLaix, *Probouleusis at Athens*, 13.

[16] DeLaix, *Probouleusis at Athens*, 13.

[17] DeLaix, *Probouleusis at Athens*, 14; see also: A. Andrewes, "The Government of Classical Sparta," 1–20.

[18] DeLaix, *Probouleusis at Athens*, 17, 19–22. For a much less tentative statement concerning the functioning of a probouleutic council during the sixth century see Josiah Ober, *Mass and Elite in Democratic Athens*, 67. Ober argues that under Peisistratus, "The Assembly continued to meet, presumably advised by the council of 400."

[19] W. G. Forrest, *The Emergence of Greek Democracy 800–400 B.C.*, 164–67. A fragment of the inscription reads that " . . . there shall be appeal to the popular Council which shall meet on the tenth of the month, chosen fifty from each tribe, and shall deal with the *demos'* business and the appeal cases . . ." (ellipses in original). While Forrest dates the inscription to approximately 570 B. C., Hignett dates the inscription after Cleisthenes' reforms.

governments shared the same formal institutional structures—an assumption of continuity.[20]

Aside from this fairly inconclusive evidence, Forrest also posits that Solon's reforms would have had a small chance for success if the Council of the Areopagus was the sole legislative power.[21] He thus concludes that the Council of Four Hundred was "a forerunner of the fifth-century Council of 500, to act as a check on the Areopagus."[22]

Like Forrest, Andrewes argues for a Solonian *boulê* based on its ability to function as a check. Andrewes, though, claims that this *boulê* would function to check the *demos* since a revolutionary mood prevailed among this subjugated group.[23] Andrewes' major "proof," though, rests with the continuity premise in that he refers to Cleisthenes' Council of Five Hundred as the "successor" of Solon's Council.[24]

Wade-Gerry continues the line of argument set down by Forrest and Andrewes, but with a slightly different bent. That is, he claims that the Council of Four Hundred functioned as a check on the inexperienced *ekklesia*, the eligibility and duties of which Solon had reformed.[25] On this view, the *ekklesia* was shielded from its own political naïveté by a more politically seasoned *probouleutic* council.[26] Freeman offers a similar argument in claiming that the Council's "pro-*bouleutic*" function checked the inexperienced *ekklesia*.[27] Like those who side with her, Freeman's argument ultimately assumes historical continuity: "it [the Council of Four Hundred] was retained by Kleisthenes unaltered except in the number of its members" since it was "indispensable" to the governing of Athens.[28]

Woodhead's claim for a Solonian *boulê* involves its legislative activities. Specifically, he states that the Council of Four Hundred "actually did the main business of governing."[29] Woodhead's ground for such a

---

[20] For a similar argument see A. Andrewes, *Probouleusis*, 22.
[21] Forrest, *The Emergence of Greek Democracy*, 166. See also Victor Ehrenberg, *From Solon to Socrates*, 66.
[22] Forrest, *The Emergence of Greek Democracy*, 164.
[23] Andrewes, "The Government of Classical Sparta," 16.
[24] Andrewes, "The Government of Classical Sparta," 16.
[25] H. T. Wade-Gerry, *Essays in Greek History*, 146.
[26] See Stanton, *Athenian Politics*, 72, and 75–76.
[27] Kathleen Freeman, *The Work and Life of Solon*, 78 and 83.
[28] Kathleen Freeman, *The Work and Life of Solon*, 78.
[29] Woodhead, "Isagoria and the Council of 500," 135.

claim, however, is also premised on historical continuity: "Cleisthenes intended that his *Boulê* should fulfil [*sic*] the same function [the business of government] with different personnel," and "Cleisthenes did not wish to alter either the function or the character of the council in his 'reform' of it."[30]

Several ancient historians have argued that Solon *did not* create a Council of Four Hundred; Aristotle's and Plutarch's historical accounts are merely manifestations of Athenian nationalism. The sources of the Council of Four Hundred, argues Sealey, "should be sought in fourth-century speculation" since a Solonian council would provide historical "respectability" to Cleisthenes' Council of Five Hundred.[31] Others have argued that since the historical antecedents of democracy are at issue, Aristotle "hypostatized" the Solonian *boulê* "because Solon was considered the founder of Athenian democracy and a *boulê* was commonly found in democracies."[32]

Setting political and historiographical motivations aside, ancient historians also doubt the existence of a Solonian *boulê* based on several other grounds. Hignett, perhaps the most incredulous of the naysayers, offers several reasons to doubt its validity. First, he argues that the historical circumstances mitigated against a *probouleutic* council since the presence of such a *boulê* "implies the existence of an *ekklesia* with extensive and important powers."[33] A *probouleutic* council, Hignett argues, was simply not warranted given the relatively impotent assembly. Hignett "refutes" the other textual evidence by arguing that the Council of Four Hundred referred to by the oligarchs in 411 (*AP* 31.1) was simply a rhetorical "invention" designed to legitimate their reforms by appealing to an Athenian figurehead.[34] As for Herodotus' reference to a *boulê* offering opposition to Kleomenes of Sparta's attempts to dissolve it, Hignett claims that this *boulê* was the Council of the Areopagus since this council could act "vigorously" and "effectively" in a crisis.[35]

---

[30] Woodhead, "Isagoria and the Council of 500," 135 and 136.

[31] Raphael Sealey, "Regionalism in Archaic Athens," 160.

[32] Day and Chambers, *Aristotle's History of Athenian Democracy*, 200. DeLaix notes that some skeptics of a Solonian boulê see it as a fictitious construction of fourth-century political propaganda: DeLaix, *Probouleusis at Athens*, 14.

[33] C. Hignett, *A History of the Athenian Constitution*, 92.

[34] C. Hignett, *A History of the Athenian Constitution*, 93.

[35] C. Hignett, *A History of the Athenian Constitution*, 94.

As for epigraphical evidence found in both Athens and Chios, Hignett claims that both inscriptions should be dated after the Cleisthenic reforms.[36] Regarding the Chian inscription, Hignett states that simply because there were two councils in Chios does not prove the existence of two similar councils at Athens.[37] Furthermore, "In the early sixth-century the Ionians of Asia Minor had far outstripped their Athenian kinsmen in all the arts of civilization, and were politically mature enough to experiment with constitutional novelties which would have been incongruous in a community just emerging from aristocratic control."[38]

Hignett's final argument is a refutation of Adcock's claim that the council was "needed to prevent hasty decisions in times of excitement."[39] If this was the council's objective, Hignett queries, "what was it doing when Aristion was able to propose and the *ekklesia* to approve the grant of a bodyguard to Peisistratus, who was thereby assisted to make himself tyrant?"[40]

Hignett, though, is hardly the sole ancient historian to object to a Solonian council. For instance, in addition to his rejection of the council on suspicious historiographical grounds, Sealey argues that there simply is no record of the council's activity between Solon and Cleisthenes—a span stretching nearly ninety years.[41] Such a gap, Sealey asserts, is too unusual to warrant the existence for a Solonian council. Finally, Stockton confesses "grave doubts" about the matter under question primarily because Aristotle makes no mention of it in his *Politics*, in which he speaks exclusively of the Council of the Areopagus.[42]

---

[36] The epigraphical evidence at Athens involves a stele found on the Acropolis which contains a mutilated sixth-century inscription. Some have argued that the last letter of the inscription stands for "*Boulê*," while others see it as the first letter of a proper name. Hignett, *A History of the Athenian Constitution*, 95.

[37] C. Hignett, *A History of the Athenian Constitution*, 95.
[38] C. Hignett, *A History of the Athenian Constitution*, 95.
[39] C. Hignett, *A History of the Athenian Constitution*, 96.
[40] C. Hignett, *A History of the Athenian Constitution*, 96.
[41] Sealey, "Regionalism in Archaic Athens," 160.
[42] Stockton, *The Classical Athenian Democracy*, 28.

Methodological Issues

Both "sides" of the debate have seemingly reasonable arguments supporting their respective positions. Until some new, "hard" evidence is unearthed, though, both sides will remain polarized, not exclusively by the plausibility of each other's arguments, but also by an extremely important methodological choice. Foucault calls this a choice between treating history as "continuous" or "discontinuous."[43] Whereas the former emphasizes progress (teleology), unity, and continuity, the latter view of history doubts "the possibility of creating totalities," or what some historians call "total histories."[44] It is this former view of history that I will explore in the remainder of this essay. Critiquing the view of history as continuous should not be interpreted as a sign of my blind allegiance to a discontinuous model. Historical discontinuity, ostensibly an oxymoron, has its own set of problematic assumptions that appear to question the very possibility of history.[45]

Continuous histories are as ancient as Thucydides, yet such a view holds sway even in the present.[46] In a fairly recent "state-of-the-state" review of historical scholarship, LaCapra found that "There is in general little self-critical inquiry into the premises of the discipline, and often some of its oldest tenants—the postulates of unity, continuity, and mastery of a documentary repertoire—are affirmed in no uncertain terms."[47] Owing to this lack of critical reflexivity, I will critique some of the assumptions that inhere in continuous histories—assumptions upon which many historians posit the existence of a Solonian Council of Four Hundred.

Before critiquing, one must know what is being critiqued. While there is no singular definition, several historians agree on some of the basic postulates of traditional historical approaches (e.g., continuous histories). LaCapra notes, "what is assumed in conventional approaches is the priority . . . of unity or its analogues: order, purity, closure,

---

[43] Michel Foucault, *The Archaeology of Knowledge*, 3–17.

[44] Michel Foucault, *The Archaeology of Knowledge*, 8.

[45] Such a skeptical view of writing history is known as "historical Pyrrhonism." See Herbert Butterfield, *The Origins of History*, 191.

[46] Charles William Fornara, *The Nature of History in Ancient Greece and Rome*, 47.

[47] LaCapra, *History and Criticism*, 32.

undivided origin, coherent structure."⁴⁸ Frazier claims that "the working presupposition of the historian is that the events of the past make up one intelligible whole."⁴⁹ Similarly, Gilbert adds, "The foremost task of the historian is to regain an image of the past in which history emerges as the conceptualization of a unified process. For the existence of history as a profession and as an independent field depends on the conception of the past as a totality."⁵⁰ All three views share an emphasis on historical unity and intelligibility; in fact, history as a discipline, claims Gilbert, cannot exist without them.

Such a view of history is laden with problems related to what LaCapra calls the "object of study" and "the historian's discourse about it." Stated differently, continuous histories influence three interrelated factors: what "counts" as history; the form history writing assumes; and the historian's relationship to the history s/he writes.

Continuous histories raise a methodological quandary: what does the historian do with events that do not fit a unified, intelligible model—events, to borrow from LaCapra, that challenge order? With the Solonian Council of Four Hundred as exemplar, should we do as Ober did and simply ignore the apparent incongruity between Peisistratus' tyranny and the Council's *probouleutic* role? Though DeLaix does not simply assume away the incongruity, he very tellingly refers to his position (and, by implication, others who espouse similar views) as "embarrassing."⁵¹ Who is embarrassed and, more importantly, why should a historian be "embarrassed" by a historical fact? Has the model of continuity been suddenly threatened? Quite obviously, the model has not only been threatened, but perhaps violated. The result of this violation and embarrassment, though, leads to an unfortunate consequence: DeLaix attempts to "fill in" the "far from complete" historical record. Though he cautions against creating "evidence where none exists," he proceeds to render "the unfamiliar familiar in the reader's mind" by rationalizing a historical reality that does not compromise the sacred model of unity/intelligibility.⁵² Apparently, historical method, not historical veracity, is at stake; in other words, a methodological

---

⁴⁸ Dominick LaCapra, "Rethinking Intellectual History and Reading Texts," 68.

⁴⁹ A. M. Frazier, "The Criterion of Historical Knowledge," 65.

⁵⁰ Quoted in LaCapra, *History and Criticism*, 24.

⁵¹ DeLaix, *Proboulêusis at Athens*, 17.

⁵² DeLaix, *Proboulêusis at Athens*, 17–18; LaCapra, *History and Criticism*, 24. It should not be surprising that DeLaix, among others, fails to mention

a priori that privileges unity, continuity, order, and progress conditions the historian's account as to what constitutes "valid" history. As Johnson notes, "methodological activity itself becomes the means of coming to know the past in a particular way."[53] Clearly, those events anathema to historical unity and intelligibility are often simply left out of history's "story." The problems that result from continuous histories, argue Blair and Kahl, "is that the historian frequently eliminates from his/her consideration those historical theories or aspects of theories that do not resemble the originary concept."[54] Such an explanation may account for why so few historians who claim that Solon created a Council of Four Hundred are willing even to mention a *probouleutic boulê* during the tyrannies at Athens during the sixth-century; "democracy" and tyranny simply pledge allegiance to different ideological orders.

While continuous histories largely presuppose what counts as valid, those events appropriated under the guise of continuity are amenable to a particular form of representation known as narrativity. Perhaps one of the primary reasons *why* historical continuity holds sway is its intimate association with narrative form.[55] Stated differently, historical continuity lends itself to a linear representation, in short a story or narrative. Such a relationship between narrative and continuity is not new in that even Thucydides and his acolytes emphasized putting historical data "into a continuous narrative."[56] Whether one categorizes narrativity as a literary or rhetorical genre, the effects of this form can be highly suasive. Nineteenth-century historian Augustin Thierry noted that "in history the best proof, the kind most capable of arousing and convincing all minds, the kind which permits the least resistance and leaves the fewest doubts, is complete narration."[57]

Aristotle's account that Peisistratus promised to "take care of all public affairs." Aristotle, *Athenaion Politeia*, 57.

[53] Nan Johnson, "The Politics of Historiography," 17.

[54] Carole Blair and Mary L. Kahl, "Revising the History of Rhetorical Theory," 151.

[55] Hayden White, "The Question of Narrativity in Contemporary Historical Theory," 28.

[56] Fornara, *The Nature of History in Ancient Greece and Rome*, 47. Though an ancient practice, historians have been slow to examine the implications of narrative form and its consequences for historiography. Only with the work of Hayden White in the late 1960s did historians take up the issue.

[57] Quoted in Roland Barthes, "The Discourse of History," 140.

Narratives, though, are always partial; a cogent narrative often cannot assimilate more than one plot-line. Put differently, continuity and intelligibility put the formal features of a story into motion; without them history writing might resemble a Joycean labyrinth. "The problem is that in a nonlinear part of the world," claims McCloskey, "the idea of storytelling is cast into doubt."[58] Thus, since narrative form is intimately linked with order, continuity, and intelligibility, those events not compatible with a given plot are simply not part of the story. Since many historians are willing to commence democracy's "story" with Solon's Council of Four Hundred, is it any wonder that "undemocratic" events often get brushed aside and that historians are anxious to assume Peisistratus' continuation of Solon's reforms?[59]

Despite objectivist claims to the contrary, history does not tell itself.[60] As Blair and Kahl argue, the historian, like the rhetorician, makes "inventional choices."[61] In other words, the historical agent *qua* historical agent inscribes himself/herself into history by the very act of writing. Historians of continuity, though, go beyond mere inscription to assert their control of the past. Commenting on the relationship between the historian and the past, Gilbert asserts that

> the need for reconstructing a historical consciousness that integrates the present with the past . . . is rooted in the general need of our time. Because history is the study of man in his social conditions, the establishment of the relation of the past to the present reasserts the role of man in a world that appears to slide out of human control.[62]

In fairly explicit terms, continuous histories privilege the writer and his/her need for control. Historical veracity is not only sacrificed to the dictates of methodology, but also to the mandates of humans' primordial need for control. As such, the past becomes merely a reflection

---

[58] Donald N. McCloskey, "History, Differential Equations, and the Problem of Narration," 33.

[59] For example, see Ehrenberg, *From Solon to Socrates*, 80–81; DeLaix, *Probouleusis at Athens*, 18.

[60] Barthes, "The Discourse of History," 131.

[61] Blair and Kahl, "Revising the History of Rhetorical Theory," 148.

[62] Quoted in LaCapra, *History and Criticism*, 25.

of the present, time being nothing but a totalization.[63] As Foucault concludes,

> continuous history is the indispensable correlative of the founding function of the subject: the guarantee that everything that has eluded him may be restored to him; the certainty that time will disperse nothing without restoring it in a reconstituted unity; the promise that one day the subject . . . will once again be able to appropriate, to bring back under his sway, all those things that are kept at a distance by difference, and find in them what might be called his abode.[64]

By "locating" the roots of democracy in a Solonian *probouleutic boulê*, whose existence is premised largely on a "democratic" Cleisthenic Council of Five Hundred, historians merge the present with the past, thereby becoming consubstantial with their intellectual and political ancestors.

Conclusion

All forms of writing are, to an extent, autobiographical. History writing is no exception. Yet by purposefully remaining uncritical of their own assumptions many ancient historians substitute romantic sentimentalism for critical skepticism. To borrow from Borza, continuous historians appear to resemble "sentimental philhellenes"—lovers "of classical things" whose attitude is to accept nearly "everything Greek."[65] The consequences of the obstreperous philhellenes has been profound, both in terms of historical scholarship and on modern Greek culture. Unbridled philhellenism leads to scholarship "embarrassed" by historical truths specifically and "the continuing corruption of classical studies" generally.[66] On a strictly human scale, Borza details the cultural and political consequences of philhellenism on the modern Greeks—a situation in which Greeks are forced to live out the ancient

---

[63] Foucault, *The Archaeology of Knowledge*, 12.

[64] *The Archaeology of Knowledge*, 12.

[65] Eugene N. Borza, "Sentimental Philhellenism and the Image of Greece," 5.

[66] Borza, "Sentimental Philhellenism and the Image of Greece," 22.

past even in the present.[67] In no uncertain terms, the writing of history has consequences. Blind allegiance to a model presupposing historical continuity will continue to privilege methodology, narrativity, and the historian, often at the expense of our collective past.

My purpose in this essay has not been to "set the record straight" once and for all; the historical record is simply too incomplete. Instead, I have attempted to further the progress in historical research "not merely through the discovery of new materials but at least as much through a new reading of materials already available."[68] Perhaps through such a reading historians will realize the "screening function" of an uncritical *a priori,* thereby rescuing the human past from "human nature."

---

[67] Borza, "Sentimental Philhellenism and the Image of Greece," 22–25.
[68] H. Stuart Hughes, "Contemporary Historiography," 245.

20 Recognizing a Rhetorical Theory of Figures: What Aristotle Tells Us About the Relationship Between Metaphor and Other Figures of Speech

Sara Newman

Aristotle begins the *Rhetoric* with a well-known metaphor; "rhetoric," he asserts, "is the *antistrophos* to dialectic" (1.1.1.1354a1).[1] Interestingly enough, Aristotle ends the *Rhetoric* by means of another figure, an asyndeton (or the omission of conjunctions), which "is appropriate for the end of the discourse, since this is an *epilogos*, not a *logos*: 'I have spoken; you have listened, you have [the facts], you judge'" (3.19.6.1420a2).[2] Although Aristotle minimizes the argumentative value of his figural statement, he not only practices what he preaches by selecting this asyndeton to conclude his text as he advises while choosing a provocative metaphor to open it, but figures appear throughout

---

[1] The metaphorical term to which he compares rhetoric, an *antistrophos*, is the antiphonal response to the stanza in Greek choral lyric; its importation here into the realm of "word uses" suggests that rhetoric is some kind of counterpart or analogue to dialectic. See Green (8–9). Although the term *antistrophos* has been taken as an adjective, particularly by Medieval and Renaissance commentators (see Green 10ff.), I follow the majority of modern writers who take it as noun (among them Cope, 1967 and 1877, and Most), even if they do not agree on the meaning of that noun as counterpart, analogue, correlative, etc.

[2] Aristotle has taken his asyndeton from "the end of Lysias, *Against Eratosthenes* (12.100): 'You have listened, you have seen, you have suffered, you have [the fact]. You be the judge'" (Kennedy 282, n. 268).

his corpus in prominent places and in roles quite different than the traditional approach to metaphor and to Aristotle's understanding of this subject allows.[3]

According to that traditional wisdom, language is a matter of style and thus accessory to knowledge production. Within this stylistic realm, figurative language may enhance linguistic effects if its individual figures are used with appropriate restraint and in suitable contexts. To clarify and encourage these proper uses, rhetorical treatises have characteristically divided the figures on the basis of form and function. But, because these categories have been applied in an arbitrary manner, they have mattered less than their overall message—that the figures are linguistic afterthoughts (Fahnestock 18–20). One notable exception lies outside this otherwise exclusive grouping; in contrast to the "other" figures, metaphor has always enjoyed an independent scholarly life and an ascendant theoretical status. In contemporary coinage, then, metaphor can refer either to an "implied comparison" or to "figurative language" more broadly construed. Finally, these attitudes and their attendant problems owe a considerable debt to Aristotle's definition of metaphor in the *Poetics* and the *Rhetoric* which is the source of all subsequent metaphorical theories and of metaphor's purported figural authority (in fact, his broader discussions of figures are the foundation for all subsequent systems of tropes and schemes; see Newman, Chapter Eight).

At present, the traditional approach to language and to metaphor has been superceded by others that grant to them epistemic and conceptual capacities. Their outmoded interpretation has also been disassociated from any explicit statement by Aristotle and his definition of metaphor more accurately understood as anticipating though not fully realizing conceptual capacities (Newman, Chapters Two and Three). Yet, the link between that definition and metaphor's privilege has not been similarly reexamined. Thus, while some scholars have begun to consider the possibility that the figures are not simply unsystematic and ornamental entities but can operate within a kind of figural

---

[3] In addition to his opening metaphor, the first two chapters of the *Rhetoric* include numerous other metaphors. See Newman (244–5). "The distinction between tropes and figures is not explicit in Aristotle's work and is a development of his successors in the Hellenistic period" (Kennedy 1991, 229); cf. Ricoeur (1977, 16–17; 1996, 325–6, 332). See Stanford (19) on the distinction between tropes and figures. On the history of the figures as a whole see Fahnestock ("Chapter One").

theory (Fahnestock, Murphy, and Perelman), the study of figurative language as a whole remains limited by its longstanding marginalized status and, with this, indentured to the traditional interpretation of Aristotle's accounts of metaphor.

With this background in mind, I take a closer look at Aristotle's "founding" definition of metaphor in its own context and on its own terms, and as his analysis sheds light on the prospect of a rhetorical theory of figures. I begin by describing how Aristotle's definition has been linked with metaphor's figural privilege. After identifying the problems inherent in this association, I resolve them by reassessing Aristotle's definition and offering a more accurate reading of it, one that suggests as well how to recognize a figural theory.

THE TRADITIONAL APPROACH TO ARISTOTLE'S DEFINITION OF METAPHOR

Aristotle defines metaphor in the context of appropriate *lexis*/style in two of his works on verbal *tekhnai*, the *Rhetoric* and the *Poetics*. Metaphor first appears in the *Poetics,* chapter 21, as one of several kinds of words that can contribute to clarity. Because clarity is Aristotle's *arkhe*/first principle for all linguistic expression, metaphors can help poetry to achieve its *telos*/end of *mimesis* (and tragedy its specific end of *katharsis*). Metaphors, Aristotle asserts, can produce new insights through the *epiphora*/transference of meaning between associated dissimilars because they "[consist] in giving the thing a name that belongs to something else; the transference being either from genus to species, or from species to genus, or from species to species, or on the grounds of analogy" (21.1457b7–9). That is, a metaphor allows an entity to be named by comparing it to a different or *allotrios*/alien term in any of four possible ways. The result of this association is a meaning transfer that leads to clarity and to an insight about what the ostensibly unlike entities share.[4]

Aristotle follows his definition of metaphor's parts and function with examples of metaphor which are presumably intended as models for his readers. Of the two groups represented, the first includes metaphors of the first three species and illustrates that these kinds of metaphor relate to each other as part-to-whole. That from genus to species

---

[4] On *epiphora*, see Kirby (531–2), and Ricoeur (1977, 17–18; 1996, 328ff.). On *allotrios*, see Ricoeur (1977, 18–20; 1996, 330–32).

is exemplified in "Here stands my ship"; for lying at anchor is a sort of standing. That from species to genus in "Truly ten thousand good deeds has Ulysses wrought," where "ten thousand," which is a particular large number, is put in place of the generic "a large number." That from species to species in "Drawing the life with the bronze," and in "Severing with the enduring bronze"; where the poet uses "draw" in the sense of "sever" and "sever" in that of "draw," both words meaning to "take away" something. (21.1457b9–16) The first three types depend on two or three terms that pertain to the same linguistic domain, as "lying" belongs to the more inclusive realm of "standing," and "draw" and "sever" to the broader notion of "taking away." When the characteristics of one entity are transferred to a second seemingly different one, a movement takes place that shifts some of the characteristics of the first to the other, thereby associating the two.[5]

After illustrating the first three species of metaphor, Aristotle moves on to the fourth. "That from analogy is possible whenever there are four terms related so that the second is to the first as the fourth to the third; for one may then put the fourth in place of the second, and the second in place of the fourth" (21.1457a16–18). In other words, A is to B as C is to D; B and D can also be switched to yield A is to D as C is to B. "Thus a cup [A] is in relation to Dionysus [B] what a shield [C] is to Ares [D]" (21.1457b20).

Because this fourth species involves four terms rather than two or three as the first three species, the basic analogy can be reconstructed in several ways. For example, the analogy (A/B = C/D) can be restated so that the first term is the metaphorical equivalent of the association between the third and second (A=C of B; 21.1457b18–20); that is, the cup = the shield of Dionysus, the second term being the metaphorical equivalent produced by the association between the first and fourth (C=A of D), the shield = the cup of Ares (cf. 21.1457b20–24, 25.1461a29–32, and *Rh*.3.11.11.1412b35–1413a1). Analogous metaphors can also perform other complex naming functions such as naming unnamed entities (21.1457b24–30).[6]

---

[5] Levin recognizes the relationship of the third species to the fourth and places the third as an intermediate kind between the first two, on the one hand, and the fourth, on the other.

[6] Naming the unnamed, an aspect of analogous metaphors for Aristotle, becomes *catechresis/abusio* for Cicero (*De Orat.* 27.94) and Quintilian (*Inst.* 8.6.34–8). See *Rh*. 3.2.1405a35–1405b5–6 and Stanford (19, 37ff.). Aristo-

In these statements and examples from the *Poetics*, Aristotle distinguishes the fourth metaphorical type from the other three species by its four terms; these grant to analogous metaphors a wider range of associations than two or three terms can achieve. For later commentators on metaphor, these passages express Aristotle's outright preference for the fourth metaphorical type; it alone is "metaphor" proper, they suggest, while the first three species, based as they are on part-to-whole relationships, are other figures altogether (metonymy and synecdoche as they have since been named).[7] From this perspective, metaphor overwhelms the other figures Aristotle describes, establishing a two-tiered figural hierarchy topped by metaphor and supported by metonymy and synecdoche (and by association all other figures). This reading of Aristotle's account is clearly the source of metaphor's figural dominance, of the understanding that other figures are less noteworthy and interesting, and of associated problems involving the relationship between metaphor and other figures, most notably for this discussion metonymy and synecdoche. These figures are still inadequately understood yet considered central to a more refined understanding of metaphor and of the figures as a whole.

In recent decades, various studies have examined how metaphor, metonymy, and synecdoche relate as a critical part of broader attempts to topple the figural hierarchy that Aristotle allegedly erected and to develop a more balanced understanding of the figures. Ironically, these efforts have erected new taxonomies that duplicate in reverse the problems that they had set out to remedy.[8] The failure of these efforts stems not simply from their implicit dependence on Aristotle's approach to metaphor but from their misreading of it. Any attempt to reconsider the figures must reexamine the Aristotelian source.

---

tle also indicates that analogous metaphors have yet another variation at *Po.* 21.1457b30–34.

[7] For the traditional interpretation of Aristotle's theory of metaphor, see Brooke-Rose, Cope (1867, 5, 13, 376 esp. and 1877), Lakoff and Johnson (190), and Stanford (5, 21).

[8] See Burke (1969, 503–17), Groupe Mu (107), Jakobson, Lakoff and Johnson (36), and Vico (409). In theory, synecdoche designates a part-for-whole relationship within a genus or domain, as in the prototypical sail to ship; in contrast, metonymy stands for such an association that crosses a domain, as when schooner or tugboat stands for ship. But in practice these definitions are vague, prompting these various interested parties to develop more explicit characterizations.

Aristotle's Definition of Metaphor Reconsidered

The traditional perspective on metaphor's figural status has treated Aristotle's definition of metaphor both inaccurately and incompletely, inaccurately because it distorts Aristotle's claims about how analogous metaphors and the other three metaphorical types relate and incompletely because it neglects a significant portion of his definition, his analysis in the *Rhetoric* especially. By misdirecting their focus in these ways, these studies go astray in another: they disregard two features that are central to the operation of Aristotelian metaphor. First, Aristotle's definition treats *metaphora*, a broader term than the modern notion of metaphor. Second, all *metaphorai* rely on Aristotle's regulating principle for linguistic expression, clarity, which requires that each statement accommodate the *telos*/goal of the subject in which it is articulated (in the present discussion, poetry and prose). When all of Aristotle's statements on metaphor are examined in light of these two features, a more accurate understanding of his definition emerges, one that remedies the problems that resulted from its prior misinterpretation and also suggests a new way to recognize a rhetorical theory of figures.

In both the *Poetics* and the *Rhetoric*, Aristotle specifies how the various kinds of *metaphorai* can contribute to clarity in their respective linguistic contexts. The *Poetics* not only defines *metaphora* but also describes how each type functions within the range of expression available to poetry. In general, a poetic metaphor attains clarity and contributes to the poetic goal of affecting emotions when its metaphorical comparisons blend an appropriate amount of ordinary and elevated language.

> The excellence of diction is for it to be at once clear and not mean, as is shown in the poetry of Cleophon and Sthenelus. On the other hand the diction becomes distinguished and non-prosaic by the use of unfamiliar terms, i.e. strange words, metaphors, lengthened forms, and everything that deviates from the ordinary modes of speech .... A certain admixture, accordingly, of unfamiliar terms is necessary. These, the strange word, the metaphor, the ornamental equivalent, etc., will save the language from seeming mean and prosaic, while the ordinary words

in it will secure the requisite clearness. (22.1458a17–1458b1; cf.25.1460b13–15)

Poetic metaphor transfers meanings between entities that deviate from familiar usage. Noteworthy language provides the distinctive character that is essential to poetry and more common language ensures that the expression remains comprehensible.

Within this expressive range, each poetic occasion requires a specific amount of elevated and familiar language, and clarity is still a measure against which this appropriateness is tested.

> The rule of moderation applies to all the constituents of the poetic vocabulary; even with metaphors, strange words, and the rest, the effect will be the same, if one uses them improperly and with the view of provoking laughter. The proper use of them is a very different thing. (22.1458b11–15)

Each genre, Aristotle continues, permits different degrees of the elevated and the ordinary depending on the particular genre's relative distance from prosaic language (22.1458b 15–19). Because heroic poetry is the most august poetic genre, it may use all of the poetic resources; fewer of these resources are available to iambic verse, which is closer to prose than the heroic, and fewer still to comedy, the poetic lowest genre (22.1459a11–14; cf. 23.1459b34–36). Striking language is essential to poetry though not an exclusive attribute.

Overall, poetry can accommodate more extreme contrasts than prose, and analogous metaphors most readily supply these materials. These noteworthy, context-dependent metaphors are inherently different than the other three types but not intrinsically better. Aristotle never makes any claims to the latter effect nor restricts poetic language to vivid statements alone.

If the traditional reading has misread some of what the *Poetics* has to say about metaphor, it has neglected much of the discussion of metaphor in the *Rhetoric* by treating it as a gloss on the poetic account. True, the *Rhetoric* assumes the basic metaphorical criteria from the *Poetics*, but it tallies these standards with rhetorical practice both by offering a range of appropriate uses for prose metaphor and by distinguishing these uses and their effects from those appropriate for poetry. The resulting complementary rhetorical perspective on metaphor supports and augments the *Poetics,* and is fundamental, therefore, to a complete understanding of how metaphor and the other figures relate.

Aristotle begins by locating prose metaphor in the context of clarity.

> Let the virtue of style [*lexeos arete*] be defined as "to be clear/*saphe*" (speech is a kind of sign, so if it does not make clear/*saphe* it will not perform its function)—and neither flat nor above the dignity of the subject, but appropriate [*prepon*]. The poetic style is hardly flat, but it is not appropriate for speech. The use of nouns and verbs in their prevailing [*kyrios*] meaning makes for clarity; other kinds, as discussed in the *Poetics*, make the style ornamented rather than flat. (3.2.10.1404b2–6; cf. 3.12.5.1414a19–28; cf. 3.12.3.1414b3–14)

Though clarity is prose *lexis'* regulating principle, and though it is attained by the same process as in poetry, prose metaphors require a different mixture of common and vivid language. Since clear prose *lexis* is a virtue that must instruct and persuade more ordinary audiences and subjects, it relies on a more limited set of assets than poetry and resolves accordingly to a less elevated linguistic mean. This resolution, Aristotle adds to his poetic account, leads to appropriate clarity by "bringing-before-the-eyes" of the audience an insight about what the two contrasted entities share (3.10.6.1410b32–36).

Similarly, when Aristotle turns to *eikon*/simile in chapter four of the *Rhetoric*, he characterizes its uses and their effects in relationship to metaphor in both prose and poetic situations. For Aristotle, simile is a kind of *metaphora*. Although "little difference" exists between the two besides the addition to the simile of "as" or "like" (3.4.3.1406b20; cf. 3.10.3.1410b20), simile "is poetic" compared with metaphor because similes are longer, rely on more explicit comparisons than metaphors (3.4.3.1406b24–25), and are thus subordinate to metaphor proper in rhetorical situations.[9] As a result, many statements can be framed either as simile or metaphor, but similes are more appropriate in contexts

---

[9] Cf. 3.10.3.1410b15 and 3.11.11.1412b34–1413a6. On simile in Aristotle, see McCall esp.(24–56), Ricoeur (1977, 47–48 and 249; 1996, 336ff.), and Stanford (25ff.). Interestingly enough, Aristotle makes no mention of simile in the *Poetics* (see McCall, 49–50; Ricoeur 1996, 336; and Stanford 9).

requiring a longer commentary, "when metaphors are needing an explanatory word" (3.4.3.1407a11–12). In particular, rhetorical contexts support a brief simile if they are like the most successful metaphors (cf. McCall 52).

> [A]s has been said above, similes, which are well liked in some way, are also metaphors. They always involve two terms, as does metaphor from analogy.... If poets do not do this well, they most fail with the public; and if they do it well, they are popular. (3.11.11.1412b33–34; 3.11.12.1413a5–9)

For Aristotle, the distinction between simile and metaphor is less important than their appropriate applications with respect to their subject. Like proportional metaphors, four-termed similes can be popular, that is, persuasive and instructive in prose application, although they would not necessarily affect emotions as well as longer similes in poetic usages.

While this discussion of simile rightly emphasizes the noteworthy character of analogous metaphors, the *Rhetoric* also underscores the degree to which less noteworthy metaphors of the first three species are suited to popular rhetorical situations. In his discussion of "frigidities," the opposite of clear prose *lexis*, Aristotle reiterates the centrality of appropriate balance to clear prose, opposes that clarity to the elevated poetic variety, and associates that prosaic mean with the first three species of metaphor.[10] Far-fetched metaphors result when metaphors do not approach a mean and are, therefore, elevated and "too poetic" (3.3.4.1406b10; cf.3.2.12.1405a35). Avoiding inappropriate prose metaphors (or even metaphors inappropriate to the most prose-like poetic genre of comedy) calls for less memorable metaphors.

Elsewhere in the *Rhetoric*, Aristotle associates the less striking contrasts of the first three species of metaphor with effective, witty prose. "Metaphor most brings about learning; for when he calls old age 'stubble,' he creates understanding and knowledge through the genus, since both old age and stubble are [species of the genus of] things that have lost their bloom" (3.10.2–3.1410b9–15). By using a species-

---

[10] The other kinds of frigidity involve using compound words (*Rh*.3.3.15.1405b34–35), words taken from foreign usage that confuse the listener (3.3.2.1406a8), and "long or untimely" epithets (3.3.3.1406a12). On frigidities, see Ricoeur (1996, 344–46).

to-genus metaphor to demonstrate how prose metaphors can be both familiar yet strange, Aristotle demonstrates as well that the first three species are *metaphorai* that are not only capable of contributing to clear prose *lexis* but are also well suited to that role (3.10.3.1410b20; cf.3.10.5.1410b35 and 3.11.7.1412a20).

Aristotle turns once more to the first three species of metaphor in the *Rhetoric* to illustrate a particular kind of rhetorical situation, how best to complicate and to denigrate. "And if you wish to adorn, borrow the metaphor from something better in the same genus, if to denigrate, from something worse" (3.2.10.1405a9–14). Here, Aristotle advises that selecting appropriate contrasts in prose is constrained by rhetoric's persuasive end and by the need to be familiar and strange at the same time. In particular, the first three types of metaphor can adorn and denigrate respectively by using praying and begging as species of asking.

Finally, Aristotle associates more ordinary rhetorical metaphors with another significant characteristic of rhetoric. Rhetoric must at times be "natural";

> for what is said [in poetry] about subjects and character is more out of the ordinary, but in prose much less so; for the subject matter is less remarkable. . . . As a result, authors should compose without being noticed and should seem to speak not artificially but naturally. (The latter is persuasive, the former the opposite) . . . 5. The "theft" is well done if one composes by choosing words from ordinary language. (3.2.6.1404b9–16,17–18,24–26)

Rhetorical situations sometimes require transparency, a characteristic of the first three metaphorical types.

Aristotle models various metaphors in the *Rhetoric*; these complement his account in the *Poetics* by clarifying how each metaphorical species contributes to effective prose rather than by privileging the fourth, analogical species (see Newman, Chapter Four). Following the *Poetics,* Aristotle arranges the three sets of metaphorical examples along the lines of species and, at the same time, reconciles their description with the characteristics of rhetoric. Since the first set illustrates thirteen analogous metaphors and since each example manifests the proper elements and function detailed in the *Poetics*, his label and selection are also consistent with the poetical discussion (3.10.7.1410b36). However, at least seven of the examples can be constructed in several ways. This plurality suggests that Aristotle's categories of metaphor are context-dependent.

Aristotle's second group, which he identifies as "metaphor" and "bringing-before-the-eyes," includes one analogous, seven species to genus, and one species to species (3.10.1411a25ff.).[11] Aristotle refers to them collectively as "metaphor," while associating them explicitly with "bringing-before-the-eyes." He also separates these examples from the preceding group of analogous metaphors that involve no such explicit association. These choices specify that analogous metaphors are distinct from the first three types because this type inherently "brings-before-the-eyes" insights whereas this is not always the case with the first three. Again, the examples verify the basic metaphorical function, underscoring specifically the degree to which the first three species resolve to a mean around the shared species or genus.

After an isolated antitheses (3.10.1411a25–27), a set of five metaphors follow which belong to the first three species (two species to

---

[11] The analogous metaphor is illustrated by "when Iphicrates said, 'My path of words is through the midst of Chares' actions,' it was a metaphor by analogy, and 'through the midst of' is bringing-before-the-eyes" (3.10.7.1411b1–6). The seven species-to-genus metaphors include: (1) "Aeson, moreover, said they had 'poured' the city into Sicily" (3.10.7.1411 a25–26); (2) "And [his phrase] 'so that Greece cried aloud' is in a certain way metaphor and a bringing-before-the-eyes" (3.10.7.1411a26–27); (3) "And [so is] the way Cephisodotus demanded that they not make the town meetings *syndromas*" (3.10.7.1411a29–30); (4) "And Isocrates [provides another example] in regard to 'those running together' in festivals" (3.10.7.1411a30–31); (5) "And [consider] what is found in the funeral Oration that 'it was proper at the tomb' of those dying at Salamis for Greece 'to cut her hair in mourning, since freedom was being buried with their valor.' If he had said it was proper to shed tears since their valor was being buried, it would be a metaphor and bringing-before-the-eyes" (3.10.7.1411a31–35); (6) "'Call dangers to the aid of dangers' is bringing-before-the-eyes and metaphor" (3.10.7.1411b5–6); and (7) "And [consider] Lycoleon speaking on behalf of Chabrias: 'not ashamed of his suppliant attitude in that bronze statue'; it was a metaphor at the time it was spoken, but not at all times, but it was bringing-before-the-eyes, for [then] when he was in danger, the statue [seemed to] supplicate, the lifeless for the living, the memorial of his deeds for the city-state" (3.10.7.1411b6–11).

genus, three species to species).¹² In this case, Aristotle applies to them a different label, calling them "metaphors" rather than "metaphor" and "bringing-before-the-eyes" as he did in the previous group. Apart from this terminological anomaly, these examples manifest once more the proper overall function that he describes in the *Poetics*.

Aristotle's examples of metaphor from the *Rhetoric* exhibit the same metaphorical elements and function detailed in the *Poetics*; regardless of the metaphorical species applied, each example contrasts initially unlike entities whose resolution to a mean actualizes a present action in an insight. As the *Poetics*, too, they distinguish the analogous metaphor from the other three types not because they are inherently "better" or a different type of figures, but because they are more vivid, or "well-liked" as Aristotle puts it (3.10.7.1410b36). Aristotle neither dissolves the boundaries that separate the figures nor grants to metaphor unlimited authority. Finally, many of these metaphors can be reconstructed in several ways; this and the fact that Aristotle uses these examples to identify when the first three species do and do not "bring-before-the-eyes" insights suggests that his theoretical categories are in practice context-dependent. Again, effective metaphors accommodate the situations in which they are expressed, and each expressive situation can tolerate a different range of rhetorical resources.

Conclusions

In the *Poetics* and the *Rhetoric*, Aristotle grants to metaphor a consistent function which may be performed by any of four species. The first three involve two or three terms and relatively subtle substitution, while the four terms of the fourth metaphorical type allow for greater flexibility and effect. According to the traditional reading, these char-

---

¹² The two species-to-genus metaphors include: (1) "'in every way practicing lowly thinking', for 'to practice' is to increase something" (3.10.7.1411b11–14); and (2) "that cities give 'great financial account' in the censure of mankind; for a financial account/*euthuna* is a legal form of damages" (3.10.7.1411b19–21). The three species-to-species metaphors include: (1) "that 'God kindled the mind as a light in the soul'; for both make something clear" (3.10.7.1411b14–15); (2) "'For we do not settle wars, but postpone them'; both postponement and a peace of this sort are [a species of] delaying" (3.10.7.1411b15–17); and (3) "that treatises are a much better 'trophy' than those won in wars; for a trophy honors a moment and one success, while treaties apply to the whole war; both are signs of a victory" (3.10.7.1411b17–19).

acteristics elevate the analogous kind as the metaphor proper; the other less effective types are different figures altogether. This understanding, however, neglects the *Rhetoric*, examines only part of Aristotle's analysis in the *Poetics,* and misreads what that part states. It is not Aristotle's analysis that subsumes other figures within metaphor, but subsequent commentators who reconstruct Aristotle's analysis along these lines and interpret his statements about difference as a value judgment.

In fact, Aristotle does not relate the figures on the basis of a hierarchy. While the first three metaphorical species are considered metonymy and synecdoche in subsequent linguistic terminology, the four types proceed together within Aristotle's inclusive grammatical vocabulary as kinds of *metaphora*, a figure which allows the characteristics of one entity to be transferred to a second seemingly different one and to produce an insight and appropriate clarity. Because all *metaphorai* can contribute to clear, effective prose, the fourth type is different than the other three types and more appropriate in particular situations, yet equally inappropriate in others; conversely, less noteworthy figural resources are hardly less interesting or significant.

Aristotle provides a precedent for recognizing other figures on this basis, since his accounts of style in the *Poetics* and *Rhetoric* name as *metaphorai* various other kinds of expressions that can provide contrasts and balance and lead to clarity. In addition to simile, *catachresis* and personification are fourth and third species metaphors respectively (3.2.12.1405a30, 3.11.2.1411b30ff.); "proverbs [*paroimiai*] are metaphors from species to species" (3.11.14.1413a15); and "effective hyperboles are also metaphors" (3.11.15.1413a20). This Aristotelian perspective must now be tallied with other research on the figures that accords to them generative conceptual capacities within language and that finds evidence of these patterns in Aristotle's own *Rhetoric* and *Topics* (Fahnestock 23, 26, 37, 46–9, 98ff., 131ff.). But, these matters must be deferred to another discussion. For the present, "I have spoken; you have listened, you have [the facts], you judge"(3.19.6.1420a2).

21 Disciplinary Relations in Ancient and Renaissance Rhetorics

Robert Gaines

One of the central problems in Renaissance rhetorical theory was adjudication of the relationship between rhetoric and logic. In response to this problem we have several theoretical discussions, not least in Philip Melanchthon's *Institutiones Rhetoricae* (1521), Leonard Cox's *The Arte or Crafte of Rhetoryke* (c.1530), Peter Ramus' *Dialecticae Institutiones* (1543) and *Aristotelicae Animadversiones* (1543), Omer Talon's *Rhetorica* (1548), and Francis Bacon's *Of the Proficience and Advancement of Learning, Divine and Humane* (1605). These works are generally viewed as providing accounts of rhetoric that are distinctive to the Renaissance era. For example, Cox and Melanchthon are viewed by Carpenter (1899), Conley (1990), Meerhoff (1994), Knox (1994), Plett (1995), and Kennedy (1999) as theoretical reformers in the tradition of northern European humanists. Again, Ramus and Talon are understood by Howell (1954, 1956), Ong (1958a), Vickers (1988), Conley (1990), Plett (1995), and Kennedy (1999)—among others—as leading a unique and widely influential revisionist movement in rhetorical thought. Finally, the novelty of Bacon's conceptualization of rhetoric, especially amongst the arts and sciences, is championed by Wallace (1943), Howell (1954, 1956), Stephens (1975), Conley (1990), Vickers (1996), and Kennedy (1999), to name just a few.

Still, despite the force and interest of these characterizations, the present essay questions whether the theoretical positions found in works of Melanchthon, Cox, Ramus, Talon, and Bacon are really as distinctive as we are led to believe. In fact, the purpose of my argument is to show that, insofar as the aforementioned works reflect on the relation of rhetoric and logic, they do so in ways that recapitulate ancient positions on the relation of rhetoric and philosophy. In framing this argument, I shall outline the Renaissance positions first, then briefly sketch what I consider to be their conceptual precedents in ancient rhetoric.

I

Within the Renaissance, there are at least three distinguishable positions on the relation of rhetoric and logic. One of them absorbs logic into rhetoric. This position has its origins in Philip Melanchthon's *Institutiones Rhetoricae* (1521). Here, Melanchthon's handling of invention (or *elementa rhetorices*) produces two remarkable doctrines. The first arises at the outset of the discussion. Melanchthon writes, "The parts of discourses are to invent, to judge, to dispose, and to utter."[1] The second doctrine follows a few sentences later: "As indeed, the kinds of themes are four: dialectical, demonstrative, deliberative, judicial."[2]

Taken together, these doctrines would suggest that for Melanchthon, the scope of rhetoric contains the materials of dialectic; for not only is judgment—a function of dialectic—added to the usual list of rhetorical activities, but it would appear that dialectical invention belongs to rhetoric as well. This appearance is confirmed by Melanchthon's subsequent handling of the dialectical discourse. For within his account of the simple theme of dialectical discourse he makes clear that invention is not only dialectical in the strict sense—since it exploits logical topics in philosophical inquiry—it is also relevant to the rhetorical composer as a practical matter.

> Now the dialectical kind [of discourse] is a method of teaching things surely and simply, through which are investigated the natures, causes, parts, and effects of things by means of certain principles, so that nothing can be known accurately and properly unless it has been subjected to dialectical instruments . . . .

---

[1] Partes disserentium sunt, inuenire, iudicare, disponere, & eloqui. (Melanchthon 1521, A.ii.r) Unless otherwise noted, translations are my own.

[2] Sicut caussarum ita thematum genera quatour sunt. Dialecticum, demonstratiuum, deliberatiuum, iudiciale. (Melanchthon 1521, A.ii.r) In translations here and elsewhere, materials in angle brackets represent words supplied from the syntactical or conceptual context.

The places or instruments for simple themes [are] Definition, Causes, Parts, Effects. So, if you should inquire what is justice, what are the causes of it, what are its parts, what are its effects, then you have thoroughly investigated the entire nature of justice, and concerning these things assuredly dialectical [topics] will have ascertained [the answers]. Now, in reference to this type of simple themes, the manner in which it is suitable for the rhetor, we will teach below. It is [suitable], of course, where there is use of definitions [and] divisions. And these things, just as they are sure and short under the power of the dialectician, so are they ample and splendid under the power of the rhetor.³

Melanchthon's account of the complex theme in dialectical discourse is quite comparable. Complex themes, which must be proved true or false by argument, may be rhetorical as well as dialectical. And prosecution of both requires recourse to dialectical rules and identical topics (specifically, definition, causes, parts, similarity, contrariety; 1521, A.ii. v). In the end, Melanchthon's account of dialectical discourse actually stresses the degree to which dialectical invention has been imported

---

³ Est autem dialecticum genus, certa quaedam & simplex docendi ratio, qua rerum naturae, caussae, partes, & officia certis quibusdam legibus inquiruntur, ut exacte & proprie nihil cognosci queat, nisi dialecticis organis astrictum . . . .
LOCI seu organa simplicis thematis.
   Finitio,
   Caussae,
   Partes,
   Officia, Vt si quid sit iusticia, quae caussae eius sunt, quae partes, quae officia, inquisieris, iam totam iusticiae naturam perscrutatus es, & de iis quidem dialectici uiderint. Nam huic simplicium thematum generi, quatenus cum rhetore conueniat infra docebimus. Est enim ubi definitionibus ubi diuisionibus utitur. Quae ut sunt apud dialecticum certae & compendiariae, Ita apud rhetorem amplae & splendidae. (Melanchthon 1521, A.ii.r)

into rhetoric; "Concerning topics," he says, "there is agreement for the rhetor and dialectician in all things."[4]

Melanchton's position is reproduced and in some ways extended in Leonard Cox's *The Arte or Crafte of Rhetoryke* (c. 1530 and 1532, cf. Carpenter 1899, Howell 1954, 1956). Melanchthon's four-part analysis of rhetoric is amplified by Cox with explanation and example as follows (1532, A.iiii.rv):

> Who someuer desyreth to be a good Oratour or to dyspute and commune of any maner thynge/ hym behoueth to haue foure thynges.
>
> The fyrste is called Inuencion/ for he muste fyrste of all imagin or Inuent in his mynde what he shall say.
>
> The seconde is named Iugement. For he muste haue wyt to deserne & iuge whether tho[se] thynges that he hath founde in his mynde be conuenient to the purpose or nat. For ofte[n]tymes yf a man lacke thys property/ he may aswell tell that that is against hym as with hym/ . . .
>
> The thyrde is Disposicion/ wherby he may know how to order and set euery thynge in his due place/ . . .
>
> The fourth & last is suche thynges as he hath inuented: and by Iugement knowen apte to his purpose whan they are set in theyr order so to speke them that it may be pleasaunt and delectable to the audience/ . . . And this last p[ro]perty is called among lerned men (Eloquence).[5]

Likewise, Cox develops Melanchton's analysis of rhetorical discourse types in this way (1532, A.v.rv):

---

[4] . . . omnino enim rhetori & dialectico de locis conuenit. (Melanchthon 1521, A.ii.v)

[5] In this and other quoted texts, letters between lower-half square brackets extend abbreviations used in the original edition and letters between square brackets are supplied by the editor (or myself where no other editor is indicated).

> Here is to be noted that there is no Theme but it is conteyned under one of the foure causes/ or for the more playnnes foure kyndes of Orations.
>
> The fyrste is called Logycall/ whyche kinde we call properly disputacio[n].
> The seconde is called Demonstratiue.
> The || thyrde Deliberative.
> The fourth Judiciall/ . . .

Details of Cox's *Arte* on the "Logycall kinde of Oration" need not detain us here; he translates Melanchthon essentially word for word regarding theoretical matters. Still, on the whole, Cox's work clarifies the theoretical absorption of logic into rhetoric. On the one hand, he insists that rhetorical invention pertains to logical disputation—and this provides solid proof that what he means by invention includes both dialectical and rhetorical invention. On the other hand, he explains that judgment—as a functional activity of rhetoric—pertains to evaluation of arguments and, thus, quite certainly represents logical judgment as traditionally conceived in dialectic. Accordingly, Cox, like Melanchthon, installs both functional elements of dialectic—invention and judgment—as parts in the theoretical apparatus of rhetoric.

I now turn to the second Renaissance position on the relation of rhetoric and logic—one which completely dissociates logic from rhetoric. The dissociative position received its most systematic and influential expression in the works of Peter Ramus and Omer Talon. Ramus' position on the relation of logic and rhetoric was worked out perhaps as early as 1543, when he published *Dialecticae Institutiones* and *Aristotelicae Animadversiones*. In these works he began a critique of discursive arts that allocated invention, judgment, and memory to dialectic; assigning expression and delivery to rhetoric (see Ramus and Talon 1599, 14–16; cf. Conley 1990, 128; Howell 1956, 148–49). We see the consequences of this critique quite clearly in the *Rhetorica* of Omer Talon in 1548. Early in this work, Talon—likely in collaboration with Ramus (see Ong 1958b, 82–5)—is at pains to divide logic from rhetoric along Ramistic lines:

> There are two parts of rhetoric: Style (*elocutio*) and Delivery (*pronuntiatio*); these are of course the only parts, the ones proper to the art, and so for the sake

of clear and easy teaching you should distinguish the general and common principles of Grammar, Rhetoric, and Dialectic, and not mix in matters foreign to each discipline. Each is marked off by its own proper ends: Grammar, through its four parts of etymology, syntax, prosody and orthography, will safeguard clear and correct speech; Dialectic will furnish the invention and disposition of matters, and through its disposition will provide the concomitant of memory; Rhetoric therefore will keep this particular task, that it takes the matter found and related by Dialectic, and laid out in clear and correct speech by Grammar, and then embellishes it with the splendor of the ornaments of style, and renders it acceptable with the grace of vocal tone and gesture.[6] (translated by Murphy, 1986, 27–28)

Following Ramus' intellectual program, the Talaean *Rhetorica* here specifies a relationship between logic and rhetoric which dissociates the two arts absolutely and permanently.

This brings me to the third position on the relationship between logic and rhetoric—one which associates logic and rhetoric within a larger framework of arts. Of course, I mean here the position of Francis Bacon as presented first in his *On the Proficience and Aduancement of Learning, Diuine and Humane* of 1605. In *Proficience,* book 2, Bacon addresses rhetoric within his more general account of the rational arts. These arts he introduces as follows (2: 48r):

---

[6] Partes eius duae sunt, Elocutio et Pronuntiatio: hae siquidem solae sunt, et propriae artis huius partes: nam si Grammaticam, Rhetoricam, Dialecticam generales et communes disciplinas: ita, ut ad facilè docendum, et perspicuè decet, distinxeris, ut non commisceantur alienis inter se praeceptis, sed suis et propriis finibus contineantur: Grammatica ex quatuor partibus, etimologia, syntaxi, prosodia, ortographia proprium et purum sermonem praestabit: Dialectica inuentionem re∥rum, et dispositionem, dispositionísque comitem memoriam suppeditabit: Rhetorica igitur hoc sibi proprium solum retinebit, ut res à Dialectica repertas et collocatus, à Grammatica autem puro et proprio sermone expositas, elocutionis ornamentis magnificentius expoliat, et pronuntiationis et actionis gratia commendet. (Talon 1549, 5–6) The 1549 edition quoted here has "[c]ontents and arrangement quite the same as in the 1548 *Rhetorica*" (Ong 1954b, 91–2).

> The ARTS INTELLECTUAL, are foure in number, diuided according to the ends whereunto they are referred: for mans labour is to *inuent* that which is *sought* or *propounded:* or to *iudge* that which is *inuented:* or to *retaine* that which is *iudged:* or to *deliuer* ouer that which is *retained*. So as the Arts must bee foure: ARTS of ENQUIRIE or INVENTION: ART of EXAMINATION or IVDGEMENT: ART of CVSTODIE or MEMORIE: and ART of ELOCUTION or TRADITION.

Now, with reference to these arts Bacon conceives invention as related to "arts and sciences" and to "speech and arguments." The former he allots to logic, but the latter—at least in part—he says is shared between logic and rhetoric (2: 52v). Judgment for Bacon is the sole province of logic. But when he arrives at custody, he insists that written custody is dependent on grammar and the method of commonplacing, while mental custody depends on an art of memory that many readers must have recognized as rhetorical (2: 57v–59r). It is in the treatment of tradition that Bacon eventually arrives at rhetoric itself. He distinguishes tradition into organ, method, and illustration. The organ or medium of tradition Bacon assigns principally to grammar, but he also mentions symbology and even discusses cryptology. Method, which he conceives as discursive organization, is aligned with logic (2: 61v). Finally, the illustration of tradition Bacon assigns to rhetoric. But the sort of luster he thinks that rhetoric provides is not strictly ornamental; it is also substantive and psychological. "The dutie and Office of Rhetoric is," he says, "To apply Reason to Imagination, for the better moving of the will" (2: 66v). And he explains this observation with some precision (2: 67rv):

> Reason would become Captiue and seruile, if *Eloquence of Perswasions,* did not practise and winne the *Imagination,* from the *affections* part, and contract a Confederacie betweene the *Reason* and *Imagination,* against the *Affections:* For the Affections themselues, carrie euer an appetite to good, as Reason doth: The difference is, *That the Affection beholdeth merely the present; Reason beholdeth the future, and summe of time.* And therefore, the *Present,* filling the *Imagination* more; *Reason* is commonly vanquished; But after

that force of *Eloquence* and *perswasion*, hath made things *future*, and *remote*, appeare as *present*, than vppon the reuolt of the Imagination, Reason preuayleth.

Crucial here is Bacon's insistence that rhetoric provides a special and functional address to reason. The nature of this address he clarifies as follows (2: 67v):

> It appeareth also, that *Logicke* differeth from *Rhetoricke*, not only as the *fist*, from the *pawme*, the one close, the other at large; but much more in this, that *Logicke* handleth Reason exacte, and in truth; and *Rhetoricke* handleth it, as it is planted in popular opinions and Manners.

The upshot is that even in its circumscribed role as illustration of tradition, rhetoric's relation to logic is complementary and in some ways symmetrical (cf. Vickers 1996, 208–10). Not only that, but both arts are associated with other discursive arts, each of which is essential to Bacon's scheme of the arts intellectual and, more generally, his conception of purposive communication.

II

To this point I have argued that the Renaissance produced at least three positions on the relation of rhetoric to logic; specifically, I have characterized the Melanchthon/Cox position as absorbing logic into rhetoric, the Ramus/Talon position as dissociating logic from rhetoric, and the Bacon position as associating logic with rhetoric and other discursive arts. Despite the novelty of these positions in Renaissance times, my contention is that they recapitulate ancient positions on the relationship between rhetoric and philosophy. Accordingly, in what follows I would like briefly to sketch instances of ancient rhetorical theory that apparently anticipate the strategies of absorption, dissociation, and association evident in the relevant Renaissance works. For purposes of exposition, I would like to reverse my original order of treatment of theoretical strategies.

I begin with the strategy of association. From the fourth century onward, ancient rhetoric and philosophy were separated by theoretical precept and pedagogical inclination. In fact the two disciplines engaged in a centuries-long feud over the scope, use, and artistic status of the rhetorical discipline. Among these issues, it was perhaps the scope of rhetoric that inspired the most significant debate. As early as Plato's *Gorgias*, the competence of rhetorical speakers to discuss philosophical subjects was questioned. And by the second century BCE, it was a standard view in the philosophical schools that important subjects such as the gods, friendship, virtue, and even political science were out of the reach of rhetorical speakers because they did not pertain to rhetoric. This view was still current in mid-first century when Cicero constructed a kind of response to the philosophers in his *De Oratore*. But rather than argue that rhetoric extended to subjects beyond court cases and legislative debates, Cicero here proposes that it is the speaker's knowledge which ranges fully over important subjects. Of course, such a range would require broad training, but Cicero embraces this requirement early in the first book (1.20): "[C]ertainly in my view," he says, "no one will be able to be an orator abounding in every excellence, unless he will have acquired knowledge of all great matters and arts."[7] (translated by Gaines 1995, 46)

An immediate implication of Cicero's characterization is that the ideal orator combines the eloquence available from rhetoric with the substantive knowledge available from philosophy and the other arts. In book 3 he pursues this implication in a polemical comparison of the orator and philosopher (3.143):

> If we ask what one thing is pre-eminent out of all, first place must be given to the learned orator; whom if they grant him also to be a philosopher, the controversy is eliminated. But if they separate them, they will be inferior in this, that all the knowledge of those men is present in the complete orator, however eloquence is not necessarily present in the knowledge of the philosophers; which eloquence, although it is despised by them, nonetheless, must needs be understood to add a certain consummation to the arts of those men.[8] (translated by Gaines 1995, 54)

---

[7] ac mea quidem sententia nemo poterit esse omni laude cumulatus orator, nisi erit omnium rerum magnarum atque artium scientiam consecutus. (Cic. *De orat*. 1.20, edited by Kumaniecki 1969)

[8] si quaerimus quid unum excellat ex omnibus, docto oratori palma danda est; quem si patiuntur eundem esse philosophum, sublata controversia

Now, the consummation to which Cicero refers in this passage is the ability to persuade about the subject. Accordingly, the conclusion I draw from the passage is that for Cicero the ability to persuade on any subject arose only through the practical combination of rhetoric, philosophy, and/or other important arts. Thus, anticipating Bacon, his position associates these arts in a broad theory of purposive communication.

This brings me to the strategy of dissociation. Around the time that Cicero published *De Oratore*, there was at work in southern Italy an Epicurean philosopher named Philodemus. The Epicureans had a rich tradition of opposition to rhetoric and Philodemus participated in this tradition with a polemical treatise *On Rhetoric* in at least eight books.[9] Within book 4 of this treatise, Philodemus critically addresses what others say are the parts and precepts of rhetoric, including invention, arrangement, style, and delivery. What is characteristic about Philodemus' position is that he attempts to isolate rhetoric within its disciplinary boundaries. For example, he denies that rhetoric is capable of inventing arguments on any subject but rhetoric (Sudhaus 1892, 1: 206 24a.26–207 25a.14):

> It is sufficient to say this much now, that there are certain things concerning indefinite and definite matters for each art and science, by reason of which it is for each singly to invent the possible arguments for single sciences taken individually, just as there are for rhetors definite and indefinite matters with respect to rhetoric; contention [by rhetoric] with any of the other arts sets up standards mad as Margites.[10]

---

est. sin eos diiungent, hoc erunt inferiores, quod in oratore perfecto inest illorum omnis scientia, in philosophorum autem cognitione non continuo inest eloquentia; quae quamquam contemnatur ab eis, necesse est tamen aliquem cumulum illorum artibus adferre videatur. (Cic. *De orat.* 3.143, edited by Kumaniecki 1969)

[9] Until recently, the standard view was that Philodemus' *On Rhetoric* comprised seven books (see Dorandi 1990). But Francesa Longo Auricchio (1995) has shown on papyrological grounds that the work must have contained at least eight books and may have contained as many as ten books.

[10] *to de tosouto kai nun eipein [a]po||xrê, di[o]ti ka[ta] tekhnên kai mathêsin hekastên e[s]t[i] tina kai peri aoristôn ka[i] peri hôrismenôn, huper [hon] hekaterou tous endekhomenous exeurein logous monôn esti tôn ka[th'] hekastên epistêm[o]nôn, hôste kai peri rhêtorôn ta kata tên rhêtorikê[n] hôrismena kai a <o>*

He likewise denies that rhetoric is in a position to judge arguments outside the narrow orbit of what appears to the many. The following argument on judging true and false arguments is typical (1: 208 27a.10–209 27a.17):

> And much more generally, since it follows that the true arguments are relevant, [but] not the false and groundless [ones], it is necessary that [rhetors] exercise judgment regarding the true and false, of which [thing] they are lacking much more than feathers.[11]

In all, Philodemus isolates rhetorical practice from the other arts in invention (including discovery and judgment), arrangement of discourse parts, and delivery (cf. Gaines 1985, 156–8, 162). And while his position may not be as radical and reductive as that proposed by Ramus and Talon, it nevertheless serves as a theoretical precedent for dissociating rhetoric from philosophy and the other arts.

I now turn to the strategy of absorption. The dispute between rhetoric and philosophy that animated Cicero and Philodemus lasted at least long enough for Quintilian to participate. Quintilian's addition to the dispute was to insist that any art which contributed to the education of an orator belonged to rhetoric (cf. Gaines 1997, 475). His position on this point is clear in the Preface to Book 1 where he writes as follows (10–11):

> For, I will not concede, as some have thought, that the theory of upright and honorable life ought to be relegated to the philosophers, when the man who is truly a citizen and capable of administering matters both public and private, who can rule cities with his

---

rista; to de tôn allôn tinos antipoieisthai margeitomanias horous histêsi[n]. (Phld. *Rh.*, edited by Sudhaus 1: 206 24a.26–207 25a.14; here and elsewhere in quoted texts, letters underlined represent equivocal traces in the papyrological evidence, letters in angle brackets represent editorial insertions); Margites (literally "Madman") was the central character in a comedic poem ascribed to Homer (see Arist. *Po.* 4.12 [1448b]).

[11] *Kai mallon de koin[o]teron; epei tous alêtheis eneinai sumbebêken, oukhi tous pseud[ei]s [k]ai [m]atai[o]us, anagkê krisin autous ekhein ta[lê]thous te kai pseudous, h[o]u polu mallon ê pter[ô]n endeousin.* (Phld. *Rh.*, P. Herc. 1007 col. 27a.12 *epei* P: *e[i] ti* Sudhaus; otherwise, Sudhaus 1: 208 27a.10–209 27a.17)

counsels, found [them] with laws, and correct [them] with judgments, [when this man] is assuredly none other that the orator. [10|11] Wherefore, even if certain things, which are contained in books by philosophers, shall be of use to me, nonetheless I shall contend that they justly and truly belong to my work and pertain particularly to the art of oratory.[12]

Lest we misunderstand, Quintilian specifies this property claim with special reference to philosophy later in Book 12 (12.2.10):

Since philosophy is divided in three parts, natural, moral, and logical, which of these is not combined with the work of the orator?[13]

Upon any interpretation, I think it clear that Quintilian's position absorbs the whole of philosophy into rhetoric. Accordingly, I believe he anticipates the absorption of logic into rhetoric by Melanchthon and Cox in the early Renaissance.

My conclusion is brief. In arguing that Renaissance positions on the relation of rhetoric and logic have precedents in ancient rhetorical theory, my intention is not to denigrate the one or elevate the other. Rather, I am simply trying to point out a force that motivated theoretical development in both Ancient and Renaissance rhetoric. Specifically, in both eras, innovation in rhetoric arose in response to disciplinary conflict over the rights to discuss scientific knowledge. The authority for scientific knowledge in ancient times was philosophy and by Renaissance times it was logic. Both disciplinary authorities were bound to engage in dispute with rhetoric, since rhetoric claimed to invent, organize, express, and manifest propositions and arguments on

---

[12] Neque enim hoc concesserim, rationem rectae honestaeque uitae, ut quidam putauerunt, ad philosophos relegandam, cum uir ille uere ciuilis et publicarum priuatarumque rerum administrationi accommodatus, qui regere consiliis urbes, fundare legibus, emendare iudiciis possit, non alius sit profecto quam orator. [10|11] Quare, tametsi me fateor usurum quibusdam quae philosophorum libris continentur, tamen ea iure uereque contenderim esse operis nostri proprieque ad artem oratoriam pertinere. (Quint. *Inst.* 1: Pr. 10–11, edited by Winterbottom 1970)

[13] Quae quidem cum sit in tris diuisa partis, naturalem moralem rationalem, qua tandem non est cum oratoris opere coniuncta? (Quint. *Inst.* 12.2.10, edited by Winterbottom 1970)

all subjects. The positions arrived at in the two eras represent the most obvious strategies for resolution of this conflict, namely, absorption of the authority in rhetoric, dissociation of rhetoric from the authority, and association of rhetoric with the authority in practical application. As historians of rhetoric, we should attend to the intellectual forces that shape the idea of rhetoric in every era. And intellectual forces that cross eras should have a special place in our practice; for they may serve as heuristics for yet undiscovered structures in the theoretical development of rhetoric.

22 Walter Pater and the Rhetorical Tradition: Finding Common Sense in the Particular

Lois Peters Agnew

Thomas Carlyle's 1834 claim that the time must come when "one leaves the pasteboard coulisses, and three unities, and Blair's Lectures, quite behind"[1] signals a nineteenth-century turn away from the search for collective judgment associated with the classical rhetorical tradition. This trend continues throughout the century, achieving particular force under the auspices of the aesthetic movement and its focus on intense personal aesthetic experiences above language directed toward the resolution of specific social concerns. One of the central emblems of this intellectual departure from the rhetorical tradition has been Walter Pater. As a leading advocate of the inherent subjectivity of aesthetic experience, Pater's views have generally been assumed to characterize a radical introspection that has little to do with the "common sense" rhetoricians whose thought helped to shape British rhetoric a century before. However, in spite of its unique features, Pater's work can be seen as part of a long tradition, extending through the belletristic rhetoricians of the eighteenth century backward to Cicero and Isocrates, that perceives expression to possess a socially redemptive power. Pater is a dominant influence on the aesthetic movement's perception that the value of art lies not in its representation of an existing objective reality, but in its creation of a higher form of subjective knowledge developed through intense momentary experiences that lead the individual to greater self-awareness. However, as *Plato*

---

[1] Thomas Carlyle, "To Ralph Waldo Emerson," 12 August 1834, in Volume One of *The Correspondence of Thomas Carlyle and Ralph Waldo Emerson, 1834–1872*, 22.

and Platonism reveals, Pater balances the radical subjectivity he most famously advocates in *The Renaissance* with an implicit belief in the power of language to preserve community, a view that reveals a striking ideological affinity between the rhetorical tradition and the final stages of the aesthetic movement.

Pater's radicalism is evident in one of his earliest and most controversial works, *The Renaissance* (1873), which Gerald Monsman and Samuel Wright characterize as "the manifesto of the Aesthetic Movement."[2] That text reveals Pater's determination to immerse himself in the redemptive intensity of immediate experience. This momentary and intensely personal notion of aesthetic experience represents a marked departure from the social orientation of the rhetorical tradition. Pater's notion that beauty must be experienced rather than merely discussed as an abstract ideal assumes that each individual possesses a vital role in the aesthetic transformation of society, but that transformation begins with an individual who makes judgments that are completely independent of others. Pater begins his "Preface to *The Renaissance*" by stating his agreement with Matthew Arnold's belief that the goal of criticism is "to see the object as in itself it really is," but he adds that it is only possible to achieve such a certain sense of that object through determining the impression it makes on oneself. The facts that lie within the critic's province are therefore derived from questions about his or her own impressions of the art object:

> What is this song or picture, this engaging personality presented in life or in a book, *to me*? What effect does it really produce on me? Does it give me pleasure? and if so, what sort of degree of pleasure? How is my nature modified by its presence, and under its influence?[3]

A number of critics have noted the crucial alteration of Arnold's doctrine of criticism that Pater makes in this passage, from one that emphasizes the critic's obligation to come to terms with art as an objective external reality to one that instead defines the critic's encounter with art in purely subjective terms. Pater's doctrine clearly leaves room for this interpretation, as he insists that criticism must be viewed as a soli-

---

[2] Gerald Monsman and Samuel Wright, "Walter Pater: Style and Text," 113.

[3] Walter Pater, *The Renaissance: Studies in Art and Poetry*, viii.

tary endeavor, placing individuals in "intellectual isolation" from each other.[4] Pater further reinforces the idea that criticism is essentially a solitary enterprise in summarizing Hegel's view that the Greeks can be considered free because they "have grown up on the soil of their own individuality, creating themselves out of themselves, and moulding themselves to what they were, and willed to be."[5] Art provides the spark that enables people to rejuvenate themselves and to preserve the power of this dynamic individuality through a heightened awareness of their sensory experiences; the artist is one who "steeps his thought again and again into the fire of colour,"[6] having achieved the ability to submerge "his intellectual and spiritual ideas in sensuous form."[7] Pater's vision compels him to show people how their awakened senses can attune them to the full range of experiences that art provides.

It is this same quality of intense individual experience that Pater advocates in the "Conclusion" to *The Renaissance*, the powerfully influential document Steven Marcus refers to as the "specimen text of modernism."[8] Pater stresses the value of experience for its own sake, insisting upon the need to replace the pursuit of theories and conventional knowledge with "the splendour of our experience and of its awful brevity, gathering all we are into one desperate effort to see and touch."[9] Pater's famous line, "To burn always with this hard, gemlike flame, to maintain this ecstasy, is success in life,"[10] has rightly come to be viewed as a summation of his own subjective approach to aestheticism and as the starting point for Oscar Wilde's even more radical view that an individual's experience with art transcends life and therefore cannot be prescribed by any objective standards whatsoever.

However, Pater's emphasis on the subjective experience of the individual should not be viewed as a complete departure from the social objectives advanced within the aesthetic theories that preceded his. For Pater, the cultivation of the senses creates a new version of aestheticism's political function as he asserts that the transformation of an oppressive social order can best be effected through the force of the individual personality. Linda Dowling observes that Pater envi-

---

[4] Pater, *Renaissance*, x.
[5] Pater, *Renaissance*, 219.
[6] Pater, *Renaissance*, 221.
[7] Pater, *Renaissance*, 221.
[8] Steven Marcus, "Conceptions of the Self in an Age of Progress," 445.
[9] Pater, *Renaissance*, 237.
[10] Pater, *Renaissance*, 236.

sions "the social transformation of Victorian life through an enlarged and emboldened sensuousness—his own version of the liberal ideal of aesthetic democracy."[11] Wolhee Choe agrees with this principle in arguing that, although Pater attempted to counter the prevailing belief that art should be didactic, "he insisted, throughout his life, on the ultimate affinities, not to say identities, between the processes by which art affects us and mature moral judgment is cultivated."[12] This view is apparent in *Marius the Epicurean*, where Pater describes the way in which an aesthetic education provides the ideal means of developing an individual's natural moral sense:

> the products of the imagination must themselves be held to present the most perfect forms of life—spirit and matter, alike, under their purest and most perfect conditions—the most strictly appropriate object of that impassioned contemplation, which, in the world of intellectual discipline, as in the highest forms of morality and religion, must be held to be the essential function of the "perfect."[13]

In spite of Pater's deviation from central principles of Arnold's cultural theory, he preserves the basic sense that aesthetic experience has a social and historical significance that ultimately transcends the boundaries of individual experience.

One of the modifications that Pater places upon the autonomy of the individual comes about through his respect for scientific method, which places the individual's observations within an external realm of knowledge. However, like the aesthetic theorists and rhetoricians who preceded him, Pater sees individual experience as serving a more important function than simply providing the most scientific basis for artistic judgment. Pater shares the distress over the mechanical nature of industrial society that had been expressed by aesthetic theorists extending back to De Quincey and Carlyle. His praise of Wordsworth's poetry centers upon his judgment that it offers a protest "against the predominance of machinery in our existence."[14] In his essay on Coleridge, he reinforces earlier views that this prevalence of machinery

---

[11] Linda Dowling, *The Vulgarization of Art*, 76.
[12] Wolhee Choe, "Walter Pater's 'Romantic Morality,'" 12.
[13] Walter Pater, *Marius the Epicurean*, 159.
[14] Walter Pater, *Essays on Literature and Art*, 115.

in turn creates a society ruled by monotony, as he writes, "The dominant tendency of life is to turn ascertained truth into a dead letter—to make us all the phlegmatic servants of routine."[15] For Pater, promoting the relative spirit "begets an intellectual finesse"[16] that prompts the individual to the acute perception that reconfigures and ultimately overcomes the mechanical precision of daily life.

Pater's assertion that proper aesthetic training develops the imaginative intuition and ultimately leads the individual to achieve a higher sensibility that transcends the sordidness of society resonates with classical and belletristic perspectives in addition to the ideas of nineteenth-century theorists. In an 1887 letter to George Moore, Pater writes that "the object of art is to help us forget the crude and the violent, to lead us towards certain normal aspects of nature."[17] In spite of what are at times the radical terms with which Pater expresses his doctrine of experience, in principle his thought parallels the insights of Longinus and the Stoics as he advances the claim that the individual's sensory impressions can be used to refine the intuition and develop that which is finest in human nature, an activity that in turn provides the basis for strengthening society as a whole.

Like earlier aesthetic theorists, Pater preserves certain fundamental elements of earlier traditions even as he offers new theoretical insights that reflect his own particular perspective and cultural situation. In pointing to the limits of Pater's radicalism, Hough notes, "Like other sceptics before him, Pater is forced to rebuild with different materials the edifice he has just destroyed: like Hume he is destroying our supposed intellectual certainties in order to replace them by the authority of feeling."[18]

Through replacing what he perceives to be the constraints of a formal system of metaphysics with the authority of feeling, Pater's thought is not that far removed from belletristic rhetorical theory. Linda Dowling states that Pater's vision of the sensory power of art involved liberating aesthetic experience from "the dreary spell of philosophical aesthetics,"[19] a mission that closely parallels the stated objectives of the

---

[15] Pater, *Essays*, 26.

[16] Pater, *Essays*, 26.

[17] Pater, "To George Moore," c. 3 August 1887, in *Letters of Walter Pater*, edited by Lawrence Evans, 74.

[18] Graham Hough, *The Last Romantics*, 140.

[19] Linda Dowling, *The Vulgarization of Art*, 85.

Scottish common sense philosophers who helped to shape the principles of belletristic rhetoric. She further notes that Pater's

> "unphilosophical" project . . . demands to be understood in philosophical terms as the continuation, by the "unphilosophical" means of fiction and belles lettres, of the democratic project found within the Common Sense tradition of Shaftesbury, George Berkeley, and Thomas Reid . . . .[20]

Jennifer Uglow depicts Pater's belief in the validity of the imaginative intuition as existing in strict opposition to "the rational philosophy and codified standards of taste of the eighteenth century,"[21] but the standards of taste were not as prescriptive or rationalistic in the eighteenth century as many critics familiar with later applications of the term have come to assume. In fact, Pater's opposition to existing metaphysical systems and his perception that the individual's intuitive sense develops and can be refined through experiences with art is in many respects similar to the view of belletristic rhetoricians, whose philosophical perspectives reflect the influence of Scottish common sense.

Dowling argues that Pater's willingness to describe the individual's intuitive development as an insular process removed from the influence of public life does represent a departure from belletristic rhetorical theory. She describes Kant's "assumption that taste judgments are in a vital sense public—that they are subjectively universal, or true for everybody"[22] as a principle he inherited "more or less unreflectingly from Shaftesbury and the Scottish Common Sense school."[23] She then contrasts Pater's insistence upon giving absolute authority to the individual's sensory experience ("What is this song . . . *to me?*") with this long-established tradition that assumes that the transformation of society can be effected through that aesthetic sense that is universally shared by all individuals.

Dowling aptly notes that Pater's dramatic turn toward subjectivity in the famous italicized phrase "*to me*" constitutes a shift away from

---

[20] Dowling, *The Vulgarization of Art*, 82.

[21] Jennifer Uglow, "Introduction," in *Essays on Literature and Art*, vii–xxiii (ix).

[22] Dowling, *The Vulgarization of Art*, 82.

[23] Dowling, *The Vulgarization of Art*, 82.

previous assumptions that universal and objective judgments about art are possible. The continued development of industrial society and Pater's particular position within that society led him to hold a less optimistic view of the capacity of all individuals to share a common aesthetic experience. However, the radical perspective the "Conclusion" offers is only a partial accounting of Pater's aesthetic theory. An examination of his philosophy as represented in one of his later texts, *Plato and Platonism*, reveals the way in which Pater continues to preserve the ideal of *sensus communis* even as his unique theoretical perspective leads him to vary the angle from which he approaches that goal.

Pater begins his interpretation of Plato's philosophy with the assertion that all philosophical principles have complex origins that can only be traced through recognizing the importance of the form in which those ideas are expressed,[24] a view that reflects Pater's persistent claim that to focus on particularity inevitably provides insights into the nature of the general. All modern concepts can therefore be seen to have roots in Antiquity, but to achieve their full realization later, "by good favour of the special intellectual conditions belonging to a particular generation, which, on a sudden, finds itself preoccupied by a formula, not so much new, as renovated by new application."[25] Pater applies this cyclical view of history in the particular case of the Renaissance, which he describes as an era in which "the human mind wins for itself a new kingdom of feeling and sensation and thought, not opposed to but only beyond and independent of the spiritual system then actually realized."[26] His effort involves reconstructing Platonic thought as a precursor to later interests in the aesthetic, identifying Plato as an ancient source of an idealized vision that he believes to have come to a more complete fruition due to the unique developments of his own age.

In appropriating Plato to support his own aesthetic vision, Pater describes *The Republic* as an attempt to establish a more certain reality in the form of "a very exclusive community, which shall be a refuge for elect souls from an ill-made world,"[27] an insulated environment that significantly mirrors both Pater's own academic community and the enclosed intellectual circle of the aesthetic movement. He acknowledg-

---

[24] Walter Pater, *Plato and Platonism*, 1–4.
[25] Pater, *Plato and Platonism*, 13.
[26] Pater, *Renaissance*, 7.
[27] Pater, *Plato and Platonism*, 17.

es that the circumstances of ancient life create a version of scepticism that emphasizes the importance of reason over sensation, which is the reverse of the tendency of the modern age. Describing modern scepticism as "an appeal from the preconceptions of the understanding to the authority of the senses,"[28] Pater adds that, for the Greeks, "whose metaphysic business was then still all to do, the sceptical action of the mind lay rather in the direction of an appeal from the affirmation of sense to the authority of newly awakened reason."[29] He explains Plato's "theory of ideas" as an effort to respond to the need to move from the world of sense to reason, to impose a conception of the finite on the formlessness of human experience.[30]

In contrast to most accounts of Platonic philosophy, Pater insists that the apparent finitude of Plato's philosophical system is not intended to be a method for arriving at certain truth. He identifies Plato's dialectic method as a process that reflects the "reasoning of the mind with itself."[31] Although such a process ultimately defies the acquisition of certain knowledge, Pater asserts that "the search for truth is a better thing for us than its possession."[32] Although he acknowledges the fact that Plato explicitly insists upon certainty, he adds, "he does think, or inclines his reader to think, that truth, precisely because it resembles some high kind of relationship of persons to persons, depends a good deal on the receiver."[33] Thus Pater maintains that, even for Plato, "philosophic truth consists in the philosophic temper,"[34] and maintains a subjective vector that emphasizes the process of seeking truth over the final judgment that is reached. He further identifies Cicero and Marcus Aurelius as later Latin proponents of this "philosophic temper" that earlier served as the foundation of Plato's Academy. Pater's unconventional interpretation of Plato's dialectic method is also manifested in his reconfiguration of Plato's search for a higher order. Pater recognizes that this quest for an eternal reality led Plato to oppose the fluidity and practicality of the Sophists.[35] However, he maintains that Plato's writings reveal the fact that his determination to establish order is the

---

[28] Pater, *Plato and Platonism*, 25.
[29] Pater, *Plato and Platonism*, 25.
[30] Pater, *Plato and Platonism*, 52.
[31] Pater, *Plato and Platonism*, 164.
[32] Pater, *Plato and Platonism*, 167.
[33] Pater, *Plato and Platonism*, 167–168.
[34] Pater, *Plato and Platonism*, 168.
[35] Pater, *Plato and Platonism*, 94.

result of "a variously interested, a richly sensuous nature."[36] In spite of Plato's concern with the world of forms, Pater argues that the visible world "really existed for him: exists still—there's the point!—is active still everywhere, when he seems to have turned away from it to invisible things."[37] He defines "the *formula* of Plato's genius" as the ability to bring that visible reality into the abstract realm that forms the basis of his philosophy,[38] an action that is created through his own writing style: "He breaks as it were visible colour into the very texture of his work: his vocabulary . . . has its delightful aesthetic qualities; almost every word, one might say, its figurative value."[39] Because Pater is convinced of the intrinsic relationship between thought and language,[40] he feels confident of his ability to characterize Platonic thought in a new way through viewing Plato's use of language as direct evidence of the workings of his mind.

Through connecting Plato's language use with latent sensuality, Pater identifies Platonism as a proponent of "imaginative reason,"[41] a major factor in "the redemption of matter, of the world of sense, by art, by all right education, by the creeds and worship of the Christian Church—towards the vindication of the dignity of the body."[42] He denies that Platonism can be considered a formal philosophical system, and instead chooses to define it as "a tendency" that relates the essence of individual experiences to "general forms."[43] He then further explains this Platonic connection between individual experience and the life of humanity in its totality:

> there is a general consciousness, a permanent common sense, independent indeed of each one of us, but with which we are, each one of us, in communication. It is in that, those common or general ideas really reside. And we might add just here . . . that those abstract or common notions come to the individual mind through language, through common or gener-

---

[36] Pater, *Plato and Platonism*, 113.
[37] Pater, *Plato and Platonism*, 113.
[38] Pater, *Plato and Platonism*, 125.
[39] Pater, *Plato and Platonism*, 125.
[40] Pater, *Plato and Platonism*, 127.
[41] Pater, *Plato and Platonism*, 126.
[42] Pater, *Plato and Platonism*, 131.
[43] Pater, *Plato and Platonism*, 134.

al names, *Animal, Justice, Equality,* into which one's individual experience, little by little, drop by drop, conveys their full meaning or content . . . between our individual experience and the common experience of our kind, we come to understand each other, and to assist each other's thoughts, as in a common mental atmosphere, an "intellectual world," as Plato calls it . . . .[44]

In spite of the fact that his aesthetic theory moves away from the social interaction associated with the rhetorical tradition, Pater's thought in this passage reverts to an assumption central to the rhetorical tradition: the "common sense" that binds people together is formed and defined through language. Although Pater acknowledges the modern world's disdain for the universals upon which Plato's idealism is based, he nevertheless asserts that in the nineteenth century, generalization has continued to enrich concrete experiences with the significance of external principles that provide isolated events with greater meaning.[45]

Pater's analysis of Plato's thought by implication connects his view of beauty with a "common sense" that connects particular individuals to each other. He insists that Plato departs from Socrates's view that ideas are formed through human reason in order to suggest that ideas themselves form human reason, as "those treasures of experience, stacked and stored, which, to each one of us, come as by inheritance . . ."[46] He also asserts that Plato perceives Beauty to be central to the formation of this system of ideas, as it provides a permanent representation of those thoughts that generate insight on the part of individuals and ultimately of humanity as a whole. He aligns what he characterizes as Plato's search for artistic perfection[47] to the natural appreciation for harmony that connects aesthetic experience to the human love of Justice—a concept that directly echoes the Stoic system of ethics, which through Cicero becomes an indirect force in shaping the persistent interest in style evident throughout the history of British rhetoric.

Lesley Higgins describes Pater's appropriation of Plato as part of a general Victorian trend to become "energetic cultural 'imperialists,'

---

[44] Pater, *Plato and Platonism,* 135–136.
[45] Pater, *Plato and Platonism,* 142.
[46] Pater, *Plato and Platonism,* 149.
[47] Pater, *Plato and Platonism,* 241–242.

inscribing in their accounts of previous civilizations' attitudes and values near and dear to their own nineteenth-century hearts."[48] She notes that Pater's interpretation of Plato pits him against his former teacher and ideological enemy, Benjamin Jowett, in an "intense intellectual and ideological struggle for control over the Platonic canon,"[49] and further notes that Pater's particular interest in reclaiming for Plato's philosophy "a politics of desire"[50] occasionally involves him in misconstructions of Plato's work. Whether or not Pater's reading of Plato can be regarded as strictly accurate, the details of his reading significantly highlight specific elements of his aesthetic theory that connect him to earlier rhetorical traditions. Although Pater's call for a personal judgment of what the work of art means "*to me*" appears to deny criticism any social function, he at the same time recognizes that "individual genius works ever under conditions of time and place: its products are coloured by the varying aspects of nature, and type of human form, and outward manners of life."[51] In addition to the changing public standards that help to shape the workings of genius, Pater allows that genius must also accommodate "an element of permanence, a standard of taste."[52] His notion that an individual's aesthetic experiences provide the foundation for the development of a common inner sense that is naturally related to other people within the community and across time also ties Pater's aesthetic theory to the ethical philosophy shared by Isocrates, Cicero, the Stoics, Shaftesbury, and the belletristic rhetorics informed by Scottish common sense philosophy.

In spite of his reputation as the instigator of a radically subjective approach to aesthetic criticism, Pater can in some sense be seen as a participant in the ongoing British search for *sensus communis*. Like many of his contemporaries, Pater abandoned hope for the formal systems that had at one time provided the basis for instilling civic virtue. However, his view that the senses must be trained to provide for the intense inwardness that can lead to a revelation of more general knowledge can be seen as closely related to the Stoic view that a moral society is formed by those whose highly conscious inner life enables them to transcend the corruption of government. Like his hero Marius, Pater

---

[48] Lesley Higgins, "Jowett and Pater," 43–72.
[49] Higgins, 44.
[50] Higgins, 45.
[51] Pater, *Renaissance*, 199.
[52] Pater, *Renaissance*, 199.

pursues not pleasure for its own sake, but "fulness of life," which places highest value on "sincere and strenuous forms of the moral life, as Seneca and Epictetus—whatever form of human life, in short, was impassioned and ideal."[53] Such an "impassioned and ideal" vision of aesthetic experience also serves as the controlling image of *Plato and Platonism*. At the conclusion of that work, Pater describes Plato's own aesthetic vision as "dry beauty," marked by an "irrepressible conscience of art."[54] The final sentence, "And the dry beauty,—let Plato teach us, to love that also, duly,"[55] may not exactly capture Plato's own perception of his aesthetic philosophy, but it does position Pater within the long rhetorical tradition that assumes that there is ultimately a connection between ethics and aesthetic expression. In spite of the radical claims he advances in *The Renaissance*, Pater's view of language modifies his belief that individuals achieve their creative potential in isolation from others. In insisting that great art must be devoted "to the increase of men's happiness, to the redemption of the oppressed, or the enlargement of our sympathies with each other, or to such presentment of new or old truth about ourselves and our relation to the world as may ennoble and fortify us in our sojourn here . . ."[56] Pater preserves the voices of Cicero and the Enlightenment rhetoricians even within the radical aestheticism of the *fin-de-siècle*.

---

[53] Pater, *Marius*, 163.
[54] Pater, *Plato and Platonism*, 255.
[55] Pater, *Plato and Platonism*, 256.
[56] Pater, "Style," in *Appreciations, with an Essay on Style* (London: Macmillan, 1910), 5–38 (38).

23 Contemporary Pedagogy for Classical Rhetoric: Averting the Reductionism of Classical Opposition

David Timmerman

As one who teaches various periods in the history of rhetoric, I often find myself struggling with a gut level impulse to turn my presentation of historical material into a ripping good story. I also find that this is the case with many treatments of the history of rhetorical theory and rhetorical practice as they developed in classical Greece. While this makes for an engaging experience for those who read or hear such presentations, I contend that such treatments do a disservice to the classical period and to students of it. Ultimately, they reduce a rich history to a narrative that, while it is intuitively satisfying and even memorable, hides and distorts far too much. In particular, such narratives often describe this history as a series of oppositions, which find their resolution in Aristotle. Such a treatment encourages us to skew the work of pre-Aristotelian sources to fit the identified oppositions and to skew Aristotle's project so that it works as a satisfying resolution. In this paper, I encourage those who teach the development of rhetoric in classical Greece to abandon the practice of turning this history into a ripping good story of good guys vs. bad guys and supplant it with a more varied, if less cohesive, one. I present an alternative which offers at least one means for avoiding the lure of a good story. This alternative involves a more inductive method that lets the perspectives of individual authors develop independently from one another and leaves the task of creating a master narrative to the student. Of course, at a certain level it is impossible for instructors to completely avoid offering the conceptual apparatus that largely frames this or any other subject matter. The choice of texts, the course schedule, and the time frame chosen naturally serve this framing function for students. However, I contend that in the present case, there is the possibility to reduce, rather than enlarge, this framing effect.

The focus of this essay is on the manner in which we present the history of classical rhetorical theory and practice to undergraduates. For the purposes of this essay, I rely on an analysis of several significant undergraduate texts that cover the classical period in order to describe the manner in which they construct an oppositional, "good guy vs. bad guy" narrative. This study might have, alternatively, examined the course syllabi, teaching strategies, and teaching materials of teachers of classical rhetoric. In fact, to a certain extent this has already been done, though the purposes for examining them were different. Nelms and Goggin conducted a survey in an attempt to examine the revival of classical rhetoric in the field of English Composition in which they utilized narrative accounts generated by many of the scholars who participated in this revival.[1] What they found was an interesting account of the manner in which the revival progressed, with some initial spurts, beginning in the 1960's and continuing to the present. Perhaps the most interesting finding of these authors arises from a question they asked concerning the role classical rhetoric has played in composition studies. Nelms and Goggin received answers that noted the political, methodological, theoretical, historical and epistemological contributions of classical rhetoric.

This disparate response, I think, would likely be duplicated if the same question were put to those in the National Communication Association that teach classical rhetoric. And, I think it is possible to imagine that these same issues (political, methodological, epistemological, etc.) are also part of what encourages the use of the oppositional narrative identified above. Theresa Enos examined a survey of doctoral programs in Rhetoric and Composition, conducted by Chapman and Tate.[2] She examined this survey with a particular focus on what it indicated in terms of the course in classical rhetoric. In particular, she examined the coursework of graduate students, many of whom go

---

[1] Gerald Nelms and Maureen D. Goggin, "The Revival of Classical Rhetoric for Modern Composition Studies," 11–26.

[2] David W. Chapman and Gary Tate, "A Survey of Doctoral Programs in Rhetoric and Composition," 124–189.

on to teach classical rhetoric in one form or another. Her conclusion is instructive:

> My survey shows that the classical rhetoric course, when offered in these programs, also lacks uniformity. The classical rhetoric course as taught in English departments is not as well defined, as it should be; it takes on too many forms and is too often reductionistic. If what we characteristically offer our students is one course spanning more than two thousand years, the unified framework, historical, theoretical, pedagogical, that these students need cannot be realized.[3]

The focus of this essay is not graduate courses, but undergraduate ones. It does not have the benefit of an extensive survey that Enos' study did. Instead, I have focused on two primary texts. I believe it is fair to say that they are two of the more widely used texts for courses that cover the history of rhetoric during the classical period. There are many undergraduate texts in this area, not all of them relevant to this project. For example, two well-known texts, Edward P. J. Corbett's *Classical Rhetoric for Modern Students* and the more recent text by Sharon Crowley and Debra Hawhee, *Ancient Rhetorics for Contemporary Students*, serve a different purpose than what I refer to here.[4] The primary goal of these texts is to teach students to make use of strategies (e.g., commonplaces in invention, reasoning from probability, and patterns of arrangement) and concepts arising out of the classical period (e.g., *kairos*, ethos, and stasis theory) in their writing and speaking. That being said, it is also the case that each text presents a version of the history of rhetorical theory in Greece and Rome along the way. However, for the purposes of this essay, I have limited my discussion of undergraduate texts to two of the most prominent with explicit designs for offering readers the history of classical rhetoric: *The Rhetoric of Western Thought* by Golden, Berquist, and Coleman and

---

[3] Theresa Enos, "The Course in Classical Rhetoric," 47.
[4] Edward P.J. Corbett, *Classical Rhetoric for the Modern Student*. 3rd ed.; Sharon Crowley and Debra Hawhee, *Ancient Rhetorics for Contemporary Students*. 2nd ed.

Classical Rhetoric and its Christian and Secular Tradition from Ancient to Modern Times by George Kennedy.[5]

THE RHETORIC OF WESTERN THOUGHT

The Rhetoric of Western Thought has been a widely used undergraduate textbook for courses in the history of rhetoric since the first edition was published in 1976. Golden, Berquist, and Coleman begin their description of the beginnings of rhetorical theory and practice by laying out the well-worn contrast between Plato and the sophists. They note that while the sophists were popular and successful as teachers, they generated a high degree of criticism.

> In brief, the sophists were reproached by the traditionalists because they threatened the very core of the established educational system on two fronts. First, as noted above, the sophists featured practical knowledge (subjects associated with governing and decision-making). This emphasis ran contrary to the traditional philosophers who were engaged in seeking truth. Second, the sophists were willing to teach anyone who could pay for their services.[6]

We might immediately note that this description places Plato's critique of the sophists several decades earlier than it actually occurred if we take a normal meaning for "their day." That is to say that sophists such as Protagoras and Gorgias came to Athens and began their teaching several decades prior to the earliest dates for Plato's dialogues. And the Platonic distinction of "truth seeking" vs. "how to win an argument for argument sake" comes through loud and clear.

The perspective of these authors not only exalts Plato's perspective over all others; it also accepts Plato's strategic bit of good and bad rhetoric. Later the authors bring the sophists, Plato, and roughly a half-century of rhetorical theory together in the following conclusion:

---

[5] James L. Golden, Goodwin F. Berquist, and William E. Coleman, *The Rhetoric of Western Thought*. 6th ed.; George A. Kennedy, *Classical Rhetoric and Its Christian and Secular Tradition from Ancient to Modern Times*. See also: George A. Kennedy, *The Art of Persuasion in Greece*; George A. Kennedy, *A New History of Classical Rhetoric*.

[6] James L. Golden, *The Rhetoric of Western Thought*, 7.

In sum, Plato in these well-known works conceived of two different types of rhetoric. The first or "false rhetoric," he perceived as all too common in the Athenian society around him. This rhetoric he rejected as showy in appearance, self-serving, and artificial. The second or "true rhetoric" he himself exemplified. The rhetoric he embraced was truthful, self-effacing, and real. Plato's noble lover was part philosopher, part logician, and part psychologist. He must know the truth. He must be a master of dialectic, the Platonic instrument for the discovery and dissemination of the truth. And he must understand the human soul in order that he may appeal to the better side of mankind. The moral rhetoric of Plato as conceived in the *Phaedrus* continues to represent an ideal for all of us, even though history demonstrates the ideal is seldom achieved.[7]

Plato's description of the sophists, and rhetoric more generally, is thus fixed, accepted, and even lauded as the goal of all future rhetorical efforts! The movement is complete when they place Aristotle within Plato's "good" rhetoric category. His text, *On Rhetoric*, becomes the "comprehensive," "analytical," "systematic," and "fundamental" explanation of rhetoric's many parts. Included in their description are many Aristotelian concepts and categories including the enthymeme, forms of proof, ethical and emotional appeals, types of discourse, organization, audience analysis, style, and delivery. What is not included is a clear positioning of his project in relation to the sophists or Plato. However, they do note that Aristotle's perspective on rhetoric was designed to "uphold truth and justice and play down their opposites," and that it is a "moral" view of rhetoric akin to Plato's.[8]

But, as noted above, this oppositional framework hides more than it reveals. It hides much of the uniqueness of each of the sophists. It hides the true nature of their efforts that went beyond "success at all costs." Finally, it hides much of Plato's own project by accepting and parroting his seductively simplistic sublimation of rhetoric to dialectic in the *Phaedrus*. Plato had much more to say about rhetoric. Though it might be convenient to set aside Plato's critique of rhetoric in the *Gor-*

---

[7] Golden, 20.
[8] Golden, 28.

gias, that is really not possible. Rhetoric, by its nature, is not so easily subdued or constrained, or limited as Plato wishes it to be at the end of the *Phaedrus*.

Golden, et al. discuss Plato's *Gorgias* under the heading, "The *Gorgias:* A Study of False Rhetoric," which, of course, from the Platonic perspective makes good sense. But this too sets up an oppositional framework that is based on Plato's characterization of Gorgias and of his teaching of rhetoric (logos). The *Gorgias* is also clearly done in an exaggerated manner, no doubt to help Plato distinguish himself from his competitors and highlight the advantages of his teaching and his school; yet, the narrative in the text accepts this characterization as definitive.

This oppositional construction between Plato and the sophists is not the only such opposition constructed in this narrative. The authors go on to describe what they take to be three views on rhetoric that were active during the classical period: the "moral-philosophical view" of Plato, the "scientific-philosophical" view of Aristotle, and the "educational-philosophical view" of Isocrates, Cicero, and Quintilian. Thus the text, through strategic grouping, naming, and selective focus, reduces several centuries of development and multiple authors down to three perspectives. In the case of Plato and the sophists these perspectives are explicitly pitted against one another.

Classical Rhetoric and its Christian and Secular Tradition from Ancient to Modern Times

George Kennedy's text has been a touchstone for students of the history of rhetoric for the last two decades. The text is well known for describing what Kennedy takes to be the three dominant views on rhetoric active in the classical period: Technical, Sophistic, and Philosophical. Kennedy also moves beyond this description of the classical period to claim that these three strands continued beyond ancient Greece right up to the present day in western civilization. For example, Kennedy describes the technical strand as represented in the rhetorical handbooks, which were prevalent in the fifth and fourth centuries. This technical strand "grew out of the needs of the democracies in Sicily and Greece" and it is "highly pragmatic; it shows how to present a subject efficiently and successfully but makes no attempt to judge the morality of the speaker or his effect on the audience." The characteristic definition of rhetoric in this technical tradition is "the art of persuasion."[9]

Kennedy likewise defines the additional two strands. The sophistic strand, "is responsible for pictures of an ideal orator leading society to noble fulfillment of national ideals. It is often ceremonial and cultural, rather than active and civic, and though moral in tone, tends not to press for difficult decisions or immediate action. Sophistic rhetoric is a natural spawning ground for amplification, elaborate conceits, and stylistic refinement, and thus is often criticized, but it has positive qualities which have ensured its survival."[10] Finally, philosophical rhetoric "tends to de-emphasize the speaker and to stress the validity of his message and the nature of his effect on an audience. Furthermore, it classifies speeches on the basis of the audience, whether they are only spectators or are judges of past or future events."[11]

This categorization, while clear, handy, and intuitively compelling, leaves us with a fixed set of boxes into which we are encouraged to place all rhetorical theory. We are thus motivated to ignore, overlook, or forcefully adapt those elements from the sophists, or even from Plato and Aristotle, that do not fit the prescribed box. The categorization quite naturally takes on a life of its own and, I would argue, as many others have, that the downside of this fact greatly overshadows the helpfulness of the original categorization itself. Let me cite two examples.

First, to point out a well-known illustration, under Kennedy's scheme Isocrates is placed in the sophistic category. We have in Isocrates' *Antidosis* a thorough explanation of his educational program and philosophy. And, while it seems to me that much of his perspective fits Kennedy's sophistic category, by no means does all of it. So, Kennedy's placement puts the focus on the "ideal orator leading society to noble fulfillment of national ideals."[12] This is true to Isocrates' program. However, Isocrates also viewed his education as involving "philosophy," which is, in fact, the most frequent term he uses to describe it. His may not have been a philosophy that Plato was comfortable with, but we should not, it seems to me, accept Plato's position on

---

[9] George A. Kennedy, *Classical Rhetoric and Its Christian and Secular Tradition from Ancient to Modern Times*, 16.
[10] Kennedy, 16–17.
[11] Kennedy, 17.
[12] Kennedy, 17.

this and then transmit it to our students. By placing Isocrates in the "sophistic" box and Plato and Aristotle in the "philosophical" box, we inadvertently accept and legitimate Plato's perspective.

Second, Kennedy's categorization, even though he attempts to avoid it, has something of a crescendo implicit within it. The history of rhetoric, following his scheme, is a natural progression during the classical period from something incomplete, and ethically unsound to that which is more complete, if not complete, and morally sound. Kennedy describes the continuation of each strand through the modern period, but it is his handling of theorists in the classical period that is my focus here. Plato and Aristotle come out well, the sophists less so. In addition, the aspects of the work of Plato and Aristotle, which in fact fit more closely to the technical and sophistic boxes, are devalued. Aristotle's *Rhetoric* is nothing if not a handbook which can guide the would-be speaker from topic selection through invention, arrangement, style and on to delivery. Plato's sublimation of rhetoric to dialectic, as employed by the philosopher king, would in fact seek the civic goals Kennedy identifies with the sophistic strand.

These examples are sufficient, I hope, to indicate the detriments of Kennedy's well-known categorization. Though its oppositional nature is not as obviously stated as Golden, Berquist, and Coleman, the result is the same. The positioning of classical authors and their "systems" naturally pits one against the other. It also hides and colors our understanding of rhetoric in the classical period in unhelpful ways. The end result, I think, is a ripping good story that leaves an intellectual hangover in its wake. Unfortunately, a good deal is lost in these presentations and further investigation by the students themselves is likewise constrained by the systems in which the material has been presented.

Problems with the Oppositions and Categorizations

I now shift to a description of what I take to be the chief problems with the oppositional, narrative approach. First, categorizations such as these, when they are front-loaded and allowed to guide discussion of classical figures and concepts, constrain and cloud our understanding of the classical period as much as they enlighten it. In particular, when we encourage students to categorize particular authors and their works into categories and oppositional stories we inevitably discourage them from wrestling with these thinkers and texts on their own. For example, in the two undergraduate texts I have described, Isocrates' conceptualization is reconstructed as "practical" in opposition to the "philosophical" approach of Plato and Aristotle. I believe this treatment hides the breadth of Isocrates' conceptualization by focusing attention on its "practical" characteristics to the exclusion of others. In fact, Isocrates is an excellent example of a sophist in that his instruction encompassed everything from mathematics to history to music. In this sense, we have failed Isocrates and his conceptualization. It is better, in my opinion, to teach the competing definitions of "philosophy" along side each other and leave the matter to our students themselves. In addition, we can encourage our students to look for the ways individual authors contradict themselves in their use of these terms from one text to another or even within the same text. This can lead to even broader questions such as: "What is philosophy?" "What is rhetoric?" "How does each relate to the 5th century descriptions of logos?" These are important questions and Plato's answer to them ought not be accepted and read back to earlier authors and forward to later authors.

Second, I wish to discuss what I take to be the negative results of turning classical rhetorical theory into a three or four act play that finds its resolution in Plato and/or Aristotle. This is one of the implicit lures of Kennedy's three strands. Adopting his characterization allows the classical period to crescendo and close with Aristotle as the systematizer of Plato's moral rhetoric with a pragmatic focus on argument from probability. This, in addition to the compelling nature of the three kinds of proof, three genres of oratory, and his discussion of audience analysis, naturally tends to paint all earlier efforts as deficient or incomplete in one way or another and it puts too great a burden on the works of Plato and Aristotle.

A third weakness of this approach is that students are encouraged to see rhetorical theory as a series of incessant fights and contrasts between theorists. This is particularly true with those accounts that stress the contrast between Plato's "search for truth" and the sophists' "success at all costs." By setting up the origins of the discipline in a story of conflict, we encourage students to see the field itself, in classical and contemporary times, as a battlefield. That battlefield is characterized by an ongoing struggle with ever-changing winners and losers. The supposed "fight" itself becomes the draw and students are encouraged to look for signs of it in every text. They miss the actual contribution and emphasis of individual authors and they are encouraged to set aside the historical, cultural, and social context of the texts they encounter. The history of rhetoric is not best viewed as a hostile engagement with winners and losers. Rhetorical engagement spans a variety of orientations, from agonistic to cooperative, between humans and their world, their society, and their neighbors.

A fourth weakness to the oppositional storyline is that our students may go through the course feeling as if they need to "take sides" with one theorist or strand. Once such positioning takes place it is only natural for them to differentiate their position from all others, thus pushing away the work of many other rhetorical theorists. This closing down of options and positions rubs against the notion that a course, such as an undergraduate course in classical rhetoric, is designed to expose students to a variety of perspectives and viewpoints. When students "decide" on a position or theoretical perspective they are more likely to shortchange or give only partial attention to other perspectives or view other perspectives through the lens of the one they have adopted.

A final weakness arises out of the manner in which the placement of any two concepts or objects can serve to over-determine the interpretation of those objects. Often, one object or term is explicitly or implicitly favored over another. The "lesser" of the objects or terms may end up being largely, if not completely, understood in terms of the "greater." At the very least the two objects or terms may end up in a relationship of reciprocal definition in which our understanding of one necessitates the other. This overrides all other possible ways of understanding either one in the pair. If we see the sophists only in opposition to Plato, then their placement in terms of their social, political, and even economic environment is likely to be given short shrift.

Averting the Oppositions

I don't think the solution is a different arrangement of good and bad guys, or a different resolution to the "conflict" than one currently offered. Neither would I unrealistically claim that we can completely avoid comparing and contrasting classical authors and their views on the significant concepts and issues they address. However, I do think that there are a variety of ways to avoid the focus on oppositions and the allure of a ripping good story line.

First, I believe that students benefit more from an exposure to primary materials than to secondary sources. Why have our students read a secondary account of the work of Gorgias when we can have them read and discuss his *Encomium to Helen?* Now, it is the case that our sources on the Older Sophists are limited, however, even selected fragments out of the Sprague compilation of fragments are better, in my judgment, than relying completely on secondary accounts. As an instructor, I fill in what I take to be the particularly relevant comments from a variety of secondary sources with particular emphasis on recent treatments. For example, on the days in which students read the fragments or surviving texts of the Older Sophists I lecture on recent treatments of the sophists by John and Takis Poulakos, Ed Schiappa, Susan Jarratt, as well as those by George Kerferd and George Kennedy.[13] All of this is secondary; however, to the first-hand reading and discussion I lead students through the works of Protagoras and Gorgias. For Protagoras, I employ a handout composed of a series of Protagorean fragments gleaned from the Sprague and Schiappa texts. I have also found it helpful to use the Platonic dialogues in which Plato includes the sophists. This can easily lead to an interesting discussion of the differences between Plato's presentation and what we learn about these individuals from other sources.

In addition, I tend to use secondary sources in two places in the course. First, I list key articles on the central figures and concepts of classical rhetoric on the term paper assignment sheet and require that students engage several of these secondary sources in their research. Second, I use several contemporary articles for readings and discussions such as a chapter from I. F. Stone's *The Trial of Socrates* for a discussion of Socrates and his times and George Kerferd on what the term "sophist" refers to from his text, *The Sophistic Movement*.[14] Finally, I reserve the last week or two of class for recent articles that discuss the enduring legacy of classical rhetoric. For example, John Poulakos' "Toward a Sophistic Definition of Rhetoric" works particularly well and easily leads into a discussion of potential contemporary applications as does Helen Sterk's article paralleling Helen of Troy and Marilyn Monroe and how the discourse of praise of beautiful women reveals the constraints they are under.[15]

---

[13] See Susan C. Jarratt, *Rereading the Sophists*; John Poulakos, "Rhetoric, the Sophists, and the Possible," 215–26; John Poulakos, *Sophistical Rhetoric in Classical Greece*; Takis Poulakos, "Intellectuals and the Public Sphere: The Case of the Older Sophists"; Edward Schiappa, *Protagoras and Logos*.

[14] George B. Kerferd, *The Sophistic Movement*; I. F. Stone, *The Trial of Socrates*.

[15] John Poulakos, "Toward a Sophistic Definition of Rhetoric," 35–48; Helen Sterk, "In Praise of Beautiful Women," 215–26. See also: Kathleen E.

In a similar vein, during the first third of the class, I have students learn and use the word-search program on the Perseus website.[16] I schedule a day in our computer lab, bring the class in, and demonstrate how they can, for example, locate all of Plato's uses of the word "speech" in the English translation used on the site. In this example, we find two hundred and seventy-two occurrences of the English word "speech." We then discuss ways to narrow the research project because I make this a three-five page paper assignment. They narrow their focus to a particular type of usage of the term or to a certain dialogue or set of dialogues. I then guide them in the task of examining each usage and its literary context and meaning within a particular passage. I might also guide them to examine uses of the same term by other authors or to a search of the Perseus Encyclopedia or other resources such as the *Encyclopedia of Rhetoric*. The results of this assignment have been extremely encouraging. Students gain a sense of classical authors and concepts that they did not have in my previous courses, and learn a good deal about academic research and writing. Other examples that I give students include Isocrates' use of the term "education" and the word "persuasion" in Aristophanes. Of course, given that they are using an English translation, this method has clear drawbacks from a scholarly standpoint. I discuss this fact and have them generate some of the weaknesses of it. Hopefully it is clear that this very process allows students to form their own perspectives and understandings of classical authors and the conceptions of rhetoric.

Conclusion

It is easy to see why teachers of rhetorical theory in the classical period may find it helpful to turn a chosen set of texts or authors into something akin to an old western. Depending on one's preconceptions and intellectual commitments, the period offers a full array of textual examples from which any number of "guys in white hats" vs. "guys in black hats" arguments might be drawn. In addition, Plato's depth and breadth offers an important touchstone against which to compare and contrast any number of authors, texts, and concepts. As I have indicated, at least two of the more prominent texts in this area provide

---

Welch, *The Contemporary Reception of Classical Rhetoric*.

[16] The website is maintained by Tufts University and the list of authors and texts that are accessible on the site expands continuously. The full title is "Perseus: An Evolving Digital Library." See http://www.perseus.tufts.edu/

categorizations and chronologies that encourage such an approach. The good guy vs. bad guy approach surely appeals, in some archetypal manner, to our deepest longings for clarity and the desire to be on the winning side. This story line typically places particular authors, particular texts, and particular concepts opposite one another in a kind of set piece battle. The classroom instructor then becomes a play-by-play announcer and color commentator rolled into one.

It is also not difficult to imagine a better way. It is a worthy goal, in my opinion, to open up undergraduate understandings and interpretations of the texts on rhetoric that survive from classical Greece. This can occur once we get past the traditional story line and use a more inductive approach. The specific tactics I have outlined, such as the replacement of survey textbooks with the use of primary texts, and the use of the Perseus website, represent examples of how this might take place. These are by no means exhaustive or definitive strategies but they are approaches that have worked for me. In addition to the benefits described above, this strategy empowers students as co-learners with the instructor. This makes the course an enjoyable one for me to teach and I recommend it to others.

24 Rhetoric, Civic Consciousness, and Civic Conscience: The Invention of Citizenship in Classical Greece

Christopher Lyle Johnstone

In his 1982 book, *Reconstructing Public Philosophy*, William Sullivan observes that the orthodox liberal conception of society and politics has proved incapable in this country of sustaining a system of social relations in which individualistic and communitarian impulses are balanced, and in which personal freedoms and community controls are not seen as being mutually antagonistic. Only through the political action of citizens joined in "active solidarity," he says, can the traditional liberal values of personal dignity and self-determination be preserved. "Conserving America's deepest founding values will require . . . a substantial change in the structure and direction of American society, and that will require development of a new civic consciousness, . . . a renewal of civic spirit."[1] Sullivan looks to "the classical notion of citizenship" for a vision of life that is simultaneously political and moral, one that identifies civic life as a form of "personal self-development":

> The tradition of republican citizenship stretching from Plato and Aristotle to the makers of the American Revolution links power and authority within the state with the social, economic, psychological, and religious realms. By contrast, modern discussions of citizenship that operate under largely liberal assumptions are far more abstract. . . . Setting classical and

---

[1] William M. Sullivan, *Reconstructing Public Philosophy*, 156.

> modern views side by side, [one has] the troubling sense that there have been large losses as well as gains. ... The principal loss is identifiable immediately. It is a loss of any relationship among political, social, economic, and psychological theorizing and the concreteness of citizenship as a way of life.[2]

It seems to me that Sullivan has accurately diagnosed an important source of what most troubles contemporary American society. Ordinary citizens watch with a mixture of disgust and frustration the continuing failure of our elected legislatures to move beyond narrow partisan and ideological interests and to achieve consensus about how to deal with such persistent social problems as poverty and homelessness, domestic and public violence, racial friction and discrimination, environmental degradation and sustainable economic well-being. We decry the loss of "civility" in public controversy, with the effect that fewer and fewer citizens of this country participate in our political life at all—whether simply as voters or through personal involvement in local, state, and national governance. This disgust with and apathy toward "politics" is especially pronounced among young people, who evidence a distaste for political activity and a conviction that it has no relevance to their lives. What has been lost as a result of this disenchantment with politics is both a clear sense of what it means to be a citizen and a commitment to fulfill the responsibilities of citizenship. It may sound like a quaint idea, but my own experience in local government some years ago convinced me that the idea of citizenship still has value, and that instruction in the duties and competencies of citizenship should be at the heart of "liberal education" in American schools and universities, just as it has traditionally been at the heart of liberal studies since their appearance in Greece during the fifth century BCE.

Sullivan invokes the ideals of the "classical notion of citizenship" in his call for a renewal of "civic philosophy." What are these ideals? How can they illuminate the notion of citizenship as a "way of life?" My aim in this essay is to address such questions as these by examining the classical Greek—and particularly the Athenian—conception of citizenship both as a form of consciousness—that is, as a way of being-in-the-world—and as a call to conscience—that is, as an invo-

---

[2] Sullivan, *Reconstructing Public Philosophy*, 157.

cation of civic duties and responsibilities. One thesis to be advanced through this examination is that "civic consciousness" is essentially rhetorical, just as a "rhetorical consciousness," at least in its inception and recurrently during the long tradition of rhetorical study, is fundamentally civic. Accordingly, the kinds of moral principles and responsibilities that inhere in citizenship will reflect what Thomas B. Farrell has termed "the norms of rhetorical culture."[3]

The term "citizen" emerged during the 4th millennium BCE in cities along the banks of the Tigris and Euphrates rivers in Mesopotamia.[4] Literally, a "citi-zen" is a "denizen" or inhabitant of the city. At the most fundamental level, the idea of citizenship implies participation in a politically organized community of fellow-citizens whose lives are interdependent and whose individual survival and well-being are thus intimately linked with the survival and well-being of others. "Indeed," Sullivan writes, "the notion of *citizen* is unintelligible apart from that of *commonwealth,* and both terms derive their sense from the idea that we are by nature political beings."[5]

This thought, of course, echoes Aristotle's statement (*Politics* 1253a2) that "man is by nature a political animal," that is, an animal intended by nature to live in a community. Aristotle goes on to note (1253a28–31) that "the individual, when isolated, is not self-sufficing; and therefore he is like a part in relation to the whole. But he who is unable to live in society, or who has no need [to do so] because he is sufficient for himself, must be either a beast or a god. . . . A social instinct is implanted in all men by nature. . . ." However, there is more to this observation than merely that humans generally must live together in groups in order to survive and prosper. For Aristotle it means also that our natural mode of existence consists in our membership and participation in a *polity,* and thus that the natural form of human social organization is the *polis*: an autonomous community, a *state,* in which the arrangement of political power and procedures of governance are set down in some sort of constitution or law code.[6]

---

[3] Thomas B. Farrell, *Norms of Rhetorical Culture.*

[4] Saggs comments that "the best archaeological evidence for the development of cities comes from Erech. . . . By 3000 BC it was a rapidly expanding city, with a population estimated at 50,000." H. W. F. Saggs, *Civilization Before Greece and Rome,* 33.

[5] Sullivan, *Reconstructing Public Philosophy,* 157.

[6] Indeed, Aristotle argues that the state exists by nature and that it is logically prior to both the family and the individual. See *Politics* 1253a19–20.

The classical conception of citizenship grows out of the emergence of the *polis* during the early Archaic period (ca. 750–600 BCE). Following the decline and eventual disappearance of the Mycenaean civilization around 1000 BCE, political arrangements among the Greek-speaking peoples scattered across the Aegean world were transformed from highly centralized, palace-based administrative centers managed via alliances among a fairly small number of powerful regional monarchs[7] to a fragmented scattering of local hamlets and small towns, each ruled by a warrior-chieftain. The inhabitants of these small communities lived under the authority of and owed allegiance to the local chief: they were *subjects* rather than true *citizens*.[8] With the emergence of the *polis*, however, the mechanics of governance began to change in ways that permitted increased participation by the *demos*. Even in *poleis* that retained monarchical forms, participation in political decision-making was broadened to include members of aristocratic families who advised the king as members of a council or *boulê*, and in some (for instance, Sparta) the entire citizen body advised the kings in matters of policy. In Athens, of course, this trajectory was followed to a kind of completion, and a form of government emerged by the end of the sixth century that permitted all adult male inhabitants with at least half Athenian parentage to participate directly in governance. Indeed, the Athenian constitution instituted by Kleisthenes between 510 and 507 created the possibility of full *citizenship:* the *demos* became the ground of sovereignty, and the individual Athenian could exercise political (i.e. civic) power.[9]

The idea of citizenship developed thus far features two essential characteristics: it is based on an awareness of interdependence and thus of the primacy of communal interests, and in its most developed forms it locates political sovereignty and power in the *demos*, the people. The empowerment of the citizen—properly so called—yields the idea of

---

[7] For example, Agamemnon at Mycenae, Nestor at Pylos, Menelaus at Sparta. See Homer, *Iliad*, II.

[8] For useful discussions of Greece during the Dark Ages and Archaic period, see Finley Hooper, *Greek Realities: Life and Thought in Ancient Greece*, 11–88; also M. I. Finley, *The World of Odysseus*, 2nd edition; Finley, *Early Greece*; John Forsdyke, *Greece Before Homer*; Raphael Sealey, *A History of the Greek City States*; and Chester G. Starr, *The Origins of Greek Civilization*.

[9] See Alfred Zimmern, *Greek Commonwealth: Politics and Economics in Fifth-Century Athens*, 5th edition; also Charles Hignett, *History of the Athenian Constitution to the End of the Fifth Century B. C.*

civil rights and civic responsibilities. It is, in a way, the true ground of citizenship. This sense of public empowerment was further enhanced by the emergence and dissemination of natural philosophy as an alternative to myth for explaining and understanding the world. In myth, the causal ground of such world-events as the alternation of day and night, the cycle of the seasons, the occurrence of storms, earthquakes, droughts and volcanic eruptions, a bountiful harvest and a crop failure, the visitations of war and disease, lies in the supernatural. More particularly, the causes of events that affect human life so profoundly are to be found, not in impersonal forces of nature, but in the very personal wills and caprices of individual deities. "Myth," Guthrie notes, "seeks an individual cause [for an event]—the wrath of a god, the jealousy of a goddess—whereas reason is only satisfied when it can explain in terms of a general law."[10] Precisely because the divine agents whose actions affect virtually every event—including human thought and choice—can be capricious, events are ultimately unpredictable and thus uncontrollable. Humans are at the mercy of the gods, to whom the appropriate attitude is *supplication*.

The transition from a mythopoetic and a naturalistic consciousness during the Archaic and Classical periods represents a sea-change in the human's sense of being-in-the world: because it locates the causes of events in immutable laws of nature, such a worldview creates the possibility of predictability in world events, and thus ultimately of human power over them. The greatest discovery of the first natural philosophers—Thales, Anaximander, and Anaximenes—lies not in their identification of "water" or "some unbounded nature" or "air" as the originating substance or principle of existing things, but in their recognition that the *archê* or causative principle of things is within rather than outside nature. As Charles Kahn describes Anaximander's insight, "the universe is governed by Law," and this Law imposes on natural events a regularity and consistency that make prediction and control possible.[11] Toward the idea of Nature as a causal ground the proper attitude is not supplication but *curiosity,* and the understandings that result from pursuing curiosity create in us a sense that, rather

---

[10] W. K. C. Guthrie, *Myth and Reason*, 5; also see Jean-Pierre Vernant, *The Origins of Greek Thought* and Vernant, *Myth and Thought Among the Greeks*.

[11] Charles H. Kahn, *Anaximander and the Origins of Greek Cosmology*. Also see Lawrence J. Hatab, *Myth and Philosophy*.

than being subject to the whims of divine beings whose minds we cannot fathom, we are capable—through the application of intelligence to observation—of predicting and to some extent regulating natural occurrences. This augmented sense of empowerment—the sense that over natural as well as civic events members of the community itself can exercise directive influence—contributed significantly to the emergence of a genuinely civic consciousness.

The empowerment of the individual—in political, judicial, ontological, and epistemological terms—was an especially pronounced implication of the first professional teachers of the "arts of citizenship." Such Sophists as Protagoras, Gorgias, Antiphon, Prodicus, and others claimed to be able to teach "prudence in the affairs of the city"[12] and held that the greatest human excellence was *hê politikê aretê*: "skill in political matters."[13] This "civic prudence" or "political virtue," an essential ingredient of the idea of citizenship, rests in part on the idea that human beings themselves determine the realities in terms of which they must live their lives. In their rejection of the metaphysical and scientific speculations of the natural philosophers, the earliest Sophists maintained anthropocentric and relativistic views of truth, existence, and knowledge.[14] Protagoras, in perhaps the most concise statement of this view, claimed that "of all things the measure is [the human], of things that are that they are, and of things that are not that they are not."[15] However one interprets this statement—and its interpretation is a matter of some controversy[16]—it clearly locates at least the ground of knowledge (and perhaps even the ground of existence itself) in the human subject, thus strengthening the sense that in the citizen resides the power of determining the social realities that will guide political life. To function as a citizen, then, is to participate in communal life with an awareness of one's own potency in affecting civic events. It is to act with an awareness that in the practical, political sphere, one is not at the mercy of monarchs and divinities; rather, one can affect the quality of communal experience and the course of communal life.

---

[12] See Rosamond Kent Sprague, *The Older Sophists* for translations of fragments from the Older Sophists' writings.

[13] William M. A. Grimaldi, "How Do We Get from Corax-Tisias to Plato-Aristotle in Greek Rhetorical Theory," 25.

[14] See W. K. C. Guthrie, *The Sophists*, especially, 164–75.

[15] Sprague, *The Older Sophists*, 18; also see Edward Schiappa, *Protagoras and Logos*, 117ff.

[16] See Guthrie, *The Sophists*; also Schiappa, *Protagoras and Logos*.

"In the strictest sense," Aristotle writes (*Pol.* 1275a23–24), the citizen is defined as one who "shares in the administration of justice, and in offices." The citizen is one who *takes part* in the governance of the community.

If a sense of empowerment is the "true ground" of citizenship, and if the chief criterion of true citizenship is participation in communal affairs, a genuinely "civic consciousness" also includes a sense of the fluidity and tentativeness of social experience and knowledge, and of the plurality of viewpoints in terms of which communal issues are deliberated and decisions are reached. This sense is particularly pronounced in a democratic polity, one in which the civic body is responsible for debating and deciding questions of policy, law, and justice.[17] A fundamental premise of democratic government is that such questions do not admit of resolution except through the process of argumentation and debate precisely because they arise in the sphere of contingency, probability and particularity. In this sphere there are no absolutes, no certainties, no fixed verities; what knowledge we have of it is not "scientific" or demonstrative. Rather, the realm of civic, communal, or political life is fraught with uncertainties and risks, it legitimizes a plurality of viewpoints and "truths," and what knowledge we can have of it is incomplete, probabilistic, and always open to question and revision. At its most highly developed, a genuinely "civic" consciousness embraces the notion that all social "truths" and the resolutions of all social issues are necessarily vexed, problematic, tentative, and hypothetical.

This attitude toward the social/civic realm finds its fullest expression in Aristotle's politico-ethical works—namely, the *Rhetoric*, *Ethics*, and *Politics*[18]—but it finds its initial expression in the extant writings of Protagoras and Gorgias. When Gorgias wrote that "Nothing exists; . . . even if something exists, it is inapprehensible to man; . . . [and] even if it is apprehensible, still it is . . . incapable of being expressed or explained to the next [person],"[19] he might be understood to have been

---

[17] For Aristotle, the highest "office" in which a citizen may serve is as a member of the popular assembly, which holds the "supreme power" in democratic states (*Pol.*1275a28).

[18] See Christopher Lyle Johnstone, "An Aristotelian Trilogy," 1–24.

[19] Sprague, *The Older Sophists*, 42. There is some controversy over whether Gorgias meant this series of statements to be taken literally, rather than intending it purely as a parody of Parmenides' argument concerning the unity of Being. See Guthrie, *The Sophists*, 193–200.

asserting that there are no absolute Truths in the (social) world; that even if there were, human beings could not grasp them; and that even if one could grasp such a Truth, one could not put it into words. One implication of this view is that, in the world of social realities and communal experience, the "truths" to which we have access are transient, problematic, and negotiable. Thus do we find Protagoras suggesting that "on every issue there are [at least] two arguments opposed to each other,"[20] with the implication that in the realm of civic experience every position, every stance, every resolution is always open to question, to counter-argument, and to revision. Thus is the civic realm fundamentally and essentially *rhetorical*. The form of consciousness—the sense of being-in-the-world—that is conditioned by and appropriate to this realm is most fully disclosed in Aristotle's *Rhetoric*, but it cannot be understood except in partnership with the *Ethics*.[21]

Aristotle distinguishes between two spheres of reality and two modes of knowledge, the one involving truths that are necessary, universal, and immutable and that can be known with scientific certainty, the other involving truths that are contingent, circumstantial, particular, and transient, and that can be "known" only with varying degrees of probability.[22] While both spheres admit of truth, the former centers on "those things whose first principles are invariable," while the latter is concerned with "things that are variable" (*Nic. Ethics* 1138b35–1139a16). In the realm of the invariable, the organ of inquiry and knowledge is *sophia*, philosophic wisdom, a combination of intuitive knowledge (*nous*) of first principles and scientific knowledge (*epistêmê*), which consists in apprehending the implications of first principles—what follows from them. In the contingent, practical, moral realm the organ of understanding is *phronêsis* or practical wisdom, which consists in the ability to "deliberate rightly about what is good and advantageous for [one]self . . . [and] conducive to the good life generally" (*Nic. Ethics* 1140a24ff.). The realm of the practical and of the moral—including the civic sphere—is the realm of deliberation, of probable knowledge, of choice and risk, of action and uncertainty. It is also the realm of rhetoric, for "the function of Rhetoric . . . is to deal with things about which we deliberate. . ." (*Rhetoric* 1357a1–2). Rhetoric deals in probabilities and "common beliefs" (1355a–1357a), and so

---

[20] Sprague, *The Older Sophists*, 21.
[21] See Johnstone, "An Aristotelian Trilogy."
[22] See Aristotle, *Nicomachean Ethics*, VI, i–vii.

serves to assist us in negotiating the oppositions and other tensions that permeate our socio-political experience. It is the method by which the citizen participates *as* citizen in communal decision making; it is, that is to say, the essential activity of citizenship—in the democratic assembly and in the lawcourt (1358b2–3).

If the essential act of citizenship is "doing rhetoric," then the core of "civic consciousness" is essentially rhetorical. This "sense" of citizenship originates in the recognition that we are communal beings, interdependent, social, political; and in an awareness of our personal potency in shaping the course of events through participation in communal life. However, the complete sense of citizenship—a fully developed "civic consciousness"—comes from an awareness of dwelling in a "civic space" where realities and truths are multiple and mutable, where knowledge is transitory and tentative, where different viewpoints have equal claims on attention, and where the resolutions of conflicts are achieved through persuasion.[23] Among the most significant constituents of such a way of being-in-the-world is an awareness of one's own fallibility, of the possibility that one might be mistaken.[24]

The implications of this way-of-being for the practice of citizenship are important, and they are responsive to the concerns expressed by Sullivan:

> Self-fulfillment and even the working out of personal identity and a sense of orientation in the world depend upon a communal enterprise. This shared process is the civic life, and its root is involvement with others: other generations, other sorts of persons whose differences are significant because they contribute to the whole upon which our particular sense of self depends. Thus mutual interdependency is the foundational notion of citizenship. The basic psychological dynamic of the participants in this interdependent way of life is an imperative to respond and to care.[25]

---

[23] See Farrell, *Norms of Rhetorical Culture*, 278ff.

[24] As Protagoras puts it, ".".. there is much to prevent one's knowing: the obscurity of the subject and the shortness of . . . life," in Sprague, *The Older Sophists*, translated by Michael J. O'Brien, 20.

[25] Sullivan, *Reconstructing Public Philosophy*, 158.

Beyond these imperatives, however, are others: to listen to others, to recognize the complexity of our communal lives, to be cognizant of how problematic and tentative all knowledge claims are, to think it possible that one might be mistaken; but also to express one's own thinking clearly and convincingly, to examine the circumstances of the problematic in communal life in order to identify in them the factors that can ground judgment and justify decision. These are the responsibilities of citizenship, the duties inherent in the very fact of our interdependence. Awareness of such responsibilities—to participate, to acknowledge interdependence, to approach communal issues from a rhetorical perspective—constitutes "civic conscience," the call to citizenship.

Even a cursory examination of contemporary American politics discloses that precisely these elements of citizenship—both a consciousness rooted in the ambiguities of civic life and an acknowledgement of the imperative for rhetorically directed participation in communal affairs—are lacking. The ideological certainty, the intolerance of disagreement, the incivility of so much public discourse, the willingness to subordinate the common welfare to the demands of narrow class and party interests—all bespeak an erosion of the idea of citizenship and of its influence on public life. The ultimate irony is that, for all its antiquarian patina, it is precisely this idea that animated the architects of the American political system as they drew upon and were inspired by the legacy of Athenian political life.

25 Motives for Practicing Shakespeare Criticism as a "Rational Science" in Lord Kames's *Elements of Criticism*

Beth Innocenti Manolescu

In the introduction to *Elements of Criticism* (1762) Lord Kames proposes to make criticism a rational science.[1] He claims that we can do so "by studying the sensitive part of human nature, and by learning what objects are naturally agreeable, and what are naturally disagreeable" (1: 7). Human nature was a central area of inquiry for rhetoricians making use of the new philosophy, but the way Kames practices criticism is not motivated by the new philosophy per se. I will argue that Kames's use of the new philosophy in the practice of criticism addresses social, political, and nationalistic circumstances.

Making this argument helps to map the course of this branch of rhetoric—criticism—and its positions outside of universities and in British culture more generally.[2] It also illuminates *Elements,* a work that has received little scholarly attention.[3] The oversight is significant

---

[1] Lord Kames, *Elements of Criticism*, Volume 1, 8. Subsequent citations are provided parenthetically in the text in the format (volume: page).

[2] Neil Rhodes, "From Rhetoric to Criticism," 22–36 has provided a succinct version of the transition from rhetoric to criticism, identifying Ramus and French writers on rhetoric and belles lettres as important sites of disciplinary change.

[3] There were a handful of articles published in the 1940s–60s: Vincent M. Bevilacqua, "Rhetoric and Human Nature in Kames's *Elements of Criticism*," 46–50, and "Lord Kames's Theory of Rhetoric," 309–27; Murray W. Bundy, "Lord Kames and the Maggots in Amber," 199–208; Walter John Hipple, Jr., "Lord Kames," *The Beautiful, the Sublime, and the Picturesque in Eighteenth-Century British Aesthetic Theory*, 99–121; András Horn, "Kames and the Anthropological Approach to Criticism," 211–233; Gordon McKen-

given its popularity and influence. *Elements* ran to at least five editions in Kames's lifetime and to at least thirty-two in North America alone. There it was used as a textbook and frequently cited by nineteenth-century rhetoricians.[4] Reviews of *Elements* in the *Monthly* and *Critical Review* ran to three installments. These reviewing periodicals gave significantly more space to *Elements* than to any other comparable work; the next longest review was only half as long.[5] Teachers and writers of rhetorics such as Smith, Campbell, Blair, and Priestley acknowledge debts to Kames. In 1831 one American editor described *Elements* as "a standard work of criticism," and in 1855 another noted that *Elements* "has long occupied a place in the colleges and academies in our own land. There seems to be no other work, even at this late date, that is fitted to supply its place, nor, without great disadvantage to the cause of education, can it be laid aside."[6] One scholar has asserted that *Elements* "may fairly be said to have established the nomenclature [substituting the term "criticism" for "rhetoric"] up to the present day."[7] Certainly *Elements* deserves the attention of historians of rhetoric and scholars interested in how rhetoric has been adapted to address practical needs.

I first illustrate Kames's critical practice—show what it means to practice criticism as a rational science. Then I propose to use his Shakespeare criticism as a case study to illustrate select motivations for practicing criticism as a rational science.

---

zie, "Lord Kames and the Mechanist Tradition," 93–121; Ian Simpson Ross, "Scots Law and Scots Criticism: The Case of Lord Kames," 614–623; and Leroy Shaw, "Henry Home of Kames: Precursor of Herder," 16–27. Helen Whitcomb Randall's "The Critical Theory of Lord Kames" remains authoritative. See Arthur E. McGuinness, *Henry Home, Lord Kames*. 59–60 and 93; and Rosamaria Loretelli, "Aspects of Lord Kames's *Elements of Criticism*," 1372.

[4] Nan Johnson, *Nineteenth-Century Rhetoric in North America*, 254–55; Vincent M. Bevilacqua, "The Rhetorical Theory of Henry Home, Lord Kames," 194–96.

[5] H. Lewis Ulman, "Discerning Readers," 68.

[6] John Frost, ed., "Advertisement of the American Editor," *An Abridgment of* Elements of Criticism, by Henry Home of Kames, iv; James R. Boyd, ed., "Preface by the American Editor," *Elements of Criticism*, by Henry Home of Kames, 3.

[7] Rhodes, 30.

Practicing Criticism as a Rational Science

For Kames practicing criticism as a rational science means using precepts about human nature, or psychology, as warrants for applying a rule of criticism to a performance in the fine arts. Perhaps the most well-known example of his critical practice, thanks to I. A. Richards, is Kames's praise of this line from Shakespeare's *Henry V:* "You may as well go about to turn the sun to ice by fanning in his face with a peacock's f[e]ather" (3: 176). Kames uses this example to illustrate the fourth rule or observation for narration and description: "facts and objects ought to be painted so accurately as to form in the mind of the reader distinct and lively images" (3: 174). Kames provides a psychological explanation for his approval of the description: "The peacock's feather, not to mention the beauty of the object, completes the image. An accurate image cannot be formed of this fanciful operation, without conceiving a particular feather; and the mind is at some loss, when this is not specified in the description" (3: 176–77). So approbation of the passage from *Henry V* is based on its conformity to a rule for description which, in turn, is based on a principle of human nature. One of Kames's contemporary biographers described this as philosophical criticism.[8] I prefer to call it the armchair psychology method. Since Kames offers a method of practicing criticism that involves reasoning upon matters of taste, *Elements* works as a rhetoric of criticism.[9]

Now that we have seen how to practice criticism as a rational science, we can sample Kames's critical practice to illustrate that his use of the new philosophy is not only or even primarily a response to the new philosophy per se, but rather a way of practicing criticism motivated by social, political, and nationalistic circumstances.

Shakespeare's Position in *Elements* and British Culture

I use Kames's Shakespeare criticism as a case study because of Shakespeare's presence in *Elements* and British culture. Kames cites more

---

[8] Alexander Fraser Tytler, Lord Woodhouselee, *Memoirs of the Life and Writings of the Honourable Henry Home of Kames*, Volume 1, 273.

[9] It does not seem accurate to limit its "rhetoric" to select chapters on language as some scholars have done. See for example Randall, 23; Ian Simpson Ross, *Lord Kames and the Scotland of His Day*, 273–76 and "Aesthetic Philosophy: Hutcheson and Hume to Alison," 253; McGuinness, 59–60; Bevilacqua, "Theory," 317 and "Nature," 48.

passages from Shakespeare than from any other author; about one in five citations is to one of his plays, or roughly two hundred of the book's thousand citations. Kames also cites ancient and foreign authors, such as Homer, Virgil, Tasso, and Voltaire, as well as other English authors such as Milton, Pope, and Swift. But the popularity of *Elements* is due in large part to its use of Shakespeare. Consider first the testimony of Dr. John Gregory in a 1768 letter advising an aspiring author. In this letter Gregory offers an explanation for the popularity of *Elements:* "What has made Lord Kaimes's [sic] 'Elements of Criticism' so popular in England, is his numerous illustrations and quotations from Shakespeare. If his book had wanted these illustrations, or if they had been taken from ancient or foreign authors, it would not have been so generally read in England."[10]

More significantly, consider the popularity of Shakespeare within British culture. The volume of editions of Shakespeare's works, of critical works devoted to Shakespeare, of theatrical performances, of Shakespeare merchandise helps to indicate Shakespeare's popularity. Between 1709 and 1762, at least nineteen editions and reprints of Shakespeare's works were printed.[11] Critical works were also printed, such as Thomas Edwards' *Canons of Criticism* (1748) and William Dodd's *The Beauties of Shakespear* (1752). Shakespeare was mentioned in some of the earliest and most popular periodicals: the *Tatler, Spectator,* and *Guardian.* Between 1747 and 1776, the London theaters of Drury Lane and Covent Garden performed Shakespeare's plays more often than those of any other author.[12] A statue of Shakespeare was erected in Westminister Abbey in 1741. By the 1769 Shakespeare Jubilee, Shakespeare had become an industry involving busts, medals, engravings, porcelain and pewter mementos.[13] Certainly Kames was tapping into the contemporary vogue for Shakespeare.

Shakespeare's popularity means that Shakespeare came ready-made with cultural meanings also at work in Kames's Shakespeare criticism. Over the course of the eighteenth century Shakespeare was made into

---

[10] William Forbes, *An Account of the Life and Writings of James Beattie,* 2nd ed., Volume 1, 141–42.

[11] See William Jaggard, *Shakespeare Bibliography,* 497–501.

[12] At Drury Lane during this period, almost twenty percent of the total number of performances were of Shakespeare, and at Covent Garden about sixteen percent (George Winchester Stone, Jr., "Introduction: The London Stage 1747–1776," clxii–clxvi).

[13] Paul Langford, *A Polite and Commercial People,* 309.

the national poet. Thomas Hanmer, editor of the 1745 Oxford edition of Shakespeare's works, evinces clearly a patriotic motive:

> Since therefore other nations have taken care to dignify the works of their most celebrated poets with the fairest impressions beautified with the ornaments of sculpture, well may our Shakespear be thought to deserve no less consideration: and as a fresh acknowledgment hath lately been paid to his merit, and a high regard to his name and memory, by erecting his Statue at a publick expence; so it is desired that this new Edition of his works, which hath cost some attention and care, may be looked upon as another small monument designed and dedicated to his honour.[14]

William Guthrie's *An Essay upon English Tragedy* (1747) is representative in pointing to France as a rival: "[T]o our eternal amazement it is true, that for above half a century the poets and the patrons of poetry, in England, abandoned the sterling merit of Shakespear for the tinsel ornaments of the French academy."[15] Guthrie describes England's participation in the battle of the books towards the end of the seventeenth century:

> The cry against the popular taste of poetry during the late reigns, became now more and more in fashion. Ministers took up the pen to ridicule Dryden, statesmen employed their talents to recommend the academy. England became a party in a French dispute. France by her arts avenged herself of our arms; our men of wit admitted her to be an arbiter, without seeming once to reflect that England had produced a Shakespear, a name which must have been decisive in the dispute, and which ought to strike dumb all advocates for any other superiority in the province of drama.[16]

Thus Guthrie associates Shakespeare with popular and English taste as opposed to that of the French and members of the Stuart court. And

---

[14] Thomas Hanmer, ed. *The Works of Shakespear*, Volume 1, viii–ix.
[15] William Guthrie, *An Essay upon English Tragedy*, 10.
[16] Guthrie, 17.

thus Shakespeare's popularity serves as a counterpart to the growing strength of the Hanoverian regime.

Shakespeare's popularity also serves as a counterpart to the rise of Britain's wealth and middling classes. Britain was in not only cultural battle with France but also military. England declared war on France in 1744, was involved in diplomatic maneuvers and military skirmishes in the early 1750s, and engaged in war by 1756. In the Seven Years War the British aimed to defend Hanover against the French as well as Austrians, Russians, and Swedes. At stake in these conflicts were commercial empires—overseas markets that contributed to the rise of the middling classes. Eventually Britain gained territory from the French and enjoyed significant commercial gains.[17] One scholar uses these British gains to explain Voltaire's change from boasting that he was responsible for the introduction of Shakespeare into France to vilifying Shakespeare, and another illustrates that Garrick's adaptations of Shakespeare during this time were identified with the national cause.[18] The point is that Kames—like Garrick, Voltaire, and others—wrote not in intellectual isolation but in the midst of a growing British economy and empire, growth taking place at the expense of its French rivals as well as its own social and political status quo. One scholar describes the rise of Shakespeare's pre-eminence as "one of the central cultural expressions of England's own transition from the aristocratic regime of the Stuarts to the commercial empire presided over by the Hanoverians."[19] Thus Shakespeare's popularity involved British nationalism and increased economic power among the middling classes.

Motives for Practicing Shakespeare Criticism as a Rational Science

Simply by reproducing so much Shakespeare in *Elements*, Kames taps into political, nationalistic, and social motives. Now we will see how

---

[17] Kathleen Wilson has summarized Britain's commercial gains as follows: the war "bolstered the Atlantic economy, especially the colonial trade in sugar, slaves, tobacco and rum, vastly increased exports to and imports from the North American colonies, allowed Britain to capture the China tea trade and the Senegal gum trade, and produced profits for speculator and privateers alike" (*The Sense of the People*, 193).

[18] Elaine Cuvelier, "Shakespeare, Voltaire, and French Taste," 39–40; Michael Dobson, *The Making of the National Poet*, 203–07.

[19] Dobson, 8.

his critical practice—how his use of the new philosophy, or the armchair psychology method—taps into these motives.

First we should clarify the audience and aim of *Elements*. The work is designed to help middling readers display taste by reasoning upon it. In the introduction to *Elements* Kames describes the principles of human nature as "a foundation for judging of taste, and for reasoning upon it" (1: 8). In the chapter "Standard of Taste," Kames suggests that the practice of criticism sets one apart from both the vulgar and voluptuous. Taste, according to Kames, resides in the common sense of mankind; taste is a matter of determining what is naturally agreeable and naturally disagreeable. Although it would seem as if all people could lay claim to taste, Kames notes that we cannot "collect votes indifferently" (3: 369): "those who depend for food on bodily labour, are totally void of taste" (3: 369), and others may have their taste corrupted by "voluptuousness" or riches (3: 370). Kames acknowledges that these exclusions narrow the group to a select few. In his words:

> The exclusion of classes so many and various, reduces within a narrow compass those who are qualified to be judges in the fine arts. Many circumstances are necessary to form a judge of this sort: there must be a good natural taste: this taste must be improved by education, reflection, and experience: it must be preserved alive, by a regular course of life, by using the goods of fortune with moderation, and by following the dictates of improved nature which gives welcome to every rational pleasure without deviating into excess. This is the tenor of life which of all contributes the most to refinement of taste; and the same tenor of life contributes the most to happiness in general. (3: 371)

What options were available for practicing criticism—for displaying taste? First, one could simply exclaim "wonderful" or "splendid" in response to a performance. Kames presents this as an undesirable option since he hopes to train readers to reason upon taste. He asserts that reasoning upon taste allows one to avoid "resign[ing] himself entirely to sentiment or feeling, without interposing any sort of judgment" (1: 8). Likewise, in the preface to his edition of Shakespeare's works, Pope had found fault with critics who reprint fine passages "with general Applauses, or empty Exclamations at the tail of them."[20] Apparently this was a live option, but it would not enable one to distinguish oneself in matters of taste.

A second option would be philological criticism, but this would not be feasible for members of the middling classes. To illustrate this point, we can compare a passage of philological criticism of Hamlet's "To be or not be" soliloquy with a passage of Kames's armchair psychology criticism. Kames uses part of the soliloquy to illustrate one of the sources of faulty metaphors—"[t]he jumbling different metaphors in the same sentence, or the beginning with one metaphor and ending with another" (3: 123):

> Whether 'tis nobler in the mind, to suffer
> The stings [sic] and arrows of outrag'ous fortune;
> Or to take arms against a sea of troubles,
> And by opposing end them.

Although Kames does not provide an explanation for this particular rule, other rules for metaphors include psychological explanations. For example, different metaphors should not be joined in the same period "even where they are preserved distinct. It is difficult to imagine the subject to be first one thing and then another in the same period without interval: the mind is distracted by the rapid transition; and when the imagination is put on such hard duty, its images are too faint to produce any good effect" (3: 124; see also 3: 118–19, 3: 125).

In contrast, Lewis Theobald approaches the passage philologically. He suggests that "to take arms against a sea of troubles" might be faulty; but then attempts to defend it.

> To take Arms against a Sea, literally speaking, would be as unfeasible a Project, as the Attempt (mentioned in a Speech of the Lord Haversham, in a late Reign;) to stop the Tide at Gravesend with a Man's Thumb. . . . [Perhaps "sea" should be corrected to "siege," as Pope suggests and as Theobald had guessed before him.] But, perhaps, the Correction may be, at best, but a Guess; considering the great Liberties that this Poet is observed to take, elsewhere, in his Diction,

---

[20] Alexander Pope, ed., *The Works of Shakespear*, Volume 1, xxiii.

and Connexion of Metaphors: And considering too, that a Sea (amongst the ancient Writers, sacred and prophane, in the Oriental, as well as the Greek and Latin, Tongues;) is used to signify not only the great, collected, Body of Waters which make the Ocean, but likewise a vast Quantity, or Multitude, of any thing else. [Here Theobald includes a note: "*Vid.* Schindleri *Lexic. Pentaglottum;* Kircheri *Concordanties Veteris Testamenti;* Becmannum *de Origine Linguae Latinae;* Martinii *Lexicon Philologicum*, &c."] The Prophet Jeremiah, particularly, in one Passage, calls a prodigious Army coming up against a City, a Sea.[21]

Here and elsewhere Theobald attempts to provide a correct version of Shakespeare with reference to other works of Shakespeare and to classical languages and works. Certainly more learning is involved in this kind of criticism than in armchair psychology criticism. And certainly one practicing this kind of criticism would be subject to the charge of pedantry.

A third option would be neoclassical criticism, or basing critical judgments on the practice of ancient dramatists and epic poets and on rules derived from the ancients such as Aristotle and Horace. One problem with practicing this kind of criticism is that, when judged by neoclassical standards such as the unities of time, place, and action, Shakespeare fares badly. Throughout the century critics defended Shakespeare against the judgments of rule-based criticism. In the *Spectator*, for example, Addison faults "our Criticks [who] do not seem sensible that there is more Beauty in the Works of a great Genius who is ignorant of the Rules of Art, than in those of a little Genius who knows and observes them. . . . Our inimitable Shakespear is a Stumbling-block to the whole Tribe of these rigid Criticks."[22] An essay in Theobald's periodical *Censor* prefaces praise of Shakespeare's presentation of Lear's character with this observation: "had Shakespear read all that Aristotle, Horace, and the Criticks have wrote on this Score, he could not have wrought more happily."[23] In 1765 Johnson is still

---

[21] Lewis Theobald, *Shakespeare Restored*, 82–83.

[22] *The Spectator*, Volume 5, edited by Donald F. Bond (Oxford: Clarendon Press, 1965), 28.

[23] *The Censor* (London, 1717), 71–72.

defending Shakespeare from "the censure of criticks, who form their judgments upon narrower principles."[24]

An essay in *Gray's-Inn Journal* is representative of an alternative standard by which to judge Shakespeare: "Aristotle was certainly mistaken when he called the Fable the Life and Soul of Tragedy; the Art of constructing the dramatic Story should always be subservient to the Exhibition of Character, our great Shakespear has breathed another Soul into Tragedy, which has found the way of striking an Audience with Sentiment and Passion at the same Time."[25] Kames shares this view:

> [Shakespeare's] plays are defective in the mechanical part, which is less the work of genius than of experience; and is not otherwise brought to perfection than by diligently observing the errors of former compositions. Shakespear excels all the ancients and moderns, in knowledge of human nature, and in unfolding even the most obscure and refined emotions. This is a rare faculty, and of the greatest importance in a dramatic author; and it is this faculty which makes him surpass all other writers in the comic as well as tragic vein. (2: 215)

By practicing criticism in a way that involves precepts about human nature, Kames and others find a way of praising Shakespeare, Britain's national poet, that involves no more learning than armchair psychology.

The method also has political and patriotic appeal. In the introduction to *Elements,* Kames observes that criticism

> continues to be not less slavish in its principles, nor less submissive to authority, than it was originally. Bossu, a celebrated French critic, gives many rules; but can discover no better foundation for any of them, than the practice merely of Homer and Virgil, supported by the authority of Aristotle. (1: 15)

---

[24] Samuel Johnson, ed., *The Plays of William Shakespeare*, 8 volumes, xii; see also William Warburton, ed., *The Works of Shakespear*, 8 volumes, xviii–xix.

[25] *The Gray's-Inn Journal*, Volume 2 (London, 1756), 267.

Kames blames Le Bossu for subjecting himself to the critical tyranny of the ancients:

> It could not surely be his [Le Bossu's] opinion, that these poets, however eminent for genius, were intitled to give laws to mankind, and that nothing now remains but blind obedience to their arbitrary will. (1: 15).

Human nature, according to Kames, is "the true source of criticism" (1: 16). The language Kames uses to describe neoclassical criticism is noteworthy: French criticism involves blind obedience to the arbitrary will of the ancients who are not entitled to give laws to mankind. The political resonances are unmistakable and contribute to the appeal of Kames's critical practice.

Conclusion

If we accounted for the appeal of *Elements* only by its use of the new philosophy, we would not go very far or deep into the motives for practicing criticism as a rational science. We would overlook other significant features of Kames's critical practice, including his heavy use of Shakespeare and the motives involved in his Shakespeare criticism. We would remind ourselves that Kames makes use of the new philosophy but we would not appreciate why. By not appreciating why we would be left with a rather thin account of this branch of rhetorical studies—criticism—and its position in eighteenth-century British culture.

This essay is a step toward enhancing our understanding of rhetoric and criticism in eighteenth-century Britain. It introduces select motives and alternative critical practices in broad outline. Certainly the story of criticism and *Elements* is more complex. But this study does begin to meet the need of understanding *Elements* in its historical context and understanding one version of the relationship between rhetoric and criticism. It shows that the appeal of the armchair psychology method of practicing criticism lies not simply in its intellectual heritage but also in its ease of practice, compatibility with Shakespearean drama, and in concert with the growing strength of the Hanoverian regime.

I close with two implications of Kames's critical practice. First, as we have seen, while it seems to bring criticism within the capacity of all people, in fact it confines it to a select few. Second, while it claims to break from neoclassical rule-based criticism—criticism founded on authority—it remains authoritarian. As Kames puts it in the dedication to George III:

> The fine arts have ever been encouraged by wise princes, not singly for private amusement, but for their beneficial influence in society. By uniting different ranks in the same elegant pleasures, they promote benevolence: by cherishing love of order, they inforce submission to government: and by inspiring delicacy of feeling, they make regular government a double blessing. (1: iii)

Thus Kames's critical practice is compatible with social and political submission. With one hand it gives middling readers a sense of cultural superiority and with the other helps to keep all in their places.

26 Sentimental Journey: The Place and Status of the Emotions in Hugh Blair's Rhetoric

Sean Patrick O'Rourke

To reassess the place and status of the emotions in the rhetoric of Hugh Blair (1718–1800), this paper takes gentle issue with two general (and somewhat contradictory) claims found in the Blair scholarship.[1] The first and dominant school of thought holds that Blair exemplifies the "New Rhetoric" of the Scottish Enlightenment by departing dramatically from Ciceronian approaches to discourse. The second, minority view considers Blair the last representative of neoclassical rhetoric, passing on the tenets of classicism to the nineteenth century. Both, it seems, stress different aspects of Blair's approach to emotion in rhetoric. Neither fully explains it.

The questions are of some importance. Over the last quarter century, historians of rhetoric have begun to reexamine the place and status of emotion in rhetorical theory and practice. William W. Fortenbaugh,[2] Jakob Wisse,[3] and Arthur Walzer[4] have authored revealing studies of emotion in Aristotle, Cicero, and Campbell. These studies and others like them suggest the importance of emotion in most accounts of human rhetorical activity. Furthermore, Blair remains a pivotal and contested figure in the history of rhetoric. His *Lectures on Rhetoric and Belles Lettres* (2 vols.), first published in 1783, have been revised, translated, abridged, adapted, and widely reprinted and studied

---

[1] The author wishes to thank the manuscript librarians at the National Library of Scotland and the Edinburgh University Library for their invaluable assistance in this project.

[2] William W. Fortenbaugh, *Aristotle on Emotion*.

[3] Jakob Wisse, *Ethos and Pathos from Aristotle to Cicero*.

[4] Arthur E. Walzer, "Campbell on the Passions," 72–85.

over the last two hundred years (a new edition is due out any day from Southern Illinois University Press) and, to a somewhat lesser extent, so have his *Sermons*.[5] Blair's rhetoric figured heavily in the education of many of the more prominent writers and orators of the nineteenth century and may well have been, as some have claimed, the most influential rhetoric in the English-speaking world.[6] A reassessment of the emotions in Blair's rhetoric would seem, then, to be of merit.

The paper proceeds by briefly surveying the scholarship on Blair, establishing the two dominant claims noted above. In the second section I offer an alternative reading of the place and status of the emotions in the *Lectures,* and attempt to show how Blair melded (or at least placed uneasily together in the same set of lectures) broadly belletristic concerns for sublimity, taste, and propriety with Ciceronian elements of the use of emotion in oratory to produce a theoretically unstable but nonetheless useful account of the emotions, one with implications for both criticism *and* composition. In the third section I illustrate Blair's approach by looking at his use of emotion in his rhetorical practice. In particular I examine emotion in Blair's *Observations Upon a Pamphlet Entitled, An Analysis of the Moral and Religious Sentiments . . . of Sopho and David Hume,* written during the *Episcopus Infidelium* controversy of 1755, his "Brief in the Douglas Cause" (c. 1767), and his fast-day sermon "On the Love of Our Country" (1793).

The Literature on Blair & Emotion, or: A Tale of Two Blairs

To return to the two general readings of Blair's rhetoric, the now dominant school of thought is to characterize Blair as a champion of

---

[5] See, e.g., Robert Morrell Schmitz, *Hugh Blair,* 144 (listing more than 100 editions and abridgments of Blair's *Lectures*); James Golden and Douglas Ehninger, "The Extrinsic Sources of Blair's Popularity," 16 (noting that Blair's *Lectures* constituted "one of the best selling and most widely influential textbooks of all times."); William Charvat, *The Origins of American Critical Thought 1810–1835,* 44 (noting that "half the educated English-speaking world studied [Blair's book] in its day").

[6] See, in addition to the sources discussed in note 4, *supra,* David Daiches, "Style Periodique and Style Coupe: Hugh Blair and the Scottish Rhetoric of American Independence," 209–26; Don Abbott, "Blair 'Abroad': The European Reception of the *Lectures on Rhetoric and Belles Lettres,*" 67–77; Don Paul Abbott, "The Influence of Blair's *Lectures* in Spain," 275–89; Thomas P. Miller, *The Formation of College English,* 227–52.

the "New Rhetoric." In so doing these scholars concentrate on Blair's emphasis on natural genius over "artificial" schemes of invention, his condemnation of the topics, his extensive discussions of criticism, taste, sublimity, and propriety, and his expansion of the modes or types of discourse. This view holds that Blair's rhetoric, like other belletristic rhetorics of his day, articulates what might be called a rhetoric of reception or a theory of "receptive competence": a concern for reading and criticism over composing and speaking.[7] And so, for example, Ehninger notes Blair's "managerial" view of rhetoric, wherein rhetoric becomes not an art of investigating or discovering evidence, proof, truth, and the like, but rather an art of criticism or, at least, a means of managing what has already been discerned through genius, nature, or plain common sense.[8] More recently, Warnick characterizes Blair's rhetoric as a "loosely-woven pedagogy that aimed to instruct its reader on the basic elements of good prose style and the rudiments of criticism," and argues that Blair's and other "[e]ighteenth-century Scottish rhetorics approached study of persuasive influence from a perspective entirely different from the neoclassical rhetorics that preceded them." She concludes, "They were not concerned with production, source credibility, invention, or the particular rhetorical situation. Instead, they emphasized reception, the origins and development of taste, and the aesthetic dimensions of discourse as generalized phenomena." As a result, Warnick considers Scottish rhetoricians "ill-served by studies that view them through a neoclassical lens."[9]

Others, however, characterize Blair as the last of the neoclassical rhetoricians. In so doing they concentrate on Blair's discussions of the

---

[7] While the term "receptive competence" can be found in Barbara Warnick, *The Sixth Canon*, 4, 96–97, 131–36, the position that Blair and others of his day developed rhetorics that were audience- rather than speaker-oriented, concerned more with the criticism than the production of discourse, and oriented toward achieving social competence in polite society, has a long tradition. See, e.g., Douglas Ehninger, "Selected Theories of *Inventio* in English Rhetoric, 1759–1828"; Ehninger, "Dominant Trends in English Rhetorical Thought, 1750–1800," 3–12; Ehninger, "On Rhetoric and Rhetorics," 242–49; Ehninger, "On Systems of Rhetoric," 131–44; Nancy S. Struever, "The Conversable World," 80. On this tradition and its implications, see Miller, especially, 253–76.

[8] See, e.g., Douglas W. Ehninger, "Dominant Trends in English Rhetorical Thought," 3–19.

[9] Warnick, 131, 136.

history of eloquence or public speaking, his division of the parts of the oration, his recommendations for the improvement of the orator, his use of the classical terminology of *elocutio* and *dispositio,* his discussion of the "vehement voice," and his extensive use of classical, especially Ciceronian examples of discourse. And so, for example, Kennedy, Halloran, and, more recently, Halloran and Ferreira-Buckley, emphasize Blair's indebtedness to Quintilian and his synthesis and reformulation of Quintilian's dominant themes.[10] Guthrie considers Blair to be one of the primary vehicles for the transference of neoclassical rhetorical thought to the American colonies,[11] and Ferguson claims that early American lawyers excavated Ciceronian tenets of judicial eloquence from Blair and employed them in early American legal practice.[12]

An Alternative Reading of Blair on Emotion

In this paper I wish to complicate the conclusions of both groups of readers. I argue that both claims may tend, if pushed to extremes, to oversimplify Blair's approach to discourse in general and to the emotions in particular. In short, I argue that Blair's rhetoric fits neatly into neither camp. Blair's rhetoric was provocative although pedantic, useful but not original, because he cared less for theoretical consistency and more for the practicalities demanded by the teaching of 15-year-old undergraduates at the University of Edinburgh. As a result, his lectures embrace a tension between two often contradictory and perhaps inimical systems of rhetoric. I call them the "conversational" and the "controversial," respectively.

"Conversational rhetoric" is here used to denote the belletristic project of revamping rhetoric for polite society or what David Hume called, "the conversable World."[13] In this realm, "gentlemen" of polite society are taught to employ a "proper" (that is, "simple" and "el-

---

[10] George A. Kennedy, *Classical Rhetoric and Its Christian and Secular Tradition from Ancient to Modern Times*; S. Michael Halloran, "Hugh Blair's Use of Quintilian and the Transformation of Rhetoric in the 18th Century," 183–95; Linda Ferreira-Buckley and S. Michael Halloran, "Introduction," *Hugh Blair's Lectures on Rhetoric and Belles Lettres,* edited by Ferreira-Buckley and Halloran.

[11] Warren Guthrie, "The Development of Rhetorical Theory in America, 1635–1850," 38–54.

[12] Robert A. Ferguson, *Law and Letters in American Culture.*

[13] David Hume, "Of Essay Writing," 533–37.

egant") style, fashion critical literary judgments, and cultivate the faculty of taste. Conversational rhetoric is rooted in "polite" ideology and early faculty psychology, assumes a non-skeptical epistemology (based on revealed religion, nature, and commonsense or empiricist philosophy), and seeks to prepare readers to be critics capable of aesthetic and moral judgment.[14]

By "controversial rhetoric" I refer to a more or less Ciceronian system of eloquence designed for the contentious world of public persuasion. In this system, citizen-orators are taught to employ a "vehement" style, craft legal and political judgments, and cultivate social justice. Controversial rhetoric is rooted in the ideals of civic humanism, assumes a skeptical epistemology (or at least a rhetorical situation pervaded by doubt), and prepares rhetors to use the Ciceronian notion of arguing *pro* and *contra, in utramque partem,* to understand both (or several) sides of an issue or controversy.

Blair's view of emotion is similarly two-fold, and loosely follows these two quasi-theoretical stances. To put it another way, Blair's view of the passions includes both conversational and controversial elements.

Blair discusses the conversational aspects of emotion in volume one of the first edition of his *Lectures*.[15] Volume one initiates a discussion of rhetoric as criticism, and in this way forms the basis for the claim that Blair's rhetoric is essentially a theory of "receptive competence." He covers the general nature and importance of criticism, the centrality of natural genius, and the key elements of Taste, Sublimity, and Propriety.

Blair's discussion of taste occupies all of Lecture II, a good portion of Lectures III & V, and serves as a rationale for most of volume one. As in so much of his rhetoric, Blair is here unconcerned with either theoretical consistency or originality. Barbara Warnick concurs when she notes that "Blair's views on taste consisted of a strange mixture of empiricism and commonsense stances."[16] Blair therefore opted to consider taste as an internal sense, one similar to gustatory taste. As such, taste is, like morality, fixed in the sentiments, and the standard of taste must be that which coincides with the general sentiments of

---

[14] On rhetoric and polite ideology in Blair's time, see Adam Potkay, *The Fate of Eloquence in the Age of Hume*.

[15] Hugh Blair, *Lectures on Rhetoric and Belles Lettres*, 2 vols.

[16] Warnick, 2, 114.

men. Blair therefore joined Hume's "internal reflex sense" of taste with the commonsense school's linkage to universal commonsense principles. Dismissing the large philosophical differences between the two schools of thought as differing "very little from one another,"[17] Blair emphasized *both* the sensory, emotive aspect of taste and the rational, commonsense elements.

Blair's views on the sublime are similarly derivative. In Lectures IV & V Blair situates the sublime in the emotional response of the reader or observer of the beautiful. He notes that, whenever we observe the sublime, "the emotion raised in us is of the same kind, although the objects that produce them be of widely different kinds." Further, Blair locates the sources of the sublime in literature in the traditional five sources: Boldness and grandeur of thoughts, the proper application of figures, the use of tropes and beautiful expressions, musical structure and arrangement of words, and of course, the pathetic. Finally, Blair notes that the sublime is not the product of rhetorical artifice but rather arises "unsought, if it comes at all," and is "the natural offspring of a strong imagination."[18] In this way Blair begins to bridge the gap between the conversational and the controversial, because, while most of his discussion assumes a reader assessing and appreciating a work of literature, his last comments concern the composition of sublime discourse.

Blair completes this bridge with his discussion of propriety, which he also associates with style and the pathetic. It is revealing that Blair's discussion of propriety occurs in two different places: In volume one he considers propriety as an aspect of the critical judgment of a work of art, and in volume two he considers it as a concern of orators in public assemblies such as the bar, the pulpit, and the legislature, as well as an aspect of the proper conduct of a discourse in general. In this sense Blair associates propriety, as Cicero did, with that which is suitable to the occasion and appropriate to the object under consideration.

It therefore seems quite natural for Blair to take up a view of emotion much more Ciceronian than belletristic in volume two, lectures XXVII through XXXII. Here he outlines a view of emotions consistent with our view of controversial rhetoric, albeit with an eighteenth-century twist. He begins by embracing the conviction/persuasion duality so characteristic of eighteenth-century Scottish rhetoric by noting

---

[17] *Lectures*, 1: 32.
[18] *Lectures*, 1: 75.

that, where one addresses only the conviction of one's listeners, the pathetic is unneeded.[19] However, to persuade, the emotions are indispensable. Blair notes:

> In all that relates to practice, there is no man who seriously means to persuade another, but addresses himself to his passions more or less; for this plain reason, that passions are the great springs of human action. The most virtuous man, in treating of the most virtuous subject, seeks to touch the heart of him to whom he speaks; and makes no scruple to raise his indignation at injustice, or his pity to the distressed, though pity and indignation be passions.[20]

The discussion of emotion that follows is, characteristically, less theoretical than preceptual. In this way Blair's work joins the long list of preceptual treatises that mark the European tradition of rhetoric. Blair offers a set of "directions" for the use of the "Pathetic" part of persuasion.

"First," he suggests, we must determine "whether the subject admit the Pathetic, and render it proper; and if it does, what part of the Discourse is the most proper" for its inclusion? Then, Blair notes, *rhetors* who "expect any emotion . . . to have a lasting effect" must appeal first to the understanding and judgment, for "hearers must be convinced that there are good and sufficient grounds for their entering with warmth into the cause." The appeal to the understanding is, for Blair, an attempt to assuage the audience's suspicion that emotion may carry them away "by mere delusion." While Blair hints that emotion properly may be employed at any point, he concludes that most writers have good reason to assign "the Pathetic to the Peroration or Conclusion," for the warmth of emotion can best produce its full effect when it is the last thing left in the minds of the hearers.[21]

---

[19] *Lectures*, 2: 189. On the "conviction-persuasion duality," see Edward Z. Rowell, "The Conviction-Persuasion Duality," 469–82. I wish to thank the late Dominic A. LaRusso for calling this forgotten article to my attention.

[20] *Lectures*, 2: 189.

[21] *Lectures*, 2: 190–91. In such passages (when needed) I have inserted "[*sic*]" to indicate not an error on Blair's part (as is sometimes mistakenly perceived) but rather, in keeping with the Latin, "so" or "thus": the spelling provided is in Blair's original. Of course, spelling and usage were not stan-

Blair's second precept of emotion is that orators should "never give warning that [they] are about to be pathetic," for such action "never fails to prove a refrigerant to passion." Blair advises what he calls the "indirect" method, "when you seize the critical moment that is favourable to emotion, in whatever part of the discourse it occurs; and then, after due preparation, throw in such circumstances, and present such glowing images, as may kindle their passions before they are aware." The indirect method, he urges, can be accomplished in a few sentences and must flow from the "natural warmth of the speaker."[22]

Blair's third precept of emotion is central to his approach. The speaker must observe, he urges, "that there is a great difference between showing the hearers that they ought to be moved, and actually moving them." Relying heavily on faculty psychology, which assumes that nature adapts a set of external objects (which convey sensations to the brain) to every passion or emotion, Blair argues that it is "not in the power of any Orator to raise emotion" without first setting the objects of the desired emotion before the minds of the hearers. He writes:

> I am warmed with gratitude, I am touched with compassion, not when a Speaker shows me that these are noble dispositions, and that it is my duty to feel them; or when he exclaims against me for my indifference and coldness. All this time he is speaking only to my reason or conscience. He must describe the kindness and tenderness of my friend; he must set before me the distress suffered by the person for whom he would interest me; then, and not till then, my heart begins to be touched, my gratitude or my compassion begin to flow.[23]

The "foundation" of all successful "Pathetic Oratory" is, for Blair, the verbal "painting of the object of that passion which we wish to raise." With this thought Blair participates in the kind of sentimental journey Adam Smith describes in *A Theory of Moral Sentiments*, in which Smith advances an explanation of moral judgment hinged on the ac-

---

dardized at the time of Blair's writing and I do not intend to imply that Blair was a careless or poor speller.

[22] *Lectures*, 2: 191.
[23] *Lectures*, 2: 192–93.

quisition of "fellow feeling" derived from vivid, persuasive description of the objects under moral consideration.[24]

In keeping with Smith's theory, Blair then offers a fourth precept: the orator must actually feel the emotion to be raised. "The only effectual method is," he tells his students, "to be moved yourselves. There are a thousand interesting circumstances suggested by real passion, which no art can imitate, and no refinement can supply." Blair insists that "the internal emotion of the Speaker adds a pathos to his words, his looks, his gestures, and his whole manner, which exerts a power almost irresistible over those who hear him."[25]

The final three precepts, attending to the proper language of the passions, avoiding interweaving anything that will divert the natural course of the passions, and restraining the pathetic so that it is neither too long nor raised to "unnatural heights," suggest general guidelines for achieving the kind of emotional appeal described in the first four precepts. They also reiterate the need to keep the emotions within the margins demanded by decorum and propriety.[26]

In sum then, Blair offers a two-fold view of emotion. In conversational rhetoric, emotion is the pathetic element of aesthetic response. In controversial rhetoric, however, the passions become the "great springs of human action," capable of touching the heart and raising indignation or pity, constrained only by decorum or propriety.

Blair in Practice, or: The Passions Broadly Displayed

The two-fold view of emotion described in his *Lectures* can be more readily apprehended by attending to Blair's rhetorical practice. In what follows I seek to show how Blair's use of emotion ranges over the entire breadth of the preceptual ground set forth in the *Lectures,* from conversational to controversial.

Observations Upon a Pamphlet (1755):

Written anonymously in 1755, Blair's pamphlet was part of the *Episcopus Infedelium* controversy, in which the Reverend Bonar and other leaders of the conservative faction of the Scottish Kirk attacked Blair's friends, Henry Home (Lord Kames) and David Hume. Blair and his moderate

---

[24] Adam Smith, *A Theory of Moral Sentiments*, 7th Edition.
[25] *Lectures*, 2: 193–94.
[26] *Lectures*, 2: 194–96.

allies rose to the defense of Kames and Hume, and the *Observations* is one of their tracts written, we now know, by Blair.[27]

In it, Blair seeks to show how Bonar distorts, misquotes, and otherwise misrepresents the writings of Kames and Hume. The tract is addressed primarily to the understanding and conviction of his hearers, at least insofar as he appears to be following his own precepts for "enquiries after mere truth." There are, however, points at which Blair seems to persuade and it is at these points that we find revealed his practice of "raising" the emotions.

Early in the tract, Blair notes:

> The freedom of inquiry and debate, tho' it may have published some errors to the world, has undoubtedly been the source from whence many blessings have flowed upon mankind. As free inquiry alone could at first have made way for Christianity, and have borne down the opposition of synagogues, senates and schools; it is to the same noble principle we owe the Reformation, and are enabled to set at defiance the tyrannical decisions of Popes and Councils. By means of free inquiry, the church of *Scotland* was originally established. In this country, therefore, all attempts to infringe so valuable a privilege in cases where the peace of society is not concerned, must ever be regarded with concern by all reasonable men. The proper objects of censure and reproof are not freedom of thought, but licentiousness of action; not erroneous speculations, but crimes pernicious to society.[28]

In this brief passage Blair seeks, it seems, to follow his own precepts on appealing to the understanding and judgment of the audience before addressing the emotions, for the passage appeals primarily to the principle of free speech and the benefits of open inquiry. The passage evokes little passion. Nonetheless, the argument does tend to emphasize a shared commitment and fidelity to freedom of speech and, to

---

[27] *Observations upon a Pamphlet, Intitled, An Analysis of the Moral and Religious Sentiments contained in the Writings of Sopho, and David Hume, Esq.* (Edinburgh: np, 1755).

[28] *Observations* 1–2.

this extent, raises an emotional response, however soft, to the object he sets forth as the central feature of the controversy.

Later Blair raises the emotional stakes by setting forth the standards of fair inquiry and debate. He suggests that, "If there should be found passages which are neither the words, nor the meaning of the author, the falshood [*sic*] cannot be palliated, nor excused."[29] Operating here is the continued commitment to a sense of fair play, a sense that he urges has been violated by Bonar's attack on Hume and Kames. Blair pleads:

> And I here ask, If it be candid or honest to cite an author in this manner, and to aver that the very expressions are quoted? To glean disunited sentences, to patch them together arbitrarily, to omit the limitations or remarks with which a proposition is delivered; can this be stiled [*sic*] exhibiting the sentiments of an author? . . . [This is] the inquisitorial method of interpretation used in the church of *Rome* [which is] by so just and so severe raillery rendered detestable. . . . This is the genuine logic of persecution. From arts such as these have the unhappy divisions which so long distracted the church been derived. At a period when mankind are fully sensible of the blessings they enjoy, and the liberty both civil and ecclesiastical is become the dearest possession of the people, and the favorite care of the Prince; what sentiments ought the revival of those insidious and Jesuitical principles to excite in every sincere friend to our present constitution in Church and State![30]

In this passage, of course, the object of Blair's probing comment is Bonar's "scholarly" method, and the emotion Blair seeks to raise is something like disgust, a sense of foul play, a feeling that the fairness standard he had set forth earlier has been violated. By associating Bonar's practices with the inquisitorial methods of the Catholic Church, widely held by the Scottish Kirk's conservative Calvinists to be diabolical, and by raising the spectre of the reviled Jesuits, Blair seeks to place before his readers the objects of moral derision and ridicule.

---

[29] *Observations* 11.
[30] *Observations* 13–14.

To ensure that his allusions are not mistaken, Blair urges that, "To affect a zeal against heresy, and at the same time to disregard truth, must appear to every one highly culpable and very unchristian."[31] Then, after a favorable review of Hume's work, Blair observes:

> Justice demands this acknowledgment as due to an elegant and agreeable writer, even though a Free-Thinker; and it must at the same time be observed, that it appears very like a contradiction to accuse a man in one page of scepticism and infidelity, and in the following page to tax him with an attachment to Popery and superstition.[32]

Here again we can discern the psychological roots of Blair's use of emotion: the object is still Bonar's method, the emotional response a kind of repugnance for Bonar's violation of the rules of fair play and even-handed treatment, the looming spectre the fearful methods of the Catholic inquisitors.

In the *Observations,* then, Blair appears to use elements of both controversial and conversational rhetoric. To the extent that the controversial setting demands it, Blair's use of emotion is heavily controversial, following, it seems, the precepts outlined in volume two of his *Lectures.* Still, Blair is writing for a learned audience and, however much he may disagree with his opponents, carefully constrains his use of "the pathetic" within the bounds of that community's sense of taste and propriety. His rhetoric contains no Ciceronian invective, evidences no vitriolic vituperation, and reviles no one, not even the good Rev. Bonar. The Ciceronian mode is constrained by his sense of decorum and the emotional appeals follow the prescriptions of "proper" taste. In the Douglas Cause, however, Blair feels less constrained, perhaps because, as will be seen, the subjects of his passion appear less deserving of restraint.

Brief in the Douglas Cause (c. 1767):

The Douglas Cause was a patrimony suit for the Douglas estate, in which the Duke of Hamilton sued Sir John and Lady Jane Douglas for fraud and falsely putting forth their son as heir to the estate. Blair wrote a brief for the Hamilton side, perhaps the only example of legal

---

[31] *Observations* 15.
[32] *Observations* 27.

writing we have from his hand.³³ That brief and the many others in the case offer more issues than can be discussed in this essay. Two, however, are of special interest here: The Hamilton side contended that Sir John and Lady Jane faked Lady Jane's pregnancy and then faked the birth of a child, instead purchasing a boy (actually two) from a poor family in France.

As in his *Observations* on the Bonar charges, in his Douglas "Brief" Blair first sets forth standards of judgment, in this case a basis for a factual claim. He writes, "What are usually regarded as the symptoms of Pregnancy, may either take their rise from some natural distemper incident to the Female Sex or may be assumed in order to lay the foundation for imposing on the world a false delivery."³⁴ He then proceeds to describe Lady Jane and Sir John's account of her putative pregnancy, only to indicate that "[t]his monstrous account of Lady Jane's pregnancy stands confuted by evidence the most clear and undeniable."³⁵ Blair follows with a lengthy review of the evidence that contradicts the account offered by his opponents. The entire account proceeds rationally, appealing, as perhaps Blair would say, to the understanding. Indeed, he underscores the rationality of his treatment of the evidence as he begins to address the passions. He writes,

> The only rational account that can be given, is that Lady Jane in fact was not pregnant. That a plan had been formed of imposing upon the World[,] and that Paris had been orriginally [sic] pexct [sic] upon as the Scene of the imposture both upon acco[un]t of the facility of procuring Children there and the great probability of their remaining undiscovered in that large and populous City.³⁶

To further strengthen the conclusion of fraud, Blair colors the story by noting that "So material a falsehood at first deliberately averred both by Sir John & Mrs. Hewitt [the couple's servant] and afterwards corrected at so critical a period, gives but an unfavourable impression

---

³³ "Case for the Respondents," [c. 1767], ms. 5356, ff. 59–122v., National Library of Scotland, Edinburgh. All subsequent references to this are as "Brief."

³⁴ "Brief," 1 (f. 59r.).

³⁵ "Brief," 4 (f. 60v.).

³⁶ "Brief," 8 (f. 62v.).

of the story which they {alledge} [*sic*] relate."[37] At this point Blair apparently feels free to raise indignation, for he follows with a condemnation in what for him is strong emotional language. He concludes, "Every part of this amazing history when attended to demonstrates the whole to be an absolute falsehood."[38]

In the Douglas "Brief" Blair can be seen once again invoking a controversial rhetoric and using the emotions in a manner still constrained by his station and his sense of propriety. In the "Brief," however, he goes well beyond the emotional play of the *Observations*. Here Blair employs much stronger language, describing Lady Jane and Sir John's story as "monstrous," their history "amazing," and their falsehood as "absolute." He seeks to raise, it seems, an emotional response much closer to outrage than to the somewhat weaker emotions at play in the *Observations*. While still quite a bit short of Ciceronian pathetic appeal, the emotion in the "Brief" is nonetheless laden with a deeper or, as Blair might say, "warmer" emotion.

"*On the Love of Our Country*" (1793):

"On the Love of Our Country" is a fast-day sermon delivered near the end of Blair's life and published in the posthumous fifth volume of his *Sermons*.[39] Fast-day sermons were delivered on special national holidays called by the crown and devoted to prayer and sacrifice (usually fasting) for a specific cause. The fast-day sermon of 1793 is devoted to the struggle with France and the perceived threat of French revolutionary thinking. Blair, a church moderate but a political conservative, responds with what is for him a ringing denunciation of the revolution and a strong call for allegiance and loyalty. The sermon unfolds in two neat parts, the first devoted to undermining the claims of the revolution and the second concerned with bolstering patriotic fervor and "love of our country."

In the first section Blair characterizes the spark of revolution as an irrational spirit, unrealistically ideal, focused on grievances, and ungrateful for the many blessings of society. At one point he asks,

---

[37] "Brief," 13 (f. 65r.). I have retained {alledge} in brackets because Blair seems to have written it then scratched it out in favor of, it appears, "relate."
[38] "Brief," 17 (f. 67r.).
[39] "On the Love of Our Country," *Sermons*, 2nd ed., 5 volumes, 5:114–39; ms. Dc 3.63, ff. 84–99, Edinburgh University Library.

> Nay, is it not much to be lamented that there should have sprung up among us an unaccountable spirit of discontent and disaffection, feeding itself with ideal grievances and visionary projects of reformation, till it has gone nigh to light the torch of sedition?[40]

After raising the wraith of sedition, he seeks to undermine the "false philosophy" of the revolution, an ideology that places love of ideas above love of one's country. In rebuttal, Blair writes:

> He who contends that he is not bound to have any more concern for the interests of Great Britain, than for those of France, or any other country, ought to hold, on the same grounds, that he is under no obligation to consult the welfare of his children and family, his brothers and friends, more than that of a distant stranger; being equally connected, as he holds, with all, by the common brotherhood of the human race. It is much to be suspected, that this wonderful extensive philanthropy is only the language of those who have no affections at all; or perhaps, that it is the language assumed by some, who, bearing in their hearts a secret preference to the interests of another country above their own, but a preference which they choose not to avow, affect to cover it under the disguise, of a liberal, enlarged spirit.
>
> Let us, my friends, disclaiming all such refinements of false philosophy, and following the dictates of plain good sense, and natural affection, resolve to love our native country.[41]

Here Blair's adherence to his own preceptual advice can be seen clearly. He places the objects of his emotions directly in front of his audience, painting a verbal picture that contrasts love of family, friends, and country with scorn for a "false philosophy" out of sync with common sense and natural affection. The result is admittedly striking for, even

---

[40] "On the Love of Our Country," *Collected Sermons*, Volume 5:115; "On the Love of Our Country," ms. 85.

[41] CS 5: 118; ms. 86–87.

without the strong language employed in the Douglas "Brief," Blair is able to color and highlight the key contrast at issue.

The second section of the sermon makes an affirmative case for patriotism by outlining three grounds on which love of country rests. He argues first that his native country is

> the seat of all our best enjoyments in private life. There, my brethren, after we first drew breath, was our tender infancy reared with care; there, our innocent childhood sported; there our careless youth grew up amidst companions and friends; there, after having passed the happiest years of our life, we look forward to our old age to rest in peace.—These are circumstances which endear, and ought to endear a home, a native land, to every human heart.... When we name our own country, we name the spot of the earth within which all that is most dear to us lies.[42]

The imagery (enhanced by anaphora) of infancy, youth, family, friends, and domestic peace seeks, it seems, to raise a kind of longing for home, an emotional tie to both the land and the society of "private life." The images are warm, even tender, and the conclusion rests almost solely on emotion.

Blair seeks to evoke stronger emotion in his second ground, religion. He claims:

> We love our country as the seat of true religion. Freed from the dominion of Popish superstition and darkness which so long overspread the earth, here the light of the blessed reformation continues to shine in its greatest splendour. Here the forms of religious worship are encumbered with no pageantry of vain rites; but, agreeably to God's word, are plain and simple, yet solemn and venerable....
>
> As soon as under the guise of philosophy, and with pretense of unlimited toleration, the established forms of religion were demolished in France, the flood-gates were opened to pour a torrent of avowed infidelity, atheism, and all the grossest immoralities, over that

---

[42] CS 5: 120; ms. 88.

> devoted country. We have beheld the throne and alter overthrown together; and nothing but a wretched ruin left, where once stately fabric stood.[43]

As was the case in the *Observations,* Blair here seeks to evoke fidelity to religion by describing the Catholic "pageantry of vain rights" while, at the same time, noting that even French Catholicism may have been superior to the "wretched ruin" of the revolution. The imagery is vivid and strong, the emotion, one would imagine, powerful.

Blair seeks to deepen the emotion in his third and final ground, the country as the seat of liberty and laws. He writes:

> Whereas, under a multitude of popular governours, oppression is more extensively felt. It penetrates into the interiour of families; and by republican tyranny the humble and obscure are liable to be as much harassed and vexed as the great and wealthy. . . . [We] behold the republican halls hung round with monuments of proscriptions, massacres, imprisonments, requisitions, domiciliary searches, and such other trophies of the glorious victory of republicanism over monarchical power.[44]

This passage, far more than a rational argument for parliamentary monarchy, is a virtual litany of the evils of republicanism. The imagery is designed to resurrect the fear aroused by the excesses of the French revolution. The short list of horrors, from massacres to domiciliary searches, serves to remind his audience of the very real terrors of the revolution, and seeks to raise the emotional stakes even higher. Restraint seems to keep him from greater detail (although detail certainly was available), though the "trophy" imagery invites the audience to see the "false philosophy" as cruel, harsh, and uncaring.

Conclusions

In each of the texts examined above, Blair demonstrates a keen awareness of the particular needs and concerns of the rhetorical situations to which he responds. In each case the emotions are used strategically, and Blair oscillates between the conversational and the controversial

---

[43] CS 5: 122–24, ms. 89–91.
[44] CS 5: 130–31, ms. 94–95.

as the situation demands. Surely then, one point raised by this study is that we reach too far when we claim, as some have, that Scottish rhetorics were not concerned with the particular rhetorical situation.

A second point made by this study is that Blair's employment of "the pathetic part" of discourse is guided by propriety or decorum. If the framework I have provided above proves at all useful, future studies might focus on decorum as the mediating principle between Ciceronian and belletristic rhetorics, at least as those rhetorics are made real in persuasive performance.

Finally, I hope to have shown that Blair's discussion and use of emotion, while hardly innovative or revolutionary, nonetheless goes beyond the simple dichotomy of "new" versus "neoclassical" rhetoric. Neither school of thought fully accounts for Blair's approach to emotion, perhaps because Blair himself never felt constrained by theoretical consistency. Blair draws heavily on both belletristic and Ciceronian rhetorical theory, and the resulting conversational and controversial elements of his thought play out in his rhetorical practices. At the very least we can conclude that, if Scottish rhetoricians such as Blair are indeed "ill-served by studies that view them through a neoclassical lens," then they are equally ill-served by studies that view them from *any* single perspective, neoclassical, belletristic, or otherwise. Our efforts should be directed toward engaging Blair and his contemporaries on their own terms, as heirs of *multiple* rhetorical traditions, as rhetoricians *and rhetors,* as writers and speakers of complexity and nuance.

Blair will remain of concern to historians of rhetoric, if for no other reason than the long dominance of his *Lectures on Rhetoric.* If we are to develop adequate accounts of his rhetoric we must, this study suggests, continue to look at his work as it embraces contrary theoretical stances, and we should continue to be willing to allow Blair's rhetorical practices to shed light on his preceptual stance.

27 Who Measures "Due Measure"? or, *Kairos* Meets Counter-*Kairos:* Implications of *Isegoria* for Classical Notions of *Kairos*

Jerry Blitefield

Overview

This essay grows out of a larger project, one in which I look to account theoretically for ways in which underpowered groups creatively manage limited physical resources for maximum rhetorical effect.[1] My assumption in that larger project is that underpowered groups—groups whose publicness must be either granted or commandeered from some more greatly powered group (e.g., government)—such groups encounter and engage constraints of public rhetoric in ways not necessarily of concern to the overpowered. For example, the mayor of any city can, at his or her choosing, call together a press conference inside City Hall to address the issue of homelessness: the homeless do not possess that same rhetorical option. Of the three terms central to that larger project—place, kairos, *and delivery—it is upon* kairos *that I will focus this essay. My argument here is that, while I am respectful of the literature accounting for kairos as a rhetorical concern in ancient Athens, most of that literature focuses on the etymology, philosophy, or theology of the term. Fully acknowledging that literature, I wish to add a political dimension, and propose that* kairos *becomes even more complex when coupled with perhaps the most significant political development in the*

---

[1] See Blitefield.

democratization of classical Athens: isegoria, *or the right of any citizen to address the Assembly.*

Though uncertainty exists among classicists how exactly *isegoria*—the right of any citizen to address the assembly—formally came into play, whether it was directly attributable to the political reforms of Cleisthenes, or whether it was the *de jure* legalization of a *de facto* process which had been burbling in the Assembly for some time prior to becoming "law," *isegoria* as an institution clearly parallels the rise of Athenian rhetoric in the 5th and 4th centuries. Whatever its genesis, *isegoria* had profound effects on the potential of speaking before the Assembly and on the potential of rhetoric, and as such presents a way of reinterpreting *kairos* from a political, democratic perspective.

By way of making that argument, I will first touch upon a few notions regarding classical *kairos*, hoping that the points I later raise will then be seen in greater relief. Following the discussion of *kairos,* I will move on to an elaboration of *isegoria*, and make my case for augmenting our understanding of *kairos* as both a rhetorical and a political concern.

Kairos Classically Read

In his 1986 article, "*Kairos:* A Neglected Concept in Classical Rhetoric," James Kinneavy tells us that *kairos* is first used as a term by Hesiod in seventh century BCE Greece: "Observe due measure, and proportion [*kairos*] is best in all things" (80); rhetorically, however, *kairos* doesn't hit its stride until some two-hundred years later, with Gorgias in the fifth century, who, "As Untersteiner has thoroughly demonstrated, ... made *kairos* the cornerstone of his entire epistemology, ethics, aesthetics, and rhetoric" (81). Though "complex," "the two basic elements ... the principle of right timing and the principle of proper measure" as key rhetorical concepts "continue unabated through Cicero" (85). But, according to Kinneavy, "the residual influence of *kairos* is almost a negligible chapter in the history of rhetoric since antiquity, partly because of the overwhelming influence of Aristotelian rhetoric in this history" (82).

In "Toward a Sophistic Definition of Rhetoric," John Poulakos corrects for that Aristotelian influence by offering a sophistic definition of rhetoric thoroughly informed by the principle of right timing and the principle of proper measure: "Rhetoric is the art which seeks to capture in opportune moments that which is appropriate and attempts to suggest that which is possible" (56). Poulakos argues that "the Sophists were interested in the problem of time in relation to speaking… [stressing] that speech must show respect to the temporal dimension of the situation it addresses, that is, it must be timely. In other words, speech must take into account and be guided by the temporality of the situation in which it occurs" (59). Coupled with "the sense of urgency" which "compels a rhetor to speak," (59) Poulakos arrives at the Sophistic implication that "ideas have their place in time, and unless they are given existence, unless they are voiced at the precise moment they are called upon, they miss their chance to satisfy situationally shared voids within a particular audience… The choice is not whether to speak but whether to speak now; more precisely, it is whether now is the time to speak" (59). Then, citing Protagoras and the *Dissoi Logoi* for further testimony, Poulakos concludes that "Clearly, the notion of *kairos* points out that speech exists in time; but more important, it constitutes a prompting toward speaking and a criterion of *the* value of speech. In short, *kairos* dictates that what is said must be said at the right time" (61).

While I do not take issue with notions of right timing or proportion or due measure, I wish that I could be more clear in my mind how to interpret "right timing," "proportion," or "due measure"—not in the language of a 21st Century student of rhetoric but rather within the language of a 5th/4th Century teacher or even perhaps practitioner of it. For today, these terms connote an almost romanticized rhetorical judgment on the part of the speaker: based upon a reading of the situation, he chooses not only when to cast in his speaking (right timing)—the "at" of Poulakos's "at the right time"—so too does he modulate the levels of his speaking for appropriateness to the situation, e.g., suitability to his audience and occasion. These readings of *kairos* strike me as qualitative in their concerns with time and appropriateness, but not quantitative: right timing as opposed to wrong or missed timing; due measure as a constraint on appropriateness of tone, style, pitch, demeanor, even argument, of rhetor to the occasion. Again, I do not disagree with these readings of *kairos*. But alternately, I am suggesting we might read *kairos* as a volumetric constraint—a matter of *filling out/fitting in* one's discourse when regulated by the political audience of the Assembly.

In what follows, then, I will elaborate on *kairos* as a political, volumetric constraint—a temporal place—a constraint which I suggest likely affected rhetorical developments, and in turn, Athenian politics. In order to do so, I must first return to some modern scholarship on the Sophists, as I will submit that a volumetric conception of *kairos* is warranted when we shift consideration from the teachings of the Sophists to the students they taught. I begin by referring to Edward Schiappa's reply to the earlier cited piece by Poulakos. In "Sophistic Rhetoric: Oasis or Mirage?" Schiappa states,

> Whoever "the sophists" were, the ancient authorities are virtually unanimous in their assessment that the fees the sophists charged were very high (Blank). Ostwald contends that "only the wealthy" could afford to hire a sophist, and that their followers "consisted largely of ambitious young men of the upper classes" (237–42). Kerford concludes that "what the Sophists were able to offer was in no sense a contribution to the education of the masses" (*SM* 17). The verdict, in ancient times as well as the present, is that the most appreciative audience was an aristocratic one and, indeed, most of the political leaders who managed to overcome a nonaristocratic birth were rather suspicious of the sophists (Blank 14–15). (69)

If Schiappa's economic assessment is correct, and if Poulakos is also correct that *kairos* was identifiable with the teaching of the Sophists, then the pedagogy and benefits of *kairos* as a rhetorical precept would have been limited to a small, fairly homogenous and well-to-do group: *elites*.[2] Historically, then, by default of those who taught it, *kairos* can be seen as a privileged understanding by a select few. But this privilege was not without constraints.

Major Changes to the Political Equilibrium

In *Mass and Elite in Democratic Athens*, Josiah Ober shows us that by mid 5th century, Athens had undergone sweeping political reforms, of

---

[2] In ancient Athens, an *elite* was characterized by wealth, status, and education. For a discussion of *elites* in ancient Athens, see Ober 11–17.

which three bear directly on historiographical discussions of rhetoric and on a reconception of *kairos*:

(1) contrary to earlier times when political office was secured through public deeds, lineage, etc., beginning in 487/6 public officials were selected by lottery, meaning that the "elite," e.g., those students of the sophists, could not, by status, be assured of public positions and their concomitant speaking roles; (76)

(2) in 462, a movement was undertaken to "strip the 'extra powers' from the Areopagus council"[3] resulting in the probable loss of some of its legal powers, "including the authority to review and set aside as "unconstitutional" decisions of the Assembly. Assuming this is correct, the decision-making powers of the Assembly were no longer limited by a body that was demographically more narrowly constituted than the *demos* itself: the elite no longer had an institutional means to veto the decisions of the masses"; (78)

(3) finally, the third significant reform, "the introduction—or at least greater emphasis upon—*isegoria*, the right of all citizens to speak on matters of state importance in the Assembly," (78) became a formal institution within a few years of 462. Ober further observes, "But since by now [462] most offices were certainly filled by lot, the politically ambitious elite might not be able to secure an official position that would give him the right to speak to the Assembly. The result was a conviction in elite circles that a greater freedom of political debate was a good idea" (79). From this we can infer that if the elite were not the original sponsors of the *isegoria* reform, they supported it on the basis that *isegoria* would grant them by law the rightful occasion to speak of which the lottery had stripped them.

Though *isegoria* ushered out a regime of exclusive discourse as it opened wide the doors to a new paradigm of public speaking, the significance

---

[3] The Areopagus council was comprised of former archons (an Athenian chief magistrate and member of the wealthy elite), whose purpose was to "insure that magistrates obeyed the laws and that measures passed in Assembly were in accordance with the law." However: "Since the Areopagites were ex-archons, and so from the top one or two property classes, the wealthy elite would have an institutional means to control any independent tendencies that might be manifested by the citizenry in Assembly." See Ober 64.

of *isegoria* for rhetoric is perhaps too little appreciated by rhetorical scholarship, warranting in full this citation by Ober:

> *isegoria* was later considered by the Athenians to be a cornerstone of democracy, and so it was. Probably most Athenian citizens—even those who attended the Assembly regularly—never exercised their right to speak. But *isegoria* changed the nature of mass experience of the Assembly from one of passive approval (or rejection) of measures presented, to one of actively listening to and judging the merits of complex, competing arguments. *Skill in public speaking became an increasingly important leadership skill, since all matter of state policy were decided on the basis of speeches delivered in the Assembly.* The political life of the citizen became much more intense and personally meaningful, as he was forced to think about and choose among the various policy options presented to him. From a forum to ensure that responsibility for decisions would be collective and so morally binding upon the citizenry, the Assembly became the focus of public political discussion, debate, decision. (79, emphasis added)

Historically, the combined effects on rhetoric might be described this way: the lottery disclaimed the elite of their rhizomatic relationship with public office, while simultaneously enabling to take root potential discursive representation by the *idiotai* [ordinary citizens and political non-experts];[4] the "stripping" from the Areopagus of its "set aside" powers meant the council could no longer be counted on as a fail-safe mechanism to scuttle Assembly actions unfavorable to the elite; consequently, all the weight of deliberation and the power of rhetoric shifted not only *onto* the Assembly, but *into* the Assembly: *here in the assembly* is where arguments will be argued and from them decisions made *final*. Hence, with such finality, the Assembly as a political organ must have grown in importance, and its dealings must have taken on a greater urgency. In other words, the combination of the lottery and the "stripping" of the Areopagus brought the institution of *isegoria* into full relief and stepped-up rhetoric's full democratic potential. With no recourse outside or after the vote, *kairos* as "right-

---

[4] For a fuller discussion of the *idiotai*, see Ober 109–112.

timing" is wholly on the mark. Yet, there is more to be said about the machinations of the Assembly.

Placed within the amalgam of the economically heterogeneous Assembly and its potentially disputatious atmosphere (even prior to the reforms of 462), rhetoric evolves into not just a skill but a competitive skill, as Ober's quote above attests, one which well-wrought could tilt if not win the issues of the day.[5] Clearly, then, as skillful competitive public speaking could well advance the interests of an elite, paid study with the Sophists could be seen as a wise investment. As already stated, however, the lottery system placed elites in the disadvantageous role of "citizen-audience" and not "citizen-official," and though we can assume that, like any other citizen, they were granted the right to speak, like any other citizen they would not be guaranteed a quantity of time to speak. That is, although the right to rhetorical discourse in the Assembly would have been guaranteed the elite as it was the *idiotai*—and unlike the courts which allotted a fixed time for speaking[6]—deliberative speeches would have been limited by the receptivity of the audience and by the turns of discussion. Neither of these variables was marked by order or courtesy, though. Ober tells us that one was able to speak to the Assembly so long as he was able to *hold* the audience's attention:

---

[5] Though I am focusing on the rhetoric of the Assembly, the "skill" and competitive nature of public speaking as taught by the sophists become even more prominent within the Courts. Ober shows that the rhetors who pleaded, and who had undergone Sophistic training to hone their skills, were often vilified: "Popular mistrust of rhetorical ability and the skilled speakers who misused it is demonstrated by the eagerness of private trial litigants to portray their opponents as slick speakers who were using their rhetorical ability to evil ends," (Ober 173). For a more thorough discussion, see Ober 170–173.

[6] Unlike addressing the Assembly, when speaking in the courts an orator was allotted a fixed amount of time in which to speak. This time was measured by a water clock, an urn which had a small hole at the bottom which, when opened, released the water. To gauge the time spent and the time remaining, floating atop the water and rising out of the urn was a stick, which, as the water drained, would shorten. Here, in the actual "flow of time" we find yet another physical occasion of *kairos* to complement the philosophical: What can be said can only be said while the water is flowing, consequently the rhetor attuned at *kairos* will "fit" his rhetoric "in due proportion" to the volume of water to be displaced.

> Undertaking to address the Athenian Assembly must have been a daunting prospect, even to the trained orator. The audience was huge, so a strong voice was essential (Aristot. *Rhet.* 1414a16–17) [7]...The demos, as Demosthenes had discovered, felt no hesitation about shouting down any speaker who irritated them or who was wasting their time. (cf. Aristot. *Rhet.* 1355a2–3). A politician's opponents would be quick to jump in if they perceived that the audience was becoming bored. [8] Demosthenes (19.23–24, 46) recalls with some bitterness how, during a key meeting in 346, Aeschines and Philocrates stationed themselves at his side in order to mock him. Worse yet, the Assemblymen had found their quips amusing. This sort of behavior may have led to the "orderliness" *nomos* of 346/5 (above III. E.2), but Hyperides (5.12), speaking in 323, claimed that it was still possible to purchase the services of "lesser rhetores" who were specialists at causing a ruckus to disturb the speaker. (138)

It appears that the Assembly was more hurly-burly Gong Show than stately affair: the conspiracy posed by the issue at hand, and one's Aeschines and Philocrates, and to the ambushes of "lesser rhetors," and audience antsyness clearly made set-pieces of oration no sure thing (ergo, a lengthy oration could be especially unwieldy and difficult to bring off in its entirety).[9] From constraints so eddying to his equi-

---

[7] The size of the audience and the orator's challenge to "hold them" gets even further exacerbated when acoustical conditions get factored in. For a thorough acoustical analysis of the physical assembly, the Pnyx, see Johnstone 97–127.

[8] Yet another occasion for the urged timeliness of Sophistic *kairos*?

[9] Of course the orations of Demosthenes contradict this assumption, yet not entirely. First, because Demosthenes was the greatest Athenian speaker of his time, and so his orations, especially those with his career and reputation firmly established, would be attended to with increased respect and interest (having worked vociferously at his delivery, which included dramatic training with the comic actor Satyrus (Ober 114), Demosthenes could probably enthrall an audience on aesthetic grounds alone). But Demosthenes was an exceptional speaker, and therefore perhaps an exception to my assumption. How many others spoke for whom we have no record, and how might their orations have proceeded?

poise, we can surmise that a speaker would have felt tenuously about his oration, and would have felt about his oration tenuously. Given the scenario, an ability to "read the audience," spontaneous adaptation of rhetoric to occasion, and deftness at deflecting an opponent's barbs loom large as rhetorical concerns. At the risk of invoking a military metaphor, public rhetoric was perhaps less strategic theater operation than hand-to-hand discourse.

KAIROS MEETS COUNTER-KAIROS

Here then is where a new view of *kairos* may be called for, for while most conceptions of it strategically front end the notion—*when* to enter the fray, *when* to pass through the opening, *when* to fill the void, now we see clearly that a speaker could anticipate active *resistance* from the audience, so much that the *kairos* of the(ir) moment might be practically understood as time in a closing vice: *kairos* meets counter-*kairos*. From this perspective then, *kairos* can be construed as a *defensive* as well as an offensive concern, as a way of first anticipating and then warding off external negative impingements—and not simply as a concept for positive rhetorical insertion. If so, *kairos* warrants consideration as a literal limiting constraint on the rhetor/rhetoric, as much as it warrants consideration as positive rhetorical strategy. For how could a speaker tell (much) in advance how long he had before his speaking would get gonged? Under these conditions the *timeliness* and *fittingness* commonly associated with *kairos* take on added dimension, not simply as matters of judgment but also now as matters of packaging, e.g., how to fit in all one has to say before one gets shouted down.

Bearing in mind the competitive, seemingly survivalist nature of deliberation, the most imposing challenge facing any orator might then have been how best to speak not simply *at* a time but *in* time, *over* time: if we can assume that "discussion, debate, and decision" were moderated by *isegoria* (and hecklers), naturally evolving discursive lim-

---

Yet perhaps even Demosthenes was subject to the encroachments of time within the Assembly. This possibility was suggested to me in a letter from Professor Ober, who pointed out that the Assembly speeches of Demosthenes are relatively short when compared to his public prosecution speeches. While this does not in itself prove anything, it does leave open the door of possibility that speaking in the Assembly exacted an expedience that speaking in the courts did not.

its would have constrained address or rejoinder.[10] To what extent this weighed on the rhetor's mind is impossible to say, though it seems equally impossible to think that it weighed not at all.

If, as stated earlier, *kairos* was taught as a rhetorical concern by Sophists to their elite students, we might think of those elite as being better trained at keeping the audience and antagonists alike at bay. From this perspective, *kairos* would seem to have wide implications for delivery, though I will leave that for another time.

Conclusion

The selection to public office by a lottery system, the scaling back of the Areopagus powers, but most importantly the entrenchment and enhancement of *isegoria,* upset not only the balance of power in the Assembly, it elevated the importance of *kairos* as a practical political concern. To reemphasize, my argument is not to replace *kairos* as currently understood. Rather, it is to suggest that beyond being a matter of philosophical or ethical judgment, it is dimensional—volumetric—and that in Athens *kairos* was equally reflected in keeping as attuned to the involuntary and unexpected oppositional constraints upon the rhetor and rhetoric as to the opportunities for such rhetoric. Hence, *kairos* can be seen as a political concern, for how many decisions then, as now, were made based upon the ability or inability to "get out the word(s)"?

What relevance does this argument have for today? Simply this: the politically elite of modern society—here in the States or anywhere in the world—are still predominantly the rhetorically elite, though they are, through the exercises of technology and power-over-place, far less bound by either *isegoria* or *kairos* than were their Athenian counterparts. Rather, there exists today a rhetorical gap enjoyed by elites and suffered by the *idiotai*, one fully underpinned in many countries by the modern democratic progeny of *isegoria*: "free speech." That's how it looks on paper, anyway. In reality, though, making public discourse, finding a guaranteed place for that discourse, clearing and securing rhetorical space in time—*kairos*—present for the underpowered monumental obstacles. For the underpowered, *kairos* is not just about

---

[10] "Similarly, Hansen contends that, 'in an assembly attended by 6,000 citizens it was impossible to have an open discussion. The debate was bound to take the form of a string of speeches of varying length'" (Johnstone 110n).

right-timing and due-measure in their traditional, classical senses: for the underpowered making rhetoric is also about *kairos* in the volumetric sense I have been speaking of in this paper, the ability to keep their speech alive, extended, and moving to a conclusion of *their* design. Yes, there will always be the "at-ness" of *kairos,* but for the underpowered, especially, there is also the concreteness of the counter-*kairos.* The canceling of the permit. The advance of the police. The disbursing of the crowd. Even bad weather. In this sense, then, *kairos* as a rhetorical concern for the underpowered means seeing the march to the end. Getting the banner completely unfurled. Delivering dissentious arguments to their conclusion. And knowing not just when to make this rhetoric, but also for how long. In other words, to most effectively fill the spanse between *kairos* and counter-*kairos.* In a realm of disproportionate *isegoria,* no effective understanding of a radicalized rhetoric can, I believe, come about without attention to this volumetric alter-ego of *kairos.*

28 "Time Appeases Anger": The Rhetorical-Political Temporality of the Paradigmatic Passion of *Orge* in Aristotle's *Rhetoric* and *Politics*

Renu Dube

Anger is correctly recognized by modern scholars as the paradigmatic passion in Aristotelian rhetoric. Larry Arnhart observes that Aristotle "commonly treats [anger] as representative of all the passions."[1] The reasons for this scholarly interest in anger are easy to see: Aristotle's definition of anger is demonstrably the most exhaustive and rigorous of all the emotions analyzed in the *Rhetoric*. This has stimulated many a commentator to construct their entire theory of Aristotelian *pathe* through an analysis of anger, because it is generally believed that Aristotle's overarching theory of the passions is manifest in his treatment of anger.

Three Perspectives on Anger: John Cooper, Larry Arnhart, and Eugene Garver

For instance, a provocative reworking of the standard judgment about anger is offered by John M. Cooper.[2] Cooper's avowed agenda is to locate the ways in which Aristotle's analysis of anger displays philosophical exactitude and rigor. But Cooper's interest in the philosophical dimension of Aristotle's comments on anger in the *Rhetoric* is at the expense of the political dimension of Aristotelian *pathe*. He foregrounds the fact that Aristotle defines anger as desire (*orexis*); from

---

[1] *Aristotle on Political Reasoning*, 115.
[2] "An Aristotelian Theory of the Emotions."

this fact Cooper deduces that there are three ways through which Aristotle defines anger as desire, and therefore as an irrational emotion: in Cooper's view Aristotle reveals the irrationality of anger by defining it as desire, as appetite, and by associating anger with pain. In this way Cooper brings the discussion of anger in the *Rhetoric* closer to the *Topics*.[3]

I situate my argument in opposition to Cooper's thesis about anger. I suggest that Cooper's dissatisfaction with the description of anger in the *Rhetoric* as well as his identification of anger with irrationality is a product of his emphasis on the philosophical dimension of Aristotelian *pathe* at the expense of its rhetorical dimension. My own emphasis is on the temporal dimension of anger, an aspect which has received little or no attention from Aristotle scholars. I study the temporal dimension of anger because I argue that the predominant orientation of Aristotelian *pathe* is not towards philosophical exactitude but rather towards rhetorical effectiveness. It is for this reason that the civic-political implications of public anger are of great importance to Aristotle. Furthermore, in the *Rhetoric* Aristotle is careful to stay at the level of the imprecise and inexact.[4] Aristotle resists theorizing the material and discipline which is, by its very nature, imprecise and inexact. Cooper ignores the fact that Aristotle's examples in his comments on anger

---

[3] For instance Cooper writes:

In other words, it [anger] is not a cool and "rational" desire, a desire judiciously considered, to inflict pain or other punishment" and, "anger has a special relationship according to Aristotle, to the other types of nonrational desires, the appetites" (249–50).

In vain, Cooper looks for a "general theory of the underlying psychology of the emotions" and a "fully comprehensive theory" of emotions and is then disappointed when he does not find it in the *Rhetoric* (250–1).

[4] In the *Nicomachean Ethics* (translated by W. D. Ross), Aristotle explains that the degree of precision possible in the discussion of subject matters varies:

Our discussion will be adequate if it has as much clearness as the subject-matter admits of, for precision is not to be sought for alike in all discussions, any more than in all the products of the crafts . . . We must be content, then, in speaking of such subjects and with such premises to indicate the truth roughly and in outline, and in speaking about things which are only for the most part true and with premises of the same kind to reach conclusions that are no better (1094b3–23).

show that, whenever there is imprecision in emotions, the rhetor is afforded an excellent rhetorical opportunity.

Arnhart addresses the same issues about Aristotle's comments on anger as Cooper, but offers an interpretation that is very different from Cooper's. Arnhart is more attentive to the rhetorical implications of the *pathos* of *orge*, therefore he focuses on the rational and cognitive elements of public anger. He observes, "A man's anger depends upon his belief that anger is a proper response to something that has occurred" (114). While Cooper emphasizes the relationship between the treatment of anger in the *Rhetoric* and the *Topics*, Arnhart emphasizes the relationship between the *Rhetoric* and the *Nicomachean Ethics*. The intertextual relationship that each scholar examines has a strong bearing on their views concerning the rationality or irrationality of anger. Arnhart goes to *Nicomachean Ethics* because Aristotle's observation "anger follows from reason somehow" (*EN* 1149a 25) is strong proof for Arnhart's contention that Aristotle's rhetorical theory is oriented towards the rationality of anger. Therefore, while Cooper perceives the emotions as causing false judgments, Arnhart is struck by the other related and social judgments caused by passions. He says:

> Aristotle conceives of the passions not as inner feelings or sensations, but as opinions or judgments about the world... anger, then, is an apprehension or assessment of something outside himself...the existence of the anger depends upon the angry man's belief that he has grasped the situation correctly. Anger, therefore, implies some sort of judgment. (116)

Cooper and Arnhart interpret the judgments of the angry audience in contrasting ways. Cooper displays no interest in the social assessment implicit in anger, nor is he engaged by the civic-political implications of Aristotle's paradigmatic example of anger caused by a public insult or belittlement. On the other hand, Arnhart, in the above extract, foregrounds precisely the other related and worldly assessment of a situation as well as the judgment implied in anger. For Arnhart, Aristotelian anger presupposes the social and political interactions between men living in society.

In my view, the test of both interpretations is their rhetorical advice which is an outcome of their respective theories about anger. Cooper's interpretation implies the following rhetorical scene: the orator demonstrates to the angry audience that their judgment is contrary to the beliefs they hold when they are not angry; next the orator convinces the angry audience that they are out of control and irrational; finally, the orator proves to the audience that the judgment implied in their anger is a false judgment. The kinds of options that Cooper's theory makes available to the orator are likely to alienate the audience rather than make them sympathetic to the orator's point of view.

Arnhart's advice to the orator is more rhetorically sound. The orator does not alienate the audience by proving that they are irrational; instead the orator addresses precisely the reasoning through which the audience has felt anger. Arnhart's conception of the Aristotelian orator posits the angry audience as a reasoning audience, and in so doing his interpretation points to the rhetorical opportunities for the orator to show his/her audience respect and consideration by reasoning with them. In Arnhart's words the orator can "control the anger of his audience by reasoning with them" (117). In Arnhart's schema the orator makes an angry audience listen to her/him by telling them, not that their reasoning is wrong, but rather that their reasoning is hasty. Arnhart writes, "the fault with acting in the heat of anger, Aristotle indicates, is not the absence of reasoning but the hastiness of the reasoning" (117).[5] Thus the orator does not interfere with the angry audience's belief that whenever they are publicly belittled or treated unjustly, as rational and self respecting citizens they have a right to feel anger. Without interfering in this belief of the audience, the orator invites the audience to consider whether this particular case justifies their passion. Arnhart says:

> Hence a rhetorician can arouse or allay the passions of his audience with arguments: he arouses the passions by showing that the facts of the case justify such a passion, and he allays a passion by showing that the facts do not justify it . . . .Aristotle's definitions of the passions commonly rest on men's conceptions of situations; a speaker can influence these conceptions by the arguments he makes. Similarly, the other two dimensions of the passions—the conditions under which and the persons against whom the passions

---

[5] Note that Arnhart's remarks take cognizance of the temporal element of anger; unfortunately, he does not follow this line of investigation any further.

arise—generally depend upon the impassioned man's thoughts or beliefs, which the speaker can attempt to create or suppress with his speech. (115–116)

Arnhart's advice in the passage quoted above shows that he is thinking through the rhetorical opportunities presented by an angry audience. In contrast, Cooper's statements tend to imply that the orator should make philosophical and ethical judgments about the truth status of the audience's emotion. In my view, the Aristotelian orator's relation to the audience is neither that of a moralist, nor that of a priest with his congregation, not even that of a therapist with his patient. Arnhart is closer to the tenor of Aristotle's advice to the orator: to work with the audience's emotions rather than construct a speech in antagonistic relation to their feelings.

My argument is also in broad sympathy with Eugene Garver; he is the foremost commentator who foregrounds the political functions of Aristotelian passions. Garver effectively argues that the principle of selection for the particular passions discussed in detail in the *Rhetoric* lies in the fact that these are the emotions of citizens. By naming Aristotelian *pathe* the emotions of citizens or civic emotions, Garver means that they are other related.[6] In Garver's words, "These emotions are related to what we want and who we think we are."[7] In Garver's view they are essentially political emotions because they are what distinguishes a city-state from a family or a mere alliance.

Garver proves his argument through the paradigmatic passion of anger. For Garver, anger demonstrates many of the elements that he sees as the political features of the civic passions: in Aristotle's definition anger is essentially other related; furthermore anger is defined in the *Rhetoric* in terms of "the fulfilling and frustrating of expectations and evaluations of dessert"; finally, the fulfillment and frustration of what we expect and how we expect to be treated is essentially a social and political expectation (124). Like Garver, I too, view Aristotle's analysis of anger in terms of a citizen's political life in the city-state. Aristotle believes that anger is essential to political life for it is connected to justice, equity, self-defense and self-respect; civic anger makes a populace act, in decisive political moments, in ways that are

---

[6] For a brief but engaging discussion of Aristotelian emotions in the *Rhetoric* as constituting a "political economy," see Daniel M. Gross, "Early Modern Emotion and the Economy of Scarcity," 308–321.

[7] "Deliberative Rationality and the Emotions," 124.

not amenable to pacification. However, I do not concur with Garver when he takes a bold step of theorizing that the discussion of *thymos* in Aristotle's philosophical treatises is the proper framework for the political valence of anger.[8] I eschew Garver's method of examining the interconnections between anger and *thymos* or spiritedness. Instead, I locate the political valence of Aristotelian *orge* in its temporal dimension.[9]

---

[8] For Aristotle's discussion of *thymos* see the *Nicomachean Ethics* (1225b1–1126b10). The discussion of thymos in the *Politics* is more complicated because it is "the capacity of the soul whereby we love" (1328a1) and includes rage and anger when slighted by friends, and it is also "this faculty that power to command and love of freedom are in all cases derived" (1328a6).

[9] Garver's thesis about the relation between *thymos* and anger is given in the passage below:

> the first emotion considered (in the *Rhetoric*) is anger, the feeling most strongly associated with *thymos* . . . there is a broad sense of *thymos*, which equally inspires friendliness and aggression, and a narrow sense tied to reactions to insults. . . In the broad sense, *thymos* both makes us angry towards enemies and makes us show goodwill towards friends. . . Without *thymos,* one cannot participate in a political community because the *thymos* makes possible the distinction between mine and thine. And, just as centrally, without membership in a *polis,* one cannot have a properly developed *thymos:* it is an emotion which leads to desires fully possible only to a certain person who stands in certain kinds of relationships to other people . . . . In the *Politics* Aristotle explains why the *thymos* is necessary for citizenship (112–113)

In the passage above, Garver rightly points out that certain equations between people are normally hidden in everyday interactions, but are clarified in moments of crisis occasioned by anger. The angry audience seizes on a certain truth about their social and political interactions that is not otherwise available to them in a state of calmness. However, Garver's perspective on civic anger misses out on the temporal dimension of anger: the fact that Aristotle also believes that political action impelled only by anger is short-lived, it is not future oriented, therefore the action resulting solely from anger lacks an investment in the future of the city-state.

Part of the problem in Garver's argumentation is that he wishes to make an overarching umbrella term—*thymos* and its relationship to *eunoia*–that can be applied to all the passions. Garver does not consider the fact that if Aristotle had wished to speak of *thymos* in the *Rhetoric,* he could certainly have done so. The fact that Aristotle speaks of *orge* and not *thymos* should alert us

A Temporal View of Anger

Commentators have neglected Aristotle's theorizing of the relation between time and anger in the *Rhetoric*. Anger acquires a powerful and inexorable momentum only in the public-political arena. Aristotle reminds his students of this fact by alluding frequently to Homer's depiction of Achilles' anger. In Aristotle's view, public anger is a temporary emotion: once anger is set into motion and publicly manifested it is like an object in motion or a stone moving in time, and being subject to time, collective anger will be spent.

Many philosophers and theorists, Martin Heidegger amongst them, have spoken of the radical departure Aristotle makes from Plato in the determinedly this-worldliness characterizing his treatment of emotions. This is the texture of everyday reality that Heidegger applauded in Aristotle by calling it "the first systematic hermeneutic of the everydayness of Being with one another."[10] The everydayness of being, in Heidegger's sense of the term, can be discerned in Aristotle's approach to the passion of anger. Aristotle does not treat anger in terms of an imitation or mimesis of the Platonic Ideal Forms. Aristotle also makes a radical departure from the Sophistical emphasis on the mediation of language. What then takes the place of a language-based understanding of emotions or the Platonic view of anger? Aristotle's alternative is to train his students to discern the ways in which, in the public-political realm, the active principle works in *orge* or anger.

In Aristotle's schema of the passions in the *Rhetoric*, anger is the supremely active passion. He describes anger, not as a diffused and generalized emotion, but as an emotion that requires a concrete and identifiable human target. Aristotle says, "the angry man must always be angry with the particular individual" because the particular individual has done some injury to him or to those near to him.[11] Aristotle's concern in the

---

to the fact that, in the rhetorical situation, Aristotle is concerned with how a group of people can be pacified or aroused into anger. In the rhetorical situation between an orator and his audience, Aristotle does not see any relevance for the large and speculative cultural-racial generalizations about the Greek temper that is appropriate to the *Politics*. In my view, the Aristotelian discussion of *thymos* in the *Politics* in Book VII (1327b24–33) is a broad and speculative cultural-racial generalization and has limited rhetorical usefulness.

[10] *Being and Time*, translated by John Macquarrie & Edward Robinson, 178.

[11] *The Art of Rhetoric*, translated by J. H. Freese. Cambridge, MA: Harvard U P (1926), 1378b1.

Rhetoric is with isolating, studying, and teaching his students to study how the active principle in anger works. His rhetorical purpose is to demonstrate how anger can become inflammable and cause an audience to unite in order to act in the political arena. In short, how collective anger becomes the motor of political action.

From common beliefs or *endoxa*, Aristotle constructs the premise that the primary temporal orientation of anger is the present tense. As Aristotle puts it in his study of pity, anger belongs to the category of "courageous emotions" because "these emotions do not take thought of the future (*alogista gar tou esomenou tauta*) (*Rhetoric* 1385b36). It is useful for an orator—who is faced with an angry mob, angry jurors, or an enraged public figure like Achilles—to know that unlike the emotion of fear which is primarily oriented towards the future, anger is an emotion in which the audience's cognitive processes are oriented towards the present and take no heed of the future.

How can a rhetorician make use of the notion that anger is primarily oriented towards the present tense of time? In order to answer this question, Aristotle examines the common belief that time makes anger cease. Commentators have ignored the rhetorical strategies hinted at by Aristotle. Aristotle says of anger "of long standing" is "not in its full flesh (*me hypognioi*), for time appeases anger" (*Rhetoric* 1380b12). Here Aristotle invites the student orators to judge whether the audience's anger "is of long standing." The orator's judgment on this point will help him to construct a speech which either utilizes the audience's angry mood or exhorts the audience to eschew its angry mood. If the orator finds that the audience's anger is "in its full flesh" then the better part of wisdom for the orator whose oratorical objective cannot utilize the active passion, is to wait till the anger runs its course. If the audience's anger has been appeased and died down with time, the speech is more likely to be persuasive.

Aristotle's second statement in the section on hatred accentuates the temporal dimension of anger, "Anger is curable (*iatonkronoi*) by time, hatred not . . . one who is angry might feel compassion in many cases, but one who hates, never" (*Rhetoric* 1382a31). Here he asks his students to discriminate between the allied emotions of anger and hatred in terms of their opposing relationship to time. The Aristotelian orator must take into account that hatred is unchanging and not amenable to time. Public anger, on the other hand, is wholly a product of a particular political moment. This is not to say that events in the past do not influence the presentness of anger. For example, a populace may suffer the privations caused by the tyrant for a long time, but an ostensibly minor infraction of their rights can cause them to lose their fear of the tyrant and rise up in anger against him. In this case, the ostensible cause is conjoined with the public's memories of past wrongs. Thus, the past fuels their anger in the present. In Aristotle's view, anger is unmoored from the future. But, the presentness of anger is strongly related to the events in the past in a city-state's political history.

However, Aristotle is less interested in how the past influences the presentness of anger and far more engaged as a rhetorician by the fact that a populace cannot sustain their angry mood forever. Scholars like Arnhart have been preoccupied with the relation between anger and pain (*lupe*). Their interpretations imply that anger is of temporary duration because it is a predominantly painful emotion even though it has elements of pleasure in the angry audience's thoughts of revenge. I avoid this purely physiological explanation and suggest instead that anger is of temporary duration because, as Aristotle points out, there is a strong relationship between anger and action.

The strong relationship between anger and action is, for Aristotle, a political relationship. The collective anger of a people is powerful enough to cause a riot, incite a revolution, or make an assembled body sanction executions. The point is not that these actions are painful to the angry people; the point is that these actions cannot be sustained indefinitely. A revolutionary mob's actions are so extreme that sooner or later their anger has to run its course. The actions that they are capable of in the heat of anger are unthinkable for them in a state of calmness.

The Aristotelian orator can make use of the fact that anger changes with the duration of time. For instance, Aristotle says in the section on hatred: "One who is angry might feel compassion in many cases, but one who hates, never; for the former wishes that the object of his anger should suffer in his turn, the latter, that he should perish" (*Rhetoric* 1382a31–2). The rhetorical strategies implicit in the above statement consist of either enhancing the angry audience's active emotion and causing them to act against injustice, overthrowing the tyrant; or to make an appeal to an angry audience's compassion. An orator can gauge whether his audience's anger is rising or on the downward curve, and if the audience is not in the first flush of anger, the orator can incite their compassion, because thoughts of compassion, in Aristotle's view, supplant anger.

My formulation about the temporal dimension of anger is incomplete. I have not yet stated what I view as Aristotle's political agenda in highlighting the temporal dimension of anger in particular and the passions in general in the *Rhetoric*. A politically informed rhetoric must foreground its political agenda; we may recall that Aristotle is dissatisfied with the Sophistical position that all rhetoric is political by its very nature.[12] However, Aristotle also does not wish to go to the other extreme and assert an apolitical rhetoric; therefore, if we are to pay attention to the Aristotelian discriminations, we have to ask what is the political agenda behind the Aristotelian emphasis on the relation between time and anger.

Garver believes that Aristotle's political agenda in the treatment of anger is to valorize the warlike aggression and spiritedness of the Greeks as a people who are ready to retaliate if they are insulted or slighted and resist those who treat them as inferior by slighting them. My own view of Aristotle's political agenda in his treatment of anger is the following: he treats anger as a timebound emotion because he is committed to the principle of difference. Time is important to him because it produces difference in the audience's emotions. Thus, Aristotle's political agenda is best understood in terms of difference producing time.

It is my suggestion that Aristotle's comments on anger in the *Rhetoric* and the references to anger in the political sphere in the *Politics* should be read together. Aristotelian rhetoric is an "offshoot (*paraphues*)" of his political theory (*Rhetoric* 1356a7). I say this in order to redress the imbalance caused by the excessive reliance on the *De Anima*, *Topics* and *Nicomachean Ethics* by scholars like Martha Nussbaum, A.O. Rorty, and Cooper in illuminating Aristotle's comments

---

[12] In the *Rhetoric* Aristotle says:

> Thus it appears that Rhetoric is as it were an offshoot of dialectic and of the science of Ethics, which may be reasonably called politics. That is why Rhetoric assumes the character of Politics, and those who claim to possess it, partly from ignorance, partly from boastfulness, and partly from other human weaknesses, do the same" (1356a7).

on anger in the *Rhetoric*.[13] This section highlights the political dimension of anger in Aristotelian theory.

THE POLITICAL VALENCE OF A TEMPORAL VIEW OF ANGER

In the Aristotelian vision of rhetoric, anger is associated with the practical exigencies of revolutions and political injustice. Anger acquires a powerful and inexorable momentum only in the public-political arena. Aristotle reminds his students of this fact by alluding frequently to Homer's depiction of Achilles' anger. In the Homeric text, Achilles' anger causes Agamemnon's army to suffer heavy casualties, and nearly results in losing the war. The text of the *Rhetoric* has eight quotations from the Homeric representation of Achilles' anger in the *Iliad* and most of these allusions are contained in the section on anger. This is a sure indication that Aristotle's thoughts dwell on his favorite Homeric text when he embarks on his analysis of anger. Aristotle's definition of anger states: "Let us then define anger as a longing, accompanied by pain, for a real or apparent revenge for a real or apparent slight, affecting a man himself or one of his friends, when such a slight is undeserved" (*Rhetoric* 1378b1–2). Aristotle often refers to Achilles' anger through the phrase "real or apparent (*phainomene*) revenge for a real or apparent slight (*me prosekontos*)."

In his comments on anger in the *Rhetoric*, Aristotle is not interested in constructing an aesthetic theory based on the passion of anger in a manner similar to his aesthetic theory of catharsis in the *Poetics* which is based on the spectator's emotions of pity and terror.[14] Aristotle's multiple references to Achilles' anger underscores the fact that rhetoric is not concerned with the private emotions of anger, but anger in the arena of the public meeting or *agora*. It is in a public assembly that Agamemnon conspicuously insults Achilles and arouses his anger in the Homeric text. It follows that Aristotle's numerous references to Achilles' anger are calculated to recall for his students the political dimension in which Achilles' anger is played out, and the political-military consequences of his actions occasioned by anger.

---

[13] A. O. Rorty, "Aristotle on the Metaphysical Status of Pathe," 521–546; Cooper op. cit.; Martha C. Nussbaum, "Aristotle on Emotions and Rational Persuasion" in *Essays on Aristotle's Rhetoric*.

[14] For a new and interesting reworking of the catharsis thesis, see Jeffrey Walker, "*Pathos* and *Katharsis* in 'Aristotelian' Rhetoric," 74–92.

For Aristotle, public anger is explosive and rarely stoppable. Anger can cause the overthrow of the ruling elite and/or the political leader. An angry public can sanction the execution of the ruling oligarchy. Anger can also motivate an army to reject its generals. Anger can induce a senate or an audience to pass a new law and change the constitution. At times collective anger can lead to riots, looting and disorderly behavior. In short, public anger is volatile and can stir people to revolt.

In the *Politics* and the *Rhetoric,* collective anger is viewed as sometimes playing a politically beneficial role, and at other times anger functions in a politically destructive way. This dual role underlines the centrality of public emotion in the political sphere. In Aristotle's view, the world of politics is not governed by reason alone. He takes cognizance of the fact that publicly manifested collective emotions can either make or break the state. The positive aspect of anger in the *Politics* is that it can spur peoples' rebellion against tyranny. In Aristotle's words, "There are two causes that chiefly lead men to attack tyranny. . . anger must be counted as an element in the hatred felt for them [tyrants] for in a way it occasions the same actions (*morion de ti tou misous kai ten orgen dei tithenai, tropon gar tina ton auton aitia ginetai praxeon*)."[15] This remark indicates that, as a political theorist, he wishes to understand those collective emotions like anger that can cause an entire people to turn against the tyrant. The negative aspect of anger in the *Politics* is that public anger is one of the two causes of revolutions and therefore public anger is the greatest threat to the state's stability.

The political consequences of unappeased public anger determines the study of anger in Aristotelian rhetoric. Earlier I argued that, as a theorist of a politically informed rhetoric, Aristotle is interested in the active principle in passion. This is abundantly clear in the *Politics,* where he observes that anger "is even more active (*praktikoteron*) than hatred" and causes "angry men to attack more vigorously (*syntonoteron*)" (*Politics* 1312b27–8). In the *Rhetoric,* Aristotle frequently defines the active political role of anger in terms of public belittling. The frequent reference in the *Rhetoric* to the anger caused by a public slight must be read in conjunction with the following remark, "anger is not aroused against what is just (*dikaion*)" (*Rhetoric* 1380b15). Both the Aristotelian emphasis on public belittling and his view that anger is antithetical to justice, highlight the relation between public anger

---

[15] *Politics*, translated by H. Rackham, 1312b25.

and political injustice. Aristotle thought of the positive aspect of anger in these terms: it is an emotion that becomes publicly explosive and publicly activated in the context of injustice.

My argument about the specific temporality of the Aristotelian pathos of *orge* or anger gains strength from the fact that it is close to the Aristotelian definition of rhetoric as *dunamis* or potentiality. We can see this particularly in Aristotle's rhetorical examples in the section on anger in the *Rhetoric*. He writes:

> Again vengeance previously taken upon one person appeases anger against another, even though it is greater. Wherefore Philocrates, when someone asked him why he did not justify himself when the people were angry with him, made the judicious reply, "Not yet." "When then?" "When I see someone else accused of the same offense" (*Rhetoric* 1380b13).

This rhetorical example exemplifies Aristotle's advice to the orator concerning the strategic use of the temporality of anger. Philocrates remains silent and does not defend himself before the angry audience. Aristotle gives the highest praise to Philocrates, he calls him judicious because Philocrates bides his time. He waits for an opportunity when the audience has expended its anger on "someone else accused of the same offense." The rhetorical premise of Philocrates' decision is that collective anger is weaker once the angry audience has taken the action that satisfies the angry audience's thirst for revenge, namely punish the object of its anger. It is at that time, when anger is exhausted, that the audience can listen to the orator's self-justification without getting angry.

Aristotle's second rhetorical example makes this clearer as it focuses on the interplay between anger, time and difference. He says:

> for men grow mild when they have exhausted their anger upon another, as happened in the case of Ergophilus. For although the Athenians were more indignant with him than with Callisthenes, they acquitted him, because they had condemned Callisthenes to death on the previous day (*Rhetoric*, 1380b1–4).

As Aristotle shows, the presentness of the people's anger, when publicly expressed and directed against Callisthenes, is significantly different from the now of the people's anger against Ergophilus. In rhetorical terms, Aristotle's point is that even though the intensity of the people's anger was much greater against Ergophilus, the time-frame of the people's publicly manifested anger against him was determined by the fact that their anger had been spent in executing a man the day before. This time-frame proved to be the determining factor in their public judgment, because it overrode the intensity of their feelings against Ergophilus, and caused them to let him go rather than sentence him to death.

Philocrates is the prototype of the Aristotelian orator because he does not rush headlong into flights of oratory even when faced with the crisis of public slander. He chooses not to speak before the angry public, he discerns the right moment for persuasion. In this way, Aristotle relates the temporality of an emotion with the timeliness of rhetoric; he teaches the orator that an understanding of the temporality of an emotion also equips the orator to time his response for greater effectiveness. Thus in Aristotle's *Rhetoric* the timeliness of rhetoric as *dunamis*, that is the ability to see the best available means of persuasion in each case, is a function of the temporality of an emotion. By acknowledging that the time for persuasion is "Not yet (*oupo ge*)," the orator implicitly acknowledges that there is no magic rhetorical formula to transcend the time of anger or provide a countervailing force to oppose the motion of publicly manifested anger. The orator's power lies in his capacity to accommodate this temporal feature of anger. When anger is set into motion in time, the orator knows that eventually it will cease.

29 Augustan Rhetoric: The Declining Orator

Ilon Lauer

Studying the status of rhetoric that begins with the Augustan age and roughly continues through the end of the Flavian dynasty reveals a puzzling tension: even though Romans valorized and lauded the orator, few speeches or even fragments remain from this period. Suetonius' anecdotal account of the emperor Augustus' own speaking habits narrates behavior that is highly symbolic of Roman practice in general; though skilled in public speaking, the emperor avoided a full display of his skills in *ex tempore* speech:

> From early youth he devoted himself eagerly and with the utmost diligence to oratory and liberal studies. During the war at Mutina, amid such a press of affairs, he is said to have read, written and declaimed every day. In fact he never afterwards spoke in the Senate or to the people or to the soldiers, except in a studied and written address, although he did not lack the gift of speaking offhand without preparation.[1]

Rhetorical practice after the ascent of Augustus bears little resemblance to the rhetoric of the Roman Republic. Instead of a heroic participant in vituperative debates who embodied an ideology of speech as a *means* to power, the orator became an emblem of empire symbolizing an ideology of speech as an *end* of power. This rereading of the discourse about speech and actual speeches that are found in the poetry

---

[1] Suetonius, *Augustus*, translated by J.C. Rolfe. (Cambridge: Harvard UP, 1914) LXXXIV 251.

and prose of the Augustan age reveals the extent of this transformation in rhetorical ideology.

This paper argues that the broad cultural movement toward homogenization in Roman institutions that occurred during the reign of Augustus limited the intellectual development of discourse, specifically the practice of rhetoric. Cultural histories addressing this period, notably the work of Karl Galinsky and Paul Zanker, have traced the contours of the dramatic social and political changes coinciding with the Augustan Participate and have established a proper context for evaluating Imperial rhetoric in a new light.[2] In particular, Zanker's characterization of Augustus' influence upon every aspect of Roman life helps to explain why larger conclusions about Roman rhetoric can be drawn by studying reflections of the *princeps*. This essay advocates the initiation of a new evaluation of the rhetoric from this period and points out potential topics and sources that could aid such an endeavor.

An appreciation for these sources addresses some of the problems emerging from current narrative tendencies to portray Roman rhetoric as a stable and consistent tradition. Such tendencies severely limit our ability to understand the transitions in rhetorical practice that were identified in the writings of Seneca the Elder and Tacitus, students of rhetoric in the early empire. Both men were alarmed by a general atrophy of skill in public speaking, a deficiency that developed as Roman speakers became reluctant to engage in pointed political debate. This general reluctance, far from emerging as a self-protective response to the persecutions of an oppressive tyranny, instead emerged naturally as the ideology of the orator developed, elevating his role far beyond the ambit of the average Roman citizen. Roman citizens could accept a decline in oratory as long as they could continue to laud the empty symbol of the orator. Concluding with an analysis of Augustan poetry, I will discuss how features of the new ideology generated praise for the orator, but encouraged the blaming of oratory for political and social strife.

The assumption that Roman rhetorical theories contain few distinctions of substance has arisen in histories of Roman rhetoric that generally fail to reflect upon differences in the political contexts of pre-Republican, Republican, Augustan, and Imperial Rome. Such as-

---

[2] Paul Zanker, *The Power of Images in the Age of Augustus*; Karl Galinsky, *Augustan Culture: An Interpretive Introduction*.

sumptions are typified in Conley's suggestion that the standard definition of the orator as a good man speaking well, *vir peritus dicendi bene,* which was voiced by Cicero, echoed by Quintilian, and idealized throughout the empire's duration, reveals the consistent force of rhetoric.[3] Any narratives that happen to discuss political differences typically do so in passing. At best, they casually observe that distinct political cultures flourished in the Republican and Imperial periods, but withhold commentary addressing the influence of these distinctions upon the actual discourse of the Romans. For the most part, it has remained a foregone conclusion that, in mode and manner, Roman rhetoric remained a steady practice in several varied political regimes. Such a conclusion supports the presumption that little is gained from considering differences in Republican and Imperial rhetorical practices. For instance, in what is generally an impressive collection of recent essays that serve to disrupt the canon and alter our understanding of the history of rhetoric, with critiques that range from extensive coverage of the discourse of the Greeks' rhetorical practice to varied analyses of Medieval, Renaissance, and later writings on rhetoric, there is a general omission of discussion about Roman rhetoric.[4] A few recent histories of rhetoric have identified a shift from civic (Republican) to pedagogic (Imperial), and finally to Asiatic (pre-Christian) rhetoric. Cheryl Glenn, in her new Feminist history of rhetoric, observes that Quintilian's work signals a shift in rhetoric, "maturity" in Roman rhetoric, but her discussion never elaborates upon what this maturity actually signifies. Curiously, she notes that rhetoric ceased to function "as a political force in Roman society," leaving this fascinating remark to wither without explanation and elaboration. She regards rhetoric as a pedagogic system that helps to distinguish an elite from the common subject. She is careful to stress the enduring social and cultural importance of rhetoric at the same time she acknowledges that rhetoric does

---

[3] Thomas M. Conley, *Rhetoric in the European Tradition*, 46; "Indeed, that influence continues in Roman rhetoric until the fall of Rome. Rhetoric does not wither under the empire; it simply changes tactics from those of the courtroom to those of the court." Also see James Herrick, *The History and Theory of Rhetoric*, 2–3 and 96–125. Particularly revealing is Herrick's timeline of rhetoric, running 200 BCE to 200 CE and provides 55 BCE, the date of publication of Cicero's *De Oratore* as the only date needing to be mentioned in this period.

[4] Victor Vitanza, *Writing Histories of Rhetoric*.

not operate in the political sphere.⁵ Even the foremost scholar of classical rhetoric, George Kennedy, has only provided limited discussion of the political context of Augustan rhetoric:

> Rhetoric played an important part in the intellectual and aesthetic life of the Augustan Age: it maintained its dominant position in the educational system, it continued to be the disciplinary core of literary criticism, it influenced the techniques and qualities of poetry and literary prose. Judicial oratory flourished under only slightly altered conditions; political oratory, however, lost ground while new forms of persuasion, a new rhetoric in the verbal and visual arts, arose to influence public opinion.⁶

In sum, a few treatments have recognized shifts in political practices, but they all assume that the knowledge of the orator and of oratory continued to provide a means to power.

Considering the intimate connection between any form of rhetoric and the conditions of public discourse, it is remarkable that rhetorical scholars have done so little to address the begged question: If the political climate had changed from the Republican era to the Imperial

---

⁵ Cheryl Glenn, *Rhetoric Retold*, 60; "Under Quintilian, Roman rhetorical theory matures; it is no longer dependent on the Greek practices espoused by Cicero. Yet in the spirit of Cicero, of whom he speaks with unbounded eulogy, Quintilian continues to regard the broadly educated man as the fittest candidate for a course in rhetoric and for a role in public life, though with the end of the republic came the end of rhetoric as a political force in Roman society."

⁶ George Kennedy, *The Art of Rhetoric in the Roman World*, 301–2; Kennedy provides much better coverage of the political climate surrounding Roman rhetoric in this book than in his later *Classical Rhetoric*, where he avoids the discussion of political context entirely. Kennedy's most recent work—*A New History of Classical Rhetoric*, 159—again provides insufficient context for the Augustan age; "Although not a distinguished public speaker, he had a profound understanding of the rhetoric of empire. A variety of republican titles and religious forms were used to mask the reality of his power; art, architecture, inscriptions, and urban planning conveyed the aura of a new golden age; and support was given to writers, who in turn were expected to celebrate the achievements of the emperor and the legitimacy of his rule. Yet the criticism of the age, within limits was tolerated and is often presented in the writings of its greatest poets, Virgil and Horace."

age, why hold to the view that the rhetoric and rhetorical theories of these times remained the same?

In examining the writings of the Augustan age rhetorician, Seneca the Elder, and the later work of Tacitus and Quintilian, we find that they did not believe in the stable continuity of the rhetorical tradition. Their writings contained unrefined elements that could be interpreted to constitute a larger political critique, however they were bound by a set of discursive constraints that this essay argues were part of an *ideology of the orator*. The Imperial construction of the symbol of the orator as the model citizen transferred the Romans' awe of speaking to an awe of the speaker. In other words, although they could condemn the lack of skillful oratory in their time, they needed to valorize the role of the orator. Seneca the Elder, sometimes referred to as Seneca the rhetorician, described this decline in oratory in his collection of *Controversiae*, written during the reign of Augustus:

> Moreover, you can by this means judge how sharply intellectual standards are falling every day, how far some grudge on nature's part has sent eloquence into a decline. Everything that Roman oratory has to set alongside or even above the haughty Greeks reached its peak in Cicero's day; all the geniuses that have brought brilliance to our subject were born then. Since, things have got daily worse.[7]

Seneca's passage deserves comment, most notably, where he conceptualizes oratory and public address as a living essence. Seneca voiced the complaint typical of the rhetorical manuals of the Imperial period that presumed a decline in the quality of the oratory. More significantly, this passage's heavy reliance upon the metaphors of life and death call closer attention to the distinction between Republican and Imperial oratory. Imperial rhetoric could only strive to be a facsimile of its dead antecedent. Seneca characterizes the "falling" and "peak" fortunes of oratory, which, when more literally translated as "flourished" and "decayed," call our attention to the living act of speech. At best, Seneca stated, rhetoric could only exist as a dead copy of the past. A hundred years later, with the Imperial government clearly established as the unquestionable institution of Rome, Tacitus repeated Seneca's ideology

---

[7] Seneca, *Controversiae*, vol. 1, translated by Winterbottom, vi, 6–7.

in the opening sentences of his *Dialogus De Oratoribus* by stating the assumption that oratory and orators in his time were clearly inferior:

> Justus Fabius, often you have asked me why it is that, with praise for eloquence abandoned and forgotten, the name of the orator himself barely remains, although in earlier ages so many worthy speakers prospered with glory and talent. And, with the exception of the ancient speakers, we do not even title anyone thus, and moreover, the accomplished speakers of these current times are called pleaders, defenders, jurists and anything else other than orator.[8]

These introductory comments to Tacitus' dialogue, like Seneca's comments, reflect an ideology that aestheticized the orator, an ideology that first fully manifested itself in Augustus' time. Whether it existed or not, both authors nostalgically recall a time when rhetoric denoted a tradition of civic advocacy and disputation, a time that contrasts to aesthetic preferences treating rhetorical discourse as an envisioned art. The aesthetic vision of the orator finds its best articulation in the description of Neptune found in Book I of Virgil's *Aeneid*:

> Thus he speaks, and swifter than his word he calms the swollen seas, puts to flight the gathered clouds, and brings back the sun. Cymothoë and Triton with common effort thrust the ships from the sharp rock; the god himself upheaves them with his trident, opens the vast quicksands, allays the flood, and on light wheels glides over the topmost waters. And as, when oft-times in a great nation tumult has risen, the base rabble rage angrily, and now brands and stones fly, madness lending arms; then, if haply they set eyes on a man honored for noble character and service, they are silent and stand by with attentive ears; he

---

[8] Tacitus, *Dialogus De Oratoribus*, edited by & notes by C. E. Bennett, 1. 1; "*Saepe ex me requiris, Iuste Fabi, cur, cum priora saecula tot eminentium oratorum ingeniis gloriaque floruerint, nostra potissimum aetas deserta et laude eloquentiae orbata vix nomen ipsum oratoris retineat. Neque enim ita appellamus nisi antiquos, horum autem temporum diserti causidici et advocati et patroni et quidvis potius quam oratores vocantur*" (translation mine).

with speech sways their passion and soothes their breasts.⁹

This simile of the orator emphasized the function of the ideology of the orator in the Augustan age. The portrayal of Neptune embodies the model of brevity and simplicity promoted by Augustus. The orator commands men and nature with his voice, calming the sea with a command (*dicto*) and governing of the mob's hearts and souls through words (*dictis*). Lengthy speeches are not required to rule the waves and direct the rabble. The simile illustrates the aristocratic heritage of the speaker, a genitor who is drawn by a chariot and whose arrival offers an alternative to civil chaos. A speaker who commands and does not debate will order the natural world. This passage points to a cultural framework that allowed for the glorification of the new status of the orator. Furthermore, it facilitated the citizens of Rome's acceptance of cultural norms restraining the public use of speech.

In fact, some scholars have suggested that the curtailing of speech was entirely voluntary. Kennedy, for one, holds this view: "In sum, although Augustus did not set out to limit freedom of speech or suppress oratory, his enormous personal power was inhibiting and could not help but affect the conditions of oratory."[10] Kennedy's judgment may be motivated by a sympathetic reading of some of Augustus' reported statements concerning liberty, governance, and speech. For instance, Suetonius recorded a comment made by Augustus to his eventual successor Tiberius that discussed the need to restrain from censorship. Arguably, this passage reveals Augustus' political philosophy regarding free speech: "My dear Tiberius do not be carried by the ardor of youth in this matter or take it too much to heart that anyone speak evil of me, we must be content if we can stop anyone doing evil to us."[11]

Despite the contemporary Western valorization of free speech principles, or perhaps because of it, analysis of the rhetoric of the Augustan age should be reluctant to rush to the conclusion that censorship played a significant role in curbing public discourse. A few specific cases of censorship can be found, but the broad cultural move away from public debate documented in this essay did not emerge as a re-

---

[9] Vergil, *Aeneid*, vol. 1, translated by H. Rushton Fairclough, I.143–56 251–53.
[10] Kennedy, *Rhetoric in Rome*, 303.
[11] Suetonius, *Augustus* LI 3.

sponse to banned speech and the institution of censorship.[12] At certain periods of time during the transition from Republican to Imperial rule, political tension led to an atmosphere that generally discouraged open speech, however nothing points to wholesale censorship. For instance, Macrobious attributed the following anecdote to John of Salisbury: "During the triumvirate Augustus wrote some lampoons on Pollio, but Pollio only observed: 'For my part I am saying nothing in reply; for it is asking for trouble to write against a man who can write you off.'"[13] Clarence Forbes more recently commented that Augustus' reign witnessed the first incident of book burning in Rome.[14] Possibly, Augustus himself initiated this book burning shortly before he died.[15] Granting the veracity of this account at best provides evidence for a personal vendetta undertaken by the emperor in his old age. Incidents that may have occurred and that might reflect hostility to free speech are insufficient in explaining the overall lack of political oratory at this time. A more detailed discussion of the religious and political climate of the age better explains the broad movement away from controversial speech.

Suetonius described Augustus' style of speaking in ways that curiously resemble the general aesthetic movement in religion and politics towards simplicity, clarity, and order:

---

[12] Galinsky, 370.

[13] Macrobius, *Saturnalia*. Translated by V. D. Percival. II 4–21. 173.

[14] Clarence A. Forbes, "Books for the Burning," 122–3: "In Roman history the earliest case of the destruction by fire of books deemed to be politically dangerous occurred in the Augustan Age. The elder Seneca describes the incident, but he attributes the burning not to the emperor but to a *Senatus Consultum* prompted by the many personal enemies of the free-spoken and fiery orator involved, Titus Labienus."

[15] Forbes, "Books for the Burning," 122: "Augustus succeeded fairly well in winning the support of the leading writers of his time, and he was magnanimous toward such conscientious objectors as Livy. In his declining years however, perhaps he was a little more touchy. Two years before his death, when he learned of the existence of libelous writings defaming certain individuals, he ordered that a search should be made for copies, that those found in the city should be burned by the aediles and those elsewhere by the appropriate local magistrates. It has been suggested that the books in question were those of Labienus, but, if so, the account of Dio differs from that of Seneca in making no mention of a *Senatus Consultum*."

> He cultivated a style of speaking that was chaste and elegant, avoiding the vanity of attempts at epigram and an artificial order, and, as he himself expresses it, "the noisomeness of far-fetched words," making it his chief aim to express his thought as clearly as possible. With this end in view to avoid confusing and checking his reader or hearer at any point, he did not hesitate to use prepositions with names of cities, nor to repeat conjunctions several times, the omission of which causes some obscurity, though it adds grace.[16]

Augustus' practice followed a certain logic: since words are extensions of a speaker, not calling attention to them maintains focus upon the speaker. Keeping in mind the unparalleled influence exerted by Augustus' example, Suetonius' anecdote reveals a powerful transformation in the notion of the orator, suggesting that the term itself came to serve as a trope for the good citizen, the orderly aristocrat. As Augustus himself says, "I myself transmitted exemplary practices to posterity for their imitation."[17] As long as the Romans maintained their praise for the good orator, they could tolerate his absence in public affairs.

As recorded in his *Res Gestae*, Augustus held a wide range of political and religious titles that all served to consolidate his political power: "I was triumvir for the organization of the republic for ten consecutive years. Up to the day of writing I have been *princeps senatus* for forty years. I am *pontifex maximus, augur, quindecimvir, sacris faciundis, septemvir epulonum, frater arvalis, sodalis Titius, fetialis*."[18] This remarkable catalogue of political and religious offices reveals the extent to which the Roman state had unified its political and religious systems. Augustus initiated a widespread religious revival that helped him to consolidate his rule and secure a religious authority for the emperor that would endure throughout Rome's Imperial age. Under Augustus, Rome underwent a long sustained process of unification and consolidation of its previously scattered and disparate forms of art, architecture, religious cults, social structures, political organization, and social grouping. The writings of the Augustan poets depict the

---

[16] Suetonius, *Augustus*, LXXXVI.
[17] *Res Gestae Divi Augusti*: *The Achievements of the Divine Augustus*, edited by P.A. Brunt & J.M. Moore. 8.5 23.
[18] *Res Gestae*, 20–21.

broad trend in the specialization of the orator that mirrored growth of the Imperial State and the homogenization of Rome's social hierarchy and religion.

A paradox emerged at this time as the increasing public religiosity and widening symbolism of religious practices denuded the previous religious connections that had bound private citizens to their gods. As the Roman State evolved its hierarchical pantheon of gods, the average citizen lacked good reason to continue the personal worship of deities undervalued by the state.[19] Cyril Bailey has argued that this became even more pronounced as Jupiter assumed greater prominence as the supreme god of the Roman State:

> Yet there is one feature of real vitality amid this general paralysis, namely the worship of Iuppiter; which became more and more the supreme cult and the symbol of the State-life. It has often been observed that the worship of the tribal god is likely to become more and more political, as civilization increases and the conception of the state develops, until it is little more in effect than the worship of the tribe itself.[20]

Bailey observed that this development culminated in the establishment of a state cult that, despite all of its encouragement of religious piety, emptied its people of any capacity for religious belief.[21] Several things emerged out of this transition to state-worship. First, the emperor, whether a divine being or merely the high priest, assumed religious authority for his secular deeds. In addition to modeling the

---

[19] Cyril Bailey, *Phases in the Religion of Ancient Rome*, 167.
[20] Bailey, *Phases in the Religion of Ancient Rome*, 168.
[21] Bailey, *Phases in the Religion of Ancient Rome*, 172–73: "And this kind of petrifaction in religion is particularly dangerous when the institution is not an independent Church, but a political State. For then there are two new evils: religion is liable to be subordinated to politics, as it was in Roman augury, and the State itself is apt to become the object of worship. The Roman Iuppiter had in his supreme position the germs of a monotheism, which philosophy later turned to good religious purpose. But in his place in the religion of the religion of the State he had become little else than its own impersonation: he had swamped and obscured the other cults and the lesser ideas of true religious significance for which they stood, and was himself the symbol of a religion essentially political. In all these ways institutionalism at Rome had killed the common instinct which it was intended to foster."

correct conduct in political affairs; in the eyes of the Roman citizens, the simple prepared speech of the emperor Augustus demonstrated his understanding of divine order and manners of speaking. Both Galinsky and Zanker have called our attention to Augustus' use of the power of *auctoritas,* a concept that stresses the authority, social stature, and religious standing of the emperor.[22] Augustus' own testament, *Res Gestae,* contains a critical passage in which he places greater emphasis on his authority than on his power.[23] While a full length treatment of *auctoritas* is beyond the scope of this essay, Galinsky and Zanker's own work demonstrates how Augustus changed the conduct of public speech. In holding both divine and mortal qualities, the symbol of the ideal orator congealed around the words and deeds of Augustus. Skill in oratory only resulted from the emulation of the speech of the high priest, the emperor.

A heavy dose of propaganda accompanied the deification processes of Imperial Rome.[24] This new development encouraged the association of various religious and cultural motifs with the symbolism of the state and of the emperor himself. As Paul Zanker has pointed out, this "meaningful use and repetition of images and messages was a new phenomenon, particularly when one considers that the coin types of the previous decades had seldom aimed at such effects."[25] This dramatic surge in propaganda led to a reformulation of the religious symbolism at the forum and a broad coalescence of praise for Octavian.[26] In his discussion of the above quoted passage from the *Res Gestae,* Zanker described how Augustus broadly characterized himself as the religious

---

[22] Zanker, *The Power of Images in the Age of Augustus*; Galinsky, *Augustan Culture.*

[23] *Res Gestae,* 37.

[24] Galinsky (*Augustan Culture,* 259) observes that Augustus while alive, was not worshipped as a god in Rome, but was outside of Rome.

[25] Zanker, *The Power of Images in the Age of Augustus,* 37.

[26] Zanker, *The Power of Images in the Age of Augustus,* 81; "These monuments set up by or for Octavian transformed the appearance of the Forum. Wherever one looked, there were symbols of victory. In the pediment of the recently completed Temple of Saturn, for example, instead of an image of the ancient god of the sowing season, there were Tritons gaily blowing on trumpets. Triton was widely recognized as one of those marine creatures who had assisted in the victory at Actium, and the temple's patron, Manutius Plancus, thus joined in the universal praise of Octavian."

savior of the Roman Republic and justified his unprecedented control over Rome's institutions of power:

> We know well, of course, that this sentence, drawn from the political autobiography of the aged ruler, is really a half truth. In fact, by means of a complicated system of prolonged extraordinary powers, special privileges, and long-term offices, and especially thanks to his huge personal fortune, the savior and restorer of the Republic was able to keep firm control of the army and thus of all the power. A coin minted more than ten years later makes quite explicit the relationship of savior and Republic: the *res publica,* represented in the scheme usual for a conquered province, kneels before Augustus, and he helps her to her feet. The savior stands beside the restored Republic, which is in need of his leadership. Most people will have felt the same way back in 27 B.C., but the act of relinquishing power was a great gesture which allowed the aristocracy to save face and in future to be partners in the new state.[27]

In addition to the architecture and monuments that were built during the massive building campaign, the propaganda of the Augustan regime can be appreciated in the poetry of the age.

In the sphere of poetry, we see the patronage of poets who would thematically incorporate praise for the state into their work. This relationship between patron and poet did not result in the type of propaganda that we might associate with some of the state-sponsored art of the twentieth-century. Galinsky, for one, dismisses such interpretation as an "inadequate top-down conception of the Augustan reign" and poignantly emphasizes that these poets did not solely serve the propagandistic needs of Augustus.[28] Nevertheless, the poetry of this period, like any period, reflects the ideology of its time, even while jesting and conveying irony dryly. Observing these ideological themes in Virgil's *Aeneid* even allows us to reflect upon the artistry of a master rhetori-

---

[27] Zanker, *The Power of Images in the Age of Augustus,* 91–2.
[28] Galinsky, *Augustan Culture,* 244.

cian.²⁹ His poetic use of the epic form accentuated and articulated some of the concepts that constituted the ideology of the Principate.³⁰ As David Quint has argued: "In the intervening years that had seen the reigns of such monstrous successors to Augustus as Tiberius, Caligula, Claudius, and Lucan's own contemporary, Nero, the *Aeneid* had become the prop for the one-man rule of the emperor."³¹ Zanker even observed a unified aesthetic and method for conveying the symbols of the state in the rhetorical manuals of the Augustan age.³² Far from cheapening the reading experience, I agree with Quint's view that examining these ideological workings in a text such as Virgil's *Aeneid* deepens the appreciation of its artistry.³³ In other words, the *Aeneid* is not mere propaganda, but the propagandistic themes that emerge from this multivalent text help to illustrate its broad scope.

The primary characters of the *Aeneid* represent particular speaking types, amongst other things. Their words and deeds symbolize their

---

²⁹ Macrobius, op cit., 5–1: "After this Eusebius paused for a little while; but in the meantime there was a murmur of talk among the rest of those present, and a general agreement to hold Virgil no less eminent as an orator than as a poet, so great was the knowledge he showed of oratory and so careful his regard for the rules of rhetoric." M.L. Clark, "Rhetorical Influences in the *Aeneid*," *Greece and Rome* 1949, 23; "Virgil is eloquent in this sense. He had studied well the heart of man and had found the just proportions of his discourse."

³⁰ David Quint, *Epic and Empire* (Princeton: UP, 1993) elaborates about the relationship between the epic form and the expression of state power at 45; "Narrative itself thus becomes ideologically charged, the formal cause or consequence of that Western male rationality and historical identity that epic ascribes to the imperial victors. Epic draws an equation between power and narrative. It tells of a power able to end the indeterminacy of war and to emerge victorious, showing that the struggle had all along been leading up to its victory and thus imposing upon it a narrative teleology—the teleology that epic identifies with the very idea of narrative."

³¹ Quint, *Epic and Empire*, 7.

³² Zanker, *The Power of Images in the Age Augustus*, 223; "In so doing he characterizes each one's qualities with a single term, precisely echoing the ethical standards of his age. Virtually every author is praised for either simplicity, clarity, precision, or purity of style. These are exactly the qualities which the most characteristic works of Augustan art so brilliantly display: clarity of outline, precision of form, and simplicity and clarity of composition."

³³ Quint, *Epic and Empire*, 52–3.

characters, hence we see Aeneas praying, cursing, supplicating, or negotiating, and we find Turnus using speech deceitfully, making arguments, justifying his behavior in someone else's actions, and reluctant to turn his gaze inward. Finally, we see Drances, the tragic speaker who voices what is in everyone's mind (11.132). Drances represents the incomplete orator, the half-man, who uses speech correctly, but lacks the proper station to fully take advantage of it. His unctuous flattery allows him to obtain peace, albeit only a temporary one:

> Then aged Drances, ever the foe of youthful Turnus in hate and calumny, thus speaks in reply: "O great in glory, greater in arms, thou hero of Troy, how with my praises may I extol thee to the sky? Am I to marvel first at thy justice or at thy toils in war? We indeed will gratefully bear these words back to our native city, and if fortune grant a way, will unite thee with Latinus our king. Let Turnus seek alliances for himself! Nay, it will be our delight to rear those massive walls thy destiny ordains, and on our shoulders to bear the stones of Troy." He ceased, and all with one voice murmured assent. For twice six days they made truce, and, with peace interposing, Teucrians and Latins o'er the forest heights roamed scatheless together.[34]

Drances fails to gain a more lasting peace because he uses oratory for personal gain. Kennedy has noted that commentators have pointed to the character of Drances as a representation of Cicero.[35] Virgil goes a little farther than that in his portrayal. He suggests a certain incompleteness that stems from Drances' envy and not entirely noble bloodline:

---

[34] Vergil, *Aeneid*, vol. 2, translated by H.R. Fairclough 1.122–35, 244.
[35] Kennedy, *Roman Rhetoric*, 394; "The passage of the *Aeneid* which most accurately reflects the conditions of political debate is the scene between Drances and Turnus in book eleven." Also, at 394–5; "Commentators have sometimes thought that Drances was Virgil's picture of Cicero, while Turnus might possibly be thought of as influenced by Antony; Demosthenes, Cicero, and the typical orator was thought to cut a poor figure on the battlefield, and Cicero had of course been torn between Pompey and Caesar, then became the implacable foe of Antony."

> Then Drances, hostile as before, whom the renown of Turnus goaded with the bitter stings of furtive envy, lavish of wealth and valiant of tongue, though his hand was cold for battle, in counsel deemed no mean adviser, in faction strong (his mother's high birth ennobled his lineage; from his sire obscure rank he drew), rises and with these words loads and heaps high their wrath.[36]

In this passage, Virgil foreshadows that Drances, the only hope for peace, was guaranteed to fail. Although he possessed sufficient wealth and speaking capability, he was motivated by envy and lacked the ethos of a warrior. His maternal lineage was canceled out by his father's and his "strong counsel" was undermined by his disloyal behavior (*potens seditione*). In his use of the verb *surgit* (he rose), Virgil alludes to the initiatory actions of the powerful figures of the divine orators, Iupiter and Triton, but the results suggest that Drances was not a true orator.

Controlling the image of the orator was an integral part of Augustan propaganda.[37] The new model orator was the calm and controlled figure of Neptune and Zeus. The speeches of Zeus are proclamations and statements of fact. They establish the state of affairs. Amidst the storm and strife of mundane affairs, the new orator stays calm and relaxed, never swayed by contrary opinions, already knowing the correct course of action, and ever ready to tell things as they really are. For instance, in Virgil's initial portrayal of Zeus, speech guarantees the rise of the Roman city: "On her smiling, with that look wherewith he clears sky and storms, the Father of men and gods gently kissed his daughter's lips, and then spake thus: 'Spare thy fear, Lady of Cythera; thy children's fates abide unmoved. Thou shalt see Lavinium's city and its promised walls; and thou shalt raise on high the starry heaven great-souled Aeneas. No thought has turned me.'"[38] This symbolism was congruent with the type of speaker that Augustus was trying to

---

[36] Virgil, *Aeneid*, vol. 2, op. cit., XI.336–41 257–9.

[37] Kennedy, *Roman Rhetoric*, 382; "To win men's minds without opening the door to the dangers of public debate Augustus developed new techniques of verbal and visual persuasion which took over some of the functions and adapted some of the methods of traditional oratory. The orator becomes a standard form in imperial sculpture and the iconography borrows from the rules of gesture and delivery."

[38] Virgil, *Aeneid*, vol. 1, translated by H.R. Fairclough, 1.254–60, 259.

promote. Suetonius reported the following statements from the writings of Augustus:

> Can you doubt whether you ought to imitate Annius Cimber or Veranius Flaccus that you use the words which Sallustius Crispus gleaned from Cato's *Origines*? Or would you rather introduce into our tongue the verbiage and unmeaning fluency of the Asiatic orators?"

And in a letter praising the talent of his granddaughter Agrippina he writes "But you must take great care not to write and talk affectedly."[39]

And so, we observe a valorization of the calm and controlled orator and a condemnation of furious speech. Laudable speeches emphasize synthesis and unity above strife and conflict. Zanker's extensive analysis of the propaganda of the age concluded that the populace willingly adopted the cultural and moral dictates of the new state. As he observed, the language and grammar of the official imagery eventually overwhelmed the ability of the individual to construct a personalized artistic language.[40]

This essay has argued that an appreciation for the aesthetic expressions of the Augustan age can facilitate our understanding of the social, religious, and cultural context that rhetoric operated in. As Rome underwent a radical change in its civic institutions, the religious, political, and general aesthetic tastes mutated in turn. Just as the emphasis upon religious ritual disconnected Romans from their gods, the praise of the orator supplemented for the desire to debate. In characterizing Augustan rhetoric, we might borrow a phrase from Galinsky's description of Augustan political historiography and observe that we are dealing "not so much with contradictory traditions as with the tradition of a contradiction."[41] Realizing the dramatic differences in the oratory of the Republican and Imperial periods might lead to the replacement of the simplified model of Roman rhetoric with a more nuanced one based in an understanding of the interrelationships between the speech, poetics, politics, and religion of an age.

---

[39] Suetonius, *Augustus*, LXXXVI.
[40] Zanker, *The Power of Images in the Age of Augustus*, 278.
[41] Galinsky, *Augustan Culture*, 374.

The figure of the orator is one example of the type of symbolism found in the new political climate coinciding with the Principate. As such it suggests several under-explored avenues for students of rhetoric. In characterizing the figure, this essay calls attention to unconventionally "rhetorical" texts that could help revise the standard narrative of Augustan and Imperial rhetoric. Virgil's *Aeneid* is just one of many works of art that provides a wealth of information about rhetoric under the empire. For instance, revisiting the statues of this time to analyze how they conveyed Imperial ideologies through visual representations of the speaker would benefit from Brilliant's descriptions of an aesthetically standardized orator type.[42] Zanker's work only begins to demonstrate how studies of Imperial rhetorical theory would gain from a reading of Horace's *Ars Poetica* that situates this text in the broader context of Roman rhetoric. Galinsky's description of the rhetorical uses of architecture and building structures only scratches the surface in identifying the physical conditions that molded the rhetoric of this time. Together, these sources and others can help us observe a new kind of orator, a ceremonial figure arising in response to changes in the deliberative process.

---

[42] Richard Brilliant, *Gesture and Rank in Roman Art*.

Afterword

Moments of Opportunity in the History of Rhetoric

David E. Beard

This collection of texts represents a moment in the history of rhetoric worth documenting and studying. It is the fourth in a series of key moments of opportunity in the history of rhetoric as a field of research across academic disciplines, and it may well be the model for future moments of interdisciplinary collaboration.

The first moment, the formative moment for rhetorical study, was the report of the Pedagogical Section of the MLA in the *Proceedings* of the 1900 MLA. Therein, W. E. Mead summarized the survey of the Pedagogical Section of the MLA on the possibility of graduate study in Rhetoric was possible. Respondents argued for the study of the history of rhetoric and the development of rhetorical theory from Aristotle to the present and the relations of argument to logic. Rhetoric, as a field of scholarly work, was legitimated by this survey. But it was not legitimated by the Modern Language Association, which dissolved the Pedagogical Section; the scholars in that section eventually formed the National Council of Teachers of English and for the first time, Rhetoric was both legitimated as a form of study and dispersed across professional associations to support that study. Literary scholars interested in rhetorical criticism of literature could work independently of scholars in rhetoric and composition.

The second moment was the formation of the National Association of Academic Teachers of Public Speaking. Rhetoric was not the core issue that drove teachers of public speaking away from teachers of Eng-

369

lish. The correspondence left by the founding members (in the biographical files at UW-Madison and Northwestern University) indicate that some members wanted, instead, to differentiate their work at university from the work at high schools and universities that the NCTE attempted to represent equally. Others advocated a disciplinary name like "Oral English"—indicating that it was orality, not rhetoricality, that divided the NAATPS from the NCTE. Regardless of the reason, rhetorical work was again validated in new arenas as it was dispersed across disciplinary lines. Literary, composition and speech rhetoricians could carry the flag in obliviousness to each other.

The third moment was a kind of missed opportunity—a series of events that kept inviting a collaboration that could not occur. The 1968 formation of the Rhetoric Society of America as an interdisciplinary organization was an important step in building a common community of scholars in rhetoric across disciplinary lines, but the Board at its formation was, in fact, a community of scholars in English working with one linguist, one communication scholar, and one philosopher. This was hardly a model for interdisciplinary collaboration. The 1970 Wingspread conference, sponsored by what is now the National Communication Association, was limited in much the same way. While a handful of literary scholars (notably Wayne Booth) and philosophers (notably Richard McKeon) presented, the conference produced more polemical calls for the globalization of rhetoric in Communication Studies than it did plans for bringing the work of scholars in rhetoric together across disciplinary lines.

I contend that *Advances in the History of Rhetoric* is the manifestation of the moment that the opportunities missed in the 1960s and 1970s was taken. *Advances* manifests the possibility of the interdisciplinary study of rhetoric even more thoroughly than the RSA, Wingspread, or the 2003 Conference of the Alliance of Rhetorical Societies. These marquee events failed (in my opinion) because they focused on issues of definition: What is rhetoric? What is its scope? What is its proper field of study and application? Where does it sit alongside other key terms in the disciplines? *Advances,* on the other hand, in its eleven years of publication under the editorship of Richard Leo Enos and now under the editorship of Robert Gaines, pulled those scholars together by putting them to work.

Instead of debating the definition of rhetoric, authors in *Advances in the History of Rhetoric* moved directly to explicating rhetorical texts, to contextualizing rhetorical theories, to connecting rhetorical thinkers to their contexts. Instead of creating polemics about what the field of rhetoric could be, these thinkers in communication, in English, in composition simply rolled up their sleeves. And the results speak for themselves: the American Society for the History of Rhetoric and its publication, *Advances,* represent the model for what interdisciplinary research in rhetorical studies can be. When departmental affiliations are removed and disciplinary lines are erased or at least effaced, what matters is the quality of the research. And *Advances,* by serving as a forum for connecting scholars based on a common interest in the history of rhetoric rather than a common departmental affiliation, continues to serve as a central ground for interdisciplinary research in the history of rhetoric.

Appendix

A Brief History of the American Society for the History of Rhetoric

In 1977 a small group of historians of rhetoric gathered at the then Speech Communication Association convention in Washington, D.C. Concerned about the lack of panels on the history of rhetoric at SCA conferences and encouraged by the inaugural meeting of the International Society for the History of Rhetoric (held in Zurich in June of 1977), these scholars proposed the formation of the American Branch of the ISHR. They sponsored panels under that rubric at the 1978 SCA meeting in Minneapolis.

Between 1978 and 1990 the organization grew in both size and diversity. It sponsored panels at the annual SCA conference and, in 1986, held its first "preconference" on the day before the SCA conference. In 1990 the organization changed its name to the American Society for the History of Rhetoric. In the late 1980s, ASHR affiliated with the Eastern Communication Association and, in 1996, affiliated with the Southern States Communication Association. ASHR now sponsors panels at national and regional conferences in rhetoric, communication and composition.

PRESIDENTS OF THE AMERICAN SOCIETY
FOR THE HISTORY OF RHETORIC
(formerly the ISHR-American Branch)

1977–78:   ISHR-American Branch organized
1978–79:   Michael C. Leff, *University of Wisconsin*
1979–80:   James J. Murphy, *University of California-Davis*
1980–81:   Richard Leo Enos, *Carnegie Mellon University*

1981–82:   William L. Benoit, *Bowling Green State University*
1982–83:   Beth S. Bennett, *University of Alabama*
1983–84:   James Benjamin, *Southwest Texas State University*
1984–85:   Keith V. Erickson, *Texas Tech University*
1985–86:   Charles Kneupper, *University of Texas-Arlington*
1986–87:   Robert N. Gaines, *University of Maryland*
1987–88:   Molly Meijer Wertheimer, *Pennsylvania State University-Hazleton*
1988–89:   Raymie E. McKerrow, *University of Maine*
1989–90:   Takis Poulakos, *University of Pittsburgh*
1990–91:   Jane Sutton, *Pennsylvania State University-York*
1991–92:   Victor Vitanza, *University of Texas-Arlington*
1992–93:   John Poulakos, *University of Pittsburgh*
1993–94:   Barbara Warnick, *University of Washington*
1994–95:   Beth S. Bennett, *University of Alabama*
1995–96:   Robert G. Sullivan, *University of Maryland/Ithaca College*
1996–97:   Sean Patrick O'Rourke, *Vanderbilt University*
1997–98:   Glen A. McClish, *Southwestern University*
1998–99:   James M. Tallmon, *South Dakota State University*
1999–00:   Mari Lee Mifsud, *University of Richmond*
2000–01:   Arthur E. Walzer, *University of Minnesota*
2001–02:   Sara Newman, *Kent State University*
2002-03:   David C. Hoffman, *University of North Carolina-Charlotte*
2003-04:   Ekatrina Haskins, *Rensselaer Polytechnic Institute*
2004–05:   Janet Atwill, *University of Tennessee*
2005–06:   Richard Graff, *University of Minnesota*
2006-07:   Daniel Emery, *University of Utah*

Bibliography of Classical Authors

ARISTOTLE

Aristotelis De Arte Poetica Liber. Recognovit brevique adnotatione critica instruxit Rudolfus Kassel. Scriptorum Classicorum Bibliotheca Oxoniensis. Oxonii, E Typographeo Clarendoniano, 1965.
Art of Rhetoric. Trans. J. H. Freese. Cambridge, MA: Harvard UP, Loeb Classical Library, 1926.
Complete Works. Trans. Jonathan Barnes. Princeton: Princeton UP, 1984.
Nicomachean Ethics. Trans. W. D. Ross. *The Basic Works of Aristotle.* Edited & introduction by Richard McKeon. New York: Random House, 1941.
On Rhetoric. A Theory of Civic Discourse. Trans. George Kennedy. New York: Oxford UP, 1991.
Politics. Trans. H. Rackham. Cambridge, MA: Harvard UP, 1977.
Politics. Trans. C. Lord. Chicago, IL: U of Chicago P, 1984.
Rhetoric of Aristotle. Trans. Lane Cooper. New York: Appleton-Century-Crofts, 1932.
Selected Works. Ed. Apostle, Hippocrates G. and Lloyd P. Gerson. Grinnell: The Peripatetic Press, 1983.

APTHONIUS

Progymnasmata. Trans. Ray Nadeau. *Speech Monographs* 19 (1962): 264–285.

AUGUSTINE

On Christian Doctrine. Trans. D.W. Robertson. New York: Macmillan, 1958.

CICERO

Cicero. Volume 21. Cambridge: Harvard UP, The Loeb Classical Library, 1913.

Cicero [formerly attributed to]. *Ad C. Herennium*. Trans. H. Caplan. Cambridge, MA: Harvard UP, Loeb Classical Library, 1964.
Cicero: *Ad C. Herennium de Ratione Dicendi*. Trans. H. Caplan. Cambridge: Harvard UP, Loeb Classical Library, 1954.
De Inventione. Trans. H. M. Hubbell. Vol. 2 of *Cicero*. Cambridge, MA: Harvard UP, The Loeb Classical Library, 1968.
Orator, Volume 5 of *Cicero*. Cambridge: Harvard UP, The Loeb Classical Library, 1913.
Tulli Ciceronis Scripta quae Manserunt Omnia. Fasc. 3, De Oratore. Ed. Kazimierz F. Kumaniecki. Leipzig: BSB B. G. Teubner Verlagsgesellschaft, 1969.

Dionysius

Usher, Stephen. *Dionysius of Halicarnassus: The Critical Essays in Two Volumes*. Cambridge: Harvard UP, Loeb Classical Library, 1974, 1985.

Gorgias

Encomium on Helen. Volume 3 of *Isocrates*. Trans. Larue van Hook. Cambridge: Harvard UP, Loeb Classical Library, 1961.

Isocrates

Antidosis, Volume 2 of *Isocrates*. Trans. George Norlin. Cambridge, MA: Harvard UP, The Loeb Classical Library, 1966.
"Isocrates on Gorgias (a selection of fragments on Gorgias)." Trans. G. Kennedy. *The Older Sophists*. Ed. R.K. Sprague. Columbia, SC: U of South Carolina P, 1972.
Panegyricus. Trans. George Norlin. Volume 1 of *Isocrates*. Cambridge, MA: Harvard UP, The Loeb Classical Library, 1991.

Melanchthon

De Officiis Concionatoris (1529). *Supplementa Melanchthoniana*. Ed. Paul Drews and Ferdinand Cohrs. 5 volumes. Frankfurt: Minerva, 1968.

Philodemus

Philodemi Volumina Rhetorica. 2 volumes. and Supplementum. Ed. Siegfried Sudhaus. Lipsiae: B. G. Teubner, 1892–96.

Plato

Euthyphro, Apology, Crito. Trans. F. J. Church. New York: MacMillan, 1948.
Gorgias. Trans. W. C. Hembold. New York, NY: MacMillan, 1952.
Protagoras. Trans. W.K.C. Guthrie. *Plato: The Collected Dialogues.* Ed. E. Hamilton and H. Cairns. Princeton, NJ: Princeton UP, 1961.
Republic. Trans. A. Bloom. New York, NY: Basic Books, 1968.

Pliny

Letters and Panegyricus, Volume Two. Trans. Betty Radice. Cambridge: Harvard UP, 1969.
"Panegyricus Plini Secundi Dictus Traiano Imp." *XII Panegyrici Latini.* Ed. R.A.B. Mynors. Oxford: Oxford UP, 1964.

Quintilian

Institutio Oratoria. Trans. H.E. Butler. Cambridge: Harvard UP, Loeb Classical Library, 1953, 1963, 1969.
Institutionis Oratoriae Libri Duodecem. 2 volumes. Ed. Michael Winterbottom. Oxonii: E Typographico Clarendoniano, 1970.

Res Gestae

Divi Augusti: The Achievements of the Divine Augustus. Edited & Notes by P.A. Brunt & J.M. More. Oxford: Oxford UP, 1967.

Seneca

Seneca. *Declamations in Two Volumes: Controversiae I-VI.* Trans. Michael Winterbottom. Cambridge: Harvard UP: 1974.

Suetonius

"Augustus." *The Lives of the Caesars.* Trans. J.C. Rolfe. Cambridge: Harvard UP: 1944.

Tacitus

Agricola, Germany and Dialogue on Orators. Trans. Herbert W. Benario. Revised edition. Norman: U of Oklahoma P, 1991.

Thucydides

History of the Peloponnesian War. Trans. R. Warner. New York, NY: Penguin, 1954.

Vergil/Virgil

Aeneid Books I-VI. Introduction, Notes, Vocabulary, and Grammatical Appendix by Clyde Pharr. Wauconda: Bolchazy Carducci: 1964.
Aeneid. Volume 2. Trans. H.R. Fairclough. Cambridge: Harvard UP.
Aeneid I-VI. Edited with Introduction and Notes by R.D. Williams. Edinburgh: St. Martins P, 1992.
Aeneid VII-XII. Edited with Introduction and Notes by R.D. Williams. Edinburgh: St. Martins P, 1973.
Aeneid VII-XII, The Minor Poems. With English Translation by H. Rushton Fairclough. Cambridge: Harvard UP, 1934.

Xenophon

Conversations of Socrates. Trans. H. Tredennick and R. Waterfield. New York: Penguin Books, 1990.

Bibliography

Abbott, Don. "Blair 'Abroad': The European Reception of the *Lectures on Rhetoric and Belles Lettres.*" *Scottish Rhetoric and Its Influences.* Ed. Lynee Lewis Gaillet. Mahwah, NJ: Hermagoras P, 1998. 67–77.

—. "The Influence of Blair's *Lectures* in Spain." *Rhetorica* 7 (1989): 275–89.

Adams, John Quincy. *Lectures on Rhetoric and Oratory*, 2 volumes. Cambridge: Hilliard and Metcalf, 1810.

Addison. *The Spectator*, Volume Five. Ed. Donald F. Bond. Oxford: Clarendon P, 1965.

Almond, Gabriel A., Marvin Chodorow, and Roy Harvey Harris, eds. *Progress and Its Discontents.* Berkeley: U of California P, 1982.

Anderson, James A. *Communication Theory: Epistemological Foundations.* New York: Guilford, 1996.

Anderson, Rob, and Veronica Ross. *Questions of Communication: A Practical Guide to Theory.* New York: St. Martin's, 1994.

Andrewes, A. "The Government of Classical Sparta." *Ancient Society and Institutions: Studies Presented to Victor Ehrenberg on his 75th Birthday.* New York: Barnes & Noble, 1967.

—. *Probouleusis.* Oxford: Clarendon, 1954.

Arendt, Hannah. *The Human Condition.* Chicago, IL: U of Chicago P, 1958.

Arnauld, Antoine. *The Art of Thinking: Port-Royal Logic.* Trans. James Dickoff. New York: The Bobbs-Merrill Company, Inc., 1964.

Arnhart, Larry. *Aristotle on Political Reasoning: A Commentary on the Rhetoric.* DeKalb, Illinois: Northern Illinois P, 1981.

Astin, Alan E. *Cato the Censor.* Oxford: Oxford UP, 1978.

Bacon, Francis. *The Tvvoo Bookes of Francis Bacon. Of the proficience and aduancement of Learning, diuine and humane.* London: Henrie Tomes, 1605.

Bailey, Cyril. *Phases in the Religion of Ancient Rome.* Berkeley: U of California P, 1932.

Barone, Dennis. "An Introduction to William Smith and Rhetoric at the College of Philadelphia." *Proceedings of the American Philosophical Society* 134 (1990): 111–60.

Barth, Markus. *Ephesians.* Garden City: Doubleday, 1974.

Barthes, Roland. "The Discourse of History." *The Rustle of Language*. Trans. Richard Howard. Berkeley: U of California P, 1989.
Baskerville, Barnet *The People's Voice: The Orator in American Society* (Lexington: U of Kentucky P, 1979). 32–87.
Beaudet, Arthur L., and Andrea Ballabio, "Molecular Genetics and Medicine." *Harrison's Principles of Internal Medicine*. Ed. Isselbacher *et al*. New York: McGraw-Hill, Inc., 1994.
Bennett, Julian. *Trajan Optimus Princeps*. Bloomington, IN: Indiana UP, 1995.
Benzing, Josef. *Die Hanauer Erstdrucker Wilhelm und Peter Antonius (1593–1625) Archiv für Geschichte des Buchwesens* 21:4–6. Frankfurt am Main: Buchhandler-Vereinigung, 1980.
Berlin, James A. *Writing Instruction in Nineteenth-Century American Colleges*. Carbondale, IL: Southern Illinois UP, 1984.
Bernoulli, Jakob. *Ars Conjectandi, Pars Quarta The Art of Conjecturing, Part Four*. Trans. Bing Sung. Harvard University Department of Statistics Technical Report 2, Feb. 12, 1966.
Bett, Richard. "The Sophists and Relativism." *Phronesis* 34.2 (1988): 139–69.
Bevilacqua, Vincent M. "Lord Kames's Theory of Rhetoric." *Speech Monographs* 30 (1963): 309–27.
—. "Rhetoric and Human Nature in Kames's *Elements of Criticism*." *Quarterly Journal of Speech* 48 (1962): 46–50.
—. "The Rhetorical Theory of Henry Home, Lord Kames." Dissertation. U of Illinois, 1961.
Bitzer, Lloyd F. "Aristotle's Enthymeme Revisited." *Quarterly Journal of Speech* 45 (1959): 399–408.
Blair, Carole. "Contested Histories of Rhetoric: The Politics of Preservation, Progress, and Change." *Quarterly Journal of Speech* 78 (1992): 403–28.
Blair, Carole, and Mary L. Kahl. "Revising the History of Rhetorical Theory." *Western Journal of Speech Communication* 54 (Spring 1990): 148–59.
Blair, Hugh. *Lectures on Rhetoric and Belles Lettres*. 2 volumes. London: Strahan and Cadell, 1783.
—. *Observations upon a Pamphlet, Intitled, An Analysis of the Moral and Religious Sentiments contained in the Writings of Sopho, and David Hume, Esq*. Edinburgh: np, 1755.
—. "On the Love of Our Country." *Sermons*, 2nd edition. 5 volumes. London: Cadell and Davies, 1801. 5: 114–39. From ms. Dc 3.63, ff. 84–99, Edinburgh U Library.
Blanc, O. *Last Letters: Prisons and Prisoners of the French Revolution 1793–1794*. Trans. A. Sheridan. New York: Farrar, Straus, & Giroux, 1984/1987.
—. *Olympe de Gouges: Une Femme de Libertés*: [Olympe de Gouges: A Woman of Liberties] Revised edition. Paris: Syros, 1989.

Blass, F., and A. Debrunner. *A Greek Grammar of the New Testament and Other Early Christian Literature*. Trans. Robert W. Funk. Chicago: UP, 1961.

Blitefield, Jerry. *From the Ground Up: Place, Kairos, Delivery and the Rhetoric of the Underpowered*. Diss. Rensselaer Polytechnic Institute, 2000. Ann Arbor: UMI, 2001. 9992598.

Bloomfield, Maxwell. *American Lawyers in a Changing Society, 1776–1876* Cambridge: Harvard UP, 1976. 1–58.

—. "Lawyers and Public Criticism: Challenge and Response in Nineteenth-Century America." *American Journal of Legal History* 15 (1971): 269–77.

Bonner, Stanley F. *Education in Ancient Rome*. Berkeley: U of California P, 1977.

—. *The Literary Treatises of Dionysius of Halicarnassus: A Study in the Development of Critical Method*. London: Cambridge UP, 1939.

Borza, Eugene N. "Sentimental Philhellenism and the Image of Greece." *Classics and the Classical Tradition: Essays Presented to Robert E. Dengler on the Occasion of His Eightieth Birthday*. Ed. Eugene N. Borza and Robert W. Carrubba. University Park, PA: Penn State UP, 1972.

Borza, Eugene N., and Robert W. Carrubba, eds. *Classics and the Classical Tradition: Essays Presented to Robert E. Dengler on the Occasion of His Eightieth Birthday*. University Park, PA: Penn State UP, 1972.

Botein, Stephen. "Cicero as Role Model for Early American Lawyers: A Case Study in Classical 'Influence'." *Classical Journal* 73 (1978): 313–21.

Bowers, John Waite, and Donovan Ochs. *The Rhetoric of Agitation and Control*. New York: Random House, 1971.

Boyd, James R. "Preface by the American editor." *Elements of Criticism* by Henry Home of Kames, 1855. New York, 1883.

Boylan, Anne M. "Benevolence and Antislavery Activity Among African American Women in New York and Boston, 1820–1840." *The Abolitionist Sisterhood: Women's Political Culture in Antebellum America*. Ed. Jean Fagan Yellin and John C. Van Horne. Ithaca: Cornell UP, 1994.

Boyle, Marjorie O'Rourke. *Erasmus on Language and Method in Theology*, Toronto: U of Toronto P, 1977.

Brandes, Paul D. *A History of Aristotle's* Rhetoric, *with a Bibliography of Early Printings*. Metuchen, NJ: Scarecrow, 1989.

Brilioth, Yngve. *A Brief History of Preaching*. Trans. Karl E. Mattson. Philadelphia: Fortress P, 1965.

Brilliant, Richard. *Gesture and Rank in Roman Art: The Use of Gestures to Denote Status in Roman Sculpture and Coinage*. New Haven: Connecticut Academy of Arts & Sciences, 1963.

Bruere, Richard T. "Tacitus and Pliny's *Panegyricus*." *Classical Philology* 49 (1954): 161–79.

Bundy, Murray W. "Lord Kames and the Maggots in Amber." *Journal of English and Germanic Philology* 45 (1946): 199–208.
Burke, Kenneth. *Counter-Statement*. 1931. Berkeley: UP, 1968.
—. *A Rhetoric of Motives*. 195. Berkeley: U of California P, 1969.
Burr, Vivien. *An Introduction to Social Constructionism*. London: Routledge, 1995.
Butler, Judith. *Gender Trouble: Feminism and the Subversion of Identity*. New York: Routledge, 1990.
Butler, Sister Mary Marguerite. *Hrotsvitha: The Theatricality of Her Plays*. New York: Philosophical Library, 1960.
Butterfield, Herbert. *The Origins of History*. Ed. Adam Watson. New York: Basic, 1981.
Cambier, J. "La Benediction d'Eph. 1:3–14." *Zeitschrift fur die neutestamentliche Wissenschaft* 54 (1963): 58–104.
Campbell, Karlyn Kohrs, and Kathleen Hall Jamieson. "Form and Genre in Rhetorical Criticism: An Introduction." *Form and Genre*. Ed. Karlyn Kohrs Campbell and Kathleen Hall Jamieson. Falls Church, VA: Speech Communication Association, 1978.
—. *Form and Genre*. Falls Church, VA: Speech Communication Association, 1978.
Cantor, Charles R., and Cassandra L. Smith. "Perspectives on the Human Genome Project." *Biotechnology and Human Genetic Predisposition to Disease*. Ed. Charles R. Cantor et al. New York: Wiley-Liss, 1989.
Caplan, Harry. *Of Eloquence: Studies in Ancient and Mediaeval Rhetoric*. Ithaca: Cornell UP, 1970.
Carey, John. "Gene Therapy: Promises, Promises" *Business Week*, 26 September 1994: 75.
Carlyle, Thomas. "To Ralph Waldo Emerson," 12 August 1834. *The Correspondence of Thomas Carlyle and Ralph Waldo Emerson, 1834–1872*, Volume One. Ed. Charles Eliot Norton. Boston: Ticknor, 1886.
Carpenter, Frederic Ives. "Introduction." *The Arte or Crafte of Rhethoryke* by Leonard Cox. Chicago: U of Chicago P, 1899.
Chambers, Stephen, and G. P. Mohrmann, "Rhetoric in Some American Periodicals, 1815–1850." *Speech Monographs* 37 (1970): 111–20.
Chapman, David W., and Gary Tate. "A Survey of Doctoral Programs in Rhetoric and Composition." *Rhetoric Review* 5 (1987): 124–89.
Charland, Thomas-Marie. *Artes Praedicandi: Contributions à l'histoire de la Rhétorique au Moyen Age*, Publications de l'Institut d'Etudes Medievales d'Ottowa, no. 7. Paris: 1936.
Charvat, William. *The Origins of American Critical Thought 1810–1835*. New York: A. S. Barnes, 1961.

Choate, Rufus. "The Eloquence of Revolutionary Periods." *The Works of Rufus Choate with a Memoir of His Life.* Ed. Samuel Gilman Brown. 2 volumes. Boston: Little, Brown, 1862. I: 439–63.
Choe, Wolhee. "Walter Pater's 'Romantic Morality.'" *Victorian Newsletter* 72 (1987): 12–17.
Chumakov, Ilya M. et al. "A YAC Contig Map of the Human Genome." *Nature: The Genome Directory* 377 (1995): 175–83.
Clark, Donald Lemen. *Rhetoric in Greco-Roman Education.* New York: Columbia UP, 1957.
Clark, Gregory, and S. Michael Halloran. "Introduction: Transformations of Public Discourse in Nineteenth-Century America." Clark and Halloran, eds., *Oratorical Culture in Nineteenth-Century America: Transformations in the Theory and Practice of Rhetoric.* Ed. Gregory Clark and S. Michael Halloran. Carbondale: Southern Illinois UP, 1993.
Clarke, M. L. "Rhetorical Influences in the Aeneid." *Greece and Rome* 18 (January 1949): 14–27.
Clough, Arthur Hugh. "Introduction." *The Lives of the Noble Grecians and Romans.* Trans. John Dryden, rev. Arthur Hugh Clough. New York: The Modern Library, n.d.: ix–xxiv.
Cohen, David. *Law, Violence, and Community in Classical Athens.* New York: Cambridge UP, 1995.
Collins, Francis S. "Ahead of Schedule and Under Budget: The Genome Project Passes Its Fifth Birthday." *Proceedings in National Academic Science* 92 (1995): 10821–10823.
—. "BRCA—Lots of Mutations, Lots of Dilemmas." *The New England Journal of Medicine* 334 (1996): 186–88.
—. "The Human Genome Project," The George Washington University, 23 February 1996.
—. "Sequencing the Human Genome." *Hospital Practice* (1997): 35–53.
Conley, Thomas. "The Enthymeme in Perspective." *Quarterly Journal of Speech* 70 (1984): 168–87.
—. *Rhetoric in the European Tradition.* Chicago: U of Chicago P: 1990.
Connors, Joseph M. "Homiletic Theory in the Late Sixteenth Century." *The American Ecclesiastical Review* 138 (1958): 316–32.
—. "Saint Charles Borromeo in Homiletic Tradition." *The American Ecclesiastical Review* 138 (1958): 9–23.
Connors, Robert J., ed. *Selected Essays of Edward P. J. Corbett.* Dallas: Southern Methodist UP, 1989.
Connors, Robert J., Lisa S. Ede, and Andrea A. Lunsford, eds. *Essays on Classical Rhetoric and Modern Discourse.* Carbondale: Southern UP, 1984.
Cook-Deegan, Robert. *The Gene Wars: Science, Politics, and the Human Genome.* New York: W.W. Norton & Company, 1994.

Cooper, Frederick. "To Elevate the Race: The Social Thought of Black Leaders." *American Quarterly* 24 (1972): 604–25.

Cooper, John. "An Aristotelian Theory of the Emotions" *Essays in Aristotle's Rhetoric.* Ed. Amelie Oksenberg Rorty. Berkeley: U of California P, 1986.

Cope, E. M. *An Introduction to Aristotle's Rhetoric.* London and Cambridge: MacMillan and Co., 1867.

Corbett, Edward P. J. *Classical Rhetoric for the Modern Student.* New York: Oxford UP, 1965.

—. *Classical Rhetoric for the Modern Student.* New York: Oxford UP, 1990.

—. "A New Look at Old Rhetoric." *Selected Essays of Edward P. J. Corbett.* Ed. Robert J. Connors. Dallas: Southern Methodist UP, 1989.

Corwin, Edward S. "The 'Higher Law' Background of American Constitutional Law." *Harvard Law Review* 42 (1928): 149–85, 365–409.

Cox, Leonard. *The Arte or Crafte of Rhetoryke.* [Edition B.] London: Robert Redman, 1532.

Crafton, Jeffrey. "Paul's Rhetorical Vision and the Purpose of Romans: Towards a New Understanding." *Novum Testamentum* 32 (1990): 317–39.

Cragan, John F., and Donald C. Shields. *Understanding Communication Theory: The Communicative Forces of Human Action.* Boston: Allyn and Bacon, 1998.

Crane, W. G. *Wit and Rhetoric in the Renaissance. The Formal Basis of Elizabethan Prose Style.* New York: Columbia UP, 1937.

Crawford, Robert. *The Scottish Invention of English Literature.* Cambridge: Cambridge UP, 1998.

Crick, F. H. C. "The Structure of Hereditary Material." *Scientific America in the 20th Century* 3 (1991): 82–88.

Cronjé, Jacobus Van Wyk. *Dionysius of Halicarnassus: De Demosthenes: A Critical Appraisal of the Status Quaestionis.* Zurich: Georg Olms, 1986.

Crowley, Sharon, and Debra Hawhee, *Ancient Rhetorics for Contemporary Students.* 2nd edition. Boston: Allyn and Bacon, 1999.

Cuvelier, Elaine. "Shakespeare, Voltaire, and French Taste." *Shakespeare and France.* Ed. Holger Klein and Jean-Marie Maguin. Lewiston, NY: Edwin Mellen P, 1995.

Daiches, David. "Style Periodique and Style Coupe: Hugh Blair and the Scottish Rhetoric of American Independence." *Scotland and America in the Age of Enlightenment.* Ed. Richard B. Sher and Jeffrey R. Smitten. Princeton: Princeton UP, 1990: 209–26.

Daston, Lorraine. *Classical Probability in the Enlightenment.* Princeton, NJ: Princeton UP, 1988.

Dauzat, A., Dubois, J., and Mitterand, H. *Nouveau Dictionnaire Etymologique et Historique* [*New Etymological and Historical Dictionary*] 2nd edition. Paris: Larousse, 1964.

Day, James, and Mortimer Chambers. *Aristotle's History of Athenian Democracy*. Berkeley: U of California P, 1962.
Decaux, A. *Histoire des Françaises: La Revolte*. [History of French Women: The Revolt] Vol. 2. Paris: Librairie Académique Perrin, 1972.
DeLaix, Roger Alain. *Probouleusis at Athens: A Study of Political Decision-Making*. Berkeley: U of California P, 1973.
de Meyier, K. A. *Codices Vossiani Latini. Descripsit K. A. De Meyier,* pars II codex 120 (Leiden, 1975),
de Romilly, Jacqueline. *Magic and Rhetoric in Ancient Greece*. Cambridge: Harvard UP, 1975.
De Winterfeld, Paul, ed. *Hrotsvithae Opera*. Berlin: Weidmann, 1902.
Dieter, Otto A. "*Arbor Picta*: The Medieval Tree of Preaching." *Quarterly Journal of Speech*, 51 (1965): 123–44.
Dihle, Albrecht. *Greek and Latin Literature of the Roman Empire: From Augustus to Justinian*. Trans. Manfred Malzahn. New York: Routledge, 1994.
Dobson, Michael. *The Making of the National Poet: Shakespeare, Adaptation and Authorship, 1660–1769*. Oxford: Clarendon P, 1992.
Donfried, K. P., ed. *The Romans Debate*. Minneapolis: Augsburg, 1977.
Dorandi, Tiziano. "Per una Ricomposizione dello Scritto di Filodemo sulla Retorica." *Zeitschrift für Papyrologie und Epigraphik* 82 (1990): 59–87.
Dorey, T. A., ed. *Empire and Aftermath: Silver Latin II*. London: Routledge, 1975.
Dorsch, T. S. (Translator and editor). *Classical Literary Criticism: Aristotle, Horace, Longinus*. Harmondsworth: Penguin Books, 1965.
Douglass, Frederick. *My Bondage and My Freedom. Autobiographies*. Ed. Henry Louis Gates, Jr. New York: Library of America, 1994.
Dowling, Linda. *The Vulgarization of Art: The Victorians and Aesthetic Democracy*. Charlottesville: UP of Virginia, 1996.
Dronke, Peter. "Hrotsvitha." *Women Writers of the Middle Ages: A Critical Study of Texts from Perpetua to Marguerite Porete*. Cambridge: Cambridge UP, (1984): 55–83.
Dunne, Gerald T. *Justice Joseph Story and the Rise of the Supreme Court*. New York: Simon and Schuster, 1970.
Edelman, Marion Wright. "Educating the Black Child: Our Past and Our Future." *Representative American Speeches, 1987–1988*. Ed. Owen Peterson. New York: The H. W. Wilson Company, 1988.
Edwards, Owen Dudley. "American Oratory." *American Studies* 16 (1982): 453–56.
Ehninger, Douglas. "Dominant Trends in English Rhetorical Thought, 1750–1800." *Southern Speech Journal* 18 (1952): 3–12.
—. "Introduction." *Elements of Rhetoric* by Richard Whately. Carbondale, IL: Southern Illinois UP, 1963.
—. "On Systems of Rhetoric." *Philosophy and Rhetoric* 1 (1968): 131–44.

—. "On Rhetoric and Rhetorics." *Western Speech* 31 (1967): 242–49.
—. "Selected Theories of *Inventio* in English Rhetoric, 1759–1828." Dissertation, Ohio State University, 1949.
Ehrenberg, Victor. *From Solon to Socrates: Greek History and Civilization during the Sixth and Fifth Centuries B. C.* London: Methuen, 1968.
Ellis, Richard. *The Jeffersonian Crisis: Courts and Politics in the Young Republic.* New York: Oxford UP, 1971.
Enos, Richard Leo. "The Epistemology of Gorgias' Rhetoric: A Re-Examination." *The Southern Speech Communication Journal* 42 (1976): 35–51.
—. *Greek Rhetoric Before Aristotle.* Prospect Heights: Waveland P, 1993.
—. *Roman Rhetoric: Revolution and the Greek Influence.* Prospect Heights: Waveland P, 1995.
Enos, Theresa. "The Course in Classical Rhetoric: Definition, Development, Direction," *Rhetoric Society Quarterly* 19 (1989): 45–48.
Erasmus. *Collected Works of Erasmus.* Toronto: U of Toronto P, 1974.
—. *The Colloquies of Erasmus.* Trans. Craig R. Thompson. Chicago: U of Chicago P, 1965.
—. *Ecclesiastes sive concionator evangelicus. Opera omnia Desiderii Erasmi Roterodami.* Ed. Jacques Chomarat. Amsterdam: Elsevier, 1991, 1994.
—. "Paraclesis." *Christian Humanism and the Reformation: Selected Writings of Erasmus.* Ed. John C. Olin. 3rd edition. New York: Fordham UP, 1987.
Erickson, Keith V., ed. *Aristotle: The Classical Heritage of Rhetoric.* Metuchen, NJ: Scarecrow, 1974.
Fahnestock, Jeanne. *Rhetorical Figures in Science.* New York: Oxford UP, 1999.
Fairweather, Janet. *Seneca the Elder.* Cambridge: Cambridge UP, 1981.
Farnsworth, Rodney. "Contextualizing the Pliny/Trajan Letters: A Case for Critiquing the (American) Myth of Deliberative Discourse in (Roman) Society." *Rhetoric Society Quarterly* 26 (1996): 29–46.
Farrell, James M. "*Pro Militibus Oratio*: John Adams's Imitation of Cicero in the Boston Massacre Trial." *Rhetorica* 9 (1991): 233–49.
Farrell, Thomas B. *Norms of Rhetorical Culture.* New Haven: Yale UP, 1993.
Feine, P., J. Behm, and W. Kummel. *Introduction to the New Testament.* Nashville: Abingdon, 1966.
Ferguson, John. *The Religions of the Roman Empire.* Ithaca: Cornell UP, 1970.
Ferguson, Robert A. *Law and Letters in American Culture.* Cambridge: Harvard UP, 1984.
Ferreira-Buckley, Linda, and S. Michael Halloran, "Introduction." *Blair's Lectures on Rhetoric and Belles Lettres.* Ed. Linda Ferreira-Buckley and Michael Halloran. Carbondale: Southern Illinois UP, 1994.

Filipczak, Zirka. *Hot Dry Men, Cold Wet Women: The Theory of Humours in Western European Art, 1575–1700*. New York: American Federation of Arts, 1997.
Finkenbine, Roy E. "Boston's Black Churches: Institutional Centers of the Antislavery Movement." *Courage and Conscience: Black and White Abolitionists in Boston*. Ed. Donald M. Jacobs. Bloomington: Indiana UP, 1993.
Finley, M. I. *Ancient History: Evidence and Models*. London: Chatto & Windus, 1985.
—. *Early Greece: The Bronze and Archaic Ages*. New York: W. W. Norton & Co., 1981.
—. *The World of Odysseus*, 2nd edition. New York: Penguin Books, 1979.
Fogle, Thomas. "Information Metaphors and the Human Genome Project." *Perspectives in Biology and Medicine* 38 (1995): 535–46.
Foner, Philip S. *The Voice of Black America: Major Speeches by Negroes in the United States, 1797–1971*. New York: Simon and Schuster, 1972.
Forbes, Clarence A. "Books for the Burning," *Transactions of the American Philological Association*. 67 (1936): 114–25.
Forbes, William. *An Account of the Life and Writings of James Beattie*, 2nd edition. Edinburgh, 1807.
Fordham, Monroe. *Major Themes in Northern Black Religious Thought, 1800–1860*. Hicksville, NY: Exposition P, 1975.
Forestié, E. "Olympe de Gouges." *Recueil de l'académie des Sciences, Belles-Lettres et Arts de Tarn-et-Garonne [Collection of the Academy of Sciences, Belles-Lettres and Arts of Tarn-et-Garonne] [2e série]*. 1901.
Fornara, Charles William. *The Nature of History in Ancient Greece and Rome*. Berkeley: U of California P, 1983.
Forrest, W. G. *The Emergence of Greek Democracy 800–400 B. C.* New York: McGraw-Hill, 1966.
Forsdyke, John. *Greece Before Homer*. New York: W. W. Norton, 1957.
Fortenbaugh, William W. *Aristotle on Emotion: A Contribution to Philosophical Psychology, Rhetoric, Poetics, Politics, and Ethics*. New York: Barnes & Noble, 1975.
—. "Aristotle's *Rhetoric* on Emotions." *Aristotle: The Classical Heritage of Rhetoric*. Ed. Keith Erickson. Metuchen, N. J.: Scarecrow, 1974. 205–34.
Fortenbaugh, William, and David Mirhady, eds. *Peripatetic Rhetoric After Aristotle*. New Brunswick: Transaction, 1994.
Foucault, Michel. *The Archaeology of Knowledge and Discourse on Language*. Trans. A. M. Sheridan Smith. New York: Pantheon, 1972.
Frazer, Elizabeth, and Nancy Lacey. *The Politics of Community: A Feminist Critique of the Liberal–Communitarian Debate*. Toronto: U of Toronto P, 1993.

Frazier, A. M. "The Criterion of Historical Knowledge." *Journal of Thought* 11.1 (January 1976): 60–67.

Freedman, Joseph S. "The Career and Writings of Bartholomew Keckermann (d. 1609)." *Proceedings of the American Philosophical Society*, 141.3 (1997): 307–308, 311.

—. *European Academic Philosophy in the Late Sixteenth and Early Seventeenth Centuries: The Life, Significance, and Philosophy of Clemens Timpler (1563/4–1624)*. Zurich and New York: Georg Olms Verlag Hildesheim, 1988.

Freeman, Kathleen. *The Work and Life of Solon*. London: Humphrey Milford, 1926.

Freudenburg, Kirk. *The Walking Muse: Horace on the Theory of Satire*. Princeton, NJ: Princeton UP, 1993.

Frier, Bruce W. *The Rise of the Roman Jurists: Studies in Cicero's* Pro Caecino. Princeton: Princeton UP, 1985.

Frost, John, ed. "Advertisement of the American editor." *An Abridgment of Elements of Criticism by Henry Home of* Kames. Philadelphia, 1831.

Fulton, Robert I., and Thomas C. Trueblood. *Practical Elements of Elocution: Designed as a Text for the Guidance of Teachers and Students of ExPion*. Boston: Ginn & Company, The Athenaeum P, 1903.

Fumaroli, Marc. "Rhetoric, Politics, and Society: From Italian Ciceronianism to French Classicism." *Renaissance Eloquence: Studies in the Theory and Practice of Renaissance Rhetoric*. Ed. James J. Murphy. Berkeley: U of California P, 1983.

Gabba, Emilio. *Dionysius and The History of Archaic Rome*. Berkeley: U of California P, 1991.

Gage, John T. "A General Theory of the Enthymeme for Advanced Composition." *Teaching Advanced Composition: Why and How*. Ed. Katherine H. Adam and John L. Adams. Portsmouth: Boynton/Cook, 1991: 161–78.

Gaillet, Lynée Lewis, ed. *Scottish Rhetoric and Its Influences*. Mahwah, NJ: Hermagoras P, 1998.

Gaines, Robert N. "Cicero's Response to the Philosophers in *De Oratore*, Book 1." *Rhetoric and Pedagogy: Its History, Philosophy, and Practice: Essays in Honor of James J. Murphy*. Ed. Winifred Bryan Horner and Michael Leff. Mahwah, NJ: Lawrence Erlbaum Associates, 1995.

—. "Isocrates, EP. 6.8," *Hermes* 118 (1990): 165–70.

—. "Philodemus on the Three Activities of Rhetorical Invention." *Rhetorica* 3 (1985): 155–63.

—. "Rhetoric, Greek and Roman." *Encyclopedia of Classical Philosophy*, Ed. Donald J. Zeyl, Westport, CN: Greenwood P, 1997. 472–76.

Galinsky, Karl. *Augustan Culture: An Interpretative Introduction*. Princeton, NJ: Princeton UP: 1996.

Gallant, T. W. "Agricultural Systems, Land Tenure, and the Reforms of Solon." *Annual of the British School of Athens* 77 (1982): 111–24.
Garber, Daniel, and Sandy Zabell. "On the Emergence of Probability." *Archive for History of Exact Sciences* 21 (1979): 33–53.
Garver, Eugene. "Deliberative Rationality and the Emotions" *Aristotle's Rhetoric: An Art of Character*. Chicago & London: U of Chicago P, 1994.
Gates, Jr., Henry Louis, ed. *Autobiographies*. New York: Library of America, 1994.
Gawalt, Gerald W. "Sources of Anti-Lawyer Sentiment in Massachusetts, 1740–1840." *American Journal of Legal History* 14 (1970): 283–307.
George, Carol V. R. "Widening the Circle: The Black Church and the Abolitionist Crusade, 1830–1860." *Antislavery Reconsidered: New Perspectives on the Abolitionists*. Ed. Lewis Perry and Michael Fellman. Baton Rouge: Louisiana State UP, 1979.
Giddings, Paula. *When and Where I Enter: The Impact of Black Women on Race and Sex in America*. New York: Bantam, 1985.
Gilmer, Francis Walker. *Sketches, Essays, and Translations*. Baltimore: Fielding Lucas, Jr., 1828.
—. *Sketches of American Orators*. Baltimore: Fielding Lucas, Jr., 1816.
Glenn, Cheryl. *Rhetoric Retold: Regendering the Tradition from Antiquity Through the Renaissance*. Carbondale, IL: Southern Illinois UP: 1997.
Golden, James L., and Douglas Ehninger. "The Extrinsic Sources of Blair's Popularity." *Southern Communication Journal* 22 (1956): 16–32.
Golden, James L., Goodwin F. Berquist, and William E. Coleman. *The Rhetoric of Western Thought*. 6th edition. Dubuque: Kendall, 1989, 1997.
Gomberini, Federico. *Stylistic Theory and Practice in the Younger Pliny*. Hildesheim: Olms-Weidmann, 1983.
Goodfellow, Peter. "A Big Book of the Human Genome," *Nature* 377: 6547 (1995) 285–86.
Gouges, Olympe de. *Les Droits de la Femme. A la Reine*. [*The Rights of Woman. To the Queen*]. Paris: Momoro, 1791.
—. *Oeuvres Complètes: Tome I: Théâtre* [*Complete Works: Vol. 1: Theatre*]. Montauban: Cocagne, 1993.
—. *Oeuvres*. Présentées par Benoîte Groult [*Works. Presented by Benoîte Groult*]. Paris: Mercure de France, 1986.
—. *Dernière Lettre d'Olympe de Gouges, à Son Fils*. [*Last Letter of Olympe de Gouges, to Her Son*]. n.p. 1793.
Gouldner, Alvin W. *Enter Plato: Classical Greece and the Origins of Social Theory*. New York Basic, 1965.
Grau, F. *Las Retóricas de Pedro Juan Núñez (Ediciones y Manuscritos)*, Valencia: Tesis Doctoral, Universitat de València, microcards, 1995.
Gray's-Inn Journal. Volume Two. London, 1756.

Green, Lawrence D. "Aristotelian Rhetoric, Dialectic, and the Tradition of *Antistrophos.*" *Rhetorica* 8.1 (1990): 5–27.

—. "Enthymemic Invention and Structural Predication." *College English* 41 (1980): 623–34.

Griffin, Em. *A First Look at Communication Theory.* [3rd edition] New York: McGraw-Hill, 1997.

Grimaldi, William M. A. *Aristotle, Rhetoric 1–2: A Commentary.* New York: Fordham UP, 1988.

—. "How Do We Get from Corax-Tisias to Plato-Aristotle in Greek Rhetorical Theory." *Theory, Text, Context: Issues in Greek Rhetoric and Oratory.* Ed. Christopher Lyle Johnstone. Albany: SUNY P, 1996.

Gronbeck, Bruce. "Gorgias on Rhetoric and Poetic: A Rehabilitation." *Southern Speech Communication Journal* 38 (Fall 1972): 27–38.

Gronbeck, Bruce, ed. *Spheres of Argument.* Annandale, VA: Speech Communication Association, 1984.

Gross, Daniel M. "Early Modern Emotion and the Economy of Scarcity." *Philosophy and Rhetoric* 34. 4 (2000): 308–21.

Groupe Mu: J. Dubois, F. Edeline, J. M. Klinkenberg, F. Minguet, H. Trinon. *A General Rhetoric.* Trans. Burrell and E. Slotkin. Baltimore: Johns Hopkins UP, 1981.

Grube, G. M. A. "Dionysius of Halicarnassus on Thucydides." *Phoenix* 4 (1950): 95–110.

—. *The Greek and Roman Critics.* London: Methuen, 1965.

Guillois, A. *Etude Médico-Psychologique sur Olympe de Gouges: Considérations Générales sur la Mentalité des Femmes pendant la Révolution Française.* [*Medico-Psychological Study of Olympe de Gouges: General Reflections on the Mentality of Women during the French Revolution*]. Doctoral dissertation, Université de Lyon, France. Lyon: Rey, 1904.

Guthrie, Warren. "The Development of Rhetorical Theory in America, 1635–1850." *Speech Monographs* 14 (1947): 38–54.

Guthrie, William. *An Essay upon English Tragedy With Remarks upon the Abbe de [sic] Blanc's Observations on the English Stage.* Eighteenth Century Shakespeare Series 6. New York: Augustus M. Kelley, 1971.

Guthrie, W. K. C. *Myth and Reason.* London: London School of Economics and Political Science, 1953.

—. *The Sophists.* London: Cambridge UP, 1971.

Guyer, Mark S., and Francis S. Collins. "How is the Human Genome Project Doing, and What Have We Learned So Far?" *Proceedings in National Academic Science*, 92 (1995): 10841–10847.

Hacking, Ian. *The Emergence of Probability: A Philosophical Study of Early Ideas about Probability, Induction, and Statistical Inference.* Cambridge: Cambridge UP, 1975.

Haight, Anne Lyon, ed. *Hroswitha of Gandersheim*. New York: Hroswitha Club, 1965.

Halloran, S. Michael. "The Birth of Molecular Biology: An Essay in the Rhetorical Criticism of Scientific Discourse." *Rhetoric Review* 3 (1984): 70–83.

—. "Hugh Blair's Use of Quintilian and the Transformation of Rhetoric in the 18th Century." *Rhetoric and Pedagogy: Its History, Philosophy, and Practice: Essays in Honor of James J. Murphy*. Ed. Winifred Bryan Horner and Michael C. Leff. Mahwah, NJ: Erlbaum, 1995: 183–95.

Halloran, S. Michael, and Annette Norris Bradford. "Figures of Speech in the Rhetoric of Science and Technology." *Essays on Classical Rhetoric and Modern Discourse*. Ed. Robert J. Connors, Lisa S. Ede, and Andrea A. Lunsford. Carbondale: Southern UP, 1984. 179–92.

Hamilton, William. *An Oration Delivered in the African Zion Church, on the Fourth of July, 1827, in Commemoration of the Abolition of Domestic Slavery in this State. Early Negro Writing 1760–1837*. Ed. Dorothy Porter. Boston: Beacon P, 1971.

Hample, Judy. "William Wirt's Familiar Essays: Criticism of Virginia Oratory." *Southern Speech Communication Journal* 44 (1978): 25–41.

Hanmer, Thomas, ed. *The Works of Shakespear*. London, 1745.

Harrison, E. K. *Introduction to the New Testament*. Grand Rapids: Eerdmans, 1971.

Hatab, Lawrence J. *Myth and Philosophy: A Contest of Truths*. LaSalle, IL: Open Court, 1990.

Havelock, Eric A. *Preface to Plato*. Cambridge: Harvard UP, 1963.

Heidegger, Martin. *Being and Time*. Trans. John Macquarrie & Edward Robinson. New York: Harper Row, 1962.

Hemmingsen, Niels. *The Preacher*, 1555. Trans. John Horsfal, 1574. Ed. R.C. Alston. Scolar P facsimile no. 325. Menston: Scolar P, 1972.

Herrick, James A. *The History and Theory of Rhetoric*. Needham Heights: Allyn and Bacon: 1997.

Hewett, Beth L. "Samuel Newman's *A Practical System of Rhetoric*: An American Cousin of Scottish Rhetoric—A Reappraisal." Paper presented at the 11th Biennial ISHR Conference in Edinburgh, Scotland. July 1995. Also in *Scottish Enlightenment Rhetoric and Its Influence on America*. Ed. Lynee Lewis Gaillet. Mahwah, NJ: Lawrence Erlbaum, 1997.

Higgins, Jesse. *Sampson Against the Philistines, Or the Reformation of Lawsuits; and Brought Home to Every Man's Door: Agreeably to the Principles of the Ancient Trial by Jury, before the Same was Innovated by Judges and Lawyers*. Philadelphia: B. Graves and W. Duane, 1805.

Higgins, Lesley. "Jowett and Pater: Trafficking in Platonic Wares." *Victorian Studies* 37.1 (1993): 43–72.

Hignett, C. *A History of the Athenian Constitution*. Oxford: Clarendon, 1952.

Hinks, Peter P. *To Awaken My Afflicted Brethren: David Walker and the Problem of Antebellum Slave Resistance*. University Park: Pennsylvania State UP, 1997.

Hipple, Jr., Walter John. "Lord Kames." *The Beautiful, the Sublime, and the Picturesque in Eighteenth-Century British Aesthetic Theory*. Carbondale: Southern Illinois UP, 1957: 99–121.

Hoch, Carl B. "The Significance of the SYN-Compounds for Jew-Gentile Relations in the Body of Christ." *Journal of the Evangelical Theological Society* 25 (1982): 175–83.

Honestus [Benjamin Austin]. *Observations on the Pernicious Practice of the Law*. Boston: Joshua Belcher, 1814.

—. *Observations on the Pernicious Practice of the Law*. Boston: True & Weston, 1819. Reprinted in the *American Journal of Legal History* 13 (1969): 244–302.

Honore, Anthony M. *Tribonian*. London: Duckworth, 1978.

Hook, Andrew. *The History of Scottish Literature*. Aberdeen: Aberdeen UP, 1987.

Hooper, Finley. *Greek Realities: Life and Thought in Ancient Greece*. Wayne State UP, 1978.

Horn, András. "Kames and the Anthropological Approach to Criticism." *Philological Quarterly* 44 (1965): 211–33.

Horner, Winifred Bryan, and Michael C. Leff, eds. *Rhetoric and Pedagogy: Its History, Philosophy, and Practice: Essays in Honor of James J. Murphy*. Mahwah, NJ: Erlbaum, 1995.

Horton, James Oliver. *Free People of Color: Inside the African American Community*. Washington: Smithsonian Institution P, 1993.

Horton, James Oliver, and Lois E. Horton. *Hope of Liberty: Culture, Community and Protest Among Northern Free Blacks, 1700–1860*. New York: Oxford UP, 1997.

Hosmer, William. *The Higher Law in its Relations to Civil Government, with Particular Reference to Slavery and the Fugitive Slave Law*. Auburn: Derby & Miller, 1852.

Hough, Graham. *The Last Romantics*. London: Methuen, 1961.

Howell, Wilbur Samuel. "English Backgrounds of Rhetoric." *History of Speech Education in America: Background Studies*. Ed. Karl R. Wallace. New York: Appleton Century-Crofts, Inc., 1954: 1–47.

—. *Logic and Rhetoric in England, 1500–1700*. Princeton: Princeton UP, 1956.

"Hrosvitha." *Britannica Online*. http://www.eb.com:180/cgi-bin/g?DocF=micro/279/23.html. Visited 24 January 1998.

Hubbard, R., and R.C. Lewontin. "Pitfalls of Genetic Testing." *The New England Journal of Medicine* 334 (1996): 1192–93.

Hubbell, Harry M. *The Influence of Isocrates on Cicero, Dionysius, and Aristides.* Dissertation. New Haven: Yale University and Oxford University, 1913.

Hubbell, Jay B. "William Wirt and the Familiar Essay in Virginia." *William and Mary Quarterly*, 2nd series, 23 (1943): 136–52.

Hudson, Thomas J. et al. "An STS-Based Map of the Human Genome." *Science* 270 (1995) 1945–54.

Hughes, H. Stuart. "Contemporary Historiography: Progress, Paradigms, and the Regression Toward Positivism." *Progress and Its Discontents*. Ed. Gabriel A. Almond, Marvin Chodorow, and Roy Harvey Harris. Berkeley: U of California P, 1982.

Hume, David. "Of Essay Writing." *Essays Moral, Political, and Literary*. Ed. Eugene F. Miller. Indianapolis: Liberty Classics, 1985: 533–37.

Hyperius, Andreas Gerardus. *De formandis concionibus sacris, seu de interpretatione scripturarum populari*. Marburg, 1562.

Jacobs, Donald M. *Courage and Conscience: Black and White Abolitionists in Boston*. Bloomington: Indiana UP, 1993.

Jaggard, William. *Shakespeare Bibliography: A Dictionary of Every Known Issue of the Writings of the Poet and of Recorded Opinion Thereon in the English Language*. New York: Frederick Ungar, 1959.

Jakobson, Roman. "Two Aspects of Language and Two Types of Aphasic Disturbances." *Fundamentals of Language*. [2nd edition]. Ed. Roman Jakobson and Morris Halle. The Hague: Mouton, 1971. 69–96.

Jamieson, Kathleen H. *Eloquence in an Electronic Age: The Transformation of Political Speechmaking*. Oxford: Oxford UP, 1988.

Jarratt, Susan C. *Rereading the Sophists: Classical Rhetoric Refigured*. Carbondale: Southern Illinois UP, 1991.

Johnson, Nan. *Nineteenth-Century Rhetoric in North America*. Carbondale: Southern Illinois UP, 1991.

—. "The Politics of Historiography." *Rhetoric Review* 7 (1988) 9–10 ff.

Johnson, Samuel, ed. *The Plays of William Shakespeare*. 8 volumes. London, 1768.

Johnstone, Christopher Lyle. "An Aristotelian Trilogy: Ethics, Rhetoric, Politics, and the Search for 'Moral Truths.'" *Philosophy and Rhetoric* 13 (Winter 1980): 1–24.

—. "Greek Oratorical Settings and the Problem of the Pnyx: Rethinking the Athenian Political Process." *Theory, Text, Context: Issues in Greek Rhetoric and Oratory*. Ed. Christopher Lyle Johnstone. Albany: SUNY P, 1996: 97–127.

Johnstone, Christopher Lyle, ed. *Theory, Text, Context: Issues in Greek Rhetoric and Oratory*. Albany: SUNY P, 1996.

Jordan, Vernon. "The Struggle is Not Over." *Representative American Speeches, 1994–1995*. Ed. Owen Peterson. New York: The H. W. Wilson Company, 1995.

Jordan, William. "'The Damnable Dilemma': African-American Accommodation and Protest During World War I." *Journal of American History* 81 (1995): 1562–83.

Jorde, Lynn, John Carey, and Raymond White. *Medical Genetics*. St. Louis: Mosby-Year Book, Inc., 1995.

Jourdain, Charles. "Memoire sur l'education des Femmes au Moyen Age." *Excursions Historiques et Philosophiques*. Paris, 1888. Repr. Frankfurt: Minerva, 1966: 465–509.

Kahn, Charles H. *Anaximander and the Origins of Greek Cosmology*. New York: Columbia UP, 1960.

Lord Kames. *Elements of Criticism*. Edinburgh, 1762.

Keckermann, Bartholomew. *Rhetoricae ecclesiasticae sive artis formandi et habendi conciones sacras libri duo* (1600). *Operum omnium quae extant* (Geneva, [Coloniae Allobrogum], 1614) 2 vols., Trinity College Dublin library shelf mark L.a.1., 2[nd Volume].

Kennedy, George. *The Art of Persuasion in Ancient Greece*. Princeton, NJ: Princeton UP, 1963.

—. *The Art of Rhetoric in the Roman World*. Princeton: Princeton UP: 1972.

—. *Classical Rhetoric: and Its Christian and Secular Tradition from Ancient to Modern Times*. Chapel Hill: U of North Carolina P, 1980.

—. (Translator). "Gorgias." *The Older Sophists*. Edited by. Rosamond Kent Sprague. Columbia: U of South Carolina P, 1972.

—. *Greek Rhetoric Under Christian Emperors*. Princeton: Princeton UP, 1983.

—. *A New History of Classical Rhetoric*. Princeton: Princeton UP, 1994.

—. *On Rhetoric: A Theory of Civic Discourse; Newly Translated with Introduction, Notes, and Appendices*. New York: Oxford UP, 1991.

Kerber, Linda K. "Salvaging the Classical Tradition." *Federalists in Dissent: Imagery and Ideology in Jeffersonian America*. Ithaca: Cornell UP, 1970: 95–134.

Kerferd, George B. *The Sophistic Movement*. Cambridge: Cambridge UP, 1981.

Kimball, Bruce A. "Legal Education, Liberal Education, and the Trivial Artes," *Journal of General Education* 38 (1986): 189–90.

Kinneavy, James L. "Kairos: A Neglected Concept in Classical Rhetoric." *Rhetoric and Praxis: The Contribution of Classical Rhetoric to Practical Reasoning*. Ed. Jean Dietz Moss. Washington, DC: Catholic UP, 1986: 79–105.

—. *A Theory of Discourse*. New York: W. W. Norton, 1980.

Kinshasa, Kwando M. *Emigration vs. Assimilation: The Debate in the African American Press, 1827–1861*. Jefferson: McFarland and Co., 1988.

Kirby, John. "Aristotle on Metaphor." *American Journal of Philology* 118 (1997): 517–54.

Klein, Holger, and Jean-Marie Maguin. *Shakespeare and France*. Lewiston, NY: Edwin Mellen P, 1995.

Knox, Dilwyn. "Order, Reason and Oratory: Rhetoric in the Protestant Latin Schools." *Renaissance Rhetoric*. Ed. Peter Mack, 63–80. New York: St. Martin's P, 1994.

Krause, Gerhard. *Andreas Gerhard Hyperius: Leben, Bilder, Schriften*. Tubigen: J. C. B. Mohr, 1977.

Kremers, Marshall N. "The *Practical Rhetoric* of Samuel Newman." Doctoral Dissertation, Rensselaer Polytechnic Institute, 1983. Ann Arbor: UMI. 8409512.

—. "Samuel Newman and the Reduction of Rhetoric in the Early Nineteenth-Century American College." *Rhetoric Society Quarterly* 13 (1983): 185–92.

La Capra, Dominick. *History and Criticism*. Ithaca, New York: Cornell UP, 1985.

—. "Rethinking Intellectual History and Reading Texts." *Modern European Intellectual History: Reappraisals and New Perspectives*. Ed. Dominick LaCapra and Steven L. Kaplan. Ithaca, NY: Cornell UP, 1982.

LaCapra, Dominick, and Steven L. Kaplan, eds. *Modern European Intellectual History: Reappraisals and New Perspectives*. Ithaca, NY: Cornell UP, 1982.

Lacour, L. *Trois Femmes de la Révolution: Olympe de Gouges, Théroigne de Méricourt, Rose Lacombe* [*Three Women of the Revolution: Olympe de Gouges, Théroigne de Méricourt, Rose Lacombe*]. Paris: Plon, 1900.

Laistner, M.L.W. *Thought and Letters in Western Europe, A.D. 500 to 900*. [2nd edition] Ithaca, New York: Cornell UP, 1957.

Lakoff, George and Mark Johnson. *Metaphors We Live By*. Chicago: U of Chicago P, 1980.

Langford, Paul. *A Polite and Commercial People: England 1727–1783*. Oxford: Oxford UP, 1989.

Lares, Jameela. *Milton and the Preaching Arts*. Pittsburgh: Duquesne UP, 2001.

Lattin, Bohn. "The Irenic and Sermonic Rhetorical System of Erasmus," Dissertation, University of Oregon, 1992.

Leibniz, Gottfried Wilhelm. *New Essays Concerning Human Understanding*. Trans. Alfred Gideon Langley. [3rd edition] La Salle, IL: The Open Court Publishing Company, 1949. Lincoln, Andrew T. *Ephesians*. Dallas: Word, 1990.

Levin, Samuel R. "Aristotle's Theory of Metaphor." *Philosophy and Rhetoric* 15 (1982): 24–46.

Liddell, Henry George, Robert Scott and Henry Stuart Jones, editors. *A Greek-English Lexicon*. 2 volumes. Oxford: Clarendon, 1940.

Linder, A. *The Jews in Roman Imperial Legislation*. Detroit: Wayne State UP, 1987.

Linton, Ralph. *The Cultural Background of Personality*. New York: Appleton-Century-Crofts, 1945.

Liska, Jo, and Gary Cronkhite. *An Ecological Perspective on Human Communication Theory*. Fort Worth: Harcourt Brace, 1995.

Littlejohn, Stephen W. *Theories of Human Communication*. [6th edition] Belmont: Wadsworth, 1999.

Longo, Auricchio Francesca. "New Elements for the Reconstruction of Philodemus' *Rhetorica*." *Akten des 21. Internationalen Papyrologenkongresses, Berlin (1995. Archiv für Papyrusforschung*, Beiheft 3 (1997): 631–35.

Loretelli, Rosamaria. "Aspects of Lord Kames's *Elements of Criticism*." *Studies on Voltaire and the Eighteenth Century* 305 (1992): 1372–75.

Lundy, Susan Ruth, and Wayne N. Thompson. "Pliny, A Neglected Roman Rhetorician." *Quarterly Journal of Speech* 66 (December 1980): 407–417.

MacCormack, Sabine. "Latin Prose Panegyrics." *Empire and Aftermath: Silver Latin II*. Ed. T. A. Dorey. London: Routledge, 1975.

Macrobius. *The Saturnalia*. Trans. Percival Vaughan Davies. New York: Columbia UP: 1969.

Magnin, Charles, ed. *Theatre de Hrosvitha*. French Trans. with introduction and notes. Paris: Benjamin Duprat, 1845.

Makua, Josina M. *Reasoning and Communication: Thinking Critically about Arguments*. Belmont: Wadsworth, 1990.

Marcus, Steven. "Conceptions of the Self in an Age of Progress." *Progress and Its Discontents*. Ed. Gabriel A. Almond, Marvin Chodorow, and Roy Harvey Pearce. Berkeley: U of California P, 1982.

Marrou, H. I. *A History of Education in Antiquity*. Trans. George Lamb. New York: Sheed & Ward, 1956.

Matthes, Dieter. "Hermagoras von Temnos, 1904–1955." *Lustrum* 3 (1959): 58–214.

McBurney, James H. "The Place of the Enthymeme in Rhetorical Theory." *Speech Monographs* III (1936): 49–74.

McCall, Marsh H. *Ancient Rhetorical Theories of Simile and Comparison*. Cambridge: Harvard UP, 1969.

McCloskey, Donald N. "History, Differential Equations, and the Problem of Narration." *History and Theory* 30.1 (February 1991): 21–36.

McConica, J. K. "Erasmus and the Grammar of Consent," *Scrinium Erasmianum*, Volume Two. Ed. J. Coppens. Leiden: Brill, 1969.

McGuinness, Arthur E. *Henry Home, Lord Kames.* New York: Twayne Publishers, 1970.
McKenzie, Gordon. "Lord Kames and the Mechanist Tradition." *University of California Publications in English* 14 (1943): 93–121.
Meador, Jr., Prentice A. "Quintilian and the *Institutio Oratoria*." *A Synoptic History of Classical Rhetoric.* Ed. James J. Murphy. Davis, CA: Hermagoras, 1983.
Meerhoff, Kees. "The Significance of Philip Melanchthon's Rhetoric in the Renaissance." *Renaissance Rhetoric.* Ed. Peter Mack. 46–62. New York: St. Martin's P, 1994.
Meier, August, and Elliott Rudwick. *From Plantation to Ghetto.* 3rd ed. New York: Hill and Wang, 1976.
Meijering, Roos. *Literary and Rhetorical Theories in Greek Scholia.* Grönigen, Neth.: Egbert Forsten, 1987.
["A member of the Philadelphia Bar."], ed. *American Oratory, Or, Selections from the Speeches of Eminent Americans.* Philadelphia: DeSilver, Thomas; Edward C. Biddle, 1836.
Miller, Thomas P. *The Formation of College English: Rhetoric and Belles Lettres in the British Cultural Provinces.* Pittsburgh: U of Pittsburgh P, 1997.
Miller, Thomas P., ed. *The Selected Writings of John Witherspoon.* Landmarks in Rhetoric and Public Address. Carbondale: Southern Illinois UP, 1990.
Monedas, M. "A Rhetorical Analysis of the Revolutionary Discourse of Olympe de Gouges, Phoenix of the French Revolution." Dissertation. Ohio University, 1996. UMI, 9639714.
—. "Olympe de Gouges and Friends: A Profile of Agitational Rhetoric of the Eighteenth Century." Paper presented at the Speech Communication Association annual conference, Atlanta, 1991.
Monfasani, James. "Humanism and Rhetoric." *Renaissance Humanism: Foundations, Forms, and Legacy. Humanism and the Disciples.* Ed. Albert Rabil Jr. Volume Three. Philadelphia: U of Pennsylvania P, 1988.
Monsman, Gerald, and Samuel Wright. "Walter Pater: Style and Text." *South Atlantic Quarterly* 71.1 (1972): 106–23.
Most, Glenn W. "The Uses of *Endoxa*: Philosophy and Rhetoric in the *Rhetoric*." *Aristotle's Rhetoric. Philosophical Essays.* Ed. David L. Furley and Alexander Nehamas. Princeton: Princeton UP, 1994: 167–90.
Mouton, Edna. "The Communicative Power of the Epistle to the Ephesians." *Rhetoric, Scripture and Theology: Essays from the 1994 Pretoria Conference.* Ed. Stanley E. Porter and Thomas H. Olbricht. Sheffield: Academic P, 1996: 290–91.
Muller, Richard A. "*Vera Philosophia cum sacra Theologia nusquam pugnat:* Keckermann on Philosophy, Theology, and the Problem of Double Truth." *Sixteenth Century Journal* 15.3 (1984): 343–66.

Murphy, James J. "Introduction." *Arguments in Rhetoric Against Quintilian. Translation and Text of Peter Ramus's* Rhetoricae distinctiones in Quintilianum. Trans. Carole Newlands. DeKalb, IL: Northern Illinois UP, 1986.
—. "Introduction." *Three Medieval Rhetorical Arts.* Berkeley: U of California P, 1971.
—. *Rhetoric in the Middle Ages.* Berkeley: U of California P, 1974.
—. *Renaissance Rhetoric: A Short-Title Catalogue of Works on Rhetorical Theory from the Beginning of Printing to A.D. 1700.* New York & London: Garland Publishing Inc., 1981.
Murphy, James J., ed. *Renaissance Eloquence: Studies in the Theory and Practice of Renaissance Rhetoric.* Berkeley: U of California P, 1983.
—. *Synoptic History of Classical Rhetoric.* Davis, CA: Hermagoras, 1983.
Nadeau, Ray (Translator). "Aphthonius, *Progymnasmata.*" *Speech Monographs* 19 (1952): 264–85.
Nagel, Bert. *Hrotsvit von Gandersheim.* Stuttgart: Metzler, 1965.
National Research Council. Committee on Mapping and Sequencing the Human Genome Board of Basic Biology Commission on Life Sciences. *Mapping and Sequencing the Human Genome.* Washington D.C.: National Academy P, 1988.
Nelms, Gerald, and Maureen D. Goggin. "The Revival of Classical Rhetoric for Modern Composition Studies: A Survey." *Rhetoric Society Quarterly* 23 (1994): 11–26.
Neuliep, James W. *Human Communication Theory: Applications and Case Studies.* Boston: Allyn and Bacon, 1996.
"Newman, Samuel Phillips." *Dictionary of American Biography.* Ed. Dumas Malone. New York: Charles Scribner's Sons, 1934. 466–67.
"Newman, Samuel Phillips." *The National Cyclopaedia of American Biography.* New York: James T. White & Co., 1909. 123.
Newman, Samuel P. *A Practical System of Rhetoric or the Principles & Rules of Style, Inferred from Examples of Writing.* 1st Ed. Portland: Wm. Hyde, 1827.
—. *A Practical System of Rhetoric or the Principles & Rules of Style, Inferred from Examples of Writing.* 2nd ed. Portland: Hyde & Shirley; Andover: Mark Newman, 1829.
—. *A Practical System of Rhetoric or the Principles & Rules of Style, Inferred from Examples of Writing.* 3rd ed. "Enlarged and Improved." Boston: Wm. Hyde, 1832.
—. *A Practical System of Rhetoric or the Principles & Rules of Style, Inferred from Examples of Writing. To Which Is Added an Historical Dissertation on English Style.* 4th ed. "Enlarged and Improved." Andover: Flagg, Gould, & Newman; Boston: Carter, Hendee & Co., 1834.

—. *A Practical System of Rhetoric or the Principles & Rules of Style, Inferred from Examples of Writing.* 5th ed. Andover: Gould & Newman; New York: H. Griffin, 1835.

—. *A Practical System of Rhetoric or the Principles & Rules of Style, Inferred from Examples of Writing.* 10th ed. New York: Dayton & Newman, 1842.

—. *A Practical System of Rhetoric or the Principles & Rules of Style, Inferred from Examples of Writing.* 12th ed. New York: Mark H. Newman, 1843.

—. *A Practical System of Rhetoric or the Principles & Rules of Style, Inferred from Examples of Writing.* 50th ed. New York: Mark H. Newman & Co., [n.d.].

Newman, Sara J. *Aristotle and Metaphor: His Theory and Its Practice.* Dissertation. University of Minnesota, 1998.

Nolan, Dennis R. "The Effect of the Revolution on the Bar: The Maryland Experience." *Virginia Law Review* 62 (1976): 969–90.

Nussbaum, Martha C. "Aristotle on Emotions and Rational Persuasion" in *Essays on Aristotle's Rhetoric.* Ed. A. O. Rorty. U of California P, 1996: 303–23.

Ober, Josiah. *Mass and Elite in Democratic Athens: Rhetoric, Ideology, and the Power of the People.* Princeton: Princeton UP, 1989.

Ober, Josiah, and Barry Strauss. "Drama, Political Rhetoric, and the Discourse of Athenian Democracy." *Nothing to Do with Dionysos?: Athenian Drama in Its Social Context.* Ed. John J. Winkler and Froma I. Zeitlin. Princeton: Princeton UP, 1990.

O'Brien, Michael J. "Protagoras." *The Older Sophists.* Ed. Rosamond Kent Sprague. Columbia: U of South Carolina P, 1972.

O'Brien, Peter T. "Ephesians I: An Unusual Introduction to a New Testament Letter." *New Testament Studies* 24 (1979): 504–16.

Olin, John C., ed. *Christian Humanism and the Reformation: Selected Writings of Erasmus.* 3rd Ed. New York Fordham UP, 1987.

—. *Six Essays on Erasmus and a Translation of Erasmus' Letter to Carondelet, 1523.* New York: Fordham UP, 1979.

Ong, Walter. "Agonistic Structures in Academia: Past and Present." *Interchange: A Journal of Education* 5.4 (1974): 1–12.

—. *Ramus and Talon Inventory. A Short-Title Inventory of the Published Works of Peter Ramus 1515–72 and of Omer Talon ca. 1510–1562 in their Original and in their Variously Altered Forms.* Cambridge, MA: Harvard UP, 1958.

—. *Ramus: Method, and the Decay of Dialogue. From the Art of Discourse to the Art of Reason.* Cambridge, MA: Harvard UP, 1958.

O'Rourke, Sean. "Cultivating the 'Higher Law' in American Jurisprudence: John Quincy Adams, Neo-Classical Rhetoric, and the *Amistad* Case." *Southern Communication Journal* 60 (1994): 33–43.

—. Review of White, G. Edward. *Intervention and Detachment: Essays in Legal History and Jurisprudence*. *American Journal of Legal History* 40 (1996): 374–76.

Outram, D. "Le Langage Mâle de la Vertu" ["The Male Language of Virtue]: Women and the Discourse of the French Revolution"]. Ed. Burke and R. Porter. *The Social History of Language*. Cambridge: Cambridge UP, 1987: 120–35.

Owst, Gerald R. "Sermon-Making, or the Theory and Practice of Sacred Eloquence." *Preaching in Medieval England: An Introduction to Sermon Manuscripts of the Period c. 1350–1450*. Cambridge: Cambridge UP, 1926. 309–59.

Parker, Edward G. *The Golden Age of American Oratory*. Boston: Whittemore, Niles, and Hall, 1857.

Pater, Walter. *Essays on Literature and Art*. Ed. Jennifer Uglow. London: Dent, 1973.

—. *Marius the Epicurean: His Sensations and Ideas*. New York: Garland, 1975.

—. *Plato and Platonism: A Series of Lectures*. London: Macmillan, 1928.

—. *The Renaissance: Studies in Art and Poetry*. London: Macmillan, 1910.

—. "Style." *Appreciations, with an Essay on Style*. London: Macmillan, 1910.

—. "To George Moore," c. 3 August 1887. *Letters of Walter Pater*. Ed. Lawrence Evans. Oxford: Clarendon, 1970.

Perelman, Chaim, and L. Olbrechts-Tyteca. *The New Rhetoric: A Treatise on Argumentation*. Trans. John Wilkinson and Purcell Weaver. Notre Dame: UP, 1969.

Perry, Lewis, and Michael Fellman. *Antislavery Reconsidered: New Perspectives on the Abolitionists*. Baton Rouge: Louisiana State UP, 1979.

Peterson, Owen, ed. *Representative American Speeches, 1987–1988*. New York: The H. W. Wilson Company, 1988.

—, ed. *Representative American Speeches, 1994–1995*. New York: The H. W. Wilson Company, 1995.

Pierpont, John. *The American First Class Book; or, Exercises in Reading and Recitation: Selected Principally from Modern Authors of Great Britain and America; And Designed for the Use of the Highest Class in Publick and Private Schools*. Boston: Cummings, Hilliard, & Co. and Richardson & Lord, 1825.

Plett, Heinrich F. *English Renaissance Rhetoric and Poetics: A Systematic Bibliography of Primary and Secondary Sources*. Symbola et Emblemata: Studies in Renaissance and Baroque Symbolism, 6. Leiden: E. J. Brill, 1995.

Polheim, Karl. *Die Lateinische Reimprosa*. Berlin: Weidmann, 1925. 1–40.

Polhill, John "An Introduction to Ephesians." *Review and Expositor* 76 (1977).

Pollack, Rhoda-Gale. "Hroswitha: Abraham." *A Sampler of Plays by Women*. New York: Peter Lang, 1990. 7–35.
Pope, Alexander, ed. *The Works of Shakespear*. Vol. 1. London, 1723–1725.
Porter, Dorothy. *Early Negro Writing 1760–1837*. Boston: Beacon P, 1971.
Porter, Stanley E., and Thomas H. Olbricht. *Rhetoric, Scripture and Theology: Essays from the 1994 Pretoria Conference*." Sheffield: Academic P, 1996.
Poste, George. "Genomics." *Vital Speeches of the Day* (1 January 1995): 165–69.
Potkay, Adam. *The Fate of Eloquence in the Age of Hume*. Ithaca: Cornell UP, 1994.
Poulakos, John. "Gorgias' *Encomium on Helen* and the Defense of Rhetoric." *Rhetorica* 1.2 (Autumn 1983): 1–16.
—. "Rhetoric, the Sophists, and the Possible." *Communication Monographs* 51 (1984): 215–26.
—. *Sophistical Rhetoric in Classical Greece*. Columbia: South Carolina UP, 1994.
—. "Toward a Sophistic Definition of Rhetoric." *Philosophy and Rhetoric* 16.1 (1983): 35–48. Reprinted in *Landmark Essays on Classical Greek Rhetoric*. Ed. Edward Schiappa. Davis, CA: Hermagoras P, 1994. 55–66.
Poulakos, Takis. "Intellectuals and the Public Sphere: The Case of the Older Sophists." *Spheres of Argument*. Ed. Bruce E. Gronbeck. Annandale, VA: Speech Communication Association, 1984.
Powell, Jr., Adam Clayton. "Can There Any Good Thing Come Out of Nazareth?" *The Voice of Black America: Major Speeches by Negroes in the United States, 1797–1971*. Ed. Philip S. Foner. New York: Simon and Schuster, 1972.
Pritchett, W. Kendrick (Translator and editor). *Dionysius of Halicarnassus: On Thucydides: An English Translation with Commentary*. Berkeley: U of California P, 1975.
Quarles, Benjamin. *Black Abolitionists*. New York: Oxford UP, 1969.
Quint, David. *Epic and Empire*. Princeton: Princeton: UP, 1993.
Rabaut, J. *Histoire des Féminismes Françaises*. [*History of French Feminisms*]. Paris: Stock, 1978.
Rabe, Hugo. *Prolegomenon Sylloge*. Leipzig: Teubner, 1931.
Rabil Jr.,Albert, ed. *Renaissance Humanism: Foundations, Forms, and Legacy. Humanism and the Disciples*. Volume 3. Philadelphia: U of Pennsylvania P, 1988.
Radice, Betty. "Pliny and the *Panegyricus*," *Greece and Rome* 15 (1968): 166–72.
Ramus, Peter. *Petri Rami Veromandui Aristotelicae Animadversiones*. Parisiis: Iacobus Bogardus, 1543.

—. *Petri Rami veromandui dialecticae institutiones, ad celeberrimam et illustrissimam Lutetiae Parisiorum Academiam.* Parisiis: Iacobus Bogardus, mense Septembri 1543.

Ramus, Peter, and Omer Talon. *Petri Rami Professoris Regii, et Audomari Talaei Collectaneae Praefationes, Epistolae, Orationes.* Marpurgi: Paulus Egenolphus, 1599.

Randall, Helen Whitcomb. "The Critical Theory of Lord Kames." *Smith College Studies in Modern Languages* 22.1–4 (1940–41).

Ray, Angela G. "'My Own Hand': Benjamin Banneker Addresses the Slaveholder of Monticello." *Rhetoric & Public Affairs* 1 (1998): 387–405.

Reid, Robert S. "Dionysius of Halicarnassus' Theory of Compositional Style and The Theory of Literate Consciousness." *Rhetoric Review* 15 (1996): 46–64.

—. "When Words Were a Power Loosed: Audience Expectation and *Finished* Narrative Technique in the *Gospel of Mark*." *Quarterly Journal of Speech* 80 (1994): 431–34.

Reid, Ronald F. *American Rhetorical Discourse*, 2nd ed. Prospect Heights, IL: Waveland P, 1995.

Rhodes, Neil. "From Rhetoric to Criticism." *The Scottish Invention of English Literature.* Ed. Robert Crawford. Cambridge: Cambridge UP, 1998.

Rhodes, P. J. *The Athenian Boule.* Oxford: Clarendon, 1972.

—. "Introduction." *The Athenian Constitution.* Trans. P. J. Rhodes. New York: Penguin, 1984: 9–35.

Richardson, Marilyn, ed. *Maria W. Stewart, America's First Black Woman Political Writer: Essays and Speeches.* Bloomington: Indiana UP, 1987.

Ricoeur, Paul. *The Rule of Metaphor.* Trans. R. Czerny. Toronto: U of Toronto P, 1977.

Robert of Basevorn. *Forma Praedicandi.* Trans. Leopold Krul. *Three Medieval Rhetorical Arts.* Ed. James J. Murphy. Berkeley, Los Angeles, and London: U of California P, 1971. 114–215.

Roberts, W. Rhys. *Dionysius of Halicarnassus On Literary Composition.* London: Macmillan, 1910.

Roetzel, Calvin J. "Jewish Christian-Gentile Christian Relations: A Discussion of Ephesians 2:15A," *Zeitschrift fur die neutestamentliche Wissenschaft* 74 (1983): 81–89.

Rorty, A. O. "Aristotle on the Metaphysical Status of *Pathe.*" *Essays on Aristotle's Rhetoric.* Berkeley, CA: U of California P, 1996. 521–46.

Ross, Ian Simpson. "Aesthetic Philosophy: Hutcheson and Hume to Alison." *The History of Scottish Literature*, Volume 2, edited by Andrew Hook. Aberdeen: Aberdeen UP, 1987.

—. *Lord Kames and the Scotland of His Day.* Oxford: Clarendon P, 1972.

—. "Scots Law and Scots Criticism: The Case of Lord Kames." *Philological Quarterly* 45 (1966): 614–23.

Rowell, Edward Z. "The Conviction-Persuasion Duality." *Quarterly Journal of Speech* 20 (1934): 469–82.
Russell, D. A. "The Arts of Prose: The Early Empire." *The Roman World, The Oxford History of the Classical World.* Volume Two. Ed. John Boardman, Jasper Griffin, and Oswyn Murray. Oxford: Oxford UP, 1986.
—. *Criticism in Antiquity.* Berkeley: U of California P, 1981.
Russell, D. A., and M. Winterbottom, eds. *Ancient Literary Criticism.* Oxford: Oxford UP, 1972.
Russell, D. S. *The Method and Message of Jewish Apocalyptic.* Philadelphia: Westminster, 1964.
Saggs, H. W. F. *Civilization Before Greece and Rome.* New Haven: Yale UP, 1989.
Sanders, Jack T. "Hymnic Elements in Ephesians 1–3," *Zeitschrift fur die neutestamentliche Wissenschaft* 51 (1965).
Scenters-Zapico, John. "The Case for the Sophists." *Rhetoric Review* 11.2 (1993): 352–67.
Schiappa, Edward. "Gorgias's *Helen* Revisited," *Quarterly Journal of Speech* 81 (1995): 310–24.
—. *Protagoras and Logos: A Study in Greek Philosophy and Rhetoric.* Columbia: U of South Carolina P, 1991.
—. "Sophistic Rhetoric: Oasis or Mirage?" *Rhetoric Review.* 10 (1991): 5–18. Rpt. *Landmark Essays on Classical Greek Rhetoric.* Ed. Edward Schiappa. Davis, CA: Hermagoras P, 1994. 67–80.
Schmitz, Robert Morrell. *Hugh Blair.* New York: King's Crown P, 1948.
Schultz, Lucille M. "Elaborating Our History: A Look At Mid-19th Century First Books of Composition." *College Composition and Communication* 45 Feb. (1994): 10–30.
Schulz, Fritz. *History of Roman Legal Science.* Oxford: Clarendon P, 1946.
Sealey, Raphael. *A History of the Greek City States, ca. 700–338 B. C.* Berkeley: U of California P, 1976.
—. "Regionalism in Archaic Athens." *Historia* 9 (1960): 155–80.
Segal, Charles P. "Gorgias and the Psychology of Logos." *Harvard Studies in Classical Philology* 66. Cambridge, MA: Harvard UP, 1962.
Shaw, Leroy. "Henry Home of Kames: Precursor of Herder." *Germanic Review* 35 (1960): 16–27.
Sher, Richard B., and Jeffrey R. Smitten. *Scotland and America in the Age of Enlightenment.* Princeton: Princeton UP, 1990.
Sloane, Thomas O. *On the Contrary: The Protocol of Traditional Rhetoric.* Washington, D.C.: Catholic U of America P, 1997.
—. "Reinventing *inventio.*" *College English* 51 (1989): 461–73.
—. "Schoolbooks and Rhetoric: Erasmus's Copia." *Rhetorica: A Journal of the History of Rhetoric* 9 (Spring 1991): 113–29.
Smith, Adam. *A Theory of Moral Sentiments,* 7th ed. London: Strahan, 1777.

Smith-Lovin, Lynn. "The Sociology of Affect and Emotion." *Sociological Perspectives on Social Psychology*. Ed. Karen S. Cook, Gary Alan Fine, and James S. House. Boston: Allyn and Bacon, 1995.

Solmsen, Friedrich. "The Aristotelian Tradition in Ancient Rhetoric." Ed. Keith V. Erickson. *Aristotle: The Classical Heritage of Rhetoric*. Metuchen, NJ: Scarecrow, 1974. 278–309.

—. "Aristotle and Cicero on the Orator's Playing upon the Feelings." *Classical Philology* 33 (October 1938): 390–404.

Sprague, Rosemary. "Hroswitha—Tenth-Century Margaret Webster." *The Theatre Annual* 13 (1955): 16–31.

Sprague, Rosamond Kent, ed. *The Older Sophists*. Columbia: U of South Carolina P, 1972.

St. John, Christopher. *Roswitha*. With an introduction by Cardinal Gasquet. London: Chatto & Windus, 1923. Reissued New York: Benjamin Blom, 1966.

Stanford, William B. *Greek Metaphor*. Oxford: Basil Blackwell Ltd., 1936.

Stanton, G. R. *Athenian Politics c.800–500 B. C.: A Sourcebook*. London: Routledge, 1990.

Starr, Chester G. *The Origins of Greek Civilization, 1100–650 B. C.* New York: Knopf, 1961.

Stephens, J. W. *Francis Bacon and the Style of Science*. Chicago: U of Chicago P, 1975.

Sterk, Helen. "Praise of Beautiful Women." *Western Journal of Speech Communication* 50 (1986): 215–26.

Stockton, David. *The Classical Athenian Democracy*. New York: Oxford UP, 1990.

Stone, Jr., George Winchester. "Introduction: The London Stage 1747–1776." *The London Stage 1660–1800*. Vol. 1. Ed. George Winchester Stone, Jr. Carbondale: Southern Illinois UP, 1962.

Stone, I. F. *The Trial of Socrates*. Boston: Little, Brown, 1988.

Story, W. W., ed. *Miscellaneous Writings of Joseph Story*, 3 volumes. Boston, 1852.

Strecker, K., ed. *Hrotsvithae Opera*. Leipzig: Teubner, 1930.

Struever, Nancy S. "The Conversable World." *Rhetoric and the Pursuit of Truth: Language Change in the Seventeenth and Eighteenth Centuries*. Los Angeles: William Andrews Clark Memorial Library, 1985.

Sullivan, William M. *Reconstructing Public Philosophy*. Berkeley: U of California P, 1982.

Sussman, Lewis A. *The Elder Seneca*. Leiden: Brill, 1978.

Sweet, W. E. *Sport and Recreation in Ancient Greece: A Sourcebook with Translations*. New York: Oxford UP, 1987.

Syme, Ronald. *Tacitus. Two Volumes*. Oxford: Oxford UP, 1958.

Talon, Omer. *Audomari Talaei rhetorica, ad Carolum Lotharingum Cardinalem Guisianum, Tertia editio ab authore recognita et aucta.* Parisiis: E typographia Matthai Dauidis, 1549.

—. *Audomari Talaei Rhetorica, ad Carolum Lotharingum Cardinalem Guisianum.* Parisiis: M. David, 1548.

Tcherikover, V. *Hellenistic Civilization and the Jews.* New York: Atheneum, 1974.

Tebbel, John. *A History of Book Publishing in the United States; Volume I: The Creation of an Industry, 1630–1865.* New York: R. R. Bowker, 1972.

Theobald, Lewis. *Shakespeare Restored: or, a Specimen of the many errors, as well committed, as unamended, by Mr. Pope in his late edition of this Poet.* London, 1726.

Theobald's The Censor. London, 1717.

Tracy, James R. *Erasmus: the Growth of a Mind.* Geneve: Librairie Droz, 1972.

Tytler, Alexander Fraser, Lord Woodhouselee. *Memoirs of the Life and Writings of the Honourable Henry Home of Kames.* Vol. 1. Edinburgh, 1807.

Uglow, Jennifer. "Introduction." *Essays on Literature and Art.* London: J. M. Dent, 1973.

Ulman, H. Lewis. "Discerning Readers: British Reviewers' Responses to Campbell's *Rhetoric* and Related Works." *Rhetorica* 1.8 (Winter 1990): 65–90.

Usher, Stephen. *Dionysius of Halicarnassus: The Critical Essays in Two Volumes.* Loeb Classical Library. Cambridge: Harvard UP, 1974, 1985.

Van Wyk Cronjé, Jacobus. *Dionysius of Halicarnassus: De Demosthenes: A Critical Appraisal of the Status Quaestionis.* Zurich: Georg Olms, 1986.

van Zuylen, W. H. *Bartholomäus Keckermann: Sein Leben und Wirken.* Borna-Leipzig: Robert Noske, 1934.

Vernant. Jean-Pierre. *Myth and Thought Among the Greek.* London: Routledge & Kegan Paul, 1983.

—. *The Origins of Greek Thought.* Ithaca: Cornell UP, 1982.

Versenyi, Laszlo. *Socratic Humanism.* New Haven: Yale UP, 1963.

Vickers, Brian. "Bacon and Rhetoric." *The Cambridge Companion to Bacon.* Ed. Markku Peltonen. Cambridge: Cambridge UP, 1996. 200–31.

—. *Defence of Rhetoric.* Oxford: Clarendon P, 1988.

—. "The Power of Persuasion." *Renaissance Eloquence: Studies in the Theory and Practice of Renaissance Rhetoric.* Ed. James J. Murphy. Berkeley: U of California P, 1983.

—. "Territorial Disputes: Philosophy *versus* Rhetoric." *Rhetoric Revalued: Papers from the International Society for the History of Rhetoric.* Ed. Brian Vickers. Binghamton, NY: Center for Medieval & Early Renaissance Studies, 1982.

Vickers, Brian, ed. *Rhetoric Revalued: Papers from the International Society for the History of Rhetoric*. Binghamton, NY: Center for Medieval & Early Renaissance Studies, 1982.

Vickers, Brian, and Nancy S. Struever, eds. *Rhetoric and the Pursuit of Truth: Language Change in the Seventeenth and Eighteenth Centuries*. Los Angeles: William Andrews Clark Memorial Library, 1985.

Vico, Giambattista. *The New Science of Giambattista Vico*. Trans. Thomas Bergin and Max Harold Fisch. Ithaca, New York: Cornell UP, 1991.

Vitanza, Victor J., ed. *Writing Histories of Rhetoric*. Carbondale: Southern Illinois UP, 1994.

von Gandersheim, Hrotsvitha. *Dulcitius, Abraham: Zwei Dramen*. German Trans. with afterword by Karl Langosch. Stuttgart: Philipp, 1964.

Wade-Gery, H. T. *Essays in Greek History*. Oxford: Basil Blackwell, 1958.

Walker, Jeffrey. "The Body of Persuasion: A Theory of the Enthymeme." *College English* 56 (1994): 46–65.

—. "*Pathos* and *Katharsis* in 'Aristotelian' Rhetoric: Some Implications." *Rereading Aristotle's Rhetoric*. Ed. Alan Gross and Art Walzer. Carbondale: Southern Illinois UP, 2000. 74–92.

Wallace, Karl R. *Francis Bacon on Communication and Rhetoric Or: The Art of Applying Reason to Imagination for the Better Moving of the Will*. Chapel Hill: The U of North Carolina P, 1943.

Walzer, Arthur E. "Campbell on the Passions: A Rereading of the *Philosophy of Rhetoric*." *Quarterly Journal of Speech* 85 (1999): 72–85.

Warburton, William, ed. *The Works of Shakespear*. 8 volumes. London, 1747.

Warnick, Barbara. *The Sixth Canon: Belletristic Rhetorical Theory and Its French Antecedents*. Columbia: U of South Carolina P, 1993.

Warren, Charles. *A History of the American Bar*. Boston: Little, Brown, 1911.

Welch, Kathleen. *The Contemporary Reception of Classical Rhetoric: Appropriations of Ancient Discourse*. Hillsdale, NJ: Lawrence Erlbaum, 1990.

West, Cornell. *Race Matters*. Boston: Beacon P, 1993.

Whately, Richard. *Elements of Rhetoric*. Ed. Douglas Ehninger. Carbondale, IL: Southern Illinois UP, 1963.

Whipper, William. "An Address Delivered in Wesley Church on the Evening of June 12, Before the Colored Reading Society of Philadelphia, for Moral Improvement." *Early Negro Writing 1760–1837*. Ed. Dorothy Porter. Boston: Beacon P, 1971.

White, G. Edward. *Intervention and Detachment: Essays in Legal History and Jurisprudence*. New York: Oxford UP, 1994.

White, G. Edward and Gerald Gunther. *History of the Supreme Court of the United States, Volumes. III & IV: The Marshall Court and Cultural Change, 1815–35*. New York: Macmillan, 1988.

White, Hayden. "The Question of Narrativity in Contemporary Historical Theory." *History and Theory* 23.1 (February 1984): 1–33.

Wiefel. W. "The Jewish Community in Rome and the Origins of Roman Christianity." *The Romans Debate.* Ed. K. P. Donfri. Minneapolis: Augsburg, 1977. 100–19.

Wills, Christopher. *Exons, Introns, and Talking Genes: The Science Behind the Human Genome Project.* New York: Basic Books, 1991.

Williston, E. B. (Compiler). *Eloquence of the United States*, 5 vols. Middletown, CT: E. & H. Clark, 1827.

Wilson, Katharina. *Hrotsvit of Gandersheim: A Florilegium of Her Works.* Woodbridge, UK: D. S. Brewer, 1998.

Wilson, Katharina, ed. and trans. *The Plays of Hrotsvit of Gandersheim.* New York: Garland, 1989.

Wilson, Kathleen. *The Sense of the People: Politics, Culture and Imperialism in England, 1715–178.* Cambridge: Cambridge UP, 1995.

Wiltse, Charles M., ed. *David Walker's Appeal, in Four Articles; Together with a Preamble, to the Coloured Citizens of the World, But in Particular, and Very Expressly, to Those of the United States of America*, 3rd ed. New York: Hill and Wang, 1965.

Wirt, William. *The Letters of the British Spy.* Richmond: Samuel Pleasants, Jr., 1803.

—. *The Old Bachelor.* Richmond: Thomas Ritchie & Fielding Lucas, 1814.

—. *The Rainbow; First Series.* Richmond: Ritchie & Worsley, 1804.

Wisse, Jakob. *Ethos and Pathos from Aristotle to Cicero.* Amsterdam: Hakkert, 1989.

Wittig, Monique. *The Straight Mind and Other Essays.* Boston: Beacon P, 1992.

Wollstonecraft, Mary. *The Vindication of the Rights of Woman* 1792. New York: Norton, 1975.

Wood, Julia. *Communication Theories in Action: An Introduction.* Belmont: Wadsworth, 1997.

Woodhead, A. G. "*Isegoria* and the Council of 500." *Historia* 16 (1967): 129–140.

Woodward, William H. *Desiderius Erasmus: Concerning the Aim and Method of Education.* New York: Teachers College, Columbia U, Bureau of Pub, 1964.

Wooten, Cecil. "The Peripatetic Tradition in the Literary Essays of Dionysius of Halicarnassus." *Peripatetic Rhetoric After Aristotle.* Ed. William Fortenbaugh and David Mirhady. New Brunswick: Transaction, 1994: 121–30.

X, Malcolm. *By Any Means Necessary*, 2nd ed. New York: Pathfinder, 1992.

Yellin, Jean Fagan, and John C. Van Horne, eds. *The Abolitionist Sisterhood: Women's Political Culture in Antebellum America*. Ithaca: Cornell UP, 1994.

Zanker, Paul. *The Power of Images in the Age of Augustus*. Trans. Alan Shapiro. Ann Arbor, MI: U of Michigan P, 1988.

Zeydel, Edwin H. "Authenticity of Hrotsvitha's Works." *Modern Language Notes* (January 1946): 50–55.

Zimmern, Alfred E. *Greek Commonwealth: Politics and Economics in Fifth-Century Athens*. 5th ed. Oxford: Oxford UP, 1931.

Index

Abdel-Rahman III, 197
Abdrahemen, 197
abusio, 238
Achilles (Achilleus), 343, 344, 347
Adams, John Quincy, 67, 99, 101–102, 148
Adelheid of Burgundy, 195
adjuratio, 205
admiratio, 205
Advances in the History of Rhetoric, 370
Aelius Lamia, 178
Aeneas, 364, 365
Aeschines, 333
Aesopus, 32
Agamemnon, 169, 289, 347
aganaktein, 170
Agape (martyr), 195
Agustín, Antonio (Archbishop of Lérida), 30
Alcibiades, 160, 162
Alcuin, 188, 189
allotrios, 237
Alston, R.C., 202
Ambrose, 207
American Society for the History of Rhetoric, 98, 151, 371
amplificatio, 200
Anaximander, 290
Anaximenes, 290
Andrewes, A., 225, 226
Annius Cimber, 366
Antiphon, 291
antistrophos, 235

antithesis, 3, 4, 5, 6, 7, 9, 11, 153
Aphthonius, 32
Apostle, Hippocrates, 116
apostrophe, 205
Aquinas, Saint Thomas, 207
Aratus, 190
Arendt, Hannah, 157, 158, 160, 162
Areopagus, 224, 226, 227, 228, 330, 331, 335
Aristion, 228
Aristophanes, 284
Aristotle, 10, 12, 15, 23, 82, 95, 115–117, 122, 144, 146–152, 156, 157, 167–175, 183, 192, 202, 203, 206, 222–228, 230, 235–247, 273, 277, 278, 279, 280, 281, 286, 288, 291–293, 304, 305, 308, 337–350, 369
Arnhart, Larry, 337, 339, 340, 341, 345
Arnold, Matthew, 262, 264
ars praedicandi, 199
Aschbach, Joseph, 188, 194
Ashcraft, Mike, 187
ASHR. See American Society for the History of Rhetoric, 145
Athanasius, 13
Athens, 41, 155, 158–160, 167–169, 172, 221, 222, 224–228, 230, 231, 232, 276, 289, 326, 329, 335
Atlas, 134, 135
Attilius Regulus, 36

409

Aubry, Pierre, 57
augur, 359
Augustus, 179, 351, 352, 355, 356, 357, 358, 359, 361, 362, 363, 365, 366
Avienus, 32

Bacon, Sir Francis, 74, 140, 151, 248, 253, 254, 255, 257
Barthes, Roland, 231, 232
Bashford, James W., 137, 138
Basil II, 195
Baskerville, Barnet, 100
Beattie, James, 299
Bede The Venerable, 190
Benario, 177
Bennett, C. E., 356
Bennett, Julian, 176, 356
Benzing, Josef, 205
Berkeley, George, 266
Berlin, James A., 63, 65, 74
Bernoulli, Jakob, 78, 79, 80, 81, 82, 83
Bett, Richard, 8
Bevilacqua, Vincent M., 296, 297, 298
Beza, 207
Bitzer, Lloyd F., 122, 174
Bizzell, Patricia, 145
Blair, Carol, 222, 231, 232
Blair, Hugh, 64, 65, 73, 152, 261, 297, 308, 309–325
Blanc, Olivier, 51, 52, 53, 54, 57, 58, 59
Blass, F., 94
Bloom, Allan, 160
Boethius, 188, 189, 190
Bonaventure, Saint, 207
Bonner, Stanley F., 14, 18, 26, 178
Bormann, Ernest, 146
Borza, 233, 234
Bostrom, Robert, 149
Botein, Stephen, 101
boulê, 221, 222, 224, 225, 226, 227, 231, 233, 289

Bowers, John Waite, 211, 212
Boyd, James R., 297
Boylan, Anne M., 210
Boyle, Marjorie O'Rourke, 44
Brabia, 32
Bradford, Annette Norris, 115
Brandes, Paul, 167
Brilioth, Yngve, 200
Brilliant, Richard, 367
Bruere, Richard, 175, 176, 184, 185, 186
Brunt, P.A., 359
Bucholerus, 207
Buckminster, 70, 71
Bundy, Murray W., 296
Burk, Don M., 146
Burke, Kenneth, 90, 91, 95, 97, 146, 211, 239
Burnet, 64, 74
Butler, H. E., 181, 194, 202
Butler, Judith, 4
Butterfield, Herbert, 229

Calimachus, 195, 197
Callicles, 164
Callisthenes, 349
Calvin, 89, 207
Campbell, George, 64, 65, 149, 152, 183, 297, 308
Campbell, Karlyn Kohrs, 183
Cantor, Charles R., 118
capita, 30, 38
Caplan, Harry, 13, 176, 177, 180
Carey, John, 116, 125
Carlyle, Thomas, 261, 264
Carpentarius, Johannes, 31
Carpenter, Frederic Ives, 248, 251
Cassiodorus, 188
catachresis, 247
Cato, 181, 366
Caxton, 74
Celtis, Conradus, 188
Cephisodotus, 245
Chabrias, 245

Chambers, Mortimer, 221, 222, 227
Chambers, Stephen, 100
Chancellor Bruno, 189
Channing, Edward T., 67, 70, 71
Chapman, David W., 274
Charland, Th.-M., 200
Chionia (martyr), 195
Chios, 225, 228
Choate, Rufus, 100
Choe, Wolhee, 264
chrestos, 171
Christiansen, David, 187
Chrysostom, Saint John, 207
Chumakov, Ilya M., 114, 118, 119, 121, 125, 126, 127
Church, F. J., 159
Cicero, Marcus Tullius, 13, 25, 32, 34, 44–48, 67, 82–84, 87, 101, 106, 108, 110, 146, 148–149, 152, 189, 202, 203, 207, 238, 256, 257, 258, 261, 268, 270–272, 278, 308, 313, 327, 353–355, 364
Clark, Gregory, 100, 101
Cleisthenes, 223, 224, 225, 226, 227, 228, 327
Cleophon, 240
Clough, Arthur Hugh, 223
Cohen, David, 172
Cohrs, Ferdinand, 203
Coleridge, Samuel Taylor, 264
Collins, Francies, 113, 114, 116, 119, 128, 130, 131
compellatio, 205
concordia, 41
confirmatio, 32, 200
confutatio, 200
Conley, Thomas M., 110, 145, 167, 194, 208, 248, 252, 353
Connors, Joseph M., 203
conscientia, 205
consul suffectus, 179
contentio, 46, 48

controversia, 110, 256
Cook-Deegan, Robert, 117
Cooper, Frederick, 210, 215
Cooper, John M., 337, 338, 339, 341, 346, 347
Cooper, Lane, 168, 174
copia, 139, 205
Corax, 152, 291
Corbett, Edward P. J., 42, 117, 168, 275
Cornelius, 88
Corwin, Edward S., 109
Cotta, 35
Count Mirabeau, 53
Cowley, 74
Cox, Leonard, 248, 251, 252, 255, 259
Crafton, Jeffrey, 89
Cragan, John, 145, 148, 149, 150
Craig, Robert, 151
Crane, W. G., 43
Crick, Francis, 112, 118
Cronkhite, Gary, 145, 146, 149
Crouch, Stanley, 218
Crowley, Sharon, 275
Cuomo, Mario, 152
cupiditatem gloriae/dominandi, 35
cupiditatem pecuniae, 35
Cuvelier, Elaine, 301
Cyprian, 207

Daston, Lorraine, 83
Day, James, 221, 222, 227
De Quincey, Thomas, 264
de Romilly, Jacqueline, 25
Debrunne, 94
Decaux, 51
declamatio, 178
DeLaix, Roger Alain, 221, 224, 225, 227, 230, 232
Democritus, 6
demos, 156, 158, 166, 225, 226, 289, 330, 333
Demosthenes, 19, 21, 22, 23, 207, 333, 364

Dhuoda, 193
diairesis, 16, 17, 20, 22, 26
dicta et facta memorabilia, 32
dictis, 357
dicto, 357
Dieter, Otto A. L., 199, 200
Dihle, Albrecht, 18
dikaion, 348
Diocletian, 195
Dionysius of Halicarnassus, 12, 13, 14, 16, 18, 20, 22, 26
divisio, 200
Dobson, Michael, 301
Domitian (Emperor), 176, 178, 179, 184
Donatus, 188, 189, 190
Donne, 74
Dorp, Martin, 43
Dorsch, T. S., 12
Douglass, Frederick, 209, 219
Dowling, Linda, 263, 264, 265, 266
Drances, 364, 365
Drews, Paul, 203
Dronke, 188
Drusiana, 197
Dryden, John, 74, 223, 300
Du Bois, W. E. B., 210, 217
Du Perron, Dave, 42
dunamis, 349, 350
Dunne, Gerald T., 109

Edelman, Marion Wright, 219
educatio, 202
Edwards, Martha, 187
Edwards, Owen Dudley, 100, 187, 299
Edwards, Thomas, 100
Egeria, 193
Ehninger, Douglas, 65, 309, 310
Ehrenberg, Victor, 226, 232
eikon, 242
ekklesia, 221, 226, 227, 228
eklogê, 21, 22

elementa rhetorices, 249
Ellis, Richard, 102
elocutio, 252, 311
Elyot, Thomas, 42
Emerson, Ralph Waldo, 261
Empedocles, 6
encomia, 175, 202
endoxa, 344
Enos, Theresa, 274, 275
enthymeme, 117, 122, 124, 151, 203, 277
Epictetus, 272
epideictic, 14, 27, 95, 150, 155, 167, 176, 179, 180, 183, 184
epilogos, 235
epilogus, 32
epiphora, 237
epistêmê, 293
epistolae, 33
Erasmus, Desiderius, 32, 40, 41, 43, 44, 45, 46, 47, 48, 139, 146, 202, 204, 206
Ergophilus, 349, 350
eros, 160
ethopoeia, 32, 33
ethos, 117, 123, 136, 140, 150, 168, 169, 173, 203, 275, 365
eudaimonia, 162
exclamatio, 205
exemplum, 38, 70, 193
exergasia, 16, 17, 18, 20, 24, 26
exordium, 32, 33, 34, 205, 206
exornatio, 205

Fahnestock, Jeanne, 236, 237, 247
Fairclough, H. R., 357, 364, 365
Farrell, James M., 101
Farrell, Thomas B., 288, 294
Fay, Samuel P. P., 109
Ferguson, Robert A., 101, 311
fetialis, 359
Filipczak, 192
Finley, Moses I., 223, 289
Fisher, Walter, 146

Flavius Sabinus, 178
Fleury, 57
Fogle, Thomas, 114
Forbes, Clarence, 358
Forbes, William, 299
Forestié, E., 51
Fornara, Charles William, 229, 231
Forrest, W. G., 225, 226
Forsdyke, John, 289
Fortenbaugh, William, 172, 173, 308
Foss, Karen, 147
Foucault. Michel, 229, 233
fragilitas, 187, 192
Franklin, Rosalind, 112
frater arvalis, 359
Frazer, Elizabeth, 3, 4
Frazier, A. M., 230
Freedman, Joseph S., 204, 206
Freese, J. H., 174, 343
Freudenburg, Kirk, 18
Frier, Bruce W., 110
Frost, John, 297
Fulton, Thomas C., 136, 137, 140–142
Fumaroli, Marc, 42

Gabba, Emilio, 14
Gage, John T., 122
Gaines, Robert, 23, 248, 256, 258, 370
Gaius, 79, 175
Galileo, 84
Galinsky, Karl, 352, 358, 361, 362, 366, 367
Gallant, T. W., 221
Gallicanus, A., 195
Garber, Daniel, 77, 78, 82, 83
Garrick, David, 301
Garver, Eugene, 337, 341, 342, 346
Gates, Jr., Henry Louis, 209
Gaudentia, 188
Gawalt, Gerald W., 103
George of Trebizond, 42

George, Carol V. R., 210
Gerard, Cornelis, 45, 46
Gerberga, the abbess of Gandersheim, 193, 194
Gerson, Lloyd P., 116
Gilbert, 230, 232
Glenn, Cheryl, 353, 354
Goggin, Maureen D., 274
Golden, James L., 43, 275, 276, 277, 278, 280, 309
Goldsmith, 71
Gomberini, Federico, 176
Gorgias of Leontini, 6, 7, 8, 42, 133, 149, 150, 152, 154, 155, 156, 157, 159, 160, 161, 162, 163, 164, 165, 166, 172, 256, 276, 277, 278, 282, 291, 292, 327
Gracchus, 81, 83
gratiarum actio, 175
Grau, F., 31
Gray, 71
Green, Lawrence D., 122, 235
Gregory the Great, 207
Gregory, Dr. John, 299
Griffin, Em, 145, 150, 151, 152, 153
Grimaldi, William M. A., 169, 291
Gronbeck, Bruce, 165
Gross, Daniel M., 341
Groupe Mu, 239
Grube, George M. A.,, 14, 26
Guillois, 51
Guthrie, W. K. C., 6, 65, 156, 290, 291, 292, 300, 311
Guyer, Mark S., 114, 119

Hacking, Ian, 77, 78, 84
Haight, Ann Lyon, 188
Hale, Sir Matthew, 71
Halloran, S. Michael, 100, 101, 115, 118, 311
Hamilton, William, 214, 215
Hample, Judy, 100

Hanmer, Thomas, 300
Harker, Christine, 187
Harper, Nancy, 149
Harrison, Becky, 187
Hart, Rod, 146
Hatab, Lawrence J., 290
Havelock, Eric A., 25
Hawhee, Debra, 275
Hawthorne, Nathaniel, 62
Hecataeus, 87
Heidegger, Martin, 343
Helen of Troy, 283
Hembold, W. C., 164
Hemmingsen, Niels, 202
Heraclitus, 6
Herder, Leroy, 296
Hermagoras, 12, 15, 23, 148
Hermes, 135
Hermogenes, 13, 32, 33, 34, 148
Herodotus, 15, 17, 227
Herrick, James, 145, 353
Herzberg, Bruce, 145
Hesiod, 6, 327
Higgins, Jesse, 102, 270, 271
Higgins, Lesley, 102, 270, 271
Hignett, Charles, 225, 227, 228, 289
Hill, Anita, 149
Hinks, Peter P., 210, 214
Hipple, Jr., Walter John, 296
Hippocrates, 116, 192
Hobbes, Thomas, 74
Homer, 159, 258, 289, 299, 305, 343, 347
Honore, Anthony M., 110
Hooker, 74
Hooper, Finley, 289
Horace, 12, 87, 304, 354, 367
Horsfal, John, 202
Horton, James Oliver, 210
Horton, Lois E., 210
Hosmer, William, 109
Hough, Graham, 265
Howell, Wilbur Samuel, 248, 251, 252

Hrotsvit, 187, 188, 189, 190, 192–198
Hubbard, R., 113
Hubbell, Harry, 25
Hudson, Thomas J., 119, 121, 127, 128, 129
Hughes, H. Stuart, 234
Hume, David, 265, 298, 309, 311–313, 317–319
Hyperius, Andreas Gerhard, 200, 201, 202, 203

imitatio, 133, 140, 141, 142
in bonam partem, 33
in foeminis, 36
in malam, 33
indoles, 35
interrogatio, 205
Iphicrates, 245
Irene (martyr), 195
Irving, 70, 71
Isaiah, 88, 207
isegoria, 168, 174, 327, 330, 331, 334–336
Isidore (of Seville), 189, 190
Isocrates, 15, 19, 23, 24, 25, 29, 41, 42, 140, 146, 149, 150, 152, 156, 161, 163, 245, 261, 271, 278–281, 284
Jaggard, William, 299
Jakobson, Roman, 239
Jamieson, Kathleen Hall, 42, 43, 48, 183
Jarratt, Susan, 283
Jeremiah, 207, 304
Jerome (Saint), 188, 207
Jesus, 44, 45, 88, 89, 92, 93
Johnson, Mark, 239
Johnson, Nan, 63, 65, 66, 74, 231, 297
Johnson, Samuel, 304, 305
Johnstone, Christopher, 292, 293, 333, 335
Jonson, Ben, 74

Jordan, Vernon, 219
Jordan, William, 210, 217
Jorde, Lynn, 116
Jourdain, 188
Jowett, Benjamin, 271
Junius Rusticus, 178
Justus Fabius, 356

Kahl, Mary L., 231, 232
Kahn, Charles, 290
kairos, 6, 9, 10, 275, 326, 327, 328, 329, 330, 331, 332, 333, 334, 335
Kant, Immanuel, 99, 109, 266
katharsis, 237
Keckermann, Bartholomew, 199, 203, 204, 205, 206, 207, 208
Kennedy, George, 5, 6, 7, 10, 12, 13, 14, 42, 163, 166, 167, 168, 169, 170, 171, 174, 175, 176, 177, 186, 235, 236, 248, 276, 278, 279, 280, 281, 283, 311, 354, 357, 364, 365
Kerber, Linda K., 101
Kerferd, George, 283
Kimball, Bruce A., 110
Kinneavy, James L., 113, 115, 327
Kinshasa, Kwando M., 210
Kirby, John, 237
Kleisthenes, 224, 226, 289
Kleomenes, 227
Kramarae, Cheris, 150
Krause, Gerhard, 200
Kremers, 63, 65, 66
Krul, Leopold, 200
kyrios, 242

LaCapra, Dominick, 229, 230, 232
Lacey, Nancy, 4
Laeta, 188
Laistner, M. L. W., 189
Lalius, 36
Langford, Paul, 299
Latinus, 364

Lattin, Bohn, 40
laus diuorum, 36
laus personarum, 36
Le Bossu, 306
Leibniz, Gottfried, Wilhelm, 83
Lenin, 138
Lewontin, R.C., 113
lexeos arete, 242
liberalitas, 35
Lincoln, Andrew T., 89, 92
Linder, A., 88
Linton, Ralph, 171
Liska, Jo, 145, 146, 149
Littlejohn, Stephen, 145, 146, 147, 148
Livy, 358
locus communis, 32, 33
logoi, 9, 135, 165
logos, 9, 150, 155, 156, 161, 165, 203, 235, 278, 281, 283, 291
Longfellow, Henry Wadsworth, 62, 67
Longinus, 12, 14, 177, 265
Lord Haversham, 303
Lord Kames, 296, 297, 298, 299, 301, 302, 303, 305, 306, 307, 317, 318
Loretelli, Rosamaria, 297
Louis XVI, 52, 53
Lucretia, 36
Luis de Granada, 203
Lundy, Susan Ruth, 180
Lunsford, Andrea, 144
Lycoleon, 245
Lysias, 19, 235

MacCormack, Sabine, 176, 177, 179
Macquarrie, John, 343
Macrobius, 358, 363
Maevius, 79
Makua, 49
Mandeville, 74
Marcella, 188

Marcus Aurelius, 268
Marcus, Steven, 263
Marie Antoinette, 53
Marius, 264, 271, 272
Martin Luther King, Jr., 217
Maternus, 177, 186
Matthes, D., 13
McBurney, James H., 122
McCall, 242, 243
McCloskey, Donald N., 232
McConica, J. K., 43, 44
McCroskey, James, 149
McGuinness, Arthur E., 297, 298
McKenzie, Gordon, 296
Meador, 178, 181
Meier, August, 210
Meijering, Roos, 13, 17
Melanchthon, Philip, 203, 248, 249, 250, 251, 252, 255, 259
Mendel, Gregor, 117
Menelaus, 289
Mercier, Louis-Sébastien, 51
metaphora, 240, 242, 244, 247
Metellus Numidicus, 36
Mettius Pompusianus, 178
metum, 35
Milton, John, 74, 203, 299
mimesis, 13, 25, 237
Mohrmann, Gerry P., 100
Monfasani, James, 42
Monroe, Marilyn, 283
Monsman, Gerald, 262
Moore, George, 265
Moore, J. M., 359
mores, 35, 203
Moses, 87
Murphy, James J., 31, 208, 237, 253
Mynors, R.A.B., 179

Nadeau, Ray D., 32
Nagel, 193
narratio, 200
natio, 202

Nazianzen, Gregory, 207
Nelms, Gerald, 274
nemini nocere, 35
Neptune, 356, 357, 365
Nerva (Emperor), 179
Nestor, 289
Neuliep, James, 145, 146, 152
Newman, Samuel P., 62–75
Newman, Sara, 235, 236, 244
nocemus propter iram, 35
Nolan, Dennis R., 103
nomos, 333
nous, 293
Nussbaum, Martha, 346, 347

Ober, Josiah, 155, 156, 158, 160, 166, 167, 168, 174, 225, 230, 329, 330, 331, 332, 333, 334
obsecratio, 205
Ochs, Donovan J., 211, 212
Octavian, 179, 361
oikonomia, 12, 13, 15, 19, 21, 22
Olbrechts-Tyteca, Lucie, 95, 148
oligoría, 169
Olin, John C., 40
Olympe de Gouges, 50–60
omnes litteras discant, 188
optatio, 205
oratio recta, 194
ordo artificiosus, 13
Orel, Sara, 187
orexis, 337
orgé, 170
Origines, 366
ornatum, 32
Ostwald, 329
Otto I, 193, 195
Otto II, 193, 195
Owst, Gerald R., 200

panegyric, 41, 175, 176, 179, 180, 181, 182, 184, 185
Parker, Edward G., 100

Pater, Walter, 261, 262, 263, 264, 265, 266, 267, 268, 269, 270, 271, 272
pathe, 337, 338, 341
pathos, 47, 117, 128, 150, 151, 203, 308, 316, 339, 349
Patria, 30, 35, 202
Paula, 188
Peachman, Henry, 42
Pearce, Barnett, 147
Peisistratus, 225, 228, 230–232
Pelagius (martyr), 197, 198
Perelman, Chaim, 95, 140, 148, 237
Pericles, 158, 162
peroratio, 200, 205, 206
Philistus, 15
Philocrates, 333, 349, 350
Philodemus, 98, 257, 258
Philostratus, 163
Phrinicus, 30
Pierce, Franklin, 62
Pierpont, John, 64, 69, 70, 71, 72
Plato, 8, 9, 22, 25, 37, 41, 98, 109, 134, 140, 146, 148–152, 156, 159, 160, 163, 164, 173, 256, 261, 267–272, 276–284, 286, 291, 343
Plautus, 194
Plett, Heinrich F., 248
Pliny the Younger, 175–186
Plutarch, 32, 223, 224, 225, 227
pneuma, 33
Pohill, John, 89
polemos, 42
Polheim, Karl Konrad, 190
polis, 6, 157, 159–161, 167, 174, 288, 289, 342
Pollio, 358
pontifex maximus, 359
Pope, Alexander, 299, 302, 303
Poste, George, 129
Poster, Carol, 167
potens seditione, 365

Poulakos, John, 9, 10, 154, 155, 157, 165, 283, 327, 328, 329
Poulakos, Takis, 144, 283
Powell, Jr., Adam Clayton, 209
praktikoteron, 348
praotes, 170
praünsis, 170
prepon, 242
Priestley, Joseph, 297
princeps senatus, 359
Priscian, 188, 189, 190
Pritchett, W. Kendrick, 16, 26
probouleûsis, 221–225–233
Prodicus, 149, 152, 291
proemium, 30, 200
professio, 35
progymnasmata, 32, 33, 34, 39
pronuntiatio, 31, 252–253
propositio, 200
prose oikonomia, 12, 15
prosopopeia, 205
Protagoras, 7, 8, 9, 149, 152, 156, 276, 283, 291–294, 328
Protarchus, 163
Pythagoreans, 6

Q. Caecilium, 32
Quarles, Benjamin, 210
quindecimvir, 359
Quint, David, 259, 363
Quintilian, 12, 13, 23, 67, 82, 83, 105, 106, 109, 140, 146, 148,– 150, 152, 177, 178, 181–183, 185, 202, 203, 238, 258, 259, 278, 311, 353–355

Rabaut, 51
Rabe, Hugo, 13
Rackham, Horace, 348
Radice, Betty, 175, 176, 177, 178, 179, 180
Raleigh, 74
Ramus, Peter, 31, 85, 144, 151, 248, 252, 253, 255, 258, 296

Randall, Helen Whitcomb, 297, 298
Rauh, Sister Miriam Joseph, 115, 117
Ray, Angela G., 183
Reagan, Ronald, 149
Reid, Ronald F., 109
Reid, Thomas, 266
Reschly, Steve, 187
rhetores, 333
Rhodes, Neil, 296, 297
Rhodes, P. J., 223–225
Richards, I. A., 43, 138, 298
Ricoeur, Paul, 236, 237, 242, 243
Rikkardis, Mistress, 193
Robert of Basevorn, 199, 200
Roberts, W. Rhys, 22
Robespierre, 57
Robinson, Edward, 343
robur, 187, 192
Rogerus, Servatius, 44
Rolfe, J. C., 178, 351
Rorty, A.O., 346, 347
Ross, Ian Simpson, 296–298, 338
Rudwick, Elliott, 210
Russell, D. A., 12, 18, 20, 23, 25
Russell, D. S., 88

sacris faciundis, 359
Saggs, H. W. F., 288
Saint Augustine, 146, 149, 152, 199, 200, 201, 204, 207, 208
Saint Basil, 195
Saint Bernard, of Clairvaux, 207
Saint Dionysius, 195
Sallustius Lucullus, 178
saphe, 242
Scenters-Zapico, John, 5, 9
Schiappa, Edward, 9, 155, 157, 283, 291, 329
Schott, Andreas, 30
Schulz, Fritz, 110
Scipio Africanus, 36
Sealey, Raphael, 227, 228, 289

Segal, Charles P., 156, 161
Seneca, 178, 194, 272, 352, 355, 356, 358
sensus communis, 267, 271
septemvir epulonum, 359
sermo, 40, 41, 44, 45, 46, 48, 49
sermocinatio, 205
Severus, 180, 181
Shaftesbury, 266, 271
Shakespeare, William, 71, 115, 296, 297, 298, 299, 300, 301, 302, 303, 304, 305, 306
Shannon, Claude, 150
Shaw, Leroy, 297
Sheridan, Alan, 58
Shields, Donald, 148, 149, 150
Sloane, Thomas O., 43, 110, 153
Smith, Adam,, 75, 297, 316
Smith, Craig, 145
Smith, William, 99
Smith-Lovin, Lynn, 171
Socrates, 36, 159, 160, 164, 226, 232, 270, 283
Solmsen, Friedrich, 169, 171
Solon, 221, 222, 223, 224, 225, 226, 227, 228, 231–233
sophia, 293
sophist, 3, 5–11, 42, 144, 148–149, 151, 163, 268, 276–283, 291–294, 327–329, 330, 332, 333, 335, 343, 346
sophistic, 9, 10, 11, 108, 149, 278–280, 283, 327
Sprague, Rosamund K., 163, 194, 283, 291, 292, 293, 294
St. Charles Borromeo, 203
St. Jerome, 188
St. Paul, 151, 202, 207
St. Radegonde, 188
Stanford, William B., 236, 238, 239, 242
Stanton, G. R., 224, 226
Starr, Chester G., 289
Steele, Shelby, 218

Stephens, James, 248
Sterk, Helen, 283
Stewart, John, 1470
Stewart, Maria, 215, 216, 220
Stockton, David, 222, 228
Stone, I. F, 283, 299
Story, Joseph, 109
Strauss, Barry, 168
Sudhaus, 257, 258
Suetonius, 178, 351, 357, 358, 359, 366
Sullivan, William M., 286, 287, 288, 294
Sulpitius Victor, 13
sunthesis, 15, 21, 22
superstitio barbara, 87
sustenatio, 205
suum cuique tribuere, 35
Sweet, W. E., 6
Syme, Ronald, 176
syndromas, 245
syntonoteron, 348

Tacitus, 87, 175, 176, 177, 178, 184, 185, 186, 352, 355, 356
Talon, Omer, 31, 140, 248, 252, 253, 255, 258
Tate, Gary, 274
taxis, 12, 16, 17, 20, 26
Tcherikover, V., 87
Tebbel, John, 67, 72, 73
techne, 142
tekhnai, 237
telos, 237, 240
Terence, 189, 190, 194, 196
Thais, 195
Thales, 290
Theobald, Lewis, 303, 304
Theophano, 195
Theophilus, 195
Theophrastus, 18
Theopompus, 15
thesis, 16, 25, 32, 33, 44, 103, 186, 288, 338, 342, 347

Thierry, Augustin, 231
Thompson, Wayne N., 180
Thrasymachus, 149, 152, 160
Thucydides, 15, 16, 17, 26, 157, 158, 160, 229, 231
thymos, 342
Tiberius, 357, 363
Timothy, 203, 207
Timpler, Clemens, 204
Tisias, 152, 291
Titius, 79; Paul's letter to, 207
Titus Labienus, 358, 359
topics, 31, 84, 179, 247, 249, 250, 310, 338, 339, 346, 352
topoi, 33, 34, 35, 36, 37, 38, 117, 151, 179
topos, 37, 38, 155, 178, 206, 207
tractatio intermedia, 205, 206
Trajan, 175, 176, 179, 180, 181, 182, 183, 184, 185, 186
Tredennick, H, 160
Triton, 356, 361, 365
Trueblood, Thomas C., 136, 137, 140, 141
Turnebus, Adrian, 31
tykhe, 171, 173
Tytler, Alexander Fraser, 298

Uglow, Jennifer, 266
Ulman, H. Lewis, 297
Ulysses, 238
union libre, 56
usus quintuplex, 203
Valerius Maximus, 32
van Hook, Larue, 161
Van Wyk Cronjé, Jacobus, 22
van Zuylen, W. H., 206
Venter, Craig, 125, 129, 130
Vernant, Jean-Pierre, 290
Verres, Gaius, 32
Versenyi, Laszlo, 165
Vespasian (Emperor), 178
Vibius Severus, 177
Vickers, Brian, 42, 99, 248, 255

Vico, Giambattista, 173, 239
Virgil, 299, 305, 354, 356, 362–365, 367
Virgilius Maro, 189
virtutes, 35
Vitanza, Victor, 144, 353
Voltaire, Francois Marie Arouet de, 299, 301
Vossius, J. G., 30

Wade-Gerry, H. T., 226
Walker, David, 122, 213, 214, 215, 216
Walker, Jeffrey, 347
Wallace, Karl, 248
Walzer, Arthur E., 308
Warner, R., 158
Warren, Charles, 103, 311
Washington, Booker T., 216
Waterfield, R., 160
Watson, James, 112, 118
Welch, Kathleen E., 15, 283, 284
West, Cornel, 36, 208, 218, 219
Whately, Richard, 64, 65, 66, 148, 149, 152
Whipper, William, 212, 213, 214
White, G. Edward, 98, 101
White, Hayden, 231
White, Raymond, 116
Wiefel, W., 88

Wilde, Oscar, 263
William, Bishop of Mainz, 193
Williston, E. B.,, 100
Wilson, Edmond B., 118
Wilson, Kathleen, 301
Winterbottom, Michael, 12, 259, 355
Wirt, William, 70, 100
Witherspoon, John, 99
Wittig, Monique, 4
Wollstonecraft, Mary, 50
Wood, Julia, 145, 147, 148
Woodhead, A. G., 222, 226, 227
Woodward, William H., 43
Wordsworth, William, 264
Wright Edelman, Marion, 218, 220
Wright, Samuel, 262

X, Malcolm, 209, 218, 220
Xenophon, 15, 16, 160, 162, 163

Yeates, Jasper, 99

Zabell, Sandy, 77, 78, 82, 83
Zanker, Paul, 352, 361, 362, 363, 366, 367
Zeno, 201
Zeus, 365
Zeydel, Edwin H., 188
Zimmern, Alfred, 289

www.ingramcontent.com/pod-product-compliance
Lightning Source LLC
Chambersburg PA
CBHW021937240426
43668CB00036B/73